4-7-72

YALE HISTORICAL PUBLICATIONS

MISCELLANY, 8

AMERICAN LOYALIST:
JARED INGERSOLL

BY LAWRENCE HENRY GIPSON

NEW HAVEN AND LONDON
YALE UNIVERSITY PRESS
1971

Distributed in Great Britain, Europe, and Africa by
Yale University Press, Ltd., London; in Canada by
McGill-Queen's University Press, Montreal; in Mexico
by Centro Interamericano de Libros Académicos,
Mexico City; in Central and South America by
Kaiman & Polon, Inc., New York City; in Australasia
by Australia and New Zealand Book Co., Pty., Ltd.,
Artarmon, New South Wales; in India by UBS Pub-
lishers' Distributors Pvt., Ltd., Delhi; in Japan by
John Weatherhill, Inc., Tokyo.

IN MEMORY OF
JEANNETTE REED GIPSON

AUTHOR'S FOREWORD, 1971

JARED Ingersoll was one among a very numerous group of Americans who with the outbreak or during the course of the War for American Independence refused to repudiate their allegiance to King George III and the government of Great Britain. What proportion of the adult population living within British colonial North America can be classified as Loyalists has never been accurately determined. The number certainly embraced many thousands of people of varying social and economic standing who had so committed themselves to the parent country and King George III in the course of the war that at its end exile seemed unavoidable.

Doubtless even much more numerous than the Loyalists were those who were apolitical, in other words those refusing to take a stand on public issues that tended to divide American communities between 1763 and 1783. They were people who were at least reasonably well satisfied with their lot or, if dissatisfied, either were through timidity unwilling to take a stand or were as an article of faith opposed to the use of force. Therefore, in the course of the armed conflict that ensued they sought to be neutral insofar as was possible, and at its end, with the triumph of the American patriots, they quietly accepted the results.

The history of the American patriots is the story of the unfolding of the new American nation from 1783 onward, of the flowering of American civilization—despite such terrible crises as the Civil War—and of the present vast strength of the United States in the world. This history is embodied in the Declaration of Independence of 1776 and the Constitution of 1787 and also in innumerable writings, both public documents and private expressions that crowd our libraries, from works of great learning to those of almost pure fancy—each work serving its purpose, addressed as it is to a particular group of readers. On the other hand, the history of the American Loyalists is and will doubtless remain an incomplete one, a story chiefly of disappointment, failure, and disillusionment of individuals, such as characterized the last years in England of Governor Thomas Hutchinson of Massachusetts Bay, or as in the case of the more fortunate, the beginning of a new life, as was true of the New York lawyer Justice William Smith, who reestablished himself in Canada.

How difficult it is to foretell the future! Who would have prophesied in 1754, with the outbreak of hostilities between British and French colonials in the New World, that after nine years these would terminate with a victorious British Empire and yet with many North American British colonials feeling that France was their friend and Great Britain their enemy? Indeed, one of the ironies of the history of the English-speaking peoples in the eighteenth century is that Great Britain became actively involved in hostilities in North America in 1755 only when in the face of appeals for aid its government finally decided to come to the assistance of the hard-pressed British American colonists who in the face of military reverses pleaded that their untrained troops were no match against regulars sent from France.

These hostilities, at first but petty clashes in the American wilderness, grew into what may be properly called Britain's Great War for the Empire—a war fought on land and sea wherever Great Britain or France and the latter's ally Spain had interests that could be challenged.

It was a war that in some respects was fused with the German Seven Years' War, although each of these wars began at a different time, with different objectives, and ended separately, each with its own treaty of peace. It was by far the most costly war in which Great Britain had been engaged up to that time, and it left her saddled with what was regarded as an unprecedented debt. To bring it to conclusion it seemed necessary to cut off the lucrative and well-established but illegal British colonial trade with the colonies of the enemy that Pitt declared was prolonging the war. Therefore, to terminate the war the use of writs of assistance—long employed in England against illegal trade and extended to the colonies—was tried. Attempts to use these writs aroused such intense opposition, especially among the seafaring and trading elements in such a colony as Massachusetts, that they quite failed of their purpose.

There also came the effort of the parent country at the end of the war to enforce the trade and navigation acts as strictly in the colonies as was being done in the British Isles. Parliament, feeling that the colonies were the chief beneficiaries of the victorious peace and should therefore help to finance the administration of the New World acquisitions, planned a program of colonial taxation. There was also the decision on the part of the home government to prevent colonials from discharging sterling debts owed in Great Britain with depreciated colonial bills of credit. All these regulatory steps just described, together with other measures of less importance, had the effect of gradually creating a deep division among the British North American colonials—intensified by other influences existing in the same direction by the simple fact of geographical separation from the mother country. Men equally devoted to the public interest, equally high-minded, found themselves in opposite camps.

The patriotic group, however, was much better organized for action and vastly stronger in most of the colonies, if not in all of them, and with the rising of passions
the Loyalists (commonly called Tories) found it no longer
possible freely to spread abroad their views either by
word of mouth or in print, as the experiences of John
Mein, the Boston printer, and James Rivington, publisher
of *Rivington's New-York Gazetteer,* as well as many
others, make clear.   There followed thereupon the terror,
with the tarring and feathering of some of the most outspoken of Loyalists, the outbreak of war, the fleeing of
people, and the confiscation by the revolutionary North
American governments of the estates of Loyalist refugees
living abroad.   All these things added to the bitterness
between the groups, a bitterness that was handed down
to generations still to come and that survived even into
the twentieth century.

In reissuing the 1920 publication, *Jared Ingersoll: A
Study in American Loyalism,* the Yale Press has chosen
a new title that takes into account the revived interest
today in the Loyalists as a group; and I wish to make
clear in my foreword the place this study occupies among
the growing number of publications concerning this
significant phase in early American history.   While it is
impossible and undesirable to attempt to list here *all*
works relating to the Loyalists, it is clear that the more
important of them should be assigned their proper place
in the rounding out of this story.

    It would be well first of all to refer to certain writers,
contemporaries of Ingersoll, who were generally regarded as leading Loyalists.   Among these men none
wrote more persuasively than the lawyer and politician
Joseph Galloway, who was speaker of the Pennsylvania
Assembly between 1766 and 1775.   His printed works in-

clude the following: *Cool Thoughts on the Arguments on Both Sides in the Dispute between Great-Britain and Her Colonies as Stated and Answered, and the Rights of the Colonists Explained and Asserted on New and Just Principles. By a Sincere Friend to Both Countries* (printed but not published, Philadelphia, 1774); this was followed by *A Candid Examination of the Mutual Claims of Great-Britain and the Colonies: With a Plan of Accommodation, on Constitutional Principles* (London and Philadelphia, 1775); *Consequences to Great Britain of American Independence* (London, 1780); *The Claim of the American Loyalists Reviewed and Maintained upon Incontrovertible Principles of Law and Justice* (London, 1788); and, finally, the posthumous publication, *Historical and Political Reflections on the Rise and Progress of the American Rebellion* (London, 1878).   In this connection the student should also consult Julian P. Boyd's *Anglo-American Union* (Philadelphia, 1941), largely concerned with the plan of union that Galloway sought to persuade the First Continental Congress to adopt; see also Thomas Balch, ed., *The Examination of Joseph Galloway by a Commission of the House of Commons* [in 1779] (Philadelphia, 1855).   The author of the unsigned article on Galloway in the 14th edition of the *Encyclopedia Britannica* states with reference to Galloway: "He was one of the clearest thinkers and ablest political writers among the American Loyalists." Few historians would disagree with this judgment.   Two modern studies on Galloway should also be noted: Ernest H. Baldwin, *Joseph Galloway, the Loyalist Politician* (Philadelphia, 1902), and O. C. Kuntzleman, *Joseph Galloway, Loyalist* (Philadelphia, 1941).

Doubtless among the Loyalist writers whose contributions are next in importance to those of Galloway in the influence exerted upon his contemporaries was the Rev-

erend Samuel Seabury. A native of Connecticut, he became identified for most of his active career, before the
outbreak of the American Revolution, with the province
of New York as an Anglican minister both on Long Island
and in Westchester County. A man of commanding
presence, devoted to his calling and enjoying to a remarkable extent the confidence of his parishioners, he was
most outspoken in his loyalty to the king. As a consequence he was in 1775 made prisoner by a party of ardent
Connecticut Whigs, led by the redoutable Isaac Sears.
They also imprisoned two of Seabury's Westchester
Loyalist neighbors, Jonathan Fowler, judge of the
superior court of the province of New York, and
Nathaniel Underhill, mayor of Westchester. Carried
into Connecticut, Seabury was placed in custody for a
period of six weeks before he was released. Returning
at length to New York he found his promising parochial
labors broken up. Seeking refuge in New York City he
was in 1778 appointed chaplain of the King's American
Regiment stationed there. With the coming of the peace
he decided wisely to remain an American. Chosen as
their bishop by ten Connecticut Episcopalian clergymen,
he went to England in 1784 to seek consecration. Since
as an American he could no longer take the oath of allegiance to the king, which was required of all British
subjects, he went to Scotland, where he was consecrated
by three non-juring Scottish bishops. He therefore became America's first Episcopalian bishop. In 1790 his
diocese was enlarged to include the state of Rhode Island
as well as that of Connecticut.

The most important of the Seabury Loyalist writings
is his anonymous *Free Thoughts on the Proceedings of
the Continental Congress . . . 1774; Wherein Their
Errors Are Exhibited, Their Reasonings Confuted, and
the Fatal Tendency of Their . . . Measures Are Laid*

Open ([New York], 1774). To this Alexander Hamilton, still in his teens, replied anonymously in his *Full Vindication of the Measures of the Congress from the Calumnies of Their Enemies: In Answer to a Letter under the Signature A. W. Farmer* (New York, 1774). Seabury replied to it in *The Congress Canvassed: Or an Examination into the Conduct of the Delegates at Their Grand Convention, Held in Philadelphia September 1, 1774 . . .* ([New York] 1774); to which Hamilton replied with *The Farmer Refuted: Or, a More Impartial and Comprehensive View of the Dispute between Great Britain and the Colonies . . .* (New York, 1775), with both the Seabury and Hamilton contributions remaining anonymous. The following year came Seabury's likewise anonymous *An Alarm to the Legislature of the Province of New-York Occasioned by the Present Political Disturbances in North America . . .* (New York, 1775). C. H. Vance edited these Loyalist writings in his *Letters of a Westchester Farmer, 1774–1775,* Westchester County Historical Society, Publications, 8 (White Plains, N.Y., 1930). Seabury's career has been well set forth by E. E. Beardsley in his *Life and Correspondence of the Rt. Rev. Samuel Seabury* (Boston, 1881); see also W. J. Seabury, *Memoir of Bishop Seabury* (New York, 1908); G. B. Hertz, ''Bishop Seabury,'' *English Historical Review* 26 (1911): 57–75; and Herbert Thomas, *Samuel Seabury, Priest and Physician, Bishop of Connecticut* (Hamden, Conn., 1963).

If Seabury was the most prominent writer in the province of New York engaged in supporting the Loyalist cause before and during the War for American Independence, there is little question that James Rivington was by far the most influential Loyalist printer and publisher not only in New York but in North America. In fact, the quality of *Rivington's New-York Gazetteer,* both in con-

tent and format, was scarcely equaled by any other newspaper published in the New World. Nor is it likely
that any of them had a wider circulation. According to
a statement that appeared in the issue of October 12,
1774, the *Gazetteer* was "constantly distributed thro'
every colony of North America as well as in the West
Indies and elsewhere in the English-speaking world."

Rivington's publishing venture was certainly far from
a shoestring operation. As he himself pointed out in a
letter to the Continental Congress dated May 20, 1775,
he had "lately employed no less than sixteen workmen,
at near a thousand pounds annually; and his consumption of printing-paper, the manufacture of Pennsylvania,
New York, Connecticut, and the Massachusetts Bay, has
amounted to nearly that sum." He went on to state that
"his extensive foreign correspondence, his large acquaintance in Europe and America, and his manner of education are circumstances which, he conceives, have not im-
properly qualified him for the station in which he wishes
to continue, in which he will exert every endeavour to be
useful.'"[1]

While the *Gazetteer,* as the result of pressure, opened
its columns to communications hostile to Great Britain's
American policy, the main emphasis of its articles was on
the cultivation of a spirit of loyalty to the British Empire. For example, in the November and December 1773
issues appeared the "Popicola" articles prepared by two
members of the faculty of King's College, New York,
President Myles Cooper and John Vardille. Addressed
"To the worthy Inhabitants of the City of New-York,"
their theme was that of the love of one's country and the
duty of cultivating a patriotism that would embrace not

---

[1] The letter is printed in Lorenzo Sabine, *Biographical Sketches of
Loyalists of the American Revolution* . . . , 2 vols. (Boston, 1864),
2:216–18.

simply one's own colony but *"the whole British Empire."*
For stressing this theme "Popicola" was bitterly denounced by such writers as "Legion," "Cassius," and
"A Tradesman" as a "ministerial hireling" and an
enemy of liberty. Rivington also printed many Loyalist
pamphlets, such as those written by Seabury. It is
therefore not surprising that the same party of Connecticut Whigs led by Sears that laid their hands on the
Loyalist Seabury should also determine to put an end to
Rivington's publishing activities in New York City.
They not only smashed his printing press but carried the
type back to Connecticut where it was melted into bullets
ultimately used against the British troops.

Going to England in the course of the war Rivington
returned to New York in 1777 with all needed materials
for reestablishing his New York publishing activities and
thereupon launched *The Royal Gazette.* His publication
labors, however, ceased in 1783. For three studies relating to Rivington, see George H. Sargent, "James Rivington, the Tory printer: A Study of Loyalist Pamphlets
of the Revolution," *American Collector* 2 (1926) : 336–41;
Catherine Small Crary, "The Tory and the Spy: The
Double Life of James Rivington," *William and Mary
Quarterly*, 3d ser., 16 (1959) : 61–72; and Leroy Hewlett,
"James Rivington, the Tory Printer," in *Books in America's Past,* ed. David Kaser (Charlottesville, Va., 1966).

One other prominent New York Loyalist writer must
be mentioned. He was Thomas Jones, Justice of the
Supreme Court of New York, who took his father's place
on the bench in 1773 and continued until that court ceased
to function in 1776. Jones, who received his training at
Yale College, which he later looked upon as "a nursery
of sedition, of faction, and republicanism," suffered imprisonment three times before he left with his family for
England in 1781. He settled in the village of Hoddesdon

in Hertfordshire where he remained until his death.   An
outspoken Loyalist during his exile, he composed his *History of New York during the Revolutionary War* . . . ,
published by the New-York Historical Society in two
large volumes in 1879 after being edited by Edward
Floyd de Lancey.   Relating especially to New York, it is
by far the most detailed account of the progress of the
War for American Independence prepared by any Loyalist writer.   At the same time, written apparently without
adequate reference materials in the isolated village of his
exile in rural England, it contains a good many errors,
errors which H. P. Johnston very properly pointed out
in his *Observations on Judge Jones' Loyalist History of
the American Revolution.   How Far Is It an Authority?*
(New York, 1880).

Jones not only made mistakes in his book, but he also
wrote with deep emotion, which is quite understandable
in a man who felt that he had unjustly suffered the in-
dignity of imprisonment more than once at the hands of
those he was persuaded were traitors.   He also labored
under an act of attainder passed against him by the New
York Assembly in 1779 providing not only for the confiscation of his property but likewise the death penalty
should he still be within the bounds of the state when
peace was made.

In Jones's opinion three men were chiefly responsible
for the disloyal conduct of the colony; they were William
Livingston, John Morin Scott, and William Smith, Jr.,
who together organized the Whig Club whose members
"took active parts in the late unnatural, unprovoked,
American rebellion," and who at their meetings, Jones
charged, would drink toasts to the immortal memory of
such seventeenth-century revolutionary figures as Oliver
Cromwell.

Of all these promoters of the rebellion the person most

abhorrent to Jones was Smith, who curiously shifted from ardent Whig to mild Loyalist and later became Chief Justice of the Province of Quebec. He was author of the important *History of the Late Province of New-York*. Although this work covered the period from the beginning of the province to 1783 only the first part of it, to 1733, appeared in 1757, during Jones's lifetime. In 1830 the New-York Historical Society published in two volumes that part of this history which brought it down to 1762. Then in 1956 under the editorship of W. H. W. Sabine there was issued in mimeograph form "Historical Memoirs from 16 March 1763 to 9 July 1776 of William Smith, Historian in the Province of New York. . . ." This cannot be described as Loyalist history. The author still writes as a Whig. His "Thoughts upon the Dispute between Great Britain and Her Colonies," composed in the course of the Stamp Act crisis and edited by Robert M. Colborn of the University of South Carolina for the *William and Mary Quarterly*, 3d ser., 22 (1965): 105–18, are also still those of an enlightened Whig advocating, as did the Loyalist Galloway in 1774, the creation of an American Parliament. For Smith see M. L. Delafield, "William Smith—The Historian," *Magazine of American History* 6 (1881): 418–39; especially Roger Andrew Wines, "William Smith, the Historian of New York," *New York History* 40 (1959): 3–17; and L. F. S. Upton, *The Loyal Whig: William Smith of New York & Quebec* (Toronto, 1969).

Turning from New York to Massachusetts Bay we must consider two outstanding public figures who contributed to the Loyalist writings. They were Thomas Hutchinson and Peter Oliver. As was true of William Smith who wrote the history of New York as a province, Hutchinson in his history of Massachusetts Bay covered the history of that colony to 1774, when he turned over its administration to General Gage and soon afterwards went to England. However, he did not live to see the appearance in print of more than the first two volumes, bringing the history up to 1750, which were published in Boston in 1764 and 1767. In fact it was not until 1828, long after his death, that his *History of the Province of Massachusetts from the Year 1749, until June 1774* was published, in London, in a single volume.[2]

For the most part Hutchinson remains, in these later volumes, the type of historian who distinguished the two earlier ones. Only in dealing with the activities of James Otis and Samuel Adams during this critical period, when he himself was faced with heavy responsibilities and under heavy attack, does he depart from the judicial calm and spirit of detachment embodied in the rest of his history. He was also critical of the argument introduced in the Declaration of Independence in his *Strictures upon the Declaration of the Congress at Philadelphia: In a Letter to a Noble Lord, Etc.* that appeared in London in 1776 and in 1957 was added to the *Old South Leaflet* series (Boston).

J. K. Hosmer in *The Life of Thomas Hutchinson, Royal Governor of the Province of Masachusetts Bay* (Boston, 1846), in commenting on the governor as historian, writes justly: "In the main he is fair-minded, and in the circumstances surprisingly calm" and adds that his comments on politics, finance, and religion "are full of intelligence and also full of humanity." No greater tribute to the quality of this history is available than the

---

[2] The edition particularly designed for the British market carried a rather expanded title: *The History of the Province of Massachusetts Bay from 1749 to 1774, comprising a detailed narrative on the origin and early stages of the American Revolution.* This edition also included a preface and a dedication to the Lord Chancellor, Boston-born Baron Lyndhurst, son of the distinguished Boston portrait painter, John Singleton Copley. It should be pointed out that both editions were edited by the governor's grandson, the Reverend John Hutchinson.

fact that in 1936 Lawrence Shaw Mayo brought out a new
critical edition in three volumes (Boston) and that Catherine Barton Mayo, his wife, supplemented this new edition in 1949 with *Additions to Thomas Hutchinson's
"History of Massachusetts Bay"* (Worcester, Mass.),
introducing many important comments and improvements which Hutchinson himself made respecting the
original manuscript.

As for Peter Oliver, he, like Hutchinson, was not
trained in the law. Both were graduated at Harvard;
both received a place on the Governor's Council; both
became members of the Superior Court of Judicature;
and both also attained the rank of Chief Justice of this
court. As devoted Loyalists they both suffered the confiscation of their property and became exiled in England
from their native land, and both left accounts of what
took place in Massachusetts, as each viewed it in connection with the American Revolution. There is, however,
an important difference in their respective narratives.
Hutchinson, as has been indicated, wrote in the main
with great restraint and comprehension respecting events
which affected his life and that of the people of Massachusetts. Oliver, on the other hand, laid bare his inner-
most feelings as to the treatment accorded him and other
Loyalists. In fact, it was not until our own day that his
history came into print, so unrestrained was he in denouncing his opponents. Under the able editorship of
Douglass Adair and J. A. Schutz, it finally was published
in 1961 under the title *Peter Oliver's Origin & Progress
of the American Rebellion. A Tory View* (San Marino,
Calif., Huntington Library). The spirit in which it is
written is expressed in the following statement that
Oliver addressed to the hypothetical reader:

You will be presented with such a detail of Villainy in
all its Forms, that it will require some Fortitude to

meet the Shock. You will see Religion dressed up into a Stalking horse, to be skulked behind, that Vice might perpetrate its most atrocious Crimes, while it bore so fair a Front to mislead & deceive the World around. In short, you will see every Thing Sacred & Profane, twisted into all Shapes to serve the Purposes of Rebellion; Earth & Hell ransacked for Tools to work the Fabrick with.

Nor were Oliver's observations on his individual opponents any more gentle. He affirmed that James Otis had taken to heart the maxim of one of John Milton's devils: "Better to reign in Hell than serve in Heaven." As for Samuel Adams, his outstanding characteristic, according to Oliver, was "the Malignity of his heart" and the "employing his abilities to the vilest Purposes." Nor did he spare the Boston clergy. To him the Reverend Dr. Samuel Cooper had gone "very deep in the black Art. . . . No man could, with a better Grace, utter the Word of God from his Mouth, & at the same time keep a two edged dagger concealed in his hand. His tongue was Butter & Oil, but under it was the Poison of Asps."

Here we have an honest man of ability so thoroughly embittered by the misfortunes heaped upon him in the course of political events that he could see nothing good in the conduct of those who had opposed him, even in those who were in his day and have also since been regarded as honorable men of ability. The importance of the *Origin & Progress of the American Rebellion* lies in the fact that it serves as a corrective of a good deal of the propaganda of the patriots that was really just as irresponsible in speaking contemptuously of all utterances and acts on the part of the Loyalists.

One other Loyalist writer deserves more than passing mention—the Reverend Jonathan Boucher. Reared in northern England in poverty, he nevertheless acquired an excellent education without attending college. In 1759 he went to Virginia to tutor the sons of a Port Royal planter; then in 1762 he returned to England to take holy orders. After doing so he was called to St. Mary's in Caroline County, Virginia, and to supplement his income conducted a boarding school for boys; among them was young John Park Custis, the stepson of George Washington. For years Boucher enjoyed the latter's friendship. In 1770 he became the rector to St. Anne's at Annapolis, Maryland, where he lived on terms of intimacy with Governor Eden and his family and later was given the much more desirable rectorship of the church of Queen Anne's Parish in Prince Georges County, also in Maryland.

In the midst of the developing crisis Boucher was steadfast in his loyalty to his king and the country of his nativity. When forbidden by a group of armed patriots to enter his pulpit, he refused to be intimidated, and from that time on until he left Maryland as an exile he always preached with a pair of loaded pistols lying close at hand. After being burnt in effigy and being faced with other threats, he and his wife went to England in September 1775, where he spent the rest of his days. Among Boucher's writings are the *American Revolution, In Thirteen Discourses Preached in North America between the years 1763 and 1775* (London, 1797); *Letters of Jonathan Boucher to George Washington,* ed. W. C. Ford (Brooklyn, 1889), and *Reminiscences of an American Loyalist, 1738–1789; Being the Autobiography of Jonathan Boucher . . .* , ed. Jonathan Bouchier (Boucher's grandson) (Boston and New York, 1925).

The above Loyalists, as was true of Jared Ingersoll, presented with different degrees of emphasis the authentic voice of the cause to which they had become committed.

Among those who were not Loyalists but were deeply

interested in the history of Loyalist activities none occupies a more prominent and respected place than
Lorenzo Sabine (1803–77). His *Biographical Sketches
of Loyalists of the American Revolution,* published in two
volumes in Boston in 1864 just as the Civil War was
drawing to conclusion, is a monument to his industry,
striving for accuracy and fairness to those whose views
were not in accordance with his own patriotic sentiments.
His task presented enormous difficulties. As he himself
wrote in the preface of this work:

I have repeatedly been ready to abandon the pursuit in
despair. For, to weave into correct and continuous
narratives the occasional allusion of books and State
Papers; to join together fragmentary events and incidents; to distinguish persons of the same surname or
family name, when only that name is mentioned; and to
reconcile the disagreements of various epistolary and
verbal communications, has seemed, at times, utterly
impossible.

Indeed, as one goes over the accounts of the hundreds of
American Loyalists here given, some very brief, other
requiring considerable space, the wonder grows that
Sabine was able to accomplish under the circumstances
what he did in so excellent a manner. There would also
be entire agreement among students of history with his
statement: "The *entire* correctness and fulness of detail,
in tracing the course, and in ascertaining the fate, of the
[American] adherents of the Crown, are not *now* within
the power of the most careful and industrious."

Even superior to Sabine in power of analysis in dealing with the Loyalists was Moses Coit Tyler, professor of
history at Cornell University. In 1896 he published
"The Party of the Loyalists in the American Revolution" in the first number of the newly launched *American
Historical Review.* This was followed in 1897 by his

very important *Literary History of the American Revolution* in two volumes, published in both London and New York. Although proud of his Whig descent, Tyler was totally committed to the idea that the writing of history made the utmost demands for intellectual integrity on the part of the individual engaged in this labor. He also wrote at a time when men still felt very deeply, even passionately, about the effort of the South to wreck the Union of the United States by establishing its own union and he therefore could sympathize more fully with the position of Loyalists who wanted to preserve the Old British Empire and thereby remain within its folds. Tyler's work, in fact, represents a high point in the effort to do justice to the Loyalists.

Mention must be made of an overly ambitious work which fell somewhat short of its promise. It was written by Adolphus Edgerton Ryerson and was published in 1880 in Toronto in two volumes under title *The Loyalists of America and Their Times, From 1620 to 1816*. However, the work of William H. Siebert of Ohio State University demands somewhat fuller comment. From the year 1911, when he published *The Flight of the American Loyalists to the British Isles*, to 1934, when his "General Washington and the Loyalists" appeared in the *Proceedings of the American Antiquarian Society*, he wrote a series of pieces concerned with the Loyalists, published as articles or as bulletins. Mention must be made also of his *Loyalists in East Florida, 1774 to 1783*, published in two volumes in 1929. These writings comprehended the activities of the Loyalists in most of the Thirteen Colonies and also in Canada and the provinces of East Florida and West Florida as well as the British West Indies and in the Bahamas. They are largely descriptive history and as such fulfilled their immediate purpose.

Certain works on Loyalism limited to state or local

boundaries should also be noted. Without considering many briefer studies, we have, for example, Alexander C. Flick's *Loyalism in New York during the American Revolution,* Columbia University Studies in History, Economics, and Public Law (1901); James H. Stark's *The Loyalists of Massachusetts and the Other Side of the American Revolution,* 2 vols. (Boston, 1910); Isaac S. Harrell's *Loyalism in Virginia, Chapters in the Economic History of the Revolution* (New York, 1926); Epaphroditus Peck's *Loyalists of Connecticut,* Tercentenary Commission of Connecticut, Publications, 31 (New Haven, 1934); and Robert O. DeMond's *Loyalists in North Carolina during the Revolution* (New Haven, 1940). Worthy of note in this connection are two volumes of documents each concerning the Loyalists in a particular state and compiled by Edward Alfred Jones. They are *The Loyalists of New Jersey: Their Memorials, Petitions, Claims, etc., from English Records,* New Jersey Historical Society Collections, 10 (Newark, 1927), and *The Loyalists of Massachusetts: Their Memorials, Petitions, and Claims* (Boston and London, 1933). The New Jersey volume more fully measures up to the title.

While most Loyalist studies and other writings are limited to a particular state, others are more general. There came from the press in New York in 1902 Claude H. Van Tyne's broad study, *The Loyalists in the American Revolution,* which was reprinted not only in 1929 but also in 1959. Two other equally broad studies, each of great merit, are Leonard W. Labaree's little volume on *Conservatism in Early American History* (New York, 1948)—which as a study is of course not limited to Loyalism as was his penetrating article on the sources of Loyalism published in the *Proceedings of the American Antiquarian Society* in 1945— and the equally brief study by William H. Nelson published at Oxford in 1961 under title of *The American Tory.* Again, Paul H. Smith's *Loyalists and Redcoats: A Study in British Revolutionary Policy* (Chapel Hill, N.C., 1964) emphasizes the failure of the British government to estimate properly the strength of American Loyalism.

Two studies relating to Canada deserve mention at this point: Esther Clark Wright's *The Loyalists of New Brunswick* (Fredericton, N.B., 1955), a painstaking effort to deal with Loyalists who fled from the United States to this Canadian province, and G. A. Rawlyk's *Revolution Rejected, 1775–1776* (Toronto, 1968), concerned with Nova Scotia and the attitude of New Englanders who inundated this province between 1763 and 1775 but who refused to join the Revolution. Mention should also be made of a meritorious volume of readings with critical comments that was edited by G. N. D. Evans under the title, *Allegiance in America. The Case of the Loyalists* (Reading, Mass., 1969).

It is clear that there has slowly developed a new attitude toward the Loyalists, especially since the period when this study of the life of Jared Ingersoll was first undertaken at Yale. At that time the New Haven Historical Society owned a trunk full of Ingersoll's papers. Apparently it had never been opened, and the curator seemed most reluctant to have these Tory papers inspected, doubtless fearing that they might reflect upon leading New Haven patriotic families. Only through the influence of Professor William Cortez Abbott of Yale was it finally arranged that they could be examined. The first step on my part then was to put the manuscripts in proper order, for they were a confused mass. Then, when their importance had been made known and when it was clear that they in no way reflected adversely upon the people of New Haven, Dr. Franklin D. Dexter published a collection of the more important of them for the

New Haven Historical Society as Volume 9 of its *Papers*.

Undoubtedly much of the change of attitude on the part of the public toward the Loyalists came at the end of World War I. With the United States emerging as the leading world power, with territories comprehending non-English-speaking and non-European peoples, the public began to realize much more fully than before the weight of responsibilities that any metropolitan country must necessarily carry. In fact, there is now great eagerness to uncover Loyalist papers which have in many cases lain quite neglected for over two centuries. As evidence of this there was held in New York in November 1968 the first international conference concerned with the Loyalists, attended by representatives of Great Britain, Canada, and the United States. One outcome of this conference was the creation of three permanent centers for the preservation and subsequent editing and publication of Loyalist papers. The chief center is in New York and is under the direction of Professor Robert A. East of the City University of New York. A second center, in London, is under the direction of Professor Esmond Wright, M.P., of the University of London, and a third is in Canada at Fredericton, under the direction of Dean MacNutt of the University of New Brunswick. The American Council of Learned Societies and the American Antiquarian Society and, most recently, the National Endowment for the Humanities, have lent financial support in the establishment and maintenance of these centers.

PREFACE

In the present study an attempt has been made to illumi-
nate certain aspects of the very complex relationship
existing between England and her American colonies
during the later colonial period. For this purpose the
life of Jared Ingersoll of New Haven, Connecticut, has
been selected as the central theme. Probably no one was
more intimately identified with the last disastrous phases
of the British experiment with a reorganized system for
administering American affairs than was Ingersoll, and
it is also probable that no one in America possessed a
more intelligently sympathetic comprehension of what
the home government had in mind or strove more earnestly and ably to persuade his fellow countrymen to
accept the ministerial program in good faith. Judge
Ingersoll stands as representative of a group, the importance and numerical weight of which has not, at least
until very recently, been fully appreciated. He was no
more a radical in his support of the crown than was John
Dickinson in his support of the colonists. While he
opposed the propaganda of the liberty group whenever
the occasion seemed to demand it, his opposition never
was manifested in violent reaction. In other words, he
was a loyalist but a moderate; while at times he displayed great courage in defending his position he was
characteristically cautious; he typifies the innate conservatism of the man of property who prospers and
consequently is satisfied in the midst of discontent.

In interpreting the life of Jared Ingersoll I have
sought to present as fully as space will permit what may

be called the environmental factors, and in this connection I have especially emphasized the drift of affairs and the ebb and flow of opinion in Connecticut and especially at New Haven, where Ingersoll throughout his public career, whether present or absent, had a powerful and not infrequently a dominating influence.

I first became interested in the life of Jared Ingersoll in 1910 in connection with a seminar conducted by Professor Wilbur C. Abbott of Yale University, in which certain British imperial problems of the eighteenth century were studied. At that time I prepared a paper upon the public career of Ingersoll and the present volume in a sense is an expansion of that paper. I desire to express my indebtedness to Professor Abbott for his encouragement and the help that he has so generously extended to me at all times. In returning to Yale University in 1917 as the Bulkeley Fellow in American History, I entered the seminar of Professor Charles M. Andrews in American Colonial Institutions and in this seminar I worked out the institutional problems bearing upon my subject and developed the volume along its present lines. Professor Andrews's deep knowledge of the institutional life of this period has been of the greatest value to me and has saved me from falling into more than one error. I am also under particular obligations to the Department of History of Yale University for making it possible for me to obtain transcripts of numerous documents in British archives, not otherwise accessible to me. The New Haven Colony Historical Society very generously allowed me to make use of the Jared Ingersoll manuscripts, although at the time Dr. Franklin P. Dexter was editing for publication a select group of the papers, and Mr. Albert C. Bates of the Connecticut Historical Society, among other courtesies, kindly permitted me to take notes from the manuscripts of the

Fitch Papers, which at the time he was editing for publication. Mr. Frederick Bostwick of the New Haven Colony Historical Society, Mr. George S. Godard of the Connecticut State Library, Mr. Gaillard Hunt of the Department of State, Mr. John C. Fitzpatrick of the Manuscript Division of the Library of Congress, Mr. John W. Jordan of the Historical Society of Pennsylvania, Mr. Samuel A. Green of the Massachusetts Historical Society, Mr. Robert H. Kelby of the New York Historical Society, Mr. Victor H. Paltsits of the Manuscript Division of the New York Public Library, Dr. Franklin B. Dexter of the Yale University Library, Professor Simeon E. Baldwin of the Law School, Yale University, Mr. Clarence S. Brigham of the American Antiquarian Society, Mr. George Pratt Ingersoll of Ridgefield, Connecticut, and Mr. William M. Meigs of Philadelphia, have all given to me valuable aid, as have also numerous Connecticut state, county, and municipal officials. Professor Rollo W. Brown of Carleton College, Dr. Alice Edna Gipson of New Haven, my sister, and Jeannette Reed Gipson, my wife, have assisted me in various ways in preparing the manuscript for publication.

LAWRENCE H. GIPSON.

Wabash College,
November 1, 1919.

CONTENTS

CHAPTER I

EIGHTEENTH CENTURY COLONIAL NEW HAVEN[1]

It is the purpose of this chapter to deal with the environment within which Jared Ingersoll, the subject of the present study, rose to prominence as one of the leading figures connected with the British colonial administrative system in America. This environment was the background of those developing forces in Connecticut which culminated in the dramatic appeal to arms against Great Britain on the part of the radical group within the colony in opposition to the conservative elements under the recognized leadership of Ingersoll.

Colonial New Haven of the eighteenth century, the home of Ingersoll, was a progressive town; not only Connecticut's cultural center, but, with Hartford, a joint capital, and one of the most populous and wealthy of the semi-agricultural, semi-trading communities within that colony, which, unlike Massachusetts and New York, possessed no metropolis. In 1756 it was third in population within the colony, but by 1774 had outstripped its rivals and taken first place, increasing from 5085 inhabitants

[1] As this chapter is largely introductory in character it has been deemed advisable to omit all footnotes. The following are the chief sources upon which the writer has drawn: The *Connecticut Colonial Records*, the *Connecticut Gazette* and other contemporary newspapers, *Extracts from the Itineraries and Miscellanies of Ezra Stiles*, the New Haven Town Records in manuscript, the Ingersoll Papers, partly in manuscript and partly in print, the *Acts and Laws* of the colony, the *East Haven Register*, and various town and county histories.

to 8022. These figures include the population not only
of the town proper, but also of the outlying dependent
parishes of Woodbridge, Hamden, North Haven, and
East Haven, each with its own village church and school.
The town proper numbered in 1760 only about fifteen
hundred people; which shows how predominately agricultural were the interests of the township at this period.

According to early maps, New Haven must have been
laid out with considerable care and was in marked contrast to what might be called the typical New England
settlement by reason of its regular streets and equally
regular and spacious town lots. In the '50's the town
commons, known as the Green, seems to have been a wide
expanse of boggy sward, where cart wheels had worn
deep and unexpected ruts in the turf, horses, cattle and
flocks of geese roamed at will, pigs "yoaked and ringed"
rooted under the scrubby barberry bushes, and young-
sters encased in leather breeches and splatterdashes
sailed their boats on the commons pond. Then, as now,
the Green was the center of the community's religious,
intellectual, and political activities. Within it or in close
proximity to it were located the three churches, Yale
College, the Court House, the grammar school, and the
jail with stocks, whipping post, and gibbet ominously
advertised. In the early '50's a commodious brick state
house arose on the Green, taking the place of the old
court house.

Just as the Green was the center of the more spiritual
activities of the community, so the harbor, especially
after the French and Indian War, was the center of the
growing commercial life of the town. Horses and oxen,
barrels of pork, beef, tallow, with lumber, wheat, rye,
Indian corn, flaxseed, pot and pearl ashes, were collected at the wharves to be carried by the diminutive
brigantines, sloops, and schooners, either to New York

or Boston in return for the varied European manufactures which the people of New Haven seem to have used very extensively, or to the Caribbean Sea in exchange for cargoes of molasses, sugar, cocoa, and cotton.

In addition to the expanding commercial interests of the town, there was the distilling of rum made from molasses secured from the sugar islands and the manufacture of coarse linens and woolens "done in the Family way for the Use of the poorer Sort, Labourers, and Servants"; there was also an "iron mongery" where the more common iron implements appear to have been fashioned. However, a majority of the people living about the port of New Haven during this period were not concerned so much with shipping and manufacturing as they were with the absorbing occupation of extracting the more common farm products from the reluctant Connecticut soil. That this could be conveniently done while yet residing within the town jurisdiction can be understood when we realize that its limits included some eight square miles of land lying about the harbor and along the Quinnipiac, Mill, and West rivers which flow into it.

During the '50's, especially, there took place unmistakable signs of the expanding interests and growing importance of the community. Early in the decade an Anglican church was built close to the Green; in 1755 the first newspaper of the colony, the *Connecticut Gazette,* was established here by James Parker, and in that year "by authority of the King," a regular post office was opened; while in 1756 a custom house was erected, which became the port of entry and clearance for western Connecticut, with Nicholas Lechmere as the first collector.

These characteristically sober, church-going descendants of the early "Brahmins of Puritanism" who had settled at New Haven, had developed by the middle of the eighteenth century a social system that would have seemed amazingly complex and binding to the men who, for instance, had been reared in one of the later western frontier communities of the United States. The keynote of western achievement was individual initiative; on the other hand organized action and organized responsibility and individual subordination was the keynote in colonial New Haven. This organized type of life expressed itself in many ways; there were the church communion and the ecclesiastical society, the freemen's meetings, those of the proprietors, those of the train bands, and perhaps the most important of all, the periodic gatherings of the inhabitants of the town. An examination of each of those forms of social expression will show how necessarily submerged was the individuality of the average townsman and yet, on the other hand, how thorough was the schooling that he received in serving in public affairs as a mere instrument of community action.

The church communion consisted of those in full Christian fellowship who had made a public profession of faith and had subscribed to the convenant. At first there was only one meeting house in New Haven; but in 1741 came the division brought about by the Great Awakening, with the result that the New Light or revivalist group organized a church of its own under the name of the White Haven Society, which was not, however, legally recognized as a distinct congregation until 1759. In the meantime, early in the '50's the Anglicans became strong enough to establish Trinity Church, made up largely, including its pastor, of those seceding from the Congregational communion; finally, in 1771, the Fair Haven Church was established by the separation of the minority group from the White Haven congregation. All of this represents, of course, the breaking up of the former church unity of the town, a process that was going on in practically all of the Connecticut communities. While a great deal of intolerance and bitterness was shown at New Haven in the working out of this process, there is nothing in its annals that compares with the treatment accorded the Saybrook separatists, fourteen of whom in 1744, after being arrested for ''holding a meeting contrary to law on God's holy Sabbath day,'' were herded through the deep mud to New London, twenty-five miles distant, and there thrown into prison without fire, food, or beds for refusing to pay their fines.

Normally the church communion was the inner circle of the ecclesiastical society in colonial Connecticut; but as the colony approaches the Revolutionary period this does not hold true. However, until 1746 the ecclesiastical society of New Haven legally comprehended all those living within the bounds of the New Haven parish and, unless especially exempt, all were obliged to pay the assessments made by the society for the maintenance of the pastor and for church building purposes as well as to attend the meetings of the church on pain of fine, imprisonment, or some other form of punishment. In that year the general assembly denied the privilege of voting in ecclesiastical society meeting to those—Anglicans, Quakers, and Baptists—who had been legally exempt from the paying of the taxes of the society. This marked the disappearance of the old unity and all-inclusiveness of the society. Within it there still remained, besides the convenanted, those who had never taken the covenant or made a profession of faith. If the latter possessed a freehold within the society limits rated at fifty shillings or were rated at forty pounds or more in the common list, they had the privilege of uniting with those in full communion in voting for officers of the society, in the calling of a minister, in the granting of church rates, and in providing for the care and reconstruction of the church building as well as for the regulation of the school within the parish. After the White Haven and Fair Haven societies had been established within the old limits of the First Ecclesiastical Society, the general assembly provided that all the inhabitants who did not possess the special exemption accorded to Anglicans, Quakers, and Baptists, should decide in which of the three societies they preferred to be enrolled. There was, it should be understood, no place in colonial New Haven for the individual who could not support any of the organized churches with his presence and his money, for there was utterly lacking that spirit of kindly toleration regarding religious matters which is characteristic of people of intelligence in present-day Connecticut. The town, as it were, had grown out of the planting of a church, and its atmosphere was that of a church congregation.

While every endeavor was made to embrace all within the limits of the ecclesiastical society and to place upon them the privileges and responsibilities belonging to membership, no such endeavor was made to see that all men should share in the privileges and responsibilities of freemanship. For it was only the freemen in colonial Connecticut who could vote for the filling of the offices of the government as well as become its officers. To be made a freeman, one had to be twenty-one years of age, in possession of a freehold estate of the value of forty shillings per annum, or of forty pounds personal estate in the general assessment list for that year and to be ''of a quiet and peaceable Behaviour, and Civil Conversation.'' An applicant not only had to secure a certificate of endorsement from a majority of the selectmen of the town but appear in a freemen's meeting and there take the prescribed oath; whereupon his name was enrolled by the town clerk among those admitted to freemanship.

In case, however, he should be guilty of "walking scandalously" he was to be disfranchised by action of the superior court.

Exactly what proportion of the adult male population in colonial Connecticut exercised a freeman's privileges in the decades just preceding the Revolution, is difficult to estimate accurately. However, in 1703 a list of the "freemen" living within the limits of New Haven contained the names of one hundred and fifteen persons; in 1784, at the time of incorporation, there were two hundred and fifteen freemen out of six hundred adult males then living within the limits of the town, which previously had granted East Haven, North Haven, and Woodbridge their freedom. In February, 1766, at an exceedingly important meeting held in the town regarding the affairs of the colony, it was stated that there were two hundred and seventy-four "voters" present and it is to be presumed that most of those qualified attended. Since the population of the town at that time must have been over six thousand, it would seem that about one in twenty of the total number of people or one in four of the adult males were freemen, which is probably a smaller proportion than in most of the towns of the colony and would indicate, if such is the case, certain conservative and aristocratic tendencies on the part of this community.

The freemen's meetings, which were held regularly on the Monday following the first Tuesday in April and on the third Tuesday in September, show how complicated was the political organism of the colony. At the September meeting two deputies were elected to represent the town at the approaching October session of the assembly and at this time each freeman gave his vote by written ballot for twenty persons whom he judged qualified "to stand in nomination for election in the month of

May following." These votes were then sent to the
general assembly to be counted with the votes coming
from the other freemen's meetings throughout the colony. The twenty persons getting the highest number of
votes were thereupon nominated to stand as the candi-
dates at the May election when all the elective offices of
the colony were filled. At the April meeting, after the
deputies had been selected to attend the May session of
the assembly, the freemen then proceeded to ballot for
the governor, deputy governor, the twelve assistants who
acted both as a governor's council and as an upper house
of the general assembly, and, also, for the treasurer and
secretary of the colony. Unlike the meetings of the New
Haven Ecclesiastical Society, which had to do only with
the town proper, the New Haven freemen's meetings
were for the entire township and it was the votes of this
select group of men that determined the political tone
of the community with reference to colonial issues. Only
on the approach of the Revolution would it seem that
the non-freeman element, certainly an overwhelming
majority of the inhabitants, finally through violent and
terroristic means wrenched political control from the
hands of the more cautious, legally inclined, and prop-
ertied freemen.

The meetings of the proprietors of the common and
undivided lands of the town were a type of local gathering very distinct from any of the foregoing. Prior to
1683 there does not seem to have been any well-defined
idea that the proprietors of the unoccupied land within
the town were to be distinguished from the inhabitants.
The regular town meeting of the inhabitants from time
to time had freely granted lands to individuals upon
petition. But in that year a "division" or distribution
of a portion of the common lands was made, which raised
the issue as to ownership, and in 1685, in an attempt to

settle this, there was granted by the colony under the common seal to ''the Proprietors and Inhabitants of the Town of New Haven all that certain tract of land known as New Haven then and for many years before in their peaceable and quiet seissen and possession being.'' The grant was so ambiguous that it only added to the keenness of the struggle between the old established families and the newcomers. The result was that on October 20, 1704, a confirmation of the land grant to New Haven was made, in which proprietorship in the lands was specifically limited to the two hundred and forty-eight persons who had been recognized as the proprietors in 1685 and to their heirs and assignees. From this time on, therefore, a sharp distinction was drawn between the proprietors' meetings and those of the inhabitants of the town.

In the drawing of lots for the fifth ''division'' in 1711, four hundred and twenty-two participated; which gives some idea of the number of the proprietors of the New Haven common and undivided lands in the eighteenth century. With the steady increase in population and the consequent rise in the land values the importance of the careful management of the common lands also increased. Frequent meetings of the proprietors were held. The actions of proprietors of common lands in the colony were carefully regulated by the general assembly, which provided that on the first Monday of March a special meeting in each town should be called to choose a committee to care for the lands during the year. This committee was empowered to choose fence viewers and haywards out of the number of the proprietors; those thus chosen who refused to serve were fined. The assembly also provided that at any lawful meeting of proprietors, taxes might be levied upon the members for making fences, gates, bridges, and that the collectors of these rates were to possess the same powers as the collectors of the town rate. These proprietors' meetings, limited as they were in purpose, must nevertheless have been, just as the freemen's meetings were, centers of conservative influence.

The proprietors' meeting, freemen's meetings, and meetings of the ecclesiastical societies, of course, were but offshoots of the parent gathering, the meeting of the "inhabitants" of the town, which was by far the most comprehensive of all the local assemblages, recognized by law, in its scope of action and in respect of the number of dwellers within the town admitted to its privileges.

It should be understood that a man might be a dweller in a New England colonial town and yet, technically, not be an inhabitant, just as a man might be an inhabitant and not a freeman. In colonial New Haven three classes of individuals—transients or "single persons newly come," indentured servants, and slaves—"never were or are inhabitants in the Town." The code of 1750 declared brusquely that "several Persons of Ungoverned Conversation thrust themselves into the Towns in the Colony and by some Underhand way, as upon pretense of being Hired Servants, or of Hiring Lands or Houses or by Purchasing the same endeavor to become Inhabitants in such Towns"; to prevent which it was provided that no person should be admitted an inhabitant but "such of honest conversation," and that no stranger might have liberty to abide in the town without consent of the selectmen or the major part of the town; those warned out of town by the selectmen were to forfeit ten shillings a week or be whipped ten stripes if they did not leave.

But not even all adult male inhabitants were qualified to participate in the proceedings of the town meeting. One not only had to be a lawful inhabitant and to be twenty-one years of age, but, in addition, a householder in possession either of freehold estate rated at fifty shillings in the tax list, or of personal estate rated at forty pounds. There was, however, one exception; no freeman could be debarred from voting in the town meeting. What proportion of the adult males were qualified to act in the town meeting is not clear. Ezra Stiles records the fact that at a New Haven town meeting in December, 1761, at which a close division took place, there were two hundred and thirty-four who cast votes. It is, therefore, probable that as a rule not more than one-fourth and possibly not more than one-fifth of the adult males of the town took part in the business proceedings of the community.

One of the most important functions performed by this assembling of the inhabitants was the selection of the local officials designated to carry out the multifarious activities of a Connecticut community of that period, where few matters were considered to be of so private a nature as not to be subjected to the inquisitorial scrutiny of those delegated for that purpose by the common authority. These officials were annually selected at a meeting held the last Thursday in December. It is illuminating to observe how comprehensive was this list of periodically chosen town dignitaries.

There were the seven selectmen who had the oversight of local affairs when the town meeting was not in session; a clerk to keep the minutes of the meetings and the other town records, and a treasurer who guarded and disbursed the funds of the town; in 1762, eight constables seem to have been needed to watch over the peace and quiet of the community and sixteen tithing men, for the maintenance of the ecclesiastical regulations, were commissioned faithfully to look after the moral welfare of the inhabitants during the week days, and on the Sabbath, to maintain order in the meeting houses through-

out the interminable sermons and, as the old formula
reads, ''to smite such as are unruly or of uncomely behaviour in the meeting.''   There were many other officials besides the above whose work was scarcely of less
importance.   At the same town meeting in 1762, not only
were nine former key keepers, whose duty it was to
empound stray animals, confirmed in their posts for
another year, but four others were granted liberty to
build pounds at their own cost and be key keepers of
them; eight branders were made responsible for placing
the brand on the horses owned within the town; twenty-
eight surveyors of highways were named to care for the
generally miserable country roads and to see that each
man in the township, not otherwise exempt, did his share
of the road work; and two fence viewers were given the
general supervision of the fences and boundaries of the
community.   Then, there was appointed one gauger and
packer to supervise the packing of beef, pork, and fish
in casks by those preparing these articles for the market;
a sealer of leather to prevent poorly tanned leather from
being made up into articles and sold; a sealer of measures as well as a sealer of weights—one to see that standard measures were used by venders and the other to make
sure of standard weights—and an excise master, who
collected, for the support of colonial government, an
excise of four pence on every gallon of rum, brandy, and
other distilled spirituous liquors sold by any tavern
keeper or retailer of liquor.   These, together with
twelve grand jurymen to make presentment of all misdemeanors, nine listers designated to prepare assessment lists, a collector of the rates or taxes of those living
within the town proper, and one to collect the same of
those living in the outer parishes, made up the impressive list of the community administrators in the '60's.

In other words, it was necessary to find those qualified

to fill over one hundred public posts in this little seaport which was a perfect network of officialdom. That it was sometimes considered a burden to hold an office is shown by the fact that the code of 1750 provided for a fine of twenty-six shillings from any person who refused to exercise the office to which he was elected, unless he could show that he was "Oppressed by such Choice," and that others were or are "Unjustly Exempted."

As might be anticipated, by far the largest share of matters that came before the town meeting were those logically springing out of the routine of the rather isolated life of a community that was, down to the Revolutionary War, in spite of its location, chiefly agricultural in character. Moreover, its scope of action was not infrequently limited by the restrictions placed upon it by the general assembly and a great deal of its work consisted in giving expression to the registered will of the higher body. Occasionally the assembly would pass an act, general in character, allowing to the local gatherings discretion as to whether or not it should be applied. For example, it was provided by law that no swine were to be allowed to go at large and that the town haywards were to empound such as did; but a clause was added which allowed the towns within their own precincts "to agree otherwise." As a result, with almost machinelike regularity the New Haven town meeting was accustomed to suspend the operation of the act, so that these "beasts" could roam on the commons if they were "yoked and ringed from the 10th day of March to the 10th Day of November and ringed all the year."

While such things as the straying of swine had thus been regulated by the colonial government, other matters of a similar nature were left entirely to the discretion of the individual town meetings. The straying of geese, almost as great a menace to the peace and happiness of colonial Connecticut as the straying of swine, was in this category. The New Haven town meeting, in an endeavor to placate everyone, arrived at the decision that owners of geese might have the privilege of grazing them on the commons from May to October but that should these errant birds be found doing damage in any particular field and, as a consequence, be empounded, they should be released only upon payment of two pence per head. Further to protect the crops of the inhabitants, the town meeting, of its own initiative, opened an avenue for an assault upon the town hoard by ordering four pence per head to be paid for crows by the collector of the town rate. But when it came to the destruction of barberry bushes, which were "thought to be very Hurtful by Occasioning (or at least Increasing) the Blasting of English Grain," the town was able to support its action by the express permission given to each community by the general assembly to deal with the problem as seemed best. At a meeting in December, 1763, it was, therefore, resolved after earnest deliberation that these noxious shrubs should be exterminated; and, as a result, the surveyors of the highways were instructed to "warn out" the inhabitants of their respective districts in the months of April and May to wage systematic warfare against them.

The preëminently pastoral and coöperative character of the community until well along in the eighteenth century, is further evidenced by the fact that as late as the '30's the selectmen were regularly called upon in town meeting to provide a sufficient number of bulls and boars for the town plot and to "assess the Inhabitants £8, if need be, for the use of Bulls and Boars, to be paid to the owners thereof." It was decided at another meeting that if any sheep in the several flocks in the town stray from the keepers, no man should empound these strays from off the commons. To protect the larger, common, agricultural interests, individual members of the community were occasionally compelled by these public gatherings to make important concessions. As an instance of this, the raising of doves was placed under the ban when it was concluded that they were more hurtful than profitable, and the selectmen were instructed to inform the owners "that the town expects them to destroy said Doves." Also, those inhabitants who were husbandmen were required by the same authority to provide axletrees for their carts "5 or 6 inches wider than now," and those who possessed cows that "use the walk where there is a cow keeper" were ordered to pay by the week to the cow keeper what others were paying for the tending of their cattle. It was not until 1724 that the "wilderness of New Haven" was plotted and in the '30's the leasing and care of the "Town Farms" was a matter that deeply concerned the inhabitants. In March, 1763, embracing a policy of conservation of resources, the inhabitants voted to close the oyster beds for a year.

The New Haven town meeting of the eighteenth century also concerned itself with a variety of matters that had nothing to do with the economic side of life. The constables on one occasion were even directed by this body to take notice of people opening the windows of the meeting house in time of public worship; after complaint was made at another time that mischievous boys played in the market place and that, as a result, "the meeting house windows are often shamefully broken," it was determined to prohibit boys from playing within twenty rods of the meeting house on penalty of a fine of twelve pence and the cost of damages.

The appointment of committees was a favorite method employed for getting special things accomplished by the town meeting. As examples of this, on December 10,

1753, St. Joseph Mix, Jared Ingersoll, and Thomas Howell were selected as a committee to audit the accounts arising in connection with the building of a pesthouse; on December 14 of the same year St. Joseph Mix, Phinehas Bradley, and Jared Ingersoll were designated to advise with the selectmen concerning the maintenance of one Brighton, "a distracted man now in the town"; on December 19, 1754, Jared Ingersoll and two others were asked to join a committee from the Milford town meeting for the joint construction of a bridge over "Oyster river"; and on December 12, 1763, a committee including Ingersoll was desired to lay a plan for supporting poor persons.

Fairly trivial as many of these matters now appear to be, which occupied the inhabitants at these gatherings, they were, nevertheless, among the things that bulked largest in the eyes of the average man and really conditioned his immediate welfare far more than the weightiest imperial legislation. What is more, from many angles the town meeting served as an excellent school in which to gather political experience. No colony produced a shrewder group of politicians than those that sprang from the Connecticut town meetings.

The most notable issue which came before the New Haven town meeting prior to the Revolution, was that raised by the people of East Haven parish, known more commonly as the people of the "Iron Works" or the "East Farmers," who made an attempt to break away from the jurisdiction of the town in 1707, thus precipitating a struggle which at times was carried on with great bitterness and which lasted until 1785. It centered upon three issues: the right of East Haven to be represented in the general assembly, the right to raise and dispose of its own taxes, and the right to control the common lands within its bounds. In 1707 the parish secured incorporation as a village, but the charter was very ambiguously worded and it is possible that Governor Saltonstall, as has been charged, used his influence against the little community because of a feud that had arisen between him and the East Farmers on account of the merciless war he waged upon their geese, which strayed into his near-by fields and resorted to his lake. From October, 1708, to October, 1710, the parish sent deputies to the general assembly, against the strenuous opposition of New Haven, which succeeded in that year in getting the assembly to deny them this right. In 1712 this body ordered that the East Haven assessment list be added to that of New Haven, and in 1716, that the care of the poor among the East Farmers belonged to the New Haven town meeting, not to East Haven. "Silenced by the terror of law suits and 'the powers that be,' East Haven submitted till another generation arose that had not known a Saltonstall." In 1752, at a meeting of inhabitants, called December 18, this plucky parish again renewed its fight for liberty. After resolving to take up the privileges granted by the general assembly in 1707, a group of town officers was selected and a committee was sent to the New Haven town meeting to give due notification, "in order that the said town of New Haven may hereafter exempt themselves from any further care or trouble respecting the said affairs of the said Town of East Haven, the regulations thereof or the Appointment of officers therein." But the mother town was inflexible in its opposition to this design and exerted so powerful an influence upon the colonial government that once again "the broad hand of the General Assembly" fell upon the people of the iron works. Not until after eighty years of conflict, not unmixed with disorders and violence, was the independence of East Haven finally achieved, two years after the peace which brought about the legal separation of the colonies from the mother country.

Controlled largely by the same elements that directed the freemen's meetings and those of the proprietors, the New Haven town meeting appears to have been rather consistently conservative during the decades preceding the Revolution, standing generally for the maintenance of the old order of things and discountenancing the extreme policies of the radical group dwelling in the town. In this respect New Haven stood in marked contrast to its offspring, Wallingford, which had succeeded in detaching itself from the former before the beginning of the eighteenth century. In 1766, under control of the radical influence, the Wallingford town meeting did not hesitate, as will be seen, to set itself up as superior in authority, within its own boundaries, even to parliament. No such extravagance ever characterized the action of a New Haven colonial town meeting.

Over against these influences, which could be counted on to oppose hasty and violent political action within the community, stood the train bands. Under the law all males between sixteen and fifty years of age, except those holding posts under the colonial government, those connected with the "Collegiate School," masters of arts, justices of the peace, physicians, surgeons, schoolmasters, attorneys-at-law, one miller to a gristmill, constant herdsmen, mariners and ferrymen, sheriffs and constables, as well as lame and disabled persons, Negroes and Indians, were required to attend musters and military exercises. Although it is true that, under ordinary conditions, these men gathered together but four days annually for training, yet in each town the military organization remained intact, all the while exercising an influence on the course of affairs which, it seems, has been too little appreciated by scholars up to the present.

It should be remembered that although the regimental officers were appointed by the Connecticut government, the officers of the train bands from captain downward were selected by the enrolled men and that, as the result of exemptions, the elections were controlled by the popular, more irresponsible elements which naturally put in command those who sympathized with their point of view. These popular officers, many of them adventurous characters, at times exercised, especially in eastern Connecticut, a degree of authority in political affairs which brushed aside any and all opposition. It was not until 1775, however, that the New Haven military group succeeded in acquiring any such influence; then, under the leadership of Benedict Arnold, it threatened to break open the door to the town powder house unless supplied with ammunition, and by a display of force thoroughly overawed the civil authority.

The radical tendencies of the train bands, which came to the surface when complications developed between the colonies and the mother country, seem to have been encouraged by the still more radical tendencies of traders and sailors clearing from this port, who were thoroughly aroused by the revenue acts of 1764 and 1767. Then there were the New Lights of White Haven and Fair Haven churches, both of which congregations were responsive to popular impulses, as well as the faculty and a majority of the two hundred students of Yale College, under the guidance of the acting president, Naphtali Daggett. These groups, as political agitation developed, stood in sharp opposition, not only to the conservatively inclined Old Lights, who made up the membership of the First Ecclesiastical Society, but to the Anglicans of Trinity Church and the little body of loyalist Sandemanians. The local papers, first the *Connecticut Gazette* and later its successor, the *Connecticut Journal,* while much more restrained in utterance than the *New London Gazette,* disseminated revolutionary ideas. The ten or fifteen taverns in New Haven seem to have been still more active agencies for their distribution; for the agitators appear to have made these resorts rallying centers and many of the more violent and terroristic acts preceding the actual outbreak of the war are almost inexplicable unless it be accepted that they were committed by men and youths made temporarily irresponsible by strong drink. This, in fact, was publicly charged by a writer in the local paper in 1768, after one of these scenes of wild disorder.

It should be appreciated that in regard to such a community as colonial New Haven, one is not dealing with a people possessed of democratic ideas in any modern sense of the word. Consistently enough, in the light of the prevailingly strong predestinarianism, the blessing of liberty and equality which men had so much to say about in the '60's and '70's were not for all to enjoy, but, just as in the case of salvation, rather, for the elect. Even as late as 1777, a writer in the local paper bitterly complained of the treatment of the ''separatists'' or those of the Congregational communion who had repudiated the Saybrook platform. ''They have been persecuted, oppressed and most cruelly treated, their property has most unjustly been taken from them to support ministers that in conscience they could not hear preach; and at the same time, they have had ministers of their own to support; they have been imprisoned for not paying the rates to the clergy and fined for not attending public worship with the standing churches.'' Unitarians and deists, moreover, were struck at by a colonial law providing that those denying ''any one of the Persons of the Holy Trinity to be God'' or denying the Scriptures to be of divine authority should, on conviction, be incapable of enjoying any offices ecclesiastical, civil, or military; and a penalty of ten shillings as a fine was levied against any person daring to form a "separate Company for worship in a private House."

Nor were conceptions of liberty and equality more liberally interpreted in the fields of social and industrial activities. Until well past the middle of the eighteenth century it would appear that the majority of the leading religious lights of the colony failed to record any disapproval of the institution of slavery. So devout a man as Rev. Ezra Stiles, who later became president of Yale College, was guilty of sending a barrel of rum to the Arab slavers of Guinea for the purchase of a slave; a Connecticut clergyman, acting as governor, decided that the offspring of a negro bond woman was born in slavery; indented whites were gladly purchased by the well-to-do of New Haven and set to work beside the slaves in the fields; while the town paupers were put through what would now be called the degrading spectacle of being sold at auction from the steps of the state house on the Green, to such as could keep them for the year at the lowest rate. Only a community that was fundamentally aristocratic in structure could fail to detect the hopeless incongruity of publishing in the local paper, side by side with passionate exhortations to all freemen to struggle for their disappearing and precious liberties, equally fervent appeals to the public to assist in the capture of some runaway white or black attempting to escape from his servitude. In reality the broad humanitarianism and the generous idealism manifested in American life today found little lodgment in the mind of the typical, sturdy New England colonist, for these were largely the product of that great leveling movement which at a later date swept eastward from beyond the Alleghenies.

If one were to characterize in general terms the ten-

dencies at work in eighteenth-century colonial New
Haven, it might be said that the town was going through
a notable period of transition, often accompanied by
rather violent manifestations. Although the multiplied
restraints upon individual freedom of thought and action
still largely remained, the old unity and homogeneity was
fast breaking down. The immediate result of this cen-
trifugal movement was a process of differentiation in the
institutions that expressed the organic life of the community. The unified church communion of 1700, together
with the all-embracing character of the ecclesiastical
society, had disappeared, as had the earlier identity between the dwellers in the town, the inhabitants of the
same, and the proprietors of the town lands. Caught by
this outward swing, the outlying parishes began, one
after another, to seek an independent life. The struggle
of East Haven to obtain the right of self-taxation and
self-regulation generally, undoubtedly epitomizes in
many respects those impulses that led the people of
the colony, in turn, to seek separation from the mother
country.

CHAPTER II

EARLY DAYS. THE OFFICE OF KING'S ATTORNEY

JARED INGERSOLL came of the Ingersoll line of Bedfordshire, England.[1] His grandfather, John Ingersoll, left England in 1629, the fatal year when Charles I dismissed his third parliament, introducing thereupon a decade of unrestrained political despotism. Shrouded in obscurity as are the causes which led to John's departure from England, it is probable that he, then in his fourteenth year, had already identified himself with the Puritan opponents of the prerogative party in England and, not averse to a great adventure, together with his elder brother, Richard, became a member of one of the numerous groups of the discontented that left for New England at that period. Richard settled at Salem in Massachusetts Bay where, in 1644, he died.[2] John, after stopping for a time with his brother, pushed out into the west, locating successively at Hartford and Northampton; while at the former town, he married. In 1666, caught with the pioneer spirit, he and his family went with a group of settlers into the western wilderness of Massachusetts Bay, where they established the town of Westfield, and here John became one of the "seven pillars"

[1] The name originally in England was Inkersoll. For facts relating to the early Ingersolls see C. S. Ripley, *The Ingersolls of Hampshire, A genealogical History of the Family from their settlement in America in the line of John Ingersoll of Westfield, Mass.*

[2] *Ibid.*, p. 12.

or foundation men in the local church.[1]   He was married, in all, three times and became the father of fifteen children, the youngest of whom was Jonathan.[2]   The latter, early left an orphan, went as a youth to Milford, Connecticut, where he took up the trade of a joiner. There is every reason to believe that he became a thrifty man as well as an efficient artificer, for he gradually accumulated substantial possessions in land and personal property; he even became the master of three slaves.[3]   At the age of thirty-one he married Sarah, the widow of David Miles of New Haven; their three surviving children were Jonathan, who graduated from Yale College in 1736 and became pastor of the Ridgefield church; Sarah, who married the clerk of the New Haven County Court, John Whiting; and Jared, the subject of this study, who was born in 1722.

Although nothing has been ascertained regarding his

[1] *The Ingersolls of New Hampshire*, p. 15.

[2] Jonathan's mother, Mary Hunt, came of good stock, for she was the granddaughter of John Webster, who in 1656 was chosen governor of Connecticut.   Jonathan's father died when the former was but three and a half years of age, while his mother died in his tenth year.

[3] Jonathan died in 1761.   His eldest son was administrator of his estate, and he presented to the court an itemized record of everything his father possessed even to the smallest detail, with an estimated value upon each article.   The whole amounted to £1202.13.2.   This inventory shows what a substantial Connecticut freeholder at that period was apt to possess and also furnishes an idea of the comparative prices of things.   His coat was valued at £5; a vest at 10s.; a pair of breeches at 4/6; another at 1/6; a shirt at 5/3; a pair of stockings at 1/8; a pair of shoes at 4/3; another pair 1s.; buckles at 6d.; his sole handkerchief at 1s.; his hat at 10s.; a quilt at 9d.; pewter plates and porringer at 8/3; a porridge pot at 7/11; a brass "Kittle" at 31/6; an iron "Kittle" 2/5; five knives and forks at 2/6; a tea "Kittle" at 4s.; his tankard at 10s.; his sorrel mare at £4.10; his white mare at £2; his seven sows from £2.13 to 3.17.6; his bull at £1.15; a pair of oxen at £19 and a pair of steers at £8.5; two sheep at 18s.; his negro Cradd at £50; Cyphax at £30 and Kate at £35; his lands, amounting to 135 acres, at £3.15 an acre up to £6.12; his house and barn with house lot at £158. See the New Haven Probate Records (1756-1763), IX, 636-638, 469-470.

earlier years, it is certain that Jared was allowed the leisure to prepare for college. What books came into his hands are unknown; the only works of any sort appearing in the inventory made of his father's estate at the time of the latter's death in 1761 were two Bibles and a Testament. However, the young man, after his matriculation at Yale, so distinguished himself that upon his graduation in 1742 he was awarded the much prized Berkeley scholarship, which opened the way for an additional year of study.[1] It is interesting to note, in passing, that the estimate which the college authorities placed upon the social standing of his father gave him ninth place in a graduating class of sixteen. That Jared was led early in life to the consideration of serious things is vouchsafed by the survival of a somewhat abstruse historical essay, which he prepared in his eighteenth year while at Yale, upon the cumbersome and all-inclusive topic of "An Historical Account of some affairs Relating to the church especially, in Connecticut, together with some other Things of a Different Nature."[2] In fact, a love of theological mysteries followed this busy, practical man through life.[3] But, in spite of his studious habits and serious-mindedness, Ingersoll did not neglect the opportunity of cultivating warm friendships with his fellow students. That some, at least, of these attachments were firm is apparent from a letter which one of his classmates wrote from Elizabethtown, New Jersey, a score of years after separating at Yale: "It would

[1] F. B. Dexter, *Yale Biographies and Annals, 1701-1745*, pp. 712-714.

[2] The original manuscript is in the Library of Congress. The cover is entitled "Ingersoll Historical Notes MS." It has the caption "Yale College, Oct. 20, 1740."

[3] The years from 1779 to 1781, just previous to his death, were largely taken up with an extensive correspondence with Dr. Benjamin Gale (Yale, 1733) upon scriptural problems. Eight of these letters have been preserved and are in the Yale Library.

give me high satisfaction to take my worthy friend by the hand and I almost insist that if your affairs call you again to New York you come over and spend a day or two in my country cottage where you will meet with a most cordial reception from an old chum who frequently recollects with pleasure the many agreeable social hours spent with you at *alma mater.*"[1]

But that Jared by no means confined himself to the companionship of his Yale acquaintances and his books, is evidenced by the fact that when his academic career came to a close in 1743, he was very soon afterward married to Hannah Whiting of New Haven.[2] The young people decided to make their home in the college town, and here was born to them in 1748, Jared, Jr., the only one of four children to survive.[3]

Young Ingersoll, apparently very soon after leaving college, took up the practice of law.[4] How he received his preparation for this profession is not known. Undoubtedly much of the time as Berkeley scholar was

[1] W. P. Smith of Elizabethtown, New Jersey, to Ingersoll. Endorsed 1763. Ingersoll Collection, New Haven Colony Historical Society Archives. This will be referred to as the "Ingersoll Collection."

[2] Entry Book of Births, Marriages, and Deaths, I, 509 (Office of Clerk of Vital Statistics, New Haven).

There has survived an interesting document which is entitled, "Acco. of Hannah Ingersoll alias Whiting. Advance in Settlement." It consists of the list of articles, in all valued at £350, which she brought as her marriage portion, not including her personal wardrobe. Out of this list, dining-room, kitchen and bedroom could be furnished with practical completeness. This list can be found in the "Jared Ingersoll Papers," a selection from the larger body of papers which have been recently edited by Dr. Franklin B. Dexter of Yale University, and have been published in Volume IX of the *Papers* of the New Haven Colony Historical Society (1918).

[3] New Haven Entry Book of Births, Marriages, and Deaths, I, 642.

[4] "Messrs. Samuel Andrew and Jared Ingersoll both of Milford were allowed to be attorneys in this court and were admitted to the oath before the Court by Law provided for attorneys of County Court the third Tues. of Jan. 1743/4." New Haven County Court Records, IV, 205.

spent in reading law. At least, it is certain that he was
sufficiently well trained to meet with almost immediate
success. The prosperity enjoyed by the rising young
lawyer was naturally reflected in his domestic life. The
Ingersoll home maintained in the '60's on Chapel Street,
facing the Green, must have been a commodious establishment. Like his father and many other well-to-do
New Englanders, Ingersoll came to possess an appren-
ticed servant and negro slaves. Facts relating to these
throw interesting light upon social conditions in New
Haven at this period:

Two years after their marriage, the Ingersolls acquired Lucretia Smith, a white child of eight years, the
daughter of William Smith, "a transcient person," and
Ruth Smith, "who do not take care of their children."
On May 20, 1745, the child was bound by her mother to
serve Ingersoll until she was sixteen years of age; in
consideration for which she was to receive "meat, drink,
washing, lodging, and apparel." The agreement also
provided that her master, in addition, was "to learn her
to read English."[1] However, the following year, on
March 3, "there was agreed an indenture by the selectmen of New Haven whereby Lucretia was bound to serve
until she was eighteen years of age." According to the
new indenture she was to be taught sewing, knitting,
spinning, and household work, in addition to the reading
of English. The document ends by reciting that when
dismissed "she shall have 2 gowns (one for Sabbath
Day; the other for week days' work), and give her a
Bible." The last clause making provision for her spir-

[1] New Haven Col. Hist. Soc. *Papers*, IX ("Jared Ingersoll Papers"),
208-209. Indenture in Ingersoll MS. Collection. For an account of this
system of apprenticeships see R. F. Seybolt, *Apprenticeship and Apprenticeship Education*. (Teachers College, Columbia University, Contributions
to Education, No. 85.)

itual welfare was apparently an afterthought, for it was written in another hand.[1]

The records of the slaves purchased from time to time by Ingersoll have been preserved. On May 31, 1751, he bought from Stephen Alling, Cambridge, a boy of eight years, for whom he paid £320;[2] twelve-year-old Zilphie, owned by Thaddeus Cook, June 16, 1755, cost £550; Isban, thirty years of age, purchased from Christopher Kelley, November 2, 1761, cost £50; Damon, twenty years of age, the property of his friend, Joshua Chandler, was acquired June 27, 1764, for £80, and Rachel Hubbard Leah, a mature woman, cost him, November 7, 1765, £36. One is able to get a comparison of values by noting that May 9, 1764, he paid £17 for a black horse, presumably a first-

[1] New Haven Col. Hist. Soc. *Papers*, IX (''Jared Ingersoll Papers''), 209-210. The law provided that all parents and masters should teach children under their care to read the English tongue and to know the laws against capital offenders. If unable to do so much the child was at least to be taught some short orthodox catechism ''without Book.'' Children were to be brought up to some honest calling. Selectmen with the advice of a justice of the peace were to bind neglected children out, males until twenty-one years of age and females until eighteen. *Acts and Laws of Connecticut* (1750), pp. 20-21.

[2] These purchases are recorded on loose-leaf memoranda. Ingersoll Collection. Until 1756 accounts were kept according to the purchasing power of the old tenor bills, which stood to sterling in the ratio of 5-9 to 1, varying with the year, when ''lawful money'' accounts make their appearance. ''Wheat was charged at three shillings and nine pence a bushel, which just before had been set down at forty-five or forty-eight shillings.'' Henry Bronson, *Connecticut Currency*, p. 74. This was brought about by the act of the general assembly, October, 1755, declaring that accounts of the colonial government, from November 1 on, would be kept in lawful money. *Conn. Col. Rec.*, X, 424. ''In the early part of the eighteenth century the price of slaves varied from 60s to £25; toward the middle of the century the price ordinarily was £75 to £125.'' F. Morgan, *Connecticut as a Colony and as a State*, II, 504. Morgan, however, does not make clear in what money at these respective periods the slaves were valued. For an important statement regarding Connecticut colonial currency the student should consult the New Haven Colony Hist. Soc. *Papers*, IX (''Jared Ingersoll Papers''), 223-224, footnote.

class animal, and two years previous, £100 for one and one-fourth acres of land bordering upon the Green.[1]

That Ingersoll's position as a slave holder was not an isolated one and that the leading families of New Haven were not apt to forego the opportunity of enjoying the services of at least a black or two, is shown by the fact that in 1762, according to Rev. Ezra Stiles, there were eighty-three Negroes among that part of the population living in the town proper; and according to an official report of that year there were four thousand five hundred and ninety blacks within the colony.[2] The strong financial standing of Ingersoll in the community is evidenced not only by the possession of slaves and numerous plots of real estate,[3] scattered about the town, but also by the fact that in 1761 there was owing him £986.12.5, in that day a small fortune in itself.[4]

Paintings that have survived show Jared Ingersoll, in his maturity, to have been a man of solid build, well proportioned, with features of unusual regularity and a countenance expressing frankness and amiability.[5] His natural dignity and assured culture were emphasized by his dress, which betokened that he was a man of taste and fashion, a gentleman of the old colonial school, as closely

[1] The Ingersoll Papers. His father's mares were valued at £4.10 and £2 in 1761. New Haven Probate Records, IX, 469. It appears that in 1778 Ingersoll sold Leah to Pompey Punchard, a free Negro. New Haven Col. Hist. Soc. *Papers*, IX ("Jared Ingersoll Papers"), 221, footnote.

[2] *Itineraries of Ezra Stiles*, p. 49; "Answers to Lords of Trade," 1762, *Conn. Col. Rec.*, XI, 630.

[3] See New Haven Town Records, "Real Estate Transfers," XIX, 30, 136; XX, 434.

[4] Ingersoll Account Books, I (Yale University Library).

[5] At least two oil paintings of Ingersoll have survived; one, painted by Copley, is in the possession of Mr. Ingersoll Armory of Boston and has been reproduced in Volume IX of the New Haven Col. Hist. Soc. *Papers;* the other, which is a much smaller painting, is in the possession of George Pratt Ingersoll, Esq., of Ridgefield, Connecticut.

akin in spirit to the Virginia cavalier as was likely to be found in New England.[1]   In religious matters, like his father and grandfather, he remained a Congregationalist, a communicant in the First Ecclesiastical Society at the conservative Old Light meeting house, presided over, in his day, in turn by Rev. Joseph Noyes and Rev. Chauncey Whittelsey. Together with his friend, Joshua Chandler, who later became a Tory refugee, he was a veritable pillar of this church, which stood in sharp opposition to the more democratic and emotionally inclined evangelical New Light White Haven Ecclesiastical Society, which had come into existence in the '40's as a seceding and rebellious wing of the First Society.[2]

All of Ingersoll's interests had the effect of identifying him with the most conservative element in the town,[3] and what undoubtedly added greatly to his growing prominence was that in 1751 he was appointed to the office of king's attorney for the county of New Haven.[4]

To appreciate the character of the public responsibilities thus laid upon Jared Ingersoll, there are certain facts regarding the historical significance of this post

[1] This is illustrated in a letter written by a soldier friend, in 1755, who sends him a poem for ''amusement . . . when you have nothing to do, that is, when you are smoking the last pipe before bed.'' E. Lyman to Jared Ingersoll, September 2, 1755, Ingersoll Papers.

[2] In 1759 the White Haven church was formally separated from the First Society by the general assembly. *Conn. Col. Rec.*, XI, 323-325.

[3] The reluctance of Ingersoll to break with old and tried forms, in contrast with the diverging, democratic spirit of colonials in general, which scorned the ritual and studied formalism of the institutions of the mother country, is brought out in a letter written to the latter in 1756 by his brother-in-law, Colonel Whiting, who was at Albany with the Connecticut troops. Speaking of the law, the latter wrote, ''I hate all the formalities at the Bar and would have you come to the case at once, but you say they are necessary and the world says you know well about it.'' Nathan Whiting to Jared Ingersoll, June 22, 1756, Ingersoll Papers.

[4] According to the law of May, 1730, for each action pleaded the attorney was to receive a fee of 10s. *Conn. Col. Rec.*, VII, 280.

of king's attorney which should be made clear.[1] The origin of the office in Connecticut, with its high sound of loyalty, harks back to the stirring events of the beginning of the century, when England and France were involved in the early stages of that titanic struggle for colonial empire which, beginning in 1689, was continued, with occasional breathing spells, until the Peace of Paris in 1763. In spite of certain advantages that England, with her sea supremacy, enjoyed, and in spite of the more solid character of her colonial settlements, it seemed at times as though the superior organization of the French, with a unified administration of their possessions in the New World, would more than offset these advantages. Those responsible for the guidance of England's affairs, especially the Board of Trade and Plantations under the successive presidencies of the Earl of Bridgewater, Lord Stanford, and Lord Dartmouth, had gradually reached the conclusion that it was imperative, not only for the establishment of an effective system of imperial defense but also for the proper expansion of trade and commerce within the Empire, that a centralization of colonial administration should be effected by placing all the colonies in America under direct royal control.[2]

Though bitter opposition to this plan for greater imperial unity and efficiency was not lacking, especially in the corporate and proprietary colonies, nevertheless, there were not wanting those established in America who came ardently to the support of the British authorities in their program. Edward Randolph, Joseph Dudley, Benjamin Fletcher, Jeremiah Basse, Robert Quary, and

[1] Curiously enough Professor Howard, in his *Local Constitutional History*, does not mention this important county office.

[2] For the representation of the board of March 26, 1701, see Public Record Office, Colonial Office, 5: 1289, pp. 12-17, printed in the *North Carolina Colonial Records*, I, 535-537. See also *Calendar of State Papers, Colonial* (1701), p. 386.

Lord Cornbury, all enjoying public posts in the colonies, heaped up charges against the colonial governments.[1] In Connecticut the assault on the charter was led by Rev. Gershom Bulkeley[2] of Glastonbury, Major Edward Palmes of New London, and William Rosewell of Branford. Bulkeley, as early as 1692, penned a large folio work which he entitled, "Will and Doom, or a History of the Miseries of Connecticut under the arbitrary power of the present Government."[3] In this he lamented the passing away of the Andros government, and "with great cunning and art" developed his case against the charter government of Connecticut. This able and extended philippic was placed in the hands of the board in 1703 by Lord Cornbury.[4] Two years previous, a bill for "Re-

[1] See L. P. Kellogg, *The American Colonial Charter*, printed in the American Historical Association *Report* (1903), I, Chapter IV. A large number of interesting and valuable letters relating to this are to be found in R. R. Hinman, *Letters from the English Kings and Queens . . . to the Governors of the Colony of Connecticut, Together with the Answers Thereto, from 1635 to 1749*, pp. 189 *et seq.*

[2] Rev. Gershom Bulkeley was graduated from Harvard College in 1655. He was a minister at New London and later at Wethersfield. In 1676 he removed to Glastonbury, where he devoted himself to the practice of medicine and law. Although in 1675 he had opposed Andros at Saybrook, he accepted under the latter in 1687 the appointment of justice of the peace for Hartford County. In 1689 he was supported by Major Edward Palmes of New London, a son-in-law of the first Governor Winthrop, in opposing resumption of the charter government in Connecticut, upon the collapse of the Andros régime. Bulkeley, Palmes, and Rosewell signed a petition in 1692 "in behalf of themselves and the rest of their Majesties' loyal subjects, freeholders in their Majesties' Colony of Connecticut," which was transmitted by Governor Fletcher of New York to the home government.

[3] This was edited by C. J. Hoadly and is printed with notes in the Connecticut Historical Society *Collections*, III.

[4] C. S. P. (1702-1703), p. 522; Conn. Hist. Soc. *Coll.*, III, 77. Sir Henry Ashurst, who was acting as the Connecticut agent in London, claimed that the book was sent over by Dudley's connivance. Sir Henry Ashurst to the Governor and Council of Connecticut, February 15, 1704/5; printed in Hinman, *Letters*, p. 321. Hoadly considered that Major Palmes, who had two appeals pending, was responsible. Conn. Hist. Soc. *Coll.*, III,

uniting to the Crown the governments of the several
colonies and plantations in America" was introduced in
parliament but failed of passage.[1]   This, however, did
not discourage the opponents of the charter, who, if possible, rather increased the keenness of their attacks.
Governor Cornbury wrote from New York that the people of Connecticut "hate anybody that owes subjection to
the Queen."[2]   Sir Henry Ashurst, the London agent of
the colony, warned Governor Fitzjohn Winthrop of the
effectiveness of the "vipers among you that would destroy their own native country."[3]   The members of the
board in their charges against the government of Connecticut specifically accused it of ignoring the acts of
trade and navigation, and of actually countenancing illegal trade and, what is more, piracy.   The colony was
called a receptacle of pirates harbored by the government; she was charged with protecting fugitives from
other colonies, of encouraging the migration of young
men from Massachusetts Bay and New York to escape
taxation for the prosecution of the war then being waged,
and of refusing to do her part in colonial defense; nor
would she allow her people to be sued by outsiders in her
courts, nor the laws of England to be pleaded within the
colony; nor countenance appeals to the Queen in Council;
nor recognize the royal commissions relating to the vice-
admiralty and the control of the militia; lastly she was
charged with preventing Christians "not of their own
community" to worship God without special license of

76; Sir Henry Ashurst to Governor Winthrop, February 2, 1705; R. R.
Hinman, *Letters,* p. 325.

[1] Louise P. Kellogg, *The American Colonial Charter* (Amer. Hist.
Assoc. *Rept.* (1903), I), 287-291.

[2] Lord Cornbury to the Board of Trade, September 9, 1703.   Printed in
N. Y. Col. Doc., IV, 1070.

[3] Sir Henry Ashurst to Governor Winthrop, September 9, 1704.   Printed
in R. R. Hinman, *Letters,* p. 316.

the assembly.[1] This resulted in an attempt to put through parliament a bill depriving this colony as well as Rhode Island of charter privileges.[2]

It was in the midst of this tense situation, when, for the preservation of the charter, it was vitally necessary to give the highest proofs of loyalty and good order, that the Connecticut general assembly, at its May session in 1704, shrewdly turned the tables upon those who were denouncing the colony's hatred of royalty and lawless turbulency by establishing the office of queen's attorney, and by directing the ministers in each ecclesiastical society, "in imitation of our nation," to excite and stir up their good people "in order to indeavour a reformation of what provoking evills are to be found amongst us."[3] The wording of the act creating this office was in form a tactful confession of neglect to deal effectively with the general situation and an earnest of a more dutiful attitude in the future toward the mother country. The act, it is important to notice, met the demand, as far as Connecticut was concerned, that in all the colonies justice should run in the name of the sovereign.[4] It reads as follows:

"Whereas we are often told from the public ministrie as well as from private discourses of the wise and pious persons of our age, that one crying sinne that may procure impending judgements further to come down on our

---

[1] R. R. Hinman, *Letters*, pp. 327-329. For a brief but good discussion of these charges see C. M. Andrews, Introduction to *Fane's Reports on Connecticut Laws* (Acorn Club Publ.), pp. 2-4.

[2] *Commons Journal*, XV, 151.

[3] *Conn. Col. Rec.*, IV, 468. At the October session a direct oath of loyalty to the queen was provided for all who in the future desired to become freemen. *Ibid.*, 483.

[4] This demand was incorporated in the bill of 1702, which was submitted by one of the secretaries of state to the board. See Louise P. Kellogg, *The American Colonial Charter*, Amer. Hist. Assoc. *Rept.* (1903), I, 290-291.

land as well as those that are already inflicted on us, is the neglect of putting good lawes in execution against immoral offenders, that therefore such neglect may be prevented for the future, It is ordered and enacted by this court, that henceforth there shall be in every county a sober, discreet and religious person appointed by the county courts to be attorney for the Queen, to prosecute and implead in the lawe all criminal offenders, and to doe all other things necessary or convenient to suppress vice and immoralitie.'"[1]

The significance of this rather ostentatious move in the direction of loyalty can better be appreciated when it is realized that Connecticut alone, of all the colonies, thus followed the example set by Virginia, one of the favored royal colonies, where the office of king's attorney had come into existence as early as the middle of the seventeenth century.[2]

---

[1] *Conn. Col. Rec.*, IV, 468. The "charges and encouragements" of said attorneys were to be allowed out of the county treasury.

[2] As far back as 1643 this office came into existence in Virginia, when George Rutland was appointed to prosecute a large number of citizens guilty of serious breaches of the acts of the assembly. He was to examine witnesses, take depositions, and with the local commissioner's aid, to bring the culprits to justice. In 1665 John Fawcett was chosen king's attorney by the Accomac County judges. Occasionally this officer was called "His Majesty's Attorney-General's Deputy." See Norfolk County Records, Order of July 17, 1643; Accomac County Records, Order of August 15, 1665, quoted in P. A. Bruce, *Institutional History of Virginia in the Seventeenth Century*, I, 570-571.

It should be understood that the attorney general in other royal colonies had charge of all such actions as ran in the king's name. September 10, 1696, the Privy Council, upon a representation of the Board of Trade, referred to the consideration of the attorney general the question "whether an attorney-general may not be appointed for His Majesty in each of the severall Colonys and Provinces of Carolina, Pennsylvania, East and West Jersey, Conecticutt, Road Island and the Massachusetts Bay in America; notwithstanding the Grants and charters to the said Colonys and Provinces?" *Acts of the Privy Council, Colonial*, II, §639.

Emory Washburn, in his *Judicial History of Massachusetts* (p. 87), says

As a result of this action the Connecticut county courts were provided with a county prosecutor, and criminal indictments now ran, "By information of the Queen's Attorney in her Majesties behalf."[1] Jonathan Law of Milford, a staunch supporter of the charter, was selected in 1704 as the New Haven county queen's attorney.[2] He was followed successively by John Reedy, Lieutenant William Adams, also of Milford, Daniel Edwards of New Haven, and Elisha Hall of Wallingford.[3] It was the latter that Ingersoll followed in office when, in his twenty-ninth year, he was appointed king's attorney for New Haven by the bench at the session beginning the second Tuesday of November, 1751.[4] His brother-in-law, John Whiting, who was clerk of the court from 1742

that with the establishment of the county courts in Massachusetts in 1686, it was laid down by the president and council that no information should be received by the court where the king was the principal party, unless it was drawn or signed by the king's attorney. This, however, apparently refers to the office of attorney general. See *ibid.*, pp. 88, 99, 103, 134, 141, 203. See *Massachusetts Civil List*, by W. H. Whitmore, for lists of civil officers, which show that if ever created the office could only have been temporary.

[1] See the New Haven County Court Records (1699-1712), II, 189, for the first example.

[2] *Ibid.*, II, 186.

Jonathan Law had a long public career. In 1706 he was appointed a deputy to the general assembly; he was admitted to the bar in 1708; in 1711 he became a member of the governor's council; in 1714 he was clerk of the upper house; in that year he was also appointed judge of the New Haven county court; in 1715 he became a judge of the supreme court; in 1716 he was speaker of the lower house; in 1724, deputy-governor; in 1725, chief judge of the supreme court; in 1728 he was appointed agent at London, but refused the appointment, and in 1741 he became governor. He died in office, November 6, 1750. Although a graduate of Harvard College of the class of 1695, his life was commemorated in the Yale College Hall by a funeral oration delivered in Latin by Ezra Stiles, then senior tutor. See *Conn. Col. Rec.*, IX, 219; VIII, 416.

[3] New Haven County Court Records, III, 114; IV, 68, 194.

[4] *Ibid.*, IV, 483.

to 1773, was doubtless influential in getting the appointment for him.

It would appear from the county court records that
the occupants of this post, previous to Ingersoll, had
generally forgotten the fact that criminal cases were to
be prosecuted in the king's name.   Indeed, efficient as
many of these county prosecutors may have been, there is
no evidence of the presence in the New Haven county
court of any enthusiastic supporter of the royal prerogative up to the time when Ingersoll assumed office.   Elihu
Hall, Ingersoll's immediate predecessor as king's attorney, was a rather popular figure; he was sent by radical
Wallingford to the assembly in 1743, was a captain of
the militia in 1743, and in 1755 a major.[1]   With the selection of Ingersoll, however, the office assumed a dignity
and importance previously unknown to it.   From this
time on, until the outbreak of the Revolution, the New
Haven county court register—in which previously the
king's name never appeared—most punctiliously gave
indictments in the name of ''His Majesty.''   In the court
proceedings themselves, instead of the cold formula, ''By
information of the King's attorney, on His Majesty's
Behalf,'' which was introduced in 1704, although seldom
employed in these records, actions now ran in the name
of ''The King, Our Sovereign Lord.''[2]   Indeed, a reader
of these proceedings can hardly avoid the impression,
after coming to the records for the year 1751 and following, that he is surely in touch with some devoted supporter of those conceptions wrapped up in the idea of
British sovereignty of which the king was the symbol;

[1] *Conn. Col. Rec.*, VIII, 552, 554; IX, 412.   In 1765 he became an
ardent opponent of the Stamp Act.

[2] John Whiting, the clerk, who was personally responsible for writing
up the proceedings, had been in office since 1740.   The personnel of the
bench also remained and continued to remain unchanged for years.

in touch, in other words, with an American loyalist, the successor of the earlier "prerogative man."[1]

It would be of value were we able to determine just what influences came into Ingersoll's life to produce this attitude of mind, for it seems hardly possible that he inherited it from the pioneer of Westfield who had left

[1] It is doubtless true that most American people of that period were nominally "loyal" and that it would have been difficult to draw any hard and fast line in any colonial community in 1750 between those who looked to an increase of influence on the part of the mother country in American affairs and those who sought to detach as far as possible the interests of the colony in which they lived from the imperial interests. Many personal factors, questions of religion especially, and those having to do with economic and social matters, played their part in the shaping of the colonist's position regarding England. There were of course certain shifting psychological factors and for various reasons a man at one period might assume an attitude very different from that which he might take at another period. Even Benjamin Franklin in the early '60's was drawn so sympathetically to the mother country that it was a matter of common knowledge that he was contemplating removing from America with "his Lady and Daughter to spend the remainder of their days in England." (See letter of Thomas Bridges to Jared Ingersoll, September 30, 1762. Ingersoll Papers.) Nevertheless, granting that loyalism at that period represented a certain more or less indefinable attitude of mind rather than what it later became, a political creed that assumed the proportions of a religion, there must have been a very large number of people who, together with Ingersoll in the '50's, held pronounced views in favor of exalting the connection with the mother country; otherwise the deeply ingrained loyalism that comes to the surface in America in the crisis of the '60's and '70's is inexplicable. Thousands of colonial families would hardly have been willing to surrender every personal interest in their devotion to the British crown, if their loyalty had been of a sudden growth. On the other hand, it would seem to be just as certain that a very large proportion of the people of such colonies as Massachusetts, Rhode Island, and Connecticut, while doing lip service to the king's government, were fundamentally opposed to any considerable exercise of the royal authority over them. What they wanted most of all was to be left severely alone by the king and his government. "They hate anybody who owes subjection to the Queen. That our people find every day," complained Governor Cornbury of New York in his indictment of the people of Connecticut in 1703. (*N. Y. Col. Doc.*, IV, 1070.) In other words, throughout the entire colonial period, two opposing tendencies seem to have been continually operating to shape and direct the thought of the body politic in America.

England when persecution was at its height. His father's intellectual interests, apparently, were very limited; it may be that his association at Yale with students such as his classmate, Samuel Fitch of Lebanon, of later Tory fame, produced an effect. The most plausible explanation, however, can be found in Ingersoll's taste for books, and among them, especially, English legal treatises; the Yale College library, meager as it was, doubtless had the same result in molding the political conceptions of the Berkeley scholar, as it had, some decades previous, in causing Rector Cutler to repudiate Congregationalism in favor of Anglicanism.

With great zeal young Ingersoll attacked the responsibilities of his office. At the very next session of the court, after his appointment, he arraigned, in the name of "Our Sovereign Lord the King," a group of Guilford men who had been acting in a riotous manner;[1] besides this, the grand jury seems to have been aroused into an astonishing state of activity in its search for criminals. So successful was Ingersoll in prosecuting those defying law and order in New Haven county that he was kept in office for over fourteen years.[2]

By far the most common criminal offense that came

[1] New Haven County Court Records, IV, 501-502.

[2] He was appointed the second Tuesday of November, 1751, and served until his departure for England on his first agency, whereupon, November 18, 1758, Elihu Hall was again appointed king's attorney. In 1761 a Samuel Adams was acting in this capacity, but in February, 1763, Hall was once again in office. At the November session in 1763, after his return from England, Ingersoll was reappointed and held office until in the fall of 1764 he left for England, when once again Elihu Hall was given the place, holding it till the first Tuesday in November, at which time James A. Hillhouse was given a temporary appointment. However, the week following, Ingersoll again took office and held it until January, 1771. Hillhouse again took charge upon the removal of his predecessor to Philadelphia. New Haven County Court Records, IV, 483; V, 200; VI, 98, 180; VII, 305. Records of the Superior Court, XIV, under dates February 24, 1761, and February 22, 1763.

before this tribunal for punishment was immorality. A study of the Connecticut codes[1] leaves the impression that the Puritan, by reason of the peculiar methods that he used in his strivings for community sanctity; by his suppression of sports and many wholesome forms of amusement, actually, though unintentionally, fostered vice. He, apparently, could not understand that life demands expression in ways other than the routine of daily material labor and that unfortunate consequences would be only too apt to ensue when the natural longing for joyous recreation was denied to youth.

The accused, after having been presented to a justice of the peace by the grand jury, were, as a rule, bound over, with "recognitions" amounting to from £3.6 to £15 lawful money, to make an appearance at the next session of the court.[2] These unhappy recreants found no sanctuary even in the subsequent establishment of a home, for the lynx-eyed grand juryman was almost sure to track them even there. During the years while Ingersoll was king's attorney, literally dozens of married couples were summoned to appear in open court to answer charges of pre-marital relations. The latter in their shame generally refrained from appearing, preferring to forfeit their recognition bonds. Occasionally, however, in a spirit of humility, the young couple would appear, humbly acknowledge their fault, and pay their fine.[3]

[1] L. H. Gipson, "The Evolution and Application of the Criminal Codes of Colonial Connecticut and Pennsylvania," *American Journal of Criminal Law and Criminology*, VI, 177-190; 323-345.

[2] Joshua Hempstead's *Diary* contains frequent references to couples who, before admission to the church, were required to make public confession of guilty conduct in this respect.

[3] Those who desire to investigate this unwholesome side of colonial life need only go through the county court records and examine those cases appearing in the register under the caption, "The King, Our sovereign Lord."

From the present-day point of view, there was something unwholesome, depressing, and reactionary about the whole procedure described above. The notoriety accompanying the judicial proceedings at every stage was such as could hardly do otherwise than take away the self-respect of penitent young people. This method of dealing with such cases could only lead to whisperings, retaliations, ostracisms, and to an atmosphere of suspicion and community scandal-mongering.

While Ingersoll and the other officers of the law may be blamed for their zeal in meting out punishment to these unfortunates, yet after all, the fault lay fundamentally with the law which they had bound themselves to see obeyed and it was inherent in the very conceptions of social control then prevailing in Connecticut. Still, taking all that into account, it must be admitted that Ingersoll's motto, like that of Strafford, was "thorough." Even his fellow office-holders found that they had to be on their guard against this champion of the law. In 1757, at the October session of the general assembly, in his official capacity he brought charges against Isaiah Tuttle, a New Haven justice of the peace, for having "grievously misdemeanored himself." Tuttle had been unscrupulously making capital out of the litigious spirit which at this period seems fairly to have carried away the people of this community.[1] This crafty justice of the peace, as the lawyer of one Elizabeth Ward of Wallingford, sued diverse persons whom he proceeded to summon before himself. No one else being present at these trials, he prosecuted the cases, gave judgments against the parties, and then coolly pocketed both his attorney's fees and the perquisites of his

[1] For a discussion of this point see Chapter IX.

justiceship. Through the efforts of the king's attorney he was dismissed from his office.[1]

Until 1758, Ingersoll seems to have confined his efforts strictly to his legal practice, with the result that by that year, although but thirty-six years old, he had succeeded in reaching the top of the legal ladder within the colony.[2] Indeed, his powerful, disciplined mind and marked ability in pleading at the bar became a Connecticut tradition in after years. President Timothy Dwight of Yale College,[3] with his strong Americanism, can be counted on to place a conservative estimate upon a contemporary who differed from him on the most vital questions relating to the welfare of America.

''Few men,'' declared President Dwight in later years, ''have excelled him in clear and comprehensive thought and strong powers of reasoning and few men ever managed a case with greater skill. At his entrance upon the argument, he conceded everything to his antagonist which was not in his own view of serious moment to his client, and often conceded so much, that he was believed by men of less understanding to have given up his cause. But he always reserved the essential points, which he exhibited with the utmost strength and advantage. His eloquence was remarkably calm and dispassionate, but

[1] Conn. Archives, Crimes and Misdemeanors, V, 61-62; Ingersoll Record Book; *Conn. Col. Rec.,* XI, 66.

[2] An interesting side light is thrown upon the times by the Benjamin King case, with which Ingersoll was connected. It seems that King was in debt to Jonathan Atwater, Jr., of New Haven. In November, 1752, Atwater, accompanied by Stephen Howell, started in pursuit of King, described in the records as ''a Runaway,'' and overtook him about three miles from New Haven, on the Derby road, in a cart loaded with leather. King was set upon, his wrists were bound with a leather strap, and, cowed by the presence of a threatening walnut staff, he was taken to the home of one Ephraim Morris, and there Atwater had his execution against King satisfied with ''Leather and Thong.'' Ingersoll, representing King, took the case before the general assembly. Conn. Archives, Crimes and Misdemeanors, IV, 228.

[3] Timothy Dwight was president of Yale College from 1795 to 1817.

was exhibited with so much candor and firmness as to be remarkably persuasive. Indeed of the eloquence which is designed to convince, it was almost a perfect pattern. The same candor and fairness appeared in all his deportment.''[1]

One of the first public functions of importance that Ingersoll was called upon to perform, outside of his work as king's attorney, was connected with a lottery. In October, 1754, he, with two others assisting him, was placed in charge of the affair which had been authorized for the purpose of raising £660 ''for the finishing of said warf at Ferry Point in New Haven which through the present unhappy circumstance of trade was stopped.'' The lottery in question was not a success for some reason; the speculative spirit of the people was at so low an ebb that only £150 was netted.[2] The next year Ingersoll is found acting as the agent for ''the Proprietors of the Common and Undivided Lands in New Haven,''[3] and in this capacity he petitioned the general assembly for permission to sell enough of the land to allow for the laying out of the ''eighth division.''[4] In the same year, as ''agent for the governor and company of the colony,'' he was called upon to take charge of certain important

[1] President Timothy Dwight, *A statistical account of the City of New Haven* (1811), p. 73.

[2] Conn. Archives, Travel, II, 203; *Conn. Col. Rec.*, XI, 60. One of the original tickets is preserved in the Library of Congress. It reads as follows: ''Connecticut Lottery. For the benefit of the Ferry-Point-Wharff in New Haven, 1754, Nomb. 4949, £12. The possessor of this ticket shall be entitled to such Prize as may be Drawn against the number (if Demanded within six months after the Drawing is finished) subject to no Deductions. Jared Ingersoll.'' On the reverse of the ticket is written the following: ''Five pounds paid. Received six Pounds in part for what this ticket has drawn. New Haven, Nov, 19, 1755. A. Saltonsto''

[3] This is discussed in Chapter I.

[4] Conn. Archives, Towns and Lands, VIII, 143. According to Ezra Stiles this division of lands comprehended 2350 acres. *Itineraries of Ezra Stiles*, p. 189.

financial matters in which the colony was involved.[1]
That he had now begun in many ways to wield great
influence in the affairs of the commonwealth is evidenced
from a peculiar favor that Gurdon Saltonstall, son of
the famous governor, and one of the most influential
personages in the colony, besought of him in 1756.[2] The
circumstance was as follows:

The previous year the last of the intercolonial wars
broke out. For the successful termination of this struggle Great Britain was obliged not only to mobilize her
resources but also to take steps to cut off the enemy from
supplies. This last step necessitated, on the part of
those in the colonies who had been plying a profitable
trade with the foreign West Indies, a sharp readjustment
in their commercial pursuits. Many colonial skippers,
however, appear to have persisted in trading with the
French Sugar Islands, in spite of the fact that the inhabitants were a hostile people. To check this tendency, at
least on the part of Connecticut traders, the general
assembly, loyally supporting the war, passed an act
obliging all masters of vessels to give bond not to land
provisions except in a British port, and also placed an
embargo on shipping.[3] At this juncture, October 25,
1756, Colonel Saltonstall wrote from New London ask-

[1] *Conn. Col. Rec.*, X, 356.

[2] May, 1753, Saltonstall had been chosen an assistant, and he was
repeatedly elected a deputy from New London. In 1755 he had been
appointed one of the commissioners, who were to provide transports and
provisions for the movement of the Connecticut troops. *Conn. Col. Rec.*,
X, 152, 291, 349.

[3] On August 20, 1756, Loudoun called upon the governors to prohibit
the export of provisions. As early as March, 1755, the assembly forbade
the export of provisions without special license from the governor. *Conn.
Col. Rec.*, X, 350, 424, 461, 485, 550. See also C. O. 5: 1275. On October
9, 1756, the Board of Trade sent to the colonial governors a letter instruct-
ing them to lay an embargo on shipping unless the same was carried on
with some other British colony. For a statement regarding this, see G. L.
Beer, *British Colonial Policy, 1754-1765*, pp. 82-83.

ing Ingersoll to intercede with the governor, Thomas
Fitch, to secure for him, if possible, a waiver of these
trading restrictions. He desired to make a voyage to
Surinam with a hundred barrels of beef and pork and a
hundred barrels of flour, and in return for these provisions he planned to bring back forty Surinam horses.
Saltonstall, however, was apprehensive regarding the
attitude of the public toward his project, for he significantly begged Ingersoll not to "chose to ask it of the
Assembly as there is danger they'd surmise I had some
other design.'"[1]

For reasons that are now obvious, Jared Ingersoll,
with all his abilities, his sturdy uprightness, and high-
mindedness in general, never won popularity with the
people of the colony. Many of the more thoughtful men
might confide in him and honor him, but his record of
strict law enforcement, his early sympathy with the
inherited order of things, his meticulous care that "the
King Our Sovereign Lord" should be kept before the
eyes of the people as plaintiff in all infractions of the
peace, could not stir the imaginations of those industrious husbandmen who were so intent upon the task of
digging the ever present glacial rocks from the Connecticut soil, and fashioning them into fences, in planting and
reaping, in suing their neighbors, in quarreling over the
Saybrook Platform, and in worrying over a multitude of
small community interests and scandals, that the king
and his law, the British constitution and British traditions were for most of them concerns of too remote a
nature to appeal to their sympathies or to awaken their
enthusiasm.[2]

[1] Gurdon Saltonstall to Jared Ingersoll, Ingersoll Papers.

[2] *Conn. Col. Rec.*, XI, 629. For example, Ingersoll was nominated to
stand for the election of the governor's assistants in May, 1763, and in
the election was rejected.

It was probably due to this difference in point of view
that the lower house of the general assembly, reflecting
the popular impulses, rejected a bill passed by the conservative and aristocratic upper house in 1756, which
provided for Ingersoll's appointment as the colony's
agent in London.[1] Significantly, in his stead the lower
house designated Jonathan Trumbull of Lebanon, later
Connecticut's famous war governor, a man in sympathy
with the democratic New Light faction, and with all his
tact and judicial temper inclined to clash with the supporters of the crown's interests.[2] The upper house was
finally brought to ratify this choice at the following session in May. But Trumbull, "as he had not had the small
pox prevalent in London and considering the circumstances of his family," could not see his way clear to
serve.[3] Again, in 1758, Trumbull was selected to go to
England but once more refused; the lower house thereupon gave way and agreed to the selection of Ingersoll,
who after modestly "pleading his unacquaintedness with
public affairs of the colony and total ignorance of the persons and manner of the British Court," accepted the
post, with a yearly stipend of £150 and all expenses
"except that of cloathing."[4]

[1] Conn. Archives, War, X, 363. The rule was laid down by the home
government that no colonial agent should be received who was not appointed
by the concurrence of "all branches of the colonial Legislature." C. O. 5:
216, fol. 67.

[2] Conn. Archives, War, X, 363.

[3] Ibid., X, 369, 373; Conn. Col. Rec., XI, 108.

[4] Conn. Col. Rec., X, 374, 378. The joint committee of the two houses
appointed to consider the matter of salary reported that "considering the
Importance of the Undertaking and the Danger attending it as well as for
the comfortable support of his family in his absence that there be granted
to the s^d Mr. Ingersoll the sum of one hundred and fifty pounds sterling per
annum during his continuance in the service of the colony as agent—and
further the s^d colony pay the whole expense except that of cloathing for Mr.
Ingersoll's Passage to and from there as well as during there, all which is
honorably submitted." Conn. Archives, War, X, 376-377.

In selecting Ingersoll for the London mission it is no exaggeration to say that the colony chose for this work her most able and distinguished advocate of that period, one who in the eyes of his contemporary, William Samuel Johnson, was by 1758 "particularly eminent in the practice of the Law."[1]

1 W. S. Johnson to Richard Jackson, September 25, 1758, W. S. Johnson Papers (Conn. Hist. Soc.).

CHAPTER III

INGERSOLL'S FIRST LONDON AGENCY, 1758-1761. THE AFFAIR OF THE *ST. JOSEPH AND ST. HELENA.* INGERSOLL IN LONDON

The instructions that Jared Ingersoll received before leaving for England to represent the colony as its special London agent make clear the scope of the work that confronted him.[1] First and foremost, he and Richard Partridge, the regular agent, were to make plain to those in control the extent of the burden that Connecticut had so far sustained in the defense of the English colonies in the French and Indian War then in progress; in this connection they were to seek financial reimbursements for the colony. They were called upon to take "prudent care of the affair of the Mohegan Indians," which concerned the title of lands that had belonged to these natives. They were also to guard the colony's interests in the boundary dispute with Massachusetts Bay, which, like the Mohegan question, was a century old and had at last ended in a contest over the possession of the towns of Enfield, Suffield, Woodstock, and Somers, "which lye south of the line between the two governments." And finally, they were to protect the colony against the protests that the Spanish ambassador had been making to the British government regarding the plundering of the Spanish snow, *St. Joseph and St. Helena,* while in New

[1] Conn. Archives, War, X, 381; *Conn. Col. Rec.,* XI, 127-128.

London harbor, "which doubt not when truly known will set us in a favorable light on that head."

This last-named matter, regarding the Spanish ship, so illuminates the actual workings of colonial institutions and the lack of any proper articulation of these with the institutions of imperial origin; so clearly exemplifies the extreme provincialism of the Connecticut townsman of that period in his extraordinary attitude toward the unfortunate "stranger within the gate"; and bears so intimately upon the purposes of this study, that more than a casual mention must be made of it. What, therefore, were the facts regarding it, that the assembly desired to be made "truly known" to Pitt through Ingersoll?

The Spanish snow, *St. Joseph and St. Helena*, under the command of Don Christoval de Urannago, and in company with three other large Spanish ships, left Havana, October 14, 1752, for Cadiz, with an exceedingly valuable cargo which had been placed on board at Honduras, and which consisted principally of gold, silver, indigo, sarsaparilla, and balsam, all together valued at about four hundred thousand Spanish dollars.[1] Some time after leaving Havana, it was found that the vessel was leaking and it seemed best to strike for some North American port in order to refit. While still on the high seas the snow encountered the brigantine *Susanna,* bound for New London, under the command of Captain John Simpson. At the request of the Spaniards, Simpson sent on board the *St. Joseph and St. Helena* Daniel Vosper, a pilot, and by this help the ship arrived, late in November, near the harbor of New London.

In light of the evidence, however contradictory some of it is, the conclusion can hardly be avoided that Vosper,

[1] Joseph Miguel de San Juan's "Declaration and Protestation," June 7, 1753, *Wolcott Papers*, pp. 277-279. "Examinations of Don Christoval de Urannaga," December 11, 1752, *ibid.*, pp. 201-203.

acting in conjunction with Captain Simpson, who had meanwhile reached New London, and with Andrew McKenzie, owner of the *Susanna,* and one James Gardiner, "the best pilot of that town," thereupon, for the sake of salvage, attempted to wreck the snow on the reefs that lie outside the harbor.[1] This outrageous plan was only partially executed, and the precious cargo was removed to New London by means of a schooner, belonging to Captain Richard Durfey, and a small sloop, after the great mast of the rudderless Spanish ship had been cut away in order to extricate her prow from a ledge. New London went wild with excitement and it would appear that almost everyone sought to profit in some form or other by the helpless situation of the Spanish crew, with the result that not only were many things appropriated outright, but immediately extraordinary claims were made against the cargo, then in the custody of the collector of

[1] See San Juan's "Declaration," *ibid.,* pp. 280-286; also the "Deposition of Daniel Vosper," December 12, 1752, *ibid.,* pp. 205-206; the "Examination of Manuel de Dueno," December 13, 1752, *ibid.,* pp. 206-208; Richard Partridge to Claude Amyand, 1753, *ibid.,* p. 248; Roger Wolcott to Richard Partridge, July 30, 1753, *ibid.,* pp. 318-320. Joshua Hempstead, in his *Diary,* states that the snow lost her rudder on Bartlett's Reef. *Diary of Joshua Hempstead,* p. 598. (New London County Hist. Soc. *Coll.,* I.)

Governor Fitch, in his report to the Board of Trade in 1756, emphasized the fact that "at New London is a fine, spacious and commodious harbour with good entrance for large ships." Conn. Hist. Soc. *Coll.,* I, 283.

This treatment by colonial skippers of a Spanish merchantman in distress is not an isolated instance. In October, 1750, the *Nuestra Senora Guadelupe* arrived in a helpless condition off the coast of North Carolina. The most valuable part of the cargo, according to the testimony of Don Manuel de Bonella, the commander, was placed on board two English vessels, which were fastened close to the side of the rudderless ship. On the twentieth of that month these ships suddenly sailed away. One of them, however, was stranded near by on the shoals and the crew was captured by the Spaniards and subjected to prosecution. Although the Spaniards pursued the second ship in their boats she succeeded in escaping, carrying with her, it was claimed, plate, goods, and money equal to 300,000 heavy Spanish dollars. *Wolcott Papers,* p. 524.

the port, Joseph Hull.[1] Simpson brazenly demanded one-third the value of the entire cargo on the grounds that by his exertions the Spanish ship with its contents had been saved. In fulfillment of the design of this gentleman and his co-partners, an application was made to the judge of the court of vice-admiralty for this jurisdiction, who was Chief Justice Lewis Morris of New York, to come to New London for the purpose of granting salvage on a libel against the cargo of the *St. Joseph and St. Helena.* Early in December Judge Morris arrived and set up his court. To conduct the proceedings an interpreter was required, and the owner of the *Susanna,* McKenzie, was not slow in finding a friend who could carry through that delicate work. The supercargo, and, therefore, the one responsible to the owners for the safety of the ship's cargo, Don Joseph Miguel de San Juan, felt that he had fallen into a nest of near-pirates. He would have nothing to do with McKenzie's interpreter and sent to Boston for a reliable man. The idea that these men, who had attempted, according to his conviction, to wreck the vessel, should now be demanding salvage was intolerable to him. Even Colonel Gurdon Saltonstall of New London could not see how a judgment in favor of this libel could stand. The proceedings of the court, in fact, were somewhat in the nature of a farce. Captain Durfey, who rescued most

[1] Colonel Gurdon Saltonstall, however, received into his care the gold and silver, which he deposited in his store and kept under guard. Governor Wolcott commissioned him to act as the colony's agent in this matter. During the vice-admiralty court proceedings there was an armed struggle between the collector and Saltonstall for possession of the money chests. It would appear, however, that the significance of this lies in the fact of a disputed jurisdiction between a crown officer and an agent of the colonial government. Gurdon Saltonstall to Roger Wolcott, December 28, 1752, *ibid.,* p. 224; Joseph Hull to Roger Wolcott, December 29, 1752, *ibid.,* p. 225; Lewis Morris to Roger Wolcott, December 30, 1752, *ibid.,* p. 226; *Diary of Joshua Hempstead,* p. 599.

of the cargo with his schooner and who had quarreled with McKenzie, could not be brought into the scheme. Nevertheless, Morris actually awarded to Simpson, in whose name the libel ran, twenty-three thousand pieces of eight,[1] together with costs. Dark suspicion clouded the whole proceedings; Morris had not borne an enviable reputation. San Juan thought the affair an outrage and refused payment, whereupon thirty saroons of indigo out of the cargo were sold by the court marshal, Joseph Chew, to satisfy these claims.

Durfey, who apparently did not hold the favor of Judge Morris, started common law proceedings against the owners of the ship to satisfy his claims, which were more nearly justified but which to the Spaniard were exorbitant. In fact, Don Juan had one consuming anxiety and that was to get his cargo out of the clutches of New London as soon as possible. Although Saltonstall, a member of the governor's council, had been appointed the colony's agent to arrange either for the repair of the snow or the charter of a new vessel, the supercargo, distrusting everyone in Connecticut, refused his services. His request to the governor to be allowed to appoint an agent of his own preference was denied, with the result

[1] Lewis Morris to Roger Wolcott, December 9, 1753, *Wolcott Papers,* p. 200; San Juan's ''Declaration,'' *ibid.,* p. 279; Richard Partridge to Claude Amyand, 1752, *ibid.,* p. 249; *Diary of Joshua Hempstead,* p. 600.

The proceedings in vice-admiralty seem to have been a disgraceful affair. Judge Morris, however, was apparently a man with a somewhat questionable judicial record. In fact, in 1747 he had been dismissed from his office as judge of the court of vice-admiralty, for misconduct, but had been allowed to continue in office when his successor refused to serve. C. O. 5: 1275, 44; Gurdon Saltonstall to Roger Wolcott, December 24, 1752, *Wolcott Papers,* pp. 222-223; George Clinton to Roger Wolcott, February 17, 1753, *ibid.,* pp. 240-241; Roger Wolcott to Richard Partridge, July 30, 1753, *ibid,* p. 318.

The piece of eight in Connecticut was valued at six shillings, Connecticut currency.

that the contents of the Spanish ship was destined to remain in New London for over two years.

Hoping to find protection somewhere, Don San Juan went to New York and hunted up two merchants of that city, Henry Cuyler and Henry Lane, into whose hands he placed his interests. But Lane, through trickery and the connivance of certain parties in official life, got momentary control of the cargo and with a lavish hand settled the claims against the same. He now started to load the Spanish effects on the *Nebuchadnezzar,* which had been chartered when the *St. Joseph and St. Helena* had been condemned as unseaworthy. It was then discovered that a chest containing over £5000 in gold had been opened, looted, and stuffed with trash.[1] Moreover, Lane, after demanding for his services two and a half per cent of the value of the entire cargo, proceeded to abscond with four chests full of silver.[2] San Juan, after appealing first to Governor Wolcott, then to Governor Clinton of New York, and then to the Connecticut general assembly for relief and protection, feeling that he had been mercilessly plundered and thwarted for over a year, deserted his cargo and went to New York, after informing the Connecticut authorities that the whole case would be presented before the high court of admiralty in London and that the colony would have to pay all damages.

The situation had become serious for Connecticut. Although the colonial government was not responsible for the disgraceful admiralty decision, nor accountable for Lane's proceedings, which Wolcott denominated ''an

---

[1] Lane made imputations against the Spaniards themselves, ''Least it should prevent a further discovery, it may be prudent not to mention this to Dⁿ Jⁿ or any other.'' Henry Lane to Roger Wolcott, August 28, 1753, *Wolcott Papers,* p. 367; Governor Fitch to Secretary Fox, May 29, 1756, Conn. Hist. Soc. *Coll.,* I, 298.

[2] *Wolcott Papers,* p. 433.

atrocious crime,'"[1] yet it had been, under the particular circumstances, lax, especially when the collector of the port refused to receive back into his custody the cargo, after it had once been released through Lane's duplicity. In fact, series of looting expeditions were carried out against these treasures, which were stored in buildings and on board the *Nebuchadnezzar.*[2] At first there had been an armed struggle between the collector of the port and the colony's agent for control of the cargo; later, when the scandal of the thing filled the air, the responsibility was tossed back and forth in the most extraordinary manner.[3] The conscience of the colony, however, had at last become awakened, especially when the conviction came home that the people of the colony would pay for the orgy. The governor, who was furiously assailed, at last asserted his authority and called upon the civil authorities of New London to bring to justice those who were guilty. "What a shame will it be to this Governm[t] to have the ship burnt the stores stolen and embezled and such vilanies nether prevented nor pun-

[1] Roger Wolcott to Daniel Coit, January 21, 1754, *ibid.,* p. 423.

[2] Saltonstall wrote: "I believe it my duty to advise you; that depradations are made on the Spanish effects, in Mr. Sloan's Store very frequently; but am not able to say how often; though its every three or four nights; & it was broke open even last night.

"Mr. Sloan denies his having the care of it; nor will the colector admit it in his custody; & the Spanish merchant is entirely easy at these proceedings, or rather rejoices at them." Gurdon Saltonstall to Roger Wolcott, December 13, 1753, *ibid.,* p. 402; *Diary of Joshua Hempstead,* pp. 620, 622, 623, 624, 625.

As the result of this delay at New London after the goods had been placed on board the *Nebuchadnezzar* there was filed in the court of vice-admiralty another libel, this time by one Richard Keats, engaged as chief mate. In this libel he asserted that he had been hired to sail to Spain, but after a long delay at New London was discharged. Keats asked that the process be issued against the "Ship Rigging apparel Boat and Appurtenances." *Fitch Papers,* I, 45.

[3] *Wolcott Papers,* pp. 224, 225, 264, 273, 305, 311, 361, 368, 413.

ished. If such thing shall escape with impunity there will be no living for any man much longer in this colony.''[1] Reports were spread that Governor Wolcott himself had been a leading beneficiary in the Spaniard's misfortune, with the result that in the May election of 1754 he was "thrown down with a vengeance,"[2] although the king's attorney for New London county "had succeeded in bringing to justice some of the guilty parties."[3]

But the matter did not stop there. As early as the spring of 1753, the Spanish ambassador had protested against the salvage award.[4] In January, 1754, Antonio and Rogue Aguado of Cadiz, chief owners of the cargo, sent their London legal representative, Jacob Franco, to call upon the Connecticut agent, Richard Partridge, and to inform him that the people of Connecticut were expected to make good the damage.[5] In June the English government decided to take cognizance of the affair, with the result that Sir Thomas Robinson, principal secretary of state for the southern department, wrote to the governor of Connecticut commanding him in the name of the king to see that the cargo was completely restored to its owners.[6] Thomas Fitch, now governor in place of Roger

[1] Roger Wolcott to Daniel Coit, January 21, 1754, *ibid.*, p. 423. A number were arrested and confined in jail, but Joshua Hempstead relates that "the Prisoners broke open the Door with Iron Crows and took Brooks's Boat and Rowed out of the Harbour and made their Escape. Thos Stubbins, Judah Coleman and Ebe Howard Junr for Steeling Gold, Silver from Coll Saltonstall's Cellar and Mills and Taylor for Stealing Endigo out of the Ship and 1 more for Endigo.'' *Diary*, p. 625.

[2] Roger Wolcott's *Memoir* (Conn. Hist. Soc. *Coll.*, III, 335).

[3] *Wolcott Papers*, p. 422; Governor Fitch to Secretary Fox, May 29, 1756, Conn. Hist. Soc. *Coll.*, I, 298-299.

[4] Richard Partridge to Roger Wolcott, October 19, 1753, *Wolcott Papers*, p. 390.

[5] Richard Partridge to Roger Wolcott, January 20, 1754, *ibid.*, p. 427.

[6] Governor Fitch to Sir Thomas Robinson, June 5, 1755, Conn. Hist. Soc. *Coll.*, I, 260.

Wolcott, proceeded to appoint Jonathan Trumbull and Roger Wolcott, Jr., to take charge of the remaining effects of the Spaniards and to see that they were safely loaded on board ship. This was done and, thereupon, Captain Whitwell of His Majesty's Navy, who had been sent to New London with the *Triton,* convoyed the *Nebuchadnezzar* in safety to Cadiz.[1]

However, Secretary Robinson again wrote to Fitch, in November, 1755, informing him that the Spanish minister, d'Abreu, had complained to the government that, according to the proprietors of the treasure, nearly all of their money and part of their goods were detained within Connecticut. Sir Thomas sharply reminded the governor that it was the king's intention that entire restitution should be made to the merchants, and added that another ship of war had been ordered to repair to New London to take on board the remainder of the Spanish property.[2] Soon after writing this letter Robinson resigned from the secretaryship and was succeeded by Henry Fox,[3] and to the latter Fitch addressed himself late in the spring of 1756, in an endeavor to clear the colony and to explain why the *Syren,* after arriving in Connecticut waters, had found nothing to carry to Spain.[4]

This was the status of the Spanish affair when Ingersoll's instructions were drawn up. Taken all in all, it was a shameful episode, streaked through and through with dark designs, avarice, knavery, blind suspicion, distortion of evidence, and eleventh-hour efforts at restitu-

[1] Conn. Hist. Soc. *Coll.; Diary of Joshua Hempstead,* pp. 642, 643.

[2] Secretary Robinson to the Governor of Connecticut, November 3, 1755, Conn. Hist. Soc. *Coll.,* I, 273-274.

[3] Secretary Fox to the Governor of Connecticut, November 14, 1755, *ibid.,* I, 277.

[4] Governor Fitch to Secretary Fox, May 29, 1756. It would appear that most of the effects were finally recovered, and some of the money that had been appropriated. *Ibid.,* I, 298-299.

tion and fair play; it showed that a Spanish treasure ship was almost as much a temptation to the dwellers of a colonial seaport in the eighteenth century as to the buccaneers of the days of Elizabeth. That those who had taken a leading part in the proceedings connected with the ship in no wise felt secure in 1758, is shown by a letter which Joseph Chew, who had acted as marshal in the vice-admiralty court proceedings, wrote to Ingersoll, the latter part of September of that year, upbraiding the latter for neglecting to come to New London and, as his attorney, help him in his affairs. Chew appeared to be very nervous and declared that his own deposition was ready and that the other depositions would soon be prepared.[1] He, of course, had hired Ingersoll to protect him in any proceedings that might take place in London over the matter.

Before leaving for England, Ingersoll was not only

[1] Joseph Chew to Jared Ingersoll, September 27, 1758, Ingersoll Papers.

That which made the situation even more grave regarding Spain's attitude toward the whole affair was that the privateer *Peggy*, commanded by Richard Haddon, committed certain acts of violence in 1756, against the ship of Don Felique D'Frances, who was also a subject of the king of Spain. But in this case the colony acted with decision, when notified by the English government. Fitch, on October 15, 1757, called upon the sheriffs in Connecticut to seize the vessel should she arrive. This was done, and on March 31, 1758, in a letter to Pitt, he was able to state that satisfaction was made to the Spanish agents. See *Fitch Papers*, I, 313, 332.

On September 5, 1758, Ingersoll wrote to Jonathan Trumbull asking him to send on the depositions and other documents regarding the snow, and on October 17 Governor Fitch wrote to Pitt, stating that he was sending, by Ingersoll, the colony's agent, additional papers bearing upon the affair; these, it was hoped, would ''clear the colony of negligence.'' *Ibid.*, I, 352, 358.

In the year 1771 a Spanish ship, with a cargo of sugar, and also bearing forty thousand Spanish dollars aboard, put into New London, after a storm had taken away her masts. The H. M. S. *Beaver* was at anchor there and her carpenters condemned the vessel as unseaworthy, with the result that another vessel was purchased, in which the sugar and the money were conveyed to Cadiz. *Penn. Journal*, November 14, 1771.

given the joint instructions, previously considered, but he also was specially instructed "considering Mr. Agent Partridge's advanced age and the probability that the colony may have occasion to appoint another person to transact our affairs in his stead . . . therefore, to make a prudent enquiry after some proper person of known ability, skill, and Disposition, who, when occasion shall call upon it, may be appointed our Agent."[1]

With these instructions, Ingersoll sailed to England late in the fall of 1758. Not long after his arrival, Partridge passed away and he was thereupon left in sole charge of the colony's affairs, not the least pressing of which, for the moment, was to rescue the Connecticut interests from the insolvent estate of his late co-partner in the agency.[2]

During the period that Ingersoll was accredited to the court of Great Britain as agent, by far his most important work lay in urging the claims of Connecticut to compensation for the expense she incurred at various times during the years from 1757 to 1760 inclusive, in maintaining bodies of her militia in the field.[3] According to a circular letter sent out by Pitt to the colonial governors, early in 1757, the home government agreed

[1] Conn. Archives, War, X, 379.

[2] When Partridge passed away he was owing the colony over £3000. A suit was instituted against the estate and in 1765 was terminated with a settlement of £2524.15.1. Richard Jackson to Thomas Fitch, April 13, 1765, *Fitch Papers; Conn. Col. Rec.*, XI, 258, 345.

[3] Connecticut of course did not expect entire compensation, nor did she receive it. "In these services from the year 1755 to the year 1762 inclusive, the expenses of the colony, over and above the parliamentary grants (which have been received with the most sensible and humble Gratitude) amounts to upwards of four hundred thousand Pounds; the large arrears of which sum will remain a heavy, distressing Burden upon the People for many years to come." *Reasons why the British Colonies in America should not be Charged with Internal Taxes* (1764); reprinted in *Conn. Col. Rec.*, XII, Appendix.

to furnish the troops raised by the colonies with ammunition, tents, and subsistence. All that the colonies were to do was to levy, clothe, arm, and pay the men.[1] In later circular letters, the secretary of the southern department offered not only to take from the shoulders of the colonies the expense of providing arms but, regarding the clothing and pay of the soldiers, assured the colonies that strong recommendations would be made to parliament at its next session to grant a proper compensation for such expenses as above, "according as the active rigor and strenuous efforts of the respective Provinces shall justly appear to merit."[2]

Upon the basis of this encouragement, Connecticut sent repeated reënforcements to the relief of Fort William Henry which, however, was captured by Montcalm, August 9, 1757, resulting in serious losses to the colony. Early in 1758 she voted to put at the service of Abercrombie five thousand men,[3] in order to help make up the quota of twenty thousand that Pitt expected New England, together with New York and New Jersey, to furnish for the mismanaged Ticonderoga expedition and the other immediate military enterprises. In order to meet the extraordinary expenses, bills of credit were issued by the colony, with the provision that the reimbursement secured from England should be applied to discharging the same.[4]

As early as 1756 parliament granted to New England, New York, and New Jersey, as a "free gift and reward for their past services and an encouragement to them to continue to exert themselves," the sum of £715,000, out of

[1] See Pitt's circular letter of February 4, 1757. *N. Y. Col. Doc.*, VII, 216.

[2] Those letters were sent out December 30, 1759, and December 9, 1758. *Ibid.*, VII, 340, 351.

[3] *Conn. Col. Rec.*, XI, 72-93; *Cal. Home Office Papers, 1760-1765*, §98.

[4] *Conn. Col. Rec.*, XI, 101.

which £26,000 was apportioned to Connecticut.[1] After the fees at the exchequer and the treasury office, and the cost of insurance, carting, and shipping, amounting to £1098.15, had been paid,[2] the remainder of the money, made up principally of Spanish milled pieces and Portuguese gold coins, was packed in twenty-five chests and eighteen bags and sent to America.[3] This appropriation was the beginning of a series of grants to the colonies during the period of the war. In order to facilitate repayment, Pitt had impressed upon the governors the importance of having in the hands of duly authorized agents in London, the necessary documents relating to the colonial military expenditures.[4]

The part played by Ingersoll and his fellow agents in securing reimbursement was, in fact, very important; they laid before the Board of Trade and other departments and branches of the government statements of expenses when desired; they actively urged the claims of the colonies with those in positions of influence; they saw that the various fees, for sign manuals and warrants, for orders and the writing of bonds, as well as the other charges against the colony at the exchequer, were met after parliament had acted; they took charge of the money, deposited the same in some bank of standing and drew upon it at the order of the colonial governments.[5]

[1] See the letter of John Thomlinson and John Hanbury to Governor Fitch, April 5, 1756, with appended documents, printed in Conn. Hist. Soc. *Coll.*, I, 285-291.

[2] *Ibid.*, I, 289.

[3] *Ibid.*, I, 286-287.

[4] Pitt to the Governors of North America, December 29, 1758, *N. Y. Col. Doc.*, VII, 355.

[5] Ingersoll patronized the house of Hinton, Brown & Son, bankers, of Lombard Street. In a letter explaining his action he stated that the Bank of England would not enter any moneys for any body corporate or for any individual who resided at a distance and who must negotiate by proxy. He was convinced that this private bank had ''nearly or quite as good a repu-

During the later period of the war, instead of sending to America chests of gold and silver, as was the case in 1756 and in 1758,[1] the Connecticut agents were instructed by the general assembly to leave the specie in England "on account of the price that foreign coins bear" in London. Bills of exchange signed by the governor were thereupon issued against these funds, after the specie had been purchased by the highest bidder.[2]

The only serious difficulty that Ingersoll met with in his efforts to secure reimbursements was in connection with the expenses entailed by the colony in the billeting of the militia sent to the relief of Fort William Henry. Although the general assembly had appointed two different committees to prepare "the most material facts attending the affair," with authenticated evidence,[3] although the committee of the pay table forwarded a statement of the number of troops employéd and the amount of rations consumed, with their affidavits attached thereto, on account of the lack of the necessary vouchers, claims to the amount of £912.8.7 were left unpaid.[4] Gov-

tation as the Bank of England." The Connecticut assembly had ordered him to place the money on interest. As the English banks did not, as he informed Governor Fitch, "ever allow interest for monies in their hands," he felt impelled to lay out the money "in a particular species of the funds carrying an interest of £4. pr cent;" although he had flattered himself that the colony could benefit by this, he found when he came to dispose of these stocks "that the Public funds sunk so low in the Capital" that he was scarcely able to save the colony from loss. Jared Ingersoll to Thomas Fitch, August 10, 1761. Agents Letters (Conn. Hist. Soc.); *Conn. Col. Rec.*, XI, 490.

1 *Ibid.*, XI, 102, 574.

2 *Ibid.*, XI, 437, 490, 502.

3 *Ibid.*, XI, 108.

4 The following item from the Treasury Papers shows what difficulty Connecticut had with this account: "Connecticut's claims for repayment of expenses in victualling the provincials (1757), as stated by J. Ingersoll, Jan. 29, 1761, Endorsed. June 30, read, reconsidered the application of Connecticut, agreed that the former Minute do stand." Treasury, 1: 377 (Andrews, *Guide*, II, 162.)

ernor Fitch, in fact, was so concerned lest this sum should
slip through the hands of the colony, that late in 1761,
after Ingersoll's return to New Haven, he sent to the
latter his stallion from Norwalk with an appeal to ride
the animal to New York in haste in order to see Lord
Amherst, who was in charge of the military affairs in
America, and bring the negotiations to a settlement before the latter left that city.[1]

The other matters referred to in the joint instructions
dragged along beyond the period of Ingersoll's agency.[2]
However, by that time the affair of the *St. Joseph and St.
Helena* had lost its serious aspect for the colony, since
Pitt was urging war against Spain on account of the so-
called Bourbon Family Compact. Ingersoll's other leading activities in England at this time, in connection with
the effort to get a vice-admiralty court for Connecticut,
his contract with the Navy Board for masts, and his

[1] The Lords of the Treasury had, according to Ingersoll, directed Sir
Jeffrey Amherst to examine the colony's demands, and if found just and
true to pay them. Jared Ingersoll to Thomas Fitch, August 10, 1761,
Agents Letters (Conn. Hist. Soc.). Thomas Fitch to Jared Ingersoll,
November 12, 1761, Ingersoll Papers; Jared Ingersoll to John Ledyard,
November 11, 1761, *ibid.;* Thomas Fitch to Jared Ingersoll, November 19,
1761, *ibid.;* Thomas Fitch to Jared Ingersoll, November 28, 1761, *ibid.*

[2] Richard Jackson, the successor of Ingersoll in the agency, received
instructions covering, in all essential things, the same grounds. Conn.
Archives, War, X, 387-388.

Ingersoll returned to America during the summer of 1761, on board the
man-of-war *Alcide.* While aboard he penned, on August 10, a letter to
Governor Fitch. Among other things he said "that in conversation with
Mr. Secretary Pitt, Soon after my arrival at London I learned that no
further complaints had been made on the part of the Spaniard, Since the
Colony's Account of their proceeding's & conduct in that affair had been
laid before the Spanish Minister. . . . I believe it may Safely be Concluded there is nothing further to be apprehended from that affair.

"The Mohegan Controversy Still lies Dormant nor has anything been
moved relative to the Line between the Colony of the Massachusetts
Province." Jared Ingersoll to Thomas Fitch, August 10, 1761. Agents
Letters (Conn. Hist. Soc.).

work in behalf of the Susquehanna Company, will be dealt with in succeeding chapters.

The period of almost three years that he spent abroad afforded him, on the whole, a most delightful and profitable experience. He established himself in North Palace Yard, near Westminster Hall, in the lodgings of one Ann Davies, proceeded to get in touch with leaders in governmental affairs, became the friend of prominent Englishmen and colonials, busied himself with various Connecticut matters that took him to Whitehall, not a great distance away from his lodgings, where the Treasury Board, the Board of Trade, and the Lords of the Admiralty sat, and where in the Cockpit were the offices of the secretary of state for the southern department and the chambers of the Privy Council; he also attended sessions of parliament and spent much of his leisure time in Westminster Hall, where the common law courts and the court of chancery were established, listening to the arguments of the leading British advocates, and for entertainment of a lighter sort he attended the theater, when Garrick was acting.[1]

The man of the hour in England in 1759 was, of course, William Pitt. Ingersoll early had the opportunity of meeting the latter at his home, and also from the visitors' gallery of the House of Commons listened to his oratory.

[1] In 1759 Ingersoll wrote rather a chatty letter to his friend, William Samuel Johnson.

''You will naturally suppose I have improved some of my leisure hours in looking into the several courts—'twas term time when I came, accordingly I attended Some little at the King's Bench, Some at Chancery; at the Common pleas and at the settings of Guildhall—have also been in the House of Commons and have heard argued several Causes on appeal before the House of Lords and some at the Cock pit before the Council, etc. The late Lord Chancellor Hardwick, the present Lord Chief Justice Mansfield, and the Lord Keeper Henly seem to be very much the Triumvirate who Decide all matters of weight at whatsoever Board.'' Jared Ingersoll to William Samuel Johnson, April 17, 1759, Johnson Papers.

The quaint description that he has left of this popular leader is not entirely flattering. According to him Pitt had a "thin face, somewhat pale, a Roman nose, his legs pretty small and almost all the way of a bigness—his ankles being swelled with gout, which makes him hobble rather than walk when he goes. If he had any fault, it is his language being a little too much swollen, seeming to border on bombast and fustian. I believe he is a greater speaker than reasoner."[1]

If the great commoner failed to captivate Ingersoll, it is nevertheless certain that he was deeply and happily impressed with the new king, George III.

"As to news," he wrote to Ezra Stiles in 1761, "I know of nothing remarkable. The Parliament was dissolved yesterday. I had the pleasure of being present in the House of Lords when the young King in his Regalia, attended by a numerous and most brilliant assembly of nobility, Ladies and Gentry, received the farewell speech of that venerable Personage, Mr. Onslow, speaker of the House of Commons. . . . The scene closed with the King's speech delivered, I do assure you, with all the grace or beauty of an accomplished speaker. He is certainly not only as a King disposed to do all in his power to make his people happy, but is undoubtedly of a Disposition truly religious and to those more noble accomplishments has the at least desirable additional circumstance of a good Person and fine Elocution."[2]

It might be mentioned at this point that among the circle of friends and acquaintances that Ingersoll made during his sojourn in England there were two who were destined to play important parts with him five years hence in the Stamp Tax crisis; these were, Thomas

[1] Jared Ingersoll to William Samuel Johnson, December 22, 1759, *ibid.*
[2] Jared Ingersoll to Ezra Stiles, March 20, 1761, *Itineraries of Ezra Stiles*, p. 502.

Whately, counselor-at-law, a student of finance and later a secretary to the Treasury, and Benjamin Franklin, the colonial agent for the Pennsylvania Assembly.[1] It should be borne in mind that in sending Ingersoll to England, the Connecticut government had not expected that he would become the permanent agent, in view of the important interests he had within the colony. In fact, after settling the amount of his salary, which was £150 sterling, as was stated, the assembly cautiously empowered the governor "to draw a bill of exchange on Richard Partridge of London, Esq., for such sums as his Honor shall think needful not exceeding £300 sterling payable to Jared Ingersoll for his expenses during his stay in Great Britain to transact our affairs as agent there."[2] At that time he was particularly instructed to find, before returning to America, someone who was suitably qualified to represent the colony as permanent agent. Early in 1760 he decided to recommend to the general assembly, his friend, Richard Jackson, commonly dubbed among his acquaintances, "Omniscient" Jackson, because of his extraordinary stores of knowledge, who was, in fact, a most distinguished barrister, and later not only the standing counsel for the South Sea Company and for Cambridge University, and the legal adviser of the Board of Trade from 1770 until its dissolution in 1782, but also, from 1762 to 1784, a member of

[1] That Franklin's regard for Ingersoll was sincere and warm is evidenced by a letter which he addressed to the latter after they had both returned to America.

"I thank you," wrote Franklin, "for your Kind Congratulations. It gives me pleasure to hear from an old friend: it will give me much more pleasure to see him. I hope, therefore, nothing will prevent the journey you propose for next summer and the favor you intend me of a visit." Benjamin Franklin to Jared Ingersoll, December 11, 1762 (Ingersoll Collection).

[2] *Conn. Col. Rec.*, XI, 128.

parliament and in 1782 a lord of the Treasury. This nomination was ratified by the assembly in March.[1]

While accepting the appointment, Jackson apparently was unable to give the time necessary to care for the more routine matters of the colony. Therefore, later in the year, upon the recommendations of both Ingersoll and Jackson, Thomas Life "of Basinghall St., London, Gentleman," was designated by the assembly as joint agent,[2] with the provision "that Mr. Jackson's sallary be £100 sterling a year and Mr. Life's £50."[3]

The circumstances which led Jared Ingersoll, after thus providing for the interests of Connecticut, to tarry for an additional year in England without pay, will be considered in the following chapter.

[1] Conn. Archives, War, X, 374. Ingersoll became acquainted with Jackson through William Samuel Johnson, who gave the newly appointed London agent a letter of introduction to this brilliant barrister. William Samuel Johnson to Richard Jackson, September 25, 1758, *Fitch Papers*, I, 354-355.

[2] *Conn. Col. Rec.*, XI, 439.

[3] Conn. Archives, War, X, 391-394.

CHAPTER IV

THE CONNECTICUT VICE-ADMIRALTY JURIS-DICTION. THE PRESERVATION OF THE KING'S WOODS IN CONNECTICUT. THE STRUGGLE FOR THE MASTING TRADE OF NEW ENGLAND

LATE in the spring of 1760, Jared Ingersoll, who was still in London, received a communication from Governor Fitch, which contained a request, in the form of a resolution of the general assembly, that the home government be asked to create a court of vice-admiralty exclusively for Connecticut.[1] In light of the traditional unpopularity of the admiralty authority in America,[2] this is a surprising, if not a unique, colonial document. However, before dealing with the conditions that gave rise to this, it would be well to examine briefly the situation within the colony at that period.

When admiralty courts were erected by the crown in America, at the end of the seventeenth century,[3] under

[1] *Conn. Col. Rec.*, XI, 358.

[2] Beer's statement should be followed with great caution, when, in referring to the degree of opposition against the vice-admiralty jurisdiction in New England, he writes, ''This opposition was, however, to a great extent confined to the directly interested localities and was not supported by the governments of New England.'' As will be seen in the progress of this chapter, the Connecticut application for an admiralty court upon which he relies in support of his statement was made under pressure of such peculiar motives that it can hardly be used legitimately as setting forth any characteristic attitude of the Connecticut government. *British Colonial Policy, 1754-1765*, p. 289.

[3] It should also be borne in mind that Connecticut, under the terms of

the provisions of the Navigation Act of 1696,[1] the colonies were brought together into two jurisdictions, the first including New England, New York, and the Jerseys, and the second, all the colonies lying to their south.[2] When it was later found expedient to separate the colonies into smaller jurisdictions, Connecticut, New York, and New Jersey were combined for that purpose,[3] and this was the situation in 1760. The complete personnel of a vice-admiralty court was a judge, a register, a marshal, and an advocate.[4] The judge, by the terms of his commission, possessed very wide powers in dealing not only with maritime cases,[5] but also on the basis of a law passed in the eighth year of the reign of George I, with cases arising out of trespasses committed against the king's woods.[6]

As far back as 1699, when William Attwood was selected as the first judge of vice-admiralty for the northern jurisdiction, the practice arose of making the chief justice of the province of New York also an admiralty judge.[7] In 1760 Colonel Lewis Morris was serving in

her charter, laid claim to admiralty jurisdiction, and as early as October, 1681, by an act of the general assembly, the court of assistants was invested with the powers of a court of vice-admiralty in Connecticut. *Conn. Col. Rec.*, III, 132.

[1] 7 and 8 William III, c. 22.

[2] *A. P. C. Col., 1688-1720*, §815.

[3] "Mem^d by Mr. Ingersoll of Sundry Matters relative to the present Circumstances of the Court of Vice Admiralty at New York, etc." C. O. 5: 1275, W 43.

[4] The latter also was called a king's advocate and a judge advocate. C. O. 5: 1276, X 3; 1275, W 43.

In addition to the judge, a surrogate, who was in the nature of an acting judge, might be appointed, as was the case at the time of the creation of the court for all America in 1764. Admiralty Papers, Out Letters, 1057. (Andrews, *Guide*, II, 37.)

[5] See Chapter X for a discussion of this.

[6] 8 George I, c. 12, sec. 5.

[7] *A. P. C. Col., 1688-1720*, §815.

this double capacity, although apparently holding his vice-admiralty post under a clouded commission.[1] As was noticed in the preceding chapter, whenever it was necessary for Judge Morris to take cognizance of cases that arose in Connecticut or New Jersey, instead of summoning the parties to appear before him in New York, he was obliged, according to his commission, to go into the colony in question and there hold court, a practice that involved delays and considerable expense, which had to be borne by those who called upon him, unless it so happened that the costs were saddled upon the defendants.[2]

While important cases occasionally arose within this jurisdiction, it would appear that Judge Morris's court was not pressed with the sort of business, as a rule, requiring the services of an advocate, whose work was to prosecute cases in this court in the name of the king. In 1730 Richard Bradley, attorney general for the province of New York, had been given a commission also as advocate; which was co-extensive with the jurisdiction of the court of vice-admiralty.[3] However, according to information furnished the Board of Trade in 1760, Bradley

[1] According to data furnished to Jared Ingersoll at the Admiralty, Morris had been set aside as judge of vice-admiralty in 1747 on account of misconduct, and in his place, James Alexander, also of New York, had been commissioned. But Alexander happened to belong to the same political faction in the province as did his predecessor, and declined to serve, excusing himself "from tenderness to Mr. Morris." The latter thereupon resumed his office, although there was no revival of his commission. Jared Ingersoll, in presenting the situation to the Board of Trade in 1760, raised the question whether Morris, under the circumstances, could claim any warrant for exercising these powers. C. O. 5: 1275, W 44.

[2] C. O. 5: 1275, W 43.

[3] Sampson Shelton Broughton, who was the first advocate for the northern admiralty jurisdiction, was also attorney general for New York. His appointment was in 1699. *A. P. C. Col., 1688-1720*, §815. *N. Y. Col. Doc.,* IV, 599. In 1723-1724 Bradley had become attorney general. He continued in office until his death in 1752. *N. Y. Col. Doc.,* V, 982, note VI, 17.

had been dead for years and there had been no renewal of the office.[1] The reason then assigned was that there was little occasion for the office, since the work of the admiralty court, when sitting at New York, consisted largely of determining questions relative to prizes brought into New York in time of war.[2] So little, in fact, was known about this post of king's advocate, pertaining to this jurisdiction, in 1753, that the surveyor general of the king's woods in America, Benning Wentworth, in urging the appointment of a Connecticut "Judge Advocate," by the general assembly, that year, contended in a letter to the governor that the king's advocate for New York had no jurisdiction in Connecticut.[3] In reply to Wentworth, Governor Wolcott was forced to confess that "A Judge Advocate being an officer wholy New to us, it will be proper for you in your Answer to this to enclose me a form for his Apointment or Commission with advice of the duty and business of this post."[4]

In fact, Connecticut had had very little experience with the operation of a vice-admiralty court and this experience had not been of a happy nature. At the very time that Wentworth made his request, the colony was still discussing the scandal arising out of the admiralty proceedings at New London in December of the previous year, in connection with the Spanish ship affair, and there is every reason to believe that the Connecticut gov-

[1] C. O. 5: 1275, W 43.

[2] *Ibid.*

[3] "My reason for this request is founded upon an Information that the Judge Advocates' commission for New York does not extend to your Honor's government, Although the Judge of Vice Admiralty's Commission gives Him Jurisdiction in both Governments, and if this be fact there is an absolute necessity for the Appointment of such an officer." *Wolcott Papers*, p. 232.

[4] *Ibid.*, p. 236.

ernment was anxious to have just as little contact as possible with this particular type of court. Not only had there been an armed conflict between the guards appointed by the colony's agent, Gurdon Saltonstall, and the admiralty marshal, Joseph Chew, over the possession of the Spanish treasure,[1] which certainly did not spread good feeling, but Judge Morris had seen fit to write a very threatening letter to the governor. ''What treatment,'' he declared, ''I have met with myself, I shall take some other opportunity to acquaint your Honour, at the same time I must acquaint your Honour that I shall represent the affair to His Majesty and his Ministers in the strongest Terms Imaginable at the same time I hope your Honour and the Government by your future Conduct will mittigate the just Resentment of the British ministry.''[2]

But, in spite of this unhappy experience in 1752, which for years plagued the colony; in spite of the open hostility of Massachusetts and of Rhode Island in 1760 toward the vice-admiralty jurisdiction,[3] the Connecticut general assembly in March voluntarily appealed to the crown to establish a court of vice-admiralty exclusively for the colony. This resolution, it may be suggested, before going further, represents perhaps the most notable reversal of public policy, the most radical change of attitude toward the direct interference of Great Britain with the administration of affairs in Connecticut, in the entire history of that colony. It can, indeed, be ventured with little fear of contradiction that the expectations of gain from this move must have been very large to have led these representatives of the people to swallow their

1 See the preceding chapter for an account of this.
2 *Wolcott Papers*, pp. 226-227; and see Joshua Hempstead's *Diary*, pp. 91, 502, 598, 600, 604, 620, 622, 624, 625, 642-643, 654.
3 *R. I. Col. Rec.*, VI, 371-372; Quincy, *Mass. Reports*, 541-547, 557.

inherited distrust and dislike of this civil law court,[1] operating without jury, under an autocratic and sometimes venal judge and deriving its authority and vitality solely from the British crown.

The reasons for this, as set forth by the assembly, were that it was believed necessary to begin getting masts by way of the Connecticut River; this would be of some advantage to the people of the colony as it would enable the importer to make remittances for his goods, in place of draining the colony of its cash; since this was so, it was felt that effectual care should be taken to preserve the woods,[2] which protection could be provided for by the erection of a court of vice-admiralty within the colony.

In dealing with this question of timber preservation, the fact cannot be overlooked that efforts previously made to preserve the king's woods in Connecticut had not been at all popular. In 1747 Governor Jonathan Law, in addressing the general assembly, took occasion to refer to the appointment of a deputy surveyor of the woods for Connecticut, remarking that he should like to know the sentiment of the deputies, "I know its neither silver

[1] The legal history of Connecticut should not be ignored in this connection. Both Connecticut and New Haven colonies, in the beginning, repudiated the English common law and set up the Pentateuch. It was only very gradually that any modification of this attitude took place. While it is true that the eighteenth century witnessed a change, the people were, nevertheless, strongly devoted to the legal system inaugurated by the Connecticut pioneers. The civil law procedure, of pagan origin, was not only foreign to their own legal system but to the legal conceptions of the Anglo-Saxon race and could hardly have been otherwise than distasteful. L. H. Gipson, "The Connecticut Codes," Amer. Jour., Crim. Law, VI, nos. 2 and 3.

When the vice-admiralty jurisdiction of Judge Attwood of New York was extended in 1701 so as to include Connecticut and the rest of New England as well as New Jersey, the governor of the colony did not hesitate to denounce this as a direct violation of the charter. A. P. C. Col., 1688-1720, §815; C. O. 5: 1287, pp. 201, 203.

[2] Conn. Col. Rec., XI, 358.

or gold.'"[1] Both in 1753 and 1755 the colony had treated with extreme coolness the appeals of Surveyor General Benning Wentworth and those of his deputy, Daniel Blake, that action should be taken (for the sake of the preservation of the woods) to make the vice-admiralty jurisdiction effective within the colony. January 17, 1753, Wentworth wrote to Governor Wolcott apprizing him of the fact that his deputy had met with resistance in the execution of his duty within Connecticut, and asking him to publish the surveyor general's commission and to issue a warrant to all civil officers to aid those in charge of the king's woods in the performance of their duties; in addition he requested, as was noticed above, the appointment by the colony of a judge advocate to prosecute trespassers against the king's woods, in the court of vice-admiralty.[2] This last request was repeated June 25 of the same year, when Wentworth complained of the shocking treatment of Blake, who, while in the execution of his office of deputy surveyor, had been hurled into a mill pond by his fellow townsman, Daniel Whitmore of Middletown. The surveyor general warned the governor that ''these are offenses of a Dangerous nature & upon a due Representation thereof by me to His Majesty may be injurious to your colony.'"[3] Although Wolcott had promised to lay before the general assembly at its May session the question of appointing a Connecticut ''Judge Advocate,'"[4] although Daniel Blake had petitioned the assembly in its October session to appoint Samuel Johnson, advocate general, Samuel Merriman, registrar, and William Wright, marshal for the vice-admiralty court, when sitting in Connecticut,[5] the depu-

1 *Wolcott Papers*, p. 467.

2 *Ibid.*, p. 232; C. O. 5: 1276, X 3.

3 *Wolcott Papers*, p. 310.

4 *Ibid.*, p. 236.

5 *Ibid.*, p. 378.

ties were cold to all suggestions. As a result, two years later Wentworth again wrote to the governor of Connecticut in a spirit of loud complaint, demanding that Whitmore, the assailant of Blake, be punished, and threatened to take the case through the Connecticut courts and then appeal to his majesty the king, in case ample satisfaction were not given to him; he also significantly gave notice that he had applied for the establishment of a court of vice-admiralty for Connecticut.[1] But the menacing letters of Wentworth seemed to fall on deaf ears, with the result that the unfortunate Blake, after being subjected to other indignities, among which was ''unlawful imprisonment by William Pitkin,'' in despair resigned this office, and in 1759 wrote a pathetic appeal to the Board of Trade asking for redress against the people of Connecticut for the hostility shown him while trying to care for the king's woods.[2]

The question, therefore, immediately arises, How did it happen that the people of Connecticut, previously so utterly indifferent to the preservation of his majesty's woods, came suddenly to appreciate the advantages that might flow from it, with such ardor that they were now anxious to see established in their midst a court foreign to their most cherished political ideals?

[1] C. O. 5: 1276, X 3. Although Wolcott went out of office in 1754, on May 15, 1755, Wentworth addressed the communication to him as governor of Connecticut.

[2] At the meeting of the Board of Trade, held April 25, 1759, there was read a memorial from Blake ''complaining of several Hardships and personal Injuries sustained by him in the execution of that office. It appearing to their Lordships upon consideration of the said memorial that the Injuries and Hardships complained of were of a private nature, and that it was not within their power and department to give any relief in, or take cognizance of this Affair as the matters complained of had reference to an Officer Acting under the Direction of the Lords Commissioners of the Admiralty, the Petition was laid aside. . . . '' Board of Trade Journals, 1675-1782, vol. LXVII.

Connecticut, it should be remembered, had always labored under the serious handicap of lacking an important export staple which New Hampshire with its timber, Massachusetts with its fish, Rhode Island with its rum, New York with its furs, Virginia with its tobacco, North Carolina with its naval stores, and South Carolina with its rice and indigo, fortunately possessed. These export staples naturally served not only to keep within the favored colonies the specie circulating there, but also to provide the means for an important direct commerce with England and the outside world under the more or less formal restrictions of the navigation and trade acts—thus adding greatly to the wealth of the people. But Connecticut was unhappily situated, hidden behind Long Island and close to the most superb harbor of the North American coast. She, therefore, had been obliged to witness the practical monopolization of the direct foreign trade to England and the other parts of the Old World by New York and her New England neighbors, with the consequent economic subjection of her people to outside commercial interests. Although it would appear that in the '50's, before the outbreak of the Seven Years' War, the colony had been fairly prosperous, the tide, by 1760, had turned against her, steeped as she was in debt,[1] and a truly alarming decline in the value of Connecticut lands took place, as people began streaming away to newer and more hopeful sections of the country.[2]

Now, however, a way seemed to open for clearing away

[1] *Conn. Col. Rec.*, XII, Appendix.

[2] Ezra Stiles was informed that by 1761 land had fallen one-quarter in value. In 1762 the testimony was gloomily recorded that ''a few years ago wild land was £30 and £25 Old Tenor an acre, now sold for £19 the best & good for £15. Many are selling this land in order to remove'' to New Hampshire and Lydius's patent, later known as Vermont. *Itineraries of Ezra Stiles*, p. 50.

this economic depression and placing the colony on a permanently prosperous basis. No wonder, under the circumstances, that the chance of bringing this about made
an irresistible appeal to the public.

What was known as the great New England pine belt
of that day extended from Nova Scotia west and south-
west beyond the Connecticut River. The British government had early grasped the importance of preserving
this virgin forest from waste, as an inexhaustible source
of masts and other naval supplies, which it had been compelled to draw principally from Sweden and other foreign parts. It would appear that as early as 1692, Edward Randolph was acting as surveyor general of his
majesty's woods in America,[1] an office created for the
protection of the timber; he was followed in turn by
Jahleel Brinton,[2] John Bridger, Charles Burniston,
Charles Armstrong, and David Dunbar, which latter, in
1744, surrendered his office to Benning Wentworth,[3] who
retained this post until, in 1767, he turned it over to his
nephew, John Wentworth. The surveyor general was
charged with the responsibility of encouraging, by all
legal and proper methods, the production of naval stores,
of preventing the destruction of trees fit for masts, and
of bringing to justice violators of the law regulating the
use of the pine woods. For, by a series of parliamentary
acts, the timber of North America, and especially the
white pine belts, had been placed under the special protection of the king.[4] An act passed in the second year of

[1] *C. S. P. 1689-1692*, §1830. For a discussion of the early preservation
of the woods, see E. L. Lord, *Industrial Experiments in the British Colonies
of North America*, Chapter II.

[2] See ''Calendar of New Hampshire Papers in English Archives,'' New
Hamp. Hist. Soc. *Coll.*, X, for a great deal of information in very brief
form regarding these surveyors general and the care of the woods.

[3] C. O. 391: 51, p. 52.

[4] 3 and 4 Anne, c. 9, sec. 2; 9 Anne, c. 22; 8 George I, c. 72; 2 George
II, c. 35.

the reign of George II provided that, without special license from the crown, no white pine trees, except the property of private persons, should be cut within Nova Scotia, New England, New York, and New Jersey. The surveyor general was aided in his work of executing these laws and other regulations, by deputies, who went about, placing the king's broad arrow on the finest and most accessible trees measuring over twenty-four inches in girth three feet from the ground. The struggles of these deputies with the loggers of New England is a very dramatic phase of colonial history.[1]

The chief logging centers in North America, in 1760, were in New Hampshire and Maine. By far the most important of these was the Piscataqua River district, which for over a century had maintained its supremacy in spite of the transference to Maine, in 1727, of important mast contracts for the royal navy, by the agent, Colonel Westbrook. Along the banks of the Piscataqua and its tributaries scores of sawmills were located, and ships, large and small, were built. At its mouth were Portsmouth and the custom house, the former the most important shipping and commercial center north of Massachusetts Bay, where the headquarters of the surveyor general of the king's woods in America were maintained and whence, according to his energy and motives, the surveyor general carried on a more or less continuous struggle with the New England lumbermen, who were inclined, as a rule, to pay but scant respect to the timber regulations.

The constant activities, legitimate and otherwise, of the loggers had resulted in the clearing away of the pine woods from the most easily accessible regions along the northeastern New England coast, so that by 1760 it had become more difficult and costly to procure from these

1 2 George II, c. 35.

parts logs that were suitable for ship masts.[1]   The idea
was then conceived by Connecticut parties of tapping the
New England white pine belt by way of the Connecticut
River and, by this means, of building up for Connecticut
an export staple of great value and importance.

In order to realize this ambition, however, two things
appeared to the promoters not only desirable but necessary.   One was to prove to the Navy Board that the Connecticut River was now the logical avenue for the tapping of the great pine belt for that portion of the masts
and other ship timber which the British government was
drawing from America for the use of the royal navy.
The other was to secure the erection of a vice-admiralty
court.   There were two reasons why a court seemed imperative for the success of the enterprise.   In the hands
of strong friends, it would take active steps to deal with
the constant and unlawful timber depredations carried
on by parties living in these sections along the river
where good masting could be obtained.[2]   It would help
to protect the contractors, also, from the hostility of the
settlers in those localities where the trees were to be cut.
While Connecticut contained some little timber suitable
for masting,[3] yet the white pine trees for this purpose,

[1] C. O. 5: 1275, W 43.

[2] In case the logs were floated down the Connecticut River, libels could
be gotten out against them and the court could thereupon condemn them.

[3] This fact is made clear in the following exchange of views between
Governor Wolcott and Surveyor General Wentworth in 1753: ''There are
no White pine Trees,'' wrote Wolcott, ''fitt for His Majesties Navey as I
hear of Growing in this Colony but on the lands Lying on the North west
of it.   These Lands were Granted by the Corporation to the Inhabitants of
the Towns of Hartford and Windsor in the year 1686 and have since been
setled into Towns and Divided in severalty into particular Lotts and Devi-
sions among the first Grantees and their Assynes who are liveing and Im-
proving upon them according to such Devissions.''   To which Wentworth
replied that ''nothing is lookt upon as private property, but Lands under
Actual improvement & Inclosures, so that the grants made in Your Colony

significantly, were, according to the plans of the promoters, to be procured farther north along the river, in
Massachusetts and in the wilderness beyond the northern
boundary of that colony. The people living in these
upper sections would not be apt to submit tamely while
their country was being denuded of its wealth and the
benefits were flowing into Connecticut coffers. Not only
would the court help crush this opposition but would
stand out against the even more dangerous hostility that
was almost sure to come from the powerful interests
centered at Portsmouth, in the person of Benning Wentworth.

Probably no one living in America during the later
colonial period occupied a more semi-regal position than
did Wentworth down to the date of his retirement from
public life. For he was not only the surveyor general of
all the king's woods in America, but also governor of
New Hampshire. It would be little exaggeration to say
that for a generation he held the political and economic
destinies of that province in the hollow of his hand. His
father, John Wentworth,[1] who for years was the acting
governor of New Hampshire, under the title of lieutenant
governor, was a man of wealth and influence, and it was
he who established the Wentworth régime within the
province. Benning, before attaining high station in political life, became exceedingly wealthy through commercial activities which frequently carried him to England
and to Spain. What New Hampshire had to offer above
everything else was lumber, and it appears that he was
principally interested in the exportation of this article.
In 1734 he entered his father's council, together with his

in the Year 1686 cannot defend the trespassers in the Court of Vice
Admiralty.'' *Wolcott Papers,* pp. 235, 309-310.

[1] For facts regarding the history of the Wentworth family see John
Wentworth, *The Wentworth Genealogy,* two vols.

brother-in-law, Theodore Atkinson. In 1741, upon the
death of the lieutenant governor, that office was abolished
and Benning was commissioned to the governorship. In
consolidating his power, he pursued his father's policy of
filling up the important provincial offices, as far as possible, with near relatives; his brother-in-law, George
Jaffrey, at one time was president of the council, also
treasurer and chief justice; Jotham Odiorne, Henry Sher-
burne, Ellis Huske, Samuel Solley, and Thomas Parker,
all closely connected with the Wentworth family by
birth or marriage, were awarded important public posts.[1]
Although by 1760 most of these men had passed away,
the lack of their presence and support in political life
was made up by their successors in office and by the entrance into the council in 1768 of Mark Hunking Wentworth, the governor's brother.[2] Some idea of the commanding position of Benning Wentworth in 1760 may be
gained by the fact that his home at Little Harbor was a
palatial mansion of fifty-two rooms, containing a pretentious council chamber, with its armory and guards in
times of danger. It was here at Little Harbor that much
of the provincial business was disposed of; here, also,
the councilors and other men of influence were entertained in the great billiard room with its inviting buffet.[3]

Now there were two reasons why the Wentworth group
that gathered at Little Harbor would be hostile to this
Connecticut plan. First of all, it was well known that
Benning Wentworth, at that moment, was getting control of the pine and other lands north of Massachusetts,
lying on either side of the Connecticut River, and it was
natural to expect that if anybody was to secure an ad-

[1] John Wentworth, *Wentworth Genealogy*, I, 287.

[2] "Calendar of New Hampshire Papers in English Archives," New
Hampshire Hist. Soc. *Coll.*, X, 469, 499.

[3] The *Portsmouth* (N. H.) *Journal*, September 5, 1857, has an interesting description of this mansion.

vantage from the exploitation of the timber of that river, the governor would see to it, if possible, that Portsmouth parties should be the beneficiaries. As early as 1750 he had laid claim, in the name of New Hampshire, to the region west of the Connecticut, after having secured a special commission from the crown to grant lands within that province upon a quit-rent basis of one shilling sterling per hundred acres;[1] and, in spite of the protests of New York, he was, in 1760, in the midst of a gigantic scheme of granting away to New Hampshire people and others, the Connecticut River lands, after they had been surveyed and laid out in townships six miles square, modestly reserving for himself, as a fee, a block of five hundred select acres in each township.[2]

But a far more direct reason for expecting hostility from Portsmouth lay in the fact that in attempting to supply mast contracts, it would be necessary to come into direct competition with the governor's brother, Mark Hunking Wentworth, one of the wealthiest men in New England, whose great commercial interests were centered in the Piscataqua and whose warehouses stood at Portsmouth, where he resided, in a home only less magnificent than that of his brother.[3] For Mark Hunking Wentworth, in 1760, was in control of the American mast trade, drawing his logs from the Piscataqua region and adjacent parts.[4] There was also a suspicion that Ben-

[1] *N. Y. Col. Doc.*, VII, 598.

[2] *Ibid.* It appears that Wentworth granted at least 140 townships lying west of the Connecticut River. *Connecticut Journal*, March, 2, 1770. For further details regarding these grants, see ''The New Hampshire Grants (so called) 1749 to 1791,'' *Documents and Records Relating to New Hampshire*, Vol. X, No. 3.

[3] New Hamp. Hist. Soc. *Coll.*, V, 239; John Wentworth, *The Wentworth Genealogy; New Hampshire Gazette*, September 13, 1765.

[4] New Hamp. Hist. Soc. *Coll.*, V, 239; Sam Willis and M. Talcott to J. Ingersoll, February 24, 1763, Ingersoll Papers. E. Dyer to Jared

ning Wentworth, on becoming governor in 1741, had not
gone out of the lumber business. In fact, it was asserted
that in order to obtain the office of surveyor general,
which was in the hands of Jeremiah Dunbar, he paid the
latter, in 1744, £2000 to get him to relinquish his commission, although the office carried with it a stipend of
but £200 a year.[1] As time went on, it became increas-
ingly apparent that the surveyor general was not a disinterested guardian of the king's woods.

No one who knew the Wentworths would be disposed
for a moment to imagine that these subtle, far-reaching,
grasping, and influential colonial magnates would allow,
without a struggle, the people of Connecticut to build up
an industry that would strike at their own prosperity
and that of New Hampshire. For the complete success
of this move might well mean, by reason of the lower
cost of production, the transfer not only of the mast contracts, but also of the lumber trade, from the Piscataqua
region to the Connecticut, with the rise of New London
into great importance as a shipping center and the consequent decline of Portsmouth, unable to meet the destructive competition of the newer section.

To combat the Wentworth and other influences that
could be counted on as hostile, a vice-admiralty court,
established by the royal authority, presided over by a
judge favorable to Connecticut, and employing a fear-
less and capable king's advocate, was the ideal weapon
for those desiring to draw the masting business to the
Connecticut River.

Who was the instigator of the plan so eagerly embraced
by the Connecticut general assembly? Circumstantial

Ingersoll, April 14, 1764. New Haven Col. Hist. Soc. *Papers*, IX ("Jared
Ingersoll Papers"), 290; C. O. 5: 1276, X 3.

[1] For a brief discussion of this point see E. L. Lord, *Industrial Experiments in the British Colonies of North America*, p. 99.

evidence of the strongest sort, as will be seen, points to
Jared Ingersoll. This evidence also leads one to feel that
he conceived the plan after leaving America, and after
coming in touch with the mast trade situation, in his association with British government officials, and those interested in the importation of lumber into England.
There is evidence, moreover, to show that he had a very
definite notion as to the person who should be appointed
judge of the court that the assembly asked to have
erected. In fact, it may here be confidently suggested
that, if every phase of his carefully framed project could
have been carried through successfully, there would have
arisen in Connecticut a group of interests, under the control of Ingersoll, as powerful as those identified with
Benning Wentworth of New Hampshire. To work out
his plans, he long deferred his departure for home, after
turning the business of the agency over to Richard Jackson.

On June 2, 1760, from his lodgings in North Palace
yard, Ingersoll addressed a letter to John Pownall, secretary to the Board of Trade, in which he pointed out the
fact that in eastern New England the pine woods had become scarce, and that ''with cost and difficulty the masting is got down the river''; but as to the Connecticut
River, ''trees or sticks for the largest masts may be
conveniently brought down the said River from the parts
above as has appeared from experiments made and 'tis
I believe, generally thought by those who are acquainted
with that country that the masting from New England
must be obtained by the way of this River, in a very considerable measure, at least after some little time longer.''
Then, turning to the question of the vice-admiralty court,
he directed the attention of the board to the fact that it
was impossible for the deputy of the surveyor general
in Connecticut to hinder ''private persons dwelling near

the river from conveying down the said River much of
his Majesty's valuable masting timber and when attempts
were made to seize said logs there had been a failure of
carrying the matter through for want of a Court of Vice
Admiralty and of the proper officers belonging to such a
court.'' He thereupon urged the appointment of a judge
of vice-admiralty, a king's advocate, and the other necessary officers for constituting a Connecticut court, supporting this by the letter from Governor Fitch in which
the desire of the general assembly was set forth.[1]

The letter was read to the board at its meeting, Friday,
June 13, and was then laid aside until there could be a
report from the attorney general and solicitor general
relative to the preservation of his majesty's woods in
North America.[2] For over a year Ingersoll exerted
himself, but without success, to bring the Board of Trade
to the point of making a representation in favor of a vice-
admiralty court for Connecticut; he was also busy with
other plans, and, before the spring of 1761, had succeeded in persuading the Navy Board to give him a contract for a shipload of masts to be procured by way of
the Connecticut River,[3] to try, as he later wrote the
board, "whether the Navy may not be supplied with that
article from that part to better advantage than at pres-

[1] C. O. 5: 1275, W 43.

[2] C. O. 5: 1275, W 43. See also Board of Trade Journals, vol. LXVIII,
entry for June 13, 1760.

[3] Among the Connecticut Papers in the Bancroft Transcripts (New
York Public Library) is an item which reads as follows: ''Tuesday, July
30, 1760. In Captain Blake arrived as passengers at Boston. Jared Ingersoll of Connecticut.'' If no mistake has been made in the date it would
appear that Ingersoll made a trip to America after withdrawing from the
agency and after petitioning the Board of Trade to establish a vice-
admiralty court for Connecticut. The trip must have been undertaken for
the purpose of making plans for the mast contract. The date of this contract was December 19, 1760. The Navy Board to Jared Ingersoll, January 26, 1762, New Haven Col. Hist. Soc. *Papers*, IX (''Jared Ingersoll
Papers''), 256-257. *Calendar Home Office Papers, 1760-1765*, §180.

ent from the several places there;'"¹—a statement clearly
disclosing the great scope of his plans. With this initial
advantage gained, he now, once more, attempted to move
the Board of Trade to action regarding the vice-admiralty court; this time, by getting the commissioners of the
navy interested in the plan. March 27, 1761, he addressed a letter to them reminding them that he had
agreed to get a load of masts by way of the Connecticut,
and emphasizing the fact that it was very important to
have established a vice-admiralty court for the purpose
of carrying into execution the contract, offering the same
reasons that he had to the Board of Trade, and closing
with the argument that "transgressors are with difficulty convicted by trials at common law." He then tact-
fully suggested that since they were about to write to
the lords commissioners of the admiralty for obtaining
permission to cut the timber required to fulfill the contract, they would also suggest at the same time the
establishment of a Connecticut vice-admiralty court.²
This the Navy Board proceeded to do, at the same time
forwarding not only Ingersoll's letters but also copies
of letters that Ingersoll shrewdly had obtained, which
Benning Wentworth had written to the governor of Connecticut in 1753 and in 1755, urging the necessity of effective admiralty jurisdiction within that colony. The
Lords of the Admiralty received the suggestion with such
favor that they instructed their secretary, John Cleveland, to lay the matter before the Board of Trade, with
the suggestion that if the plan met with its approval, fit
persons should be recommended to act as judge and
register. The project seemed on the point of consumma-
tion; but Ingersoll's hopes were dashed for the second

¹ Jared Ingersoll to the Navy Board, March 27, 1761, C. O. 5: 1276, X 3.
² *Ibid.*

time. Some unknown opposition at the Board of Trade seems to have nullified his efforts.[1]

The unwillingness of the Board of Trade to seize this opportunity to aid in vitalizing the royal authority within Connecticut, at this time, is enough to excite attention. From the days of its establishment in 1696, with remarkable consistency the board had upheld a policy in favor of subjecting the colonies to much greater direct control on the part of the home government; it had desired the placing of a crown attorney general within each colony;[2] for years it had sought the recall of the charters and the destruction of the proprietary control in America; when that had failed, it had attempted to compel Connecticut, Rhode Island, and Maryland to submit their laws to England for ratification as was the practice of the other colonies. But it did not seem at all disposed to encourage Connecticut's application. Ultimately the board was to commit itself to the reorganization of the vice-admiralty jurisdiction in the colonies; yet it was not Ingersoll's plan that was to meet with favor but, significantly, the

[1] On May 26, 1761, Pownall addressed a letter to Cleveland setting forth the position of the board, from which the following is quoted: "It appears, from the Papers enclosed in your Letter, that the Court of Vice-Admiralty of New York does still comprehend within its jurisdiction the Colony of Connecticut, and therefore the Lords Commissioners for Trade and Plantations conceive that the Propriety, or Impropriety, of any New Establishment must depend upon such Information, as the Lords Commissioners of the Admiralty shall have received of the sufficiency or Insufficiency of that Jurisdiction as it stands at present, concerning which no Complaint has been made to this Board. Their Lordships therefore under these circumstances cannot take upon them to give any Opinion as to the Expediency or Inexpediency of any new Regulations with respect to the Admiralty Jurisdiction in the Colony of Connecticut; nor are they sufficiently acquainted with the Names and Characters of Persons proper to be Officers of a separate Admiralty Court for that Colony, in case it should be thought advisable to establish such a Court." C. O. 5: 1296. This communication will be printed in full in the forthcoming Volume II of the *Fitch Papers.*

[2] *A. P. C. Col., 1688-1720,* §639.

one urged as a substitute by Benning Wentworth, who suddenly was awakened to the conviction that, after all, it would be poor policy on the part of the English government to establish an independent vice-admiralty court for Connecticut.

Probably realizing how futile it would be longer to delay his departure from England in the hope of procuring action regarding the court, and being under the necessity, moreover, of applying himself to the task of fulfilling his contract, Jared Ingersoll sailed to America in the *Calcide*, about the middle of 1761.[1] It may be said with a good deal of certainty that he never again was so popular with the people of Connecticut as at the time of his home coming. To show its appreciation of his efforts in behalf of the colony, the general assembly appointed a committee of its leading men to wait personally upon him and to congratulate him on his safe arrival, at the same time thanking him ''for the good services he hath done for this Colony, during his agency at the Court of Great Britain.''[2] In fact, no one, in 1761, was considered to be a firmer friend of Connecticut interests than Jared Ingersoll.

By November Ingersoll was prepared to take active steps regarding the procuring of the white pine sticks. On the fourteenth he dispatched Captain Willis to the surveyor general at Portsmouth, bearing a copy of the mast contract and a letter requesting Wentworth to appoint some proper person to designate the trees to be

[1] It seems that Ingersoll was interested in horse breeding, and upon his return to America brought with him an English stallion. His friend, Thomas Bridges of Headley, England, wrote him in 1762 that he was glad to hear of the welfare of his ''Gray Horse.'' ''I hope his Colts will turn out to your satisfaction & the gentlemen of the Country, & that he will mend your Breed.'' Thos. Bridges to J. Ingersoll, September 30, 1762, New Haven Col. Hist. Soc. *Papers*, IX (''Jared Ingersoll Papers''), 279.

[2] Conn. Archives, War, X, 40.

appropriated.   Willis was also authorized to acquaint
Wentworth "more particularly when & where it will be
needful to have the Service performed."[1]   A month later
he was able to inform the surveyor general that he had
agreed with Willis and Matthew Talcott, both of Middletown, Connecticut, to procure the stipulated "stores"
which would be secured along the Connecticut "from
Deerfield & the Cowhees[2] Inclusive"; at the same time
he asked for the customary licenses.[3]   Everything appeared to move smoothly.   That he was strongly en-
trenched at this time with the Navy Board, is vouched
for by the receipt of a request in January, 1762, from
that body that he should inform it as to the possibilities
of an early delivery of the masts, in order that a time
might be fixed upon "for coming to a new contract for
supply of American Masts,"[4] in reply to which he stated
his hopes of having the timber delivered at Portsmouth
by the following Christmas.[5]

However, Willis and Talcott, who by this time were up
the river in Massachusetts with their loggers, were en-
countering difficulties and unusual expense.[6]   There

[1] Jared Ingersoll to Benning Wentworth, November 14, 1761, New
Haven Col. Hist. Soc. *Papers,* IX ("Jared Ingersoll Papers"), 255.

[2] "The country in the neighborhood of Lunenburgh and Newburg, and
on the side of the river opposite the latter place was called by the Indians
'Coos' which word, in the Abenaqui language, is said to signify 'The
Pines.' " B. H. Hall, *History of Eastern Vermont,* p. 585.

[3] Jared Ingersoll to Benning Wentworth, December 18, 1761, New
Haven Col. Hist. Soc. *Papers,* IX ("Jared Ingersoll Papers"), 256.

[4] The Navy Office to Jared Ingersoll, January 26, 1762, *ibid.,* IX, 256-
257.

[5] Jared Ingersoll to G. Cockburne, Comptroller of His Majesty's Navy,
May 13, 1762, *ibid.,* IX, 258.

[6] That they, however, hoped for another contract is attested by their
letter. "We think it may not be amiss to inform the Gentm Commissioners
that if the thing proves practicable that we may have the preference for a
future contract this way in order to make up for difficulties of the first
venture." Samuel Willis to Jared Ingersoll, July 2, 1762, Ingersoll Papers.

apparently was quite a search for suitable trees. After these had been selected, it was necessary to "blaze" the way to them from the river by cutting down the obstructing trees. The contract called for eighty sticks suitable for masts; but to provide for contingencies, eighty-nine of the white pine giants were felled, some, unfortunately, breaking in the fall; eighty-four of those that were down appeared sound. After this work and the blazing had been finished, it was found that besides the big trees, sixty-three smaller ones, together with a number of defective trees, were down.[1] Then came the task of "balking" the trees to the river, which had to be done at that period by the use of numbers of oxen.[2] The men succeeded in getting one hundred and forty-seven of the pines to the water's edge. One suitable tree, alone, was left lying in the wilderness; this was on account of the opposition shown from the beginning by the people of the neighborhood, which reached such heights toward the end that, according to Willis and Talcott, Captain Zedekiah Stone of Petersham went to their camping ground in their absence and carried away their hay, which necessitated giving up the plan to "balk" the remaining tree.[3]

The log drive that thereupon ensued down the Connecticut River was not very successful by reason of the low state of the water. Twenty-one of the trees, among them one of the finest of the masts, got lodged on a rapid and had to be left there for the high spring

[1] Samuel Willis and Matthew Talcott to Jared Ingersoll, April 9, 1764, New Haven Col. Hist. Soc. *Papers*, IX ("Jared Ingersoll Papers"), 266-268.

[2] Weeden gives a very clear idea as to the methods used in handling these logs. W. B. Weeden, *Economic and Social History of New England*, II, 765, 783-785, 833.

[3] Samuel Willis and Matthew Talcott to Jared Ingersoll, April 9, 1764, New Haven Col. Hist. Soc. *Papers*, IX ("Jared Ingersoll Papers"), 266-268.

waters.[1] Another magnificent thirty-seven-inch stick
was broken in the drive. Less than the contract number
of logs reached the lower river, with the result that
drivers had to go up the river in low water to get down
the necessary number. By January, 1763, a shipment
might have been made, although a good many trees were
still held up the river.

It is not apparent that Ingersoll ever ventured, himself, into the logging country. He, however, wrote the
commissioners of the navy, in October, 1762, that the
work was progressing hopefully and that it was receiving his closest attention ''from views not only of discharging my present Obligations but also of future benefits as well to the public as to myself.''[2] The following
January he informed them that the logs were down and
that he had sent for an experienced lumber liner to give
expert judgment and proof regarding them.[3]

Up to 1763 the Wentworth group made no outward
attack, although they seem soon to have come to a complete comprehension of the scope of Ingersoll's plans,
and, in alarm, to have sent John, the talented son of Mark
Hunking Wentworth, who was associated with his father
in his commercial enterprises, to England, as early as
1762, for the protection of the family interests.[4] Each
side was playing a deep game for great stakes, and every
move was a studied one. Ingersoll would win the mast
trade by getting his white pine sticks more cheaply and
quickly than the same could be procured along the New
Hampshire and Maine rivers. Moreover, to protect his

[1] Jared Ingersoll to the Commissioners of the Navy, June 8, 1763, *ibid.*, IX, 261-262.

[2] Jared Ingersoll to the Commissioners of the Navy, October 12, 1762, *ibid.*, IX, 259.

[3] Jared Ingersoll to the Commissioners of the Navy, June 8, 1763, *ibid.*, IX, 261-262.

[4] John Wentworth, *The Wentworth Genealogy*, I, 538.

enterprise, he had now conceived of the idea—since his original plan for a district Connecticut court of vice-admiralty had come to naught—of securing something almost as desirable: an appointment as deputy judge of vice-admiralty for the colony of Connecticut. It happened that Judge Lewis Morris died, July 3, 1762; his son, Richard, thereupon fell heir, as it were, to his post. In fulfillment of this new plan, Ingersoll not only wrote to Richard Morris regarding his desires, but even to his college friend, William Livingston, also of New York, asking him to use his influence in furtherance of this end. When Livingston waited upon Morris, the latter declared that he was not in a position to make any answer to the proposal, owing to the fact that he had only up to that time received an appointment as judge of admiralty for New York. However, the latter part of December the judge wrote to Ingersoll, stating that he had received notice that his warrant for a commission as judge of admiralty "for the three provinces" had been made out, and that when he came into Connecticut to publish his commission he would "be proud" to appoint Ingersoll his deputy.[1] Clearly Jared Ingersoll's fortunes were mounting. To crush him, the Wentworths felt themselves under the necessity of raising up such a storm of disapproval against his enterprise and his ambitious plans as would condemn it in the eyes of the home government. This they now proceeded to do.

Late in January, 1763, Willis and Talcott wrote from Middletown, Connecticut, where most of the logs were being held, saying that a Colonel Symes, who claimed to be a deputy under the surveyor general, had come to

[1] Richard Morris to Jared Ingersoll, December 23, 1762, New Haven Col. Hist. Soc. *Papers,* IX ("Jared Ingersoll Papers"), 275.

Judge Lewis Morris had a Connecticut deputy judge, one Nathaniel, *Fitch Papers,* I, 45.

inspect the logs, saying that he had been informed that they had been destroying timber. They declared that upon conversation with Symes they found out that his coming "was wholy by Mr. Mark Wentworth's Motion." Symes, they also informed Ingersoll, proceeded to measure some of the smallest sticks and they suspected from the proceedings "that his coming was to furnish Mr. Mark Wentworth with a pretense to Inform the Commissioners that they had not or would not get Timber to answer the purpose."[1] A month later they wrote Ingersoll again, in haste, informing him that Colonel Symes had received orders to seize all of their logs under contract length; they were persuaded, they informed him, that this proceeding was "owing to Mark Wentworth on purpose to embarrass and bind us."[2] Ingersoll immediately took alarm. The day after getting the report, he addressed a letter to the Navy Board, informing them of this new development. He insisted that the only sticks sent down the river under contract size were those that had to be felled to blaze a way to the large timber; he presumed, however, that Wentworth would communicate with them regarding the matter and he desired to present it in its true light.[3] That he realized the seriousness of the situation is shown by a second letter, addressed to the commissioners that same day, in which he declared that "if things succeed according to Expectation tis not unlikely I may think of going over to England myself with the Masts."[4] He also immediately set out to Hart-

[1] Samuel Willis and Matthew Talcott to Jared Ingersoll, January 28, 1763, Ingersoll Papers.

[2] Samuel Willis and Matthew Talcott to Jared Ingersoll, February 24, 1763, Ingersoll Papers.

[3] Jared Ingersoll to the Commissioners of the Navy, March 1, 1763, New Haven Col. Hist. Soc. *Papers*, IX ("Jared Ingersoll Papers"), 259-260.

[4] *Ibid.*, IX, 260.

ford, where he was able to get in touch with Governor Fitch, and from that place wrote to Colonel Symes, expressing his surprise at the surveyor general's order, and protesting that the extra number of logs was only designed to cover losses of sending them down the river.[1]

Wentworth now waited until early in July, when he addressed a letter to Governor Fitch, complaining of the "uncommon waste made in the King's woods in the hinter part," stating that, notwithstanding the vigilance of his officers, this timber so wasted had been transported into Connecticut; he then declared, "I must apply to you for your Protection and Countenance to my officers in proceeding against the offenders in case they may be found," and ended by demanding a proclamation to the civil and military officers to aid him in the preservation of the king's woods.[2] Fitch coolly proceeded to send a copy of this letter to Ingersoll and needlessly warned him that he had reason to believe that Wentworth had his timber in mind and, thereupon, suggested that "it may be expedient, for political ends at least, (if his case be as I guess) for me to grant his request. I acquaint you with the thing in order for your advice with Respect to the Care and Caution it may be proper to be used in drawing the Proclamation."[3]

It seems to have been Wentworth's desire to let the clamor against Ingersoll, which he had raised and was feeding gradually, take effect in London before proceeding further. However, the latter part of October he was again ready to attack. On the eighteenth, he addressed a communication to the Board of Trade in which he advo-

1 Jared Ingersoll to Colonel Symes, March 9, 1763, New Haven Col. Hist. Soc. *Papers*, IX ("Jared Ingersoll Papers"), 260-261.

2 Benning Wentworth to Governor Fitch, July 1, 1763, Ingersoll Papers.

3 Thomas Fitch to Jared Ingersoll, August 1, 1763, Ingersoll Papers.

cated the appointment of a judge of vice-admiralty whose
authority should extend over all the colonies in matters
relating to the woods set apart for his majesty's use.[1]
He, of course, was not only aware of Ingersoll's efforts
to secure the establishment of a court of vice-admiralty
for Connecticut, but, it would appear, was acquainted
with the attempts that the latter had been making to have
himself appointed deputy judge of vice-admiralty for
Connecticut. By securing the creation of a court pos-
sessing superior jurisdiction with reference to the king's
woods, Governor Wentworth must have realized that he
and his brother could, with the aid of a friendly superior
judge, keep control of the New England timber situation,
even with Ingersoll presiding over an admiralty court in
Connecticut.

What is more, Wentworth probably acquainted Judge
Richard Morris with the fact that Ingersoll had been
exerting himself to detach Connecticut from the New
York admiralty district. This, at least, is by far the most
plausible explanation for the reason why Judge Morris
apparently failed to make Ingersoll, who desired to sup-
plant him in Connecticut, his deputy, after he had written
to him that he would be proud to do so; that Judge Morris, by 1764, had joined hands with the Wentworths
against Ingersoll can hardly be questioned, in light of the
fact that in April of that year Gideon Lyman, of Northampton, Hampshire County, Massachusetts, appeared
before him and signed a deposition directed against
Ingersoll in which he asserted that although the mast
contract had called for only eighty sticks, Ingersoll's
men had cut down one hundred and sixty, "to the great
waste of the King's woods." Lyman then very significantly went on to say that for this reason, in spite of his

[1] C. O. 391: 70, pp. 361-362; Board of Trade Journals, vol. LXXI
(1763). Entry for Tuesday, December 13, 1763.

high opinion of Mr. Ingersoll's character, he conceived him to be "an Improper person to set as the Judge of the Vice Admiralty Court in the Colony of Connecticut concerning or relating to any pine Logs or Masts that may be seized or Libelled in the said colony as forfeited for the use of his Majesty for having been cut without License therefor being first obtained."[1] Lyman, it may be added, was one of Wentworth's deputies. The deposition of course was designed to be used against Ingersoll by the representatives of the Wentworth interests who were in England.

Ingersoll, meanwhile, was getting very impatient over the unaccountable delay there had been in sending a suitable ship from England for transporting the masts. Early in February, 1764, he wrote to the commissioners of the navy, voicing his disappointment, while giving his opinion that the masts could hardly be delivered before midsummer. He, however, emphasized the fact that he had spared neither pains nor expense to fulfill properly his contract, and he therefore asked that the board would not take any steps which might prejudice his affairs or disappoint his future hopes until his arrival; he was planning, he further declared, to bring to England with him, Captain Willis, experienced in the mast business, who could give information as to the practicability of securing in the future masts from the Connecticut, and he trusted that the board would receive "better information

[1] "Affidavit of Gideon Lyman. April 2. 1764," New Haven Col. Hist. Soc. *Papers*, IX ("Jared Ingersoll Papers"), 264-265. How this came into the hands of Ingersoll is a mystery; it is, however, to be found among his papers.

As late as January 1, 1768, Willis is found writing to Ingersoll from Middletown, Connecticut, that he is at a loss to know how to dispose of what "Sticks we have at New London & hear." Samuel Willis to Jared Ingersoll, Ingersoll Papers.

from him in these matters than from any Vague Accounts
which they may have from others, whose knowledge may
perhaps be justly Suspected and as it may happen, their
motives too."[1]

That Ingersoll's fears as to the type of war being
waged against his enterprise were by no means unfounded, is shown by a letter which some months later
he received from his friend, Eliphalet Dyer,[2] who wrote
from London the middle of April. Dyer had gone to England from Connecticut in a mast ship, and he said that
while on board he had gained "Considerable Intelligence
of what might be Expected to hinder Success in your
Scheme & plan about the Mast affair, . . . " He went
on to inform Ingersoll that he had disclosed this information to Richard Jackson, the Connecticut agent, and
continued, "was in hopes you would not have waited for
the arrival of your Mast Ship before you had set out for
England, if you had a design still to prosecute that affair,
for I have the greatest reason to believe that Mr Hennika
& others in Contract with Mr Wentworth are Determined
to break all your measures & frustrate your designs as
they have allready Indeavourd to propagate an Opinion
that the Masts you have got & prepared to send here are
good for Nothing for that purpose, & will not half pay
the freight, and doubt not that they will Indeavour to
procure the Inspecters here, who are much under their
influence, even to say the same when they arrive, let them

[1] Jared Ingersoll to the Commissioners of the Navy, February 7, 1764,
New Haven Col. Hist. Soc. *Papers*, IX ("Jared Ingersoll Papers"), 263-
264.

[2] Eliphalet Dyer of Windham, Connecticut, was a graduate of Yale
College of the class of 1740; for seventeen years he was a member of
the general assembly; he participated in the French and Indian War and
in 1763 was sent to England as the agent of the Susquehanna Company.
He was a delegate to the Stamp Act Congress and also to the Continental
Congress and for a time was chief justice of the superior court.

be ever so good; this I mention that you may be sufficiently guarded against all these Vile Attempts etc.''[1]
Why the English government took over two years
to send a mast ship to New London, especially since the
Navy Board sought, an early delivery, can probably only
be conjectured.[2] At last, in the fall of 1764, the ship,
Prince Henry, arrived, and by the latter part of October
the timber was loaded, and Ingersoll and Willis were
able to begin the slow voyage across the ocean, which
consumed over two months.[3]

By the time, however, that Ingersoll arrived in London, the Wentworth group seems to have gotten in firm
control again of the ship mast situation.[4] John Wentworth, in fact, so ingratiated himself with the ministry,
that in 1766, while still in England, he was appointed not
only to the governorship of New Hampshire in place of
his uncle Benning, who was becoming infirm and desirous

---

[1] Eliphalet Dyer to Jared Ingersoll, April 14, 1764, New Haven Col.
Hist. Soc. *Papers,* IX (''Jared Ingersoll Papers''), 288-290.

John Henniker, mentioned above, was a member of parliament and also
a sub-contractor for the royal masts. For further facts see *ibid.,* IX, 290,
note.

[2] On November 3, 1763, Dyer had written to Ingersoll informing him
that a mast ship would sail for Connecticut the following January. ''I
should much rejoice to see you here which shall Expect in that ship if not
before.'' *Ibid.,* IX, 287-288.

[3] *New London Gazette,* February 26, 1764. Ingersoll arrived early in
December. *Ingersoll Stamp Act Correspondence,* p. 3.

[4] Yet it is to be noted that up to the summer of 1763 Ingersoll had the
powerful support of the comptroller of the Navy Board, George Cockburne,
as the following communication indicates: ''It gives me pleasure to hear
of Mr Ingersoll. I did every thing in my power to assist that Gentleman
when he was here, and shall on all occasions continue to do the same, as I
am in great hopes by His means the Government will, not only in what He
has contracted for but in future, be furnished with Masts on better terms
than heretofore.'' G. Cockburne to an unknown party, August 19, 1763,
New Haven Col. Hist. Soc. *Papers,* IX (''Jared Ingersoll Papers''), 262-
263.

of retiring from public life, but also to the latter's post of surveyor general of his majesty's woods in America.[1]

In line also with the desires of the Wentworth family was the establishment, in 1764, by the royal authority, of a vice-admiralty court for all America, sitting at Halifax, with a concurrent jurisdiction in all matters with each and every other admiralty court that had been or might be set up in America.[2]

Ingersoll, probably realizing that he had been hopelessly outreached in this struggle for power and wealth and the control of the American mast trade, turned his attention to other issues soon after his arrival. Connecticut, therefore, was compelled to forego the pleasures of a vice-admiralty court and an export staple, and also was forced to wait patiently for the coming of prosperity. Ultimately, the Connecticut River became, as Ingersoll had predicted, the masting center of the New England white pine belt.[3] But this did not occur until after the collapse of the Wentworth interests at the outbreak of the Revolutionary War.[4]

---

[1] John Wentworth, *The Wentworth Genealogy*, I, 538.

[2] 4 George III, c. 15, sec. 41.

[3] W. B. Weeden, *Social and Economic History of New England, 1620-1789*, II, 833.

[4] Even during the early days of the Revolution, the British mast ships kept coming to Portsmouth. *N. H. Prov. Papers*, VII, 361; W. B. Weeden, *Social and Economic History of New England, 1620-1789*, II, 784.

It is of interest to note that in the spring of 1769 Wentworth, in his capacity of surveyor general, wrote to Ingersoll, after the latter had received his commission as judge of vice-admiralty for the Middle Colonies, beseeching him to take action against certain trespassers against the king's woods living about Windsor, Connecticut, who were making depredations ''in open, repeated and publicly asserted defiance and contempt of Law.'' Ingersoll referred the matter to Judge Morris as belonging to his jurisdiction. John Wentworth to Jared Ingersoll, February 3 and April 10, 1769. Ingersoll Papers.

CHAPTER V

THE PASSING OF THE STAMP ACT

THE successful conclusion of the Seven Years' War, in 1763, brought to the British ministry the necessity of organizing for administration and defense the newly acquired territory of the empire. That such organization was highly important, especially at this time, seemed patent to thoughtful and well-informed Englishmen, who were keenly aware of "how refractory was the conduct of the Colonies in the matter of trade and defense during the French and Indian War."[1]

While the prestige of England had been greatly increased as a result of the war, she was "reeling under a national debt of nearly 140 millions." At the instigation of Charles Townshend, president of the Board of Trade, the Bute ministry had come to the conclusion that no greater immediate service could be rendered to the empire than the development of additional sources of revenue. One important way of doing this appeared to be through the strict enforcement of the trade and navigation acts; for the ministry was convinced that a vast volume of trade was being carried on by Americans who

[1] This has been carefully worked out by G. L. Beer, in his volume, *British Colonial Policy, 1754-1765;* see also, E. J. McCormac, *Opposition to Imperial Authority,* Univ. of Calif. *Pub.*

The expression British "Empire" was not infrequently employed by Englishmen of that period. Richard Jackson, the Connecticut agent in England, in a communication dated November 15, 1765, says, "However, the Colonies have friends, I sh^d say, the British Empire has friends . . . " *Fitch Papers.*

were evading the customs.[1] Now that the colonies were prosperous, it did not seem fair that they should be allowed to escape their just share of responsibility in financing the imperial administration in time of peace as well as in war—more particularly in light of the fact that no small part of the peace footing expense would go to maintain garrisons along the western American frontier to guard against any repetition of the disasters that had befallen outlying communities, due to the inability and neglect of the colonial legislatures to provide adequate protection.

Bute, however, did not remain in office long enough to accomplish anything in this direction, for in April, 1763, the ministry was reconstructed with George Grenville at the head of affairs. Grenville, a hard-working, conscientious, and loquacious little man, had been in the former administration, and approved heartily of the Townshend program. This he immediately set to work to carry out. His first task was to tighten up the vice-admiralty courts and the colonial customs service for a rigid execution of the navigation and trade acts.[2] In this connection he began the effective enforcement of the Molasses Act of 1733, which, at least as far as Connecticut and Rhode Island were concerned, had been rather a dead letter, in spite of the fact that "of all the Northern Provinces their industries were most dependent upon intercourse with the French sugar Islands."[3] The news

[1] See Thomas Whately, *Considerations on the Trade and Finance of the Kingdom and on the Measures of Administration* (London, 1766); C. M. Andrews, "Colonial Commerce," in *Am. Hist. Rev.*, XX, 61-62; Frank W. Pitman, *The Development of the British West Indies, 1700-1763*, especially the chapter on illicit trading.

[2] By 4 George III, c. 15, sec. 11, the Admiralty Court for all America was provided; for other steps see *Grenville Papers*, II, 114.

[3] In "An Account of all the duties collected under the Molasses Act in each of the Northern Colonies from 1733 to 1750," nothing is credited to either Connecticut or Rhode Island, except £99 collected in Connecticut for

of this determination of the ministry threw the Connecticut importers into a panic. But the impetus to action came from the Merchants' Society at Boston, which had been established in 1763 for the express purpose of preventing the renewal of the Molasses Act.[1] The society drew up a "state of the Trade" showing the conditions of commerce in New England, and early in 1764 transmitted copies of this to the Massachusetts London agent and to the leading merchants of the neighboring colonies.[2] As a result, "Gurdon Saltonstall, Esq. & other merchants and traders" in Connecticut called upon Jared Ingersoll to draw up a memorial to the general assembly in which it was pointed out that "his Majesty had been pleased, of late, to enforce the execution of the Sugar Act, so called, in these parts of his Dominion, by which it is generally supposed, by persons acquainted with the trade of the Northern Colonies will very much Distress the Inhabitants of said Northern Colonies, & that without Serving the essential Interests of the mother country; and, as the said Sugar Act expires about this time, and will probably be again revived, unless prevented by seasonable remonstrances, it was desired that the Connecticut Government should join with other colonies in remonstrating against it, and that the Assembly should appoint some persons in behalf of this colony to collect and transmit to the agent in London material Documents and Information relative to the mat-

prizes. C. O. 5: 38, Appendix No. 5; F. W. Pitman, *The Development of the British West Indies,* pp. 275, 288, 289-290, 325, 326.

[1] The official name of the organization was, "The Society for encouraging Trade and Commerce within the Province of Massachusetts Bay."

[2] For a discussion of this, consult C. M. Andrews, "The Boston Merchants and the Non-Importation Movement," pp. 165-168, of the *Publications of The Colonial Society of Massachusetts,* vol. XIX. A copy of this memorial as well as the letter of the Boston merchants of January 9, 1764, addressed to the New London merchants can be found in the forthcoming Volume II of the *Fitch Papers.*

ter, or in some way exercise the paternal care in the matter.''[1]

However, in March, 1764, before any effective opposition could be raised against it, the famous Sugar Act was passed, providing, as is well known, for substantial duties upon various articles of common consumption, while lowering to a revenue level the duty on foreign raised molasses.[2] A system of bonding shipmasters and the issuing of cargo certificates was also added, to put an end to lawless trafficking.

The opposition that this measure aroused in Connecticut was reflected by an item in the *Connecticut Gazette,* published at New Haven, which spread the intelligence that the local people had taken practical steps to defeat the revenue plans of the British government by putting themselves to making their own grape and currant wines and ''also enough for the Gentlemen of the College,'' who, as a lofty rebuke to those disturbers of the old

---

[1] Jared Ingersoll's memorial to the General Assembly, January 20, 1764, Conn. Archives, War, I, 3, a and b.

In order to influence public sentiment in England as well as to develop opposition against the designs of the ministry in the colony, there was drawn up and published in New London in January, 1764, a pamphlet entitled, ''Remarks on the Trade of the Colony.'' It was therein asserted that the result of changes to be brought about in the sugar trade would be the ruin of the West India trade, unless the English planters there could so improve their molasses and sugar as to make up the deficiency. It was claimed that it was notorious that these products were sold ''to the Continentals at 100 per cent Increase,'' and that while the ''Northern Colonies'' have no members in parliament the sugar islands have fifty-six. ''Does this arise from the Poverty or the affluence of the West Indian planters?'' This document is also to appear in Volume II of the *Fitch Papers.*

[2] 4 George III, c. 15. Previous to this seven parliamentary acts, beginning with 25 Car. II, c. 7, sec. 2, had provided for import duties. Besides this latter, there was 6 Anne, c. 37; 9 Anne, c. 27; 6 George II, c. 13; 29 George II, c. 26; 31 George II, c. 36; and 1 George III, c. 9. In addition, 7 and 8 Will. III, c. 21; 8 and 9 Will. III, c. 23; and 10 Anne, c. 17, had laid Greenwich hospital taxes on all colonial seamen. See Brit. Mus. Addit. MS. 35,910, fo. 308.

colonial régime, had determined "to confine themselves to liquors of our own produce."[1]

Jared Ingersoll's attitude toward the Sugar Act is expressed in an important letter that he wrote July 6, 1764, to his old friend, Thomas Whately, in reply to a communication from the latter, then one of the joint secretaries to the Treasury under Grenville.[2] "I think Parliament," he declared, "have overshot their mark & you will not, in the Event, have your Expectations in any measure answered from the provisions of the late Act . . . I am of opinion that the Foreign Molasses will bear a Duty of One penny half-penny at most,[3] the raw or brown Sugar 2/6 & the Clayed 5/ per Ct."[4] Ingersoll then assured Whately that the trade to the French and Dutch West Indies was decaying very rapidly and that there was not a single voyage undertaken to these parts "with the most Distant intention to pay the Dutys." Indeed, as to the practice of smuggling, it could not easily be prevented; "a Seizure will be made of perhaps one Vessell in a Hundred"; in fact, to attempt to put an end to it under present conditions would be like "burning a Barn to roast an Egg."[5] If, however, the duty were

---

[1] *Connecticut Gazette*, July 19, 1765.

[2] Jared Ingersoll to Thomas Whately, July 6, 1764, *Ingersoll Stamp Act Correspondence* (1766), p. 3. This correspondence was printed in pamphlet form in 1766, after the Stamp Act crisis had passed.

Charles Jenkinson was the other secretary. Jenkinson seems to have been more of a political whip than a financier.

[3] "The Boston men said that the business could not be carried on if the duty on Molasses were more than one penny per gallon." Channing, *History of the United States*, III, 41. It was lowered to this level in 1766.

[4] The duties placed by the act were, for molasses, three pence per gallon, and for clayed sugar, one pound two shillings per cwt.

[5] Professor Channing holds a different opinion. Speaking of Grenville's policy, he says: "He also caused deputations to be issued to the commanders of some of the smaller ships on the American Station, giving them authority to seize vessels carrying on illicit trade. They certainly did effective work in putting an end to evasions of the laws." *History of the United States*, III, 39.

lowered to the level just suggested, he was of the opinion
that the merchants would pay it without the use of men-
of-war; "you may think me mad for saying it, but I do
say, that tis my opinion the Parliament of the two had
better have given a Premium than to have imposed the
Duty they have laid upon that branch of trade."

The revenue prospects of the Sugar Act, however, by
no means satisfied the ministry. Other avenues for
drawing on the financial resources of the people in the
colonies must be opened up.[1] One very obvious way was
to extend to America the system, successfully applied
in England, of levying stamp duties. In 1722 Archibald
Cumins made this suggestion[2] and Sir William Keith put
forward the idea in 1743.[3] Both in 1754 and in 1757,
the Treasury Board under Newcastle had thought to
utilize it in solving the problem of financing the colonial
administration; in 1754 there was prepared "An Act
for Granting to His Majesty Sev'l Duties upon Vellum
Parchment and Paper for two years towards Defraying
the Charges of the Government of Massachusetts Bay,"[4]
which provided for seventeen groups of articles that
would bear stamps, and in 1757, "An Act for Erecting
and Establishing a Stamp Office in New York," with
fourteen groups of dutiable articles.[5] Soon after enter-

[1] See Whately's undated letter to Ingersoll, printed in the *Ingersoll
Stamp Act Correspondence.*

[2] See Edward Channing, *History of the United States,* III, 48 and footnotes.

[3] Brit. Mus. Addit. MS. 33,028, fo. 376 (Newcastle Papers). "Endorsed Sr Wm Keith's Proposal / for laying a Duty on / Stampt Papers
in / America / Decr 17, 1742."

[4] Brit. Mus. Addit. MS. 35,910, fos. 160-163.

[5] *Ibid.,* 35,910, fos. 165-166. A much more interesting proposal which
appears to be of this earlier group, the date of which, however, is unknown,
has the following title, "A List of Stamp Duties intended to be used
throughout all the Colonies upon the Continent of America or in any Island
belonging thereto, And in the Islands of Bermuda and the Bahama Islands,

ing upon his new office, Grenville's attention had been called to its possibilities by Henry McCulloh who, on July 5, 1763, addressed a letter to Secretary Jenkinson of the Treasury, suggesting that ''A stamp duty on vellum and paper in America, at six pence, twelve pence, and eighteen pence per sheet, would, at a moderate computation, amount to upwards of sixty thousand sterling per annum, or, if extended to the West Indies, would produce double that sum.''[1] McCulloh's advice, it is not unlikely, carried some weight, for in 1739 he had gone to America as a ''Commissioner for Supervising, Inspecting and Controlling His Majesty's Revenue and Grants of Lands,'' and his continued interest in the revenue possibilities of the colonies was shown in a statement that he drew up and incorporated in his letter to Jenkinson, regarding ''such taxes as are usually raised in His Majesty's old settled colonies on the continent of America, viz: North and South Carolina, Virginia and Pennsylvania.''[2]

However, in considering the extension of stamp duties to America, it is a matter of surprise, not that the attempt was made at this time, but rather that it was not earlier considered as a legitimate source of revenue, especially during the periods of great financial pressure when England was at war, largely to save her colonies from

as, also, in all the British Islands or Plantations in that part of America, commonly called the West Indies.'' The one who prepared this planned to have five schedules, which were to be as follows: American duties, West India duties, Jamaica duties, New York duties, and Massachusetts Bay duties. *Ibid.*, 35,910, fos. 167-203.

Richard Jackson, in a letter to Governor Fitch, written November 15, 1765, said, in referring to the Stamp Act, ''Unfortunately the late Tax was a measure proposed long before the existence of that Ministry who afterward proposed it and carried it through the Legislature.'' *Fitch Papers.*

[1] *Grenville Papers*, II, 374.
[2] *Ibid.*

destruction. Ever since 1694, when, under William and
Mary, the first stamp act was passed, stamp duties had
been a very fruitful and not unpopular source of revenue
in England.¹ In 1760 £290,000 had been raised through
this means and this was increased in 1765 by a slight
extension of duties.²

By September, 1763, Grenville had arrived at a definite
decision regarding the American revenues, and in March
of the following year, the month of the passage of the
Sugar Act, he was ready to announce to the Commons
his intention of introducing an American stamp bill at
the next session of parliament and he secured the approval of the house to a resolution to that effect.³ In
conformity with this vote, the Board of Trade, now under
the Earl of Halifax, sent out formal requests to each
colonial governor to transmit to England the various
forms of writs, deeds, and similar legal instruments in use
within the colony.⁴

Eliphalet Dyer, a member of the governor's council
and one of the leading men of Connecticut, was in London
at this time in the interests of the Susquehanna Company's enterprise. About the middle of April, he wrote
to Ingersoll laying bare the purpose of the ministry to
bring forward a bill imposing a stamp tax, which was,
he wrote, ''to fix upon us a large Numbeʳ of regular
Troops under pretense of our Defence; but rather designed as a rod & Check over us.'' Dyer, in his anger,

¹ Beginning with 5 and 6 William and Mary, c. 21, there were twenty
acts down to and including 5 George III, c. 46, relating to English stamp
duties.

² Stephen Dowell, *A History of Taxation and Taxes in England*, III,
377. See also, *A History and Explanation of Stamp Duties*, p. 21, by the
same author.

³ *Parliamentary History of England*, XV, 1427.

⁴ Trumbull Papers. The Connecticut list of documents was ready by
October 13, 1764, Conn. Archives, War, I, 13. For these lists see Andrews
and Davenport, *Guide*, p. 26; Andrews, *Guide*, I, 241.

however, was not oblivious of the services that Richard
Jackson, the Connecticut agent, was rendering to the
colonies, "you are sensible he is in the Interest of the
present Ministry, & as such by his Influence the propos^d
Stamp duty is at present postponed.'"[1]

Meanwhile, the British Stamp Commissioners had
been directed by Grenville, in the fall of 1763, to draw up
a tentative stamp measure. Indeed, the Stamp Office had
become interested in this project even earlier than this.
From Trinity vacation of that year on, it would appear
that Henry McCulloh was in frequent consultation with
them. He drew up a plan which he entitled, "Proposals
with respect to a Stamp Duty in America," which, in
October, was embodied in a formal bill.[2] To what extent,
however, his ideas found expression in the final act, is
hard to say, for it appears certain that his plan was rejected in 1764, in favor of one which Secretary Thomas
Whately of the Treasury had drawn up.[3]

[1] Eliphalet Dyer to Jared Ingersoll, April 14, 1764, New Haven Col.
Hist. Soc. *Papers*, IX ("Jared Ingersoll Papers"), 288-292. In a letter
to Governor Fitch, written in March, 1765, Dyer says: "But, Sir, soon
after my Arrival I found there were many Things new, meditating with
Respect to the Colonies in America in general, and more especially against
those that have the most free and liberal charters. Therefore, I delayed
prosecuting the Affair I came upon, in any public way . . . I spared no
Pains, in my small Sphere, to represent the Colonies in the most favorable
Light I was capable of and have the Pleasure to say . . . that the particular
Accounts I have been able to give, of the Regularity of the government to
which I belong, the strict and impartial Administration of Justice therein,
their ready and cheerful Compliance with all Orders and Instructions from
the Crown, as well as the Peace, Happiness and Quiet that the People
possess under those Happy Privileges they enjoy, have been in some Degree
satisfactory and well approved, and I believe nothing special will be done
with Respect to these Colonies in particular." Eliphalet Dyer to Governor
Fitch. This is printed in the *Connecticut Gazette*, September 20, 1765.

[2] The following entry was made in the American Stamp Office Law Bill
Record, "Drawing Law agreeable to Mr. McCullo's Scheme." Brit. Mus.
Addit. MS. 35,911, fo. 206 (Hardwicke Papers, DLXIII).

[3] "Attending Secretarys of the Treasury settling American Bill when

Early in the spring of 1764, Whately wrote to Ingersoll acquainting him with the plans of the ministry. In
this letter he showed his hearty accord with Grenville's
position that the colonies ought to share in the payment
of the "American expense" for imperial defense. He
pointed out that since the amount to be raised from the
colonies by the late revenue act was doubtful, some other
means for making up the deficiency must be devised. A
stamp act, he declared, had been proposed, but had not
been carried into execution "out of Tenderness" and also
from a desire to allow the colonies either to furnish the
necessary information for it or to suggest a better mode
of taxation. A tax on the importation of Negroes had
been suggested, but a stamp tax was considered preferable, because it would not bear more heavily on the southern colonies than the northern colonies. On the other
hand, a stamp tax would be less easy to collect and more
liable to evasion. The revenue from a stamp tax should
be great on account of the numerous suits continually
pending. Whately thereupon asked Ingersoll pointedly,
"Would it yield a considerable Revenue if the Duty were
low upon mercantile Instruments, high upon gratuitous
Grants of Lands, & moderate upon Law Proceedings?"[1]

they refused Mr. McCullos and when received Orders to alter Draft agre-
able to Directions then given . . . 13/4.

"During Michelmas vacation, 1764. Copy Mr. Whately's Plan as approved by the Lords Commissioners, for the Board . . . £1.7." *Ibid.*

"It fell to the said Mr. W[hately] from his office as Secretary to the
Treasury to prepare and draw the Stamp Act." *Ingersoll Stamp Act
Corresp.*, p. 3, note. "Soon after my arrival I found in this gentleman's
hands the governor's Letter with the several forms of writs, Deeds and the
like, as used among us, sent to the Ministry." *Ibid.*

[1] Thomas Whately to Jared Ingersoll, not dated, *Ingersoll Stamp Act
Corresp.*, p. 4.

Joseph Trumbull wrote from London, on February 13, 1764: "The
Courts are contriving every scheme to saddle us in America with troops
and some carry it so far as not to be content with our paying and supporting them, but also would have us pay a considerable sum to the Civil

The true attitude of the Grenville administration toward America seems to be fairly reflected in this letter. Whately, it should be borne in mind, was perhaps the most ardent and able advocate of the financial policy of the ministry.[1] How foreign to this program was the idea of flying blindly in the face of American interests and of needlessly disturbing colonial tranquillity and legitimate prosperity, is shown by the solicitous desire of the man who was responsible for framing the bill, to know the truth about American conditions. Before concluding his letter to Ingersoll, he declared: "I should be happy to know the genuine Opinion of sensible Men in the Colonies upon Subjects equally interesting both to them & to us: You know I always from Inclination interested myself in their Prosperity: My present Situation necessarily employs me often in their Affairs; & I, therefore, am anxious to get all the Information I can in Relation to them." And he thereupon besought Ingersoll in case either of his suggestions regarding a tax should be found "very exceptionable," to suggest some other type of revenue bill for the colonies.[2]

Ingersoll's reply to this letter, which was in a friendly but candid spirit, came in July. It gives one an intimate insight into his attitude of mind at this period. "You

List—all of which monies are to be raised by duties on French and Dutch goods—by our paying in New England the same duties on East India goods as are paid here—by Post Office regulations in the manner they are here—and by a Stamp Office—all which the friends to America are doing everything in their power to prevent.'' Joseph Trumbull to Jonathan Trumbull. Printed in I. W. Stuart, *Life of Jonathan Trumbull*, p. 84, note.

[1] In 1765 Whately answered David Hartley's attacks on the Grenville financial program in his *Remarks on The Budget, or a Candid Examination of the Facts and Arguments in that Pamphlet.* The following year he wrote a defense of the ministerial policy in his *Considerations on the Trade and Finances of the Kingdom and on the Measures of the Administration Since the Conclusion of Peace.*

[2] *Ingersoll Stamp Act Corresp.*, p. 4; New Haven Col. Hist. Soc. *Papers*, IX ("Jared Ingersoll Papers''), 292-295.

may depend," he declared, "upon the Strictest truth
Even tho' it should offend. . . . You say America can &
ought to Contribute to its own defense. . . . we only dif-
fer about the means; we, perhaps should first of all Re-
scind great part of the present Expense & what remains
should difray by the Application of our own force &
Strength." He reminded Secretary Whately that the
people of Connecticut—"who besides their Charter of
Priviledge granted by K. Ch. 2ᵈ have . . . subsisted
hitherto without one farthing's Expense to the Crown,
except what the Nation was pleased to give to them in
Common with their neighbours in the late war"—did not
believe as yet that the British Parliament really meant
to impose internal taxes upon them without their consent.
There must be no disguise, he continued, "as to the
feeling of colonials. If the King should fix the proportion of our Duty, we all say we will do our parts in the
Common Cause, but if Parliament once interpose & Lay
a tax, tho' it may be a very moderate one, & the Crown
appoint officers of its own to Collect such tax & apply the
same without Accᵒ., what Consequences may, or rather
may not, follow? . . . The peoples minds not only here
but in the neighbouring Provinces are filled with the most
dreadfull apprehensions from such a Step's taking place,
from whence I leave you to guess how Easily such a tax
of that kind could be Collected, . . ."[1]

It seems very odd, indeed, that the man who had so
clear an understanding of the temper of the people
allowed himself, later on, to become responsible for the
execution of the Stamp Act in Connecticut. But, to do
him justice, Ingersoll was of a very open mind, and in
this same letter to Whately confessed that he might "be

[1] Jared Ingersoll to Thomas Whately, July 6, 1764, *Ingersoll Stamp Act
Corresp.*, pp. 5-11; New Haven Hist. Soc. *Papers*, IX ("Jared Ingersoll
Papers"), 295-301.

Convinced of the propriety as well as necessity of such a Step." "I long to see you & please myself much in the Expectations I have, that you & my friend, Mr. Jackson, & other Gentlemen on yᵣ Side the water will be able to tell me Some Facts & acquaint me with some reasonings upon these Subjects which I am at present a Stranger to, & that will dispell those Clouds of Darkness that now hang over my mind. . . ." But at present he was far from convinced, and in reply to Whately's desire for advice as to the most feasible plan for raising a revenue in America, he made clear that he was prevented from suggesting which of the several methods of taxation mentioned would be best, for it was plain that "every one of them or any supposable one, . . . would go down with the people like Chopt hay." However, the close intimacy between the two was shown in Ingersoll's statement, "as I expect to see you soon in London, I shall hope for the Pleasure of having an opportunity to say a Thousand Things to you on the Score of Friendship & which I will therefore pass by at present. . . .'"[1]

Ingersoll's warmth for the colonial cause at this time is also shown by the fact that immediately upon receipt of Whately's letter, he copied the most essential portions of it and dispatched them to Governor Fitch.

When the Connecticut general assembly met for its May session in 1764, Governor Fitch submitted to its consideration a letter from Richard Jackson, which acquainted the colony with the parliamentary resolution favoring a stamp tax. As a result, a committee was appointed by the assembly with the governor as its head "to collect and set in the most advantageous light all such arguments and objections as may justly and reasonably be advanced against creating and collecting a revenue" in the colony, and "especially against effecting the

[1] *Ingersoll Stamp Act Corresp.*

same by stamp duties.'"¹ Although not a member of the assembly, Jared Ingersoll was asked to serve on this committee. The result of its efforts was a very carefully framed document entitled, "Reasons why the British Colonies in America should not be charged with Internal Taxes by Authority of Parliament.'"² Governor Fitch seems to have taken the leading part in drafting this,³ although the mere fact that the assembly went outside of the governmental circle to procure Ingersoll's services would seem to indicate a feeling that, by reason of his eminence as an advocate and on account of his experience as London agent, he was peculiarly qualified to marshal against the ministerial plan the most effective arguments. That he was the best constitutional lawyer of the group can scarcely be doubted. His share in the work, therefore, must not have been unimportant.

With great skill, facts were brought forward to show how ready Connecticut had been at all times to respond to the financial needs of the home government and with what willingness and celerity she had sent her men on numerous occasions, at the call of danger along the frontier. What she had done in the past through the free action of her own assembly she would gladly do again. No reasonable cause, therefore, could be urged which would justify the denial to her people of the liberties and privileges which as Englishmen and as freemen they so highly valued. If, however, it was absolutely necessary to levy a permanent and regular charge upon America it would be better to place a duty on the importation of Negroes and also to tax the fur trade rather than to impose a stamp tax; for, with regard to the Negroes, a

¹ *Conn. Col. Rec.*, XII, 256.

² This is printed in *ibid.*, XII, Appendix.

³ Ingersoll gives Fitch the credit of being "the principal Compiler and Draughts-man" of the remonstrance. *Ingersoll Stamp Act Corresp.*, p. 2, note.

lessened importation might be attended with many salutary effects and, as to the fur trade, since its protection was one of the chief sources of expense in America, it surely should be charged to support itself.

It should be noticed that while Ingersoll, in his personal letter to Whately, refused to give the slightest endorsement to either of the proposals which he put forward, the "Book of Reasons,"[1] prepared after Ingersoll's reply, retreated somewhat from the high constitutional ground of the latter by confessing that if the British government was determined to raise a revenue in the colonies by the direct action of parliament, it might get it out of Negroes and furs—a revenue scheme which would hardly affect Connecticut of the '60's. It is important, in the light of such pronouncements as came from James Otis and Patrick Henry, to appreciate the exceedingly cautious position assumed by Connecticut at this juncture, under the control, as she was, of the more conservative elements in the colony. In a letter written to Ingersoll, in December, 1764, Governor Fitch, in referring to the remonstrance drawn up by the committee, gave his views of the constitutional position which it embodied. "In these Reasons," declared Governor Fitch, "we have avoided all Pretense of objection against the Authority or Power of the Parliament as the supreme Legislature of all the King's Dominions to tax the Colonies and have therefore Endeavored only to show that the exercise of such Power in that Particular Instance or in like Cases will take away Part of our Antient Privileges, etc. (which it is presumed the Parliament who are also Guardians of our Liberties will not do). . . ."[2]

[1] This is the title by which the Connecticut remonstrance was known and designated.

[2] Governor Fitch to Jared Ingersoll, December 7, 1764, Trumbull Papers (unbound Correspondence). A duplicate of this letter was sent to Richard Jackson.

Late in the month of October, 1764, Ingersoll, as was noted in an earlier chapter, sailed from New London for England on the ship, *Prince Henry,* which was loaded with masts that he had contracted to deliver, while in London in 1760.[1] While he was yet at sea, the general assembly desired the governor to write to him requesting him again to assist Richard Jackson in the London agency "in any matters that may concern the colony," for the people were "convinced of his skill, ability and good disposition to serve the interests of this Colony."[2] By the time that he arrived in England, which was about the tenth of December, the stamp bill had been drafted and lay at the Treasury for objections and adjustments.[3] Ingersoll, it would appear, took steps to oppose it some weeks before he received the news of his reappointment to the agency.[4] One of his first acts was to distribute, among the ministry and members of parliament, over a hundred copies of the Connecticut "Book of Reasons." He submitted a copy to Grenville, who, while admitting that it was written in good temper and that it contained good arguments, considered that it failed in its principal premise, which was that the colonies should not be taxed by parliament since they were not represented there.[5]

Numerous meetings and conferences were held among the colonial agents both before and after Ingersoll's arrival. Montague, Charles, Franklin, Garth, Jackson, and,

[1] Besides Ingersoll, there were on board, Joseph Harrison, collector of customs for the port of New Haven, Captain Samuel Willis of Middletown, and Samuel Wyllys, son of the secretary of the colony. *New London Gazette,* October 26, 1764; *Connecticut Courant,* October 29, 1764.

[2] *Ingersoll Stamp Act Corresp.,* p. 11; Conn. Archives, War, I, 15. Fitch was to let Ingersoll know that "his services would be gratefully accepted and rewarded by this Assembly." *Ibid.*

[3] *Ingersoll Stamp Act Corresp.,* p. 3, note.

[4] This fact is emphasized in a letter written February 1, 1766, to an unknown party. Emmet Collection (New York Public Library).

[5] *Ingersoll Stamp Act Corresp.,* p. 31, note.

later, Ingersoll probably made up the circle,[1] though there were other colonial agents in London at that time. The London merchants engaged in the business of trading with America also went into opposition to the program of the ministry. They appointed a committee which was to exert itself to that end. This committee of merchants invited the agents to a joint conference. According to Ingersoll, they were frequently together, working hand and glove, and several times the two groups went before the ministry upon the pending issues relating to America.[2]   The principal spokesman of the merchants on these occasions was Barlow Trecothick, who had been raised in Boston and had moved to London, where he acquired ''a great estate with the fairest character'' and became an alderman.

At one of these gatherings of the agents it was decided that Franklin and Ingersoll should wait upon Grenville, together with Jackson and Garth, who were members of parliament. As a result of this and other conferences, if his own statement can be accepted without reservation, Ingersoll's entire attitude was altered regarding the justification of the stamp measure. It is certain that a change of view took place. Was the prospect of an office accountable for it, or was it a change of conviction? While it is clear that Ingersoll was a seeker after preferment, he was, at the same time, a man of strong character and high ideals, with very liberal opinions and with unusual openness of mind. The explanation would, therefore, appear to lie in the fact, as he himself suggested to Whately in his letter of June, 1764, that in the end he was ''Convinced as to the propriety as well as necessity of such a Step.'' It is safe to say that there exist nowhere else such full and faithful accounts of

1 *Ingersoll Stamp Act Corresp.*, pp. 17, 22-23.
2 John Wentworth, *The Wentworth Genealogy*, I, 538.

the conferences with Grenville as in Ingersoll's letters, written to Governor Fitch and to the Connecticut general assembly.[1] The emphasis that he placed upon Grenville's arguments would seem to indicate the weight and importance that he felt they deserved. Grenville's statements must, therefore, be followed with care as offering an explanation for Ingersoll's conversion. "Mr. Grenville gave us a full hearing," wrote Ingersoll to Governor Fitch, February 11, 1765, "told us he took no pleasure in giving the Americans so much uneasiness as he found he did;—that it was the Duty of his Office to manage the Revenue;—that he really was made to believe that considering the whole Circumstances of the Mother Country & the Colonies, the latter could and ought to pay something,[2] & that he knew of no better way than that now pursuing to lay such a Tax; but that if we could tell of a better he would adopt it.'"[3]

In reply to this, Jackson urged that the measure in question, "by enabling the Crown to keep up an armed Force of its own in America & to pay the Governours in the Kings Governments, & all with the Americans own Money, the Assembles *in* the Colonys would be subverted. . . ." But Grenville rejected the idea warmly.

[1] See "An Account of a Conference between the late Mr. Grenville and the Several Colony Agents in 1764, previous to the passage of the Stamp Act." Mass. Hist. Soc. *Coll.*, IX (1804) (reprinted in 1857). Benjamin Franklin to John Ross, February 14, 1765, *The Writings of Benjamin Franklin* (Smyth), IV, 362; Benjamin Franklin to Charles Thomson, 1765, *The Penn. Magazine of Hist. and Biog.*, VIII, 426. "A True History of the Differences between the Colonies and the Author of the Stamp Act," written by Franklin, in 1778, to an unknown party. *Writings*, VII, 119-120.

[2] Professor Channing has figured that, owing to the operation of the colonial system, America contributed nearly two million pounds sterling yearly to the income of the homeland. *History of the United States*, III, 33-34.

[3] *Ingersoll Stamp Act Corresp.*, pp. 17 *et seq.*, for this and following quotations and abstracts from the interviews.

When Franklin pleaded that the old method by king's requisition should be followed in the present case, the minister asked in return if they could "agree upon the several proportions Each Colony should raise?"   To which the agents were forced to confess that they could not; which gave Grenville the upper hand in the discussion, and he thereupon pointed out that he did not think that anybody in England was furnished with the materials for that purpose, and what is more, there would be no certainty that every colony would raise the sum enjoined.   The colonies, moreover, by their increase, he suggested, would be constantly varying in their proportion of numbers and ability to pay, which a stamp bill would keep pace with.[1]   Completely baffled by these arguments, the protesting committee withdrew.

At a later conference with these spokesmen for America, Grenville urged the necessity of the act. He asked them to lay aside all considerations of past services on the part of the colonies, on the one hand, and on the part of England, on the other.   There was an immense national interest-bearing debt of not less than £140,000,000 lying heavy on the nation. By the best information that he could secure, the whole public debt of all the colonies together was £800,000,[2] yet the annual civil establishment in England required £800,000, while that of all the colonies "we find to be about £40,000." In addition, the military and naval establishments were immense, but without considering that, the annual amount of the expense of the army now placed in America, "as well on Account of the Troubles with the Indians as for the general Defense against other Nations & the like in so Ex-

[1] *Ingersoll Stamp Act Corresp.*

[2] *Ibid.*, p. 25. The outstanding debts incurred by the colonies in connection with the war alone amounted to over £757,000, according to a report of the Board of Trade. C. O. 323:19, sec. 88, p. 27.

tensive a Country,'' amounted to about £300,000. Yet he would be glad, he informed the agents, if he should find that the stamp duties would bring in forty or fifty thousand pounds, so that the entire revenue from America, including that from the duty on molasses and from the post office and other sources, would amount to £100,000, which would be but one-third of the cost of maintaining the army in America.

Evading the financial question, which was of such serious moment, the agents placed before Grenville the proposition already brought forward in colonial protests that it ''will be for ever inconvenient; 'twill for ever be dangerous to America, that they should be taxed by the Authority of a British parliament,'' urging at the same time the great distance, the want of mutual knowledge and acquaintance with one another and the want of personal friendship between England and America.[1] But Grenville was not to be drawn away from what to him were the practical issues. He proceeded, therefore, to point out the difficulties of leaving the colonies responsible for the supply of the military forces; ''don't some of you Complain,'' he asked, ''& perhaps very justly, that in the late War, while some of you did much, others did but little, or perhaps nothing at all—and would not that be the Case again, was you left to Defend yourselves?''

In answer, the agents set forth the prevailing American apprehension, saying that ''without any Persons . . . to speak for us in the great Council of the Nation,—we fear a Foundation will be laid for mutual Jealousy and ill Will, and that your Resentments being kindled, you will be apt to lay upon us more & more, even to a Degree that will be truly grievous. . . .'' But Grenville replied that the colonies had never intimated that they desired representation in parliament, and that there were ''many

[1] *Ingersoll Stamp Act Corresp.*, p. 26.

Reasons why they should not desire it"; since members received no pay, the expense would be very great to the colonies in sending representatives and already they were pleading poverty; again, the influence of these representatives would not be dominant; the colonies appreciated that they could not hope to have a majority of members in the House of Commons; colonial representatives would also be confronted by many inconveniences, by reason of the great distance and want of connection with England. If it were not feasible to introduce such representation, "What then? Shall no Steps be taken & must we and America be two distinct Kingdoms, & that now immediately, or must America be Defended entirely by us, & be themselves quite excused or left to do just what they shall please to do? Some, perhaps, will do something, & others Nothing.'"[1] He then made an interesting and prophetic admission, that perhaps "from the nature of our Situations, it will happen & must be Expected that one Day we shall be two distinct Kingdoms"; but he trusted that the colonies did not consider themselves "ripe for that Event as yet." Let those possible events, he counseled, be left to the disposal of Providence. For his own part, he declared that he did not choose to predict nor yet to hasten the time of this supposed period and thought that a separation would be mutually disadvantageous. And in conclusion, he urged, "Let mutual Confidence and mutual Uprightness of Intention take Place & no considerable Ills can follow.'"[2]

These statements attributed to Grenville—after due allowance is made for the inaccuracy of his information

[1] According to Mr. Beer, Massachusetts, Connecticut, and New York were the only colonies that could be brought to respond in any proper manner during the war. Some of the other colonies hung back disgracefully. G. L. Beer, *British Colonial Policy, 1754-1765*, p. 68 *et seq.*

[2] Jared Ingersoll to Governor Fitch, March 6, 1766, *Ingersoll Stamp Act Corresp.*, pp. 25-28.

respecting the colonial financial situation, regarding which the agents themselves seem to have been ignorant—tend to soften the charge that he was simply a reactionary, narrow-grooved, mechanistic type of closet politician. While it is true that during his political career he occasionally showed a lack of finesse in dealing with men and measures,[1] yet in the main, his ideas on government were not unsound. In justice to him, it should be pointed out that he was capable of something that few men in his age had the vision to appreciate; he could think in terms of imperial welfare; he sought what in our present political parlance is termed a mobilization of the imperial resources, through a proper articulation of every unit in the empire with the central authority. The ministry, of course, was unfortunately obliged to rely upon an antiquated and inflexible parliamentary system, due to the innate conservatism of the English-speaking people; still more unfortunately, it was forced to encounter the extremely particularistic spirit that prevailed in the American colonies, the weight of which at that time was not suspected by even so close an observer of American conditions as Benjamin Franklin. Nevertheless, casting aside inherited prejudices and the political opportunism of the older historians, both British and American, who demanded a scapegoat in order to interpret the history of this period, it is not clear how the Grenville program can be regarded as other than a sincere and not unenlightened attempt to accomplish something of vast importance to the nation, which would have gone far toward making the British people, scattered as they were even in 1765, ready to face any emergency.

[1] It will be remembered that the prosecutions of Wilkes were energetically pushed by Grenville at the behest of George III. He also fathered the exceedingly unpopular and unremunerative Cider Bill of 1763. He even, finally, alienated the king, ''who had a horror of his interminable arguments.''

Indeed, as has been pointed out, the hard experiences of the Seven Years' War seemed to have proved the need of some such reorganization as was now sought. Might not the Grenville program of centralization and unification be regarded, in other words, as a premature step, taken in good faith, in the direction of realizing a federal system for the British empire; something that men to-day are demanding? For, surely, where the great common affairs of the nation were decided, there the different units of the empire would inevitably, before long, have secured a voice.[1]

[1] In other words, there is every reason to believe that the American colonies would have secured representation in parliament after submitting to taxation. As Richard Jackson, himself a member of parliament, pointed out in a letter to Governor Fitch, parliament did not think the County of Durham ought to be free from taxation because it was unrepresented. They were of opinion that it was represented, though it chose no members, and continued to tax it, but the House of Commons thought this so good a reason for giving it members that they passed several bills for that purpose and at last a bill passed both houses of parliament. See the *Fitch Papers*.

Among the Chatham Papers is a ''Scheme for the better uniting and cementing the mutual interest and peace of Great Britain and her Colonies by representation in the Parliament of Great Britain and Dominions thereto belonging.'' According to this scheme, which is without date, the colonies were to have the following representation:

1. Massachusetts, Pennsylvania, and Virginia, each four members or a smaller number at their option.

2. Connecticut, New York, and Jamaica, each three members.

3. Canada, the East and West Jerseys, Maryland, and South Carolina, each two members.

4. Nova Scotia, New Hampshire, Rhode Island, the Lower Counties of Pennsylvania, North Carolina, Georgia, East Florida, West Florida, Bahamas, Bermuda, Barbadoes, Antigua, St. Christopher, Nevis, Granados, one member each. For this plan see the *English Historical Review*, XXII, 756-758.

But it should be pointed out that the colonies were not asking or desiring representation in the British parliament and this scheme would have suited them as little as Grenville's. The fourth resolution of the Stamp Act Congress reads, ''that the people of these colonies are not, and, from their local circumstances, cannot be, represented in the House of Commons in Great Britain.''

It can now be appreciated that the colonial problem of the period subsequent to 1763 was, in truth, a glowing ember ready to sear the hand of any British statesman who attempted to carry it to a solution. No one better understood this than Grenville's opponent, the great Pitt.

In studying the cause for the failure of this taxation experiment, it must be done in light of the causes for the failure of the confederation of the United States, established in 1781. In each case, there was an unwillingness on the part of the American people to think in terms other than that of local welfare, which culminated in bitter interstate conflicts; in each case, it was the unwillingness of the people to surrender the notion that a group of detached, practically independent political units could serve the interests of all effectively; in each case, it was an attachment to the requisition idea, which caused Patrick Henry, even in 1788, to maintain, in opposing the Constitution,—which had been submitted to the states for ratification,—that he could never give up his "darling requisitions," unjust and hopelessly defective as the idea was in practice. If the American people were suspicious of giving to parliament the right of taxation in 1765, they were hardly less willing to entrust it to their own congress of the Confederation, which pleaded for it in vain in 1781, in 1783, and in 1788. Indeed, there is abundant evidence to show that almost from the very beginning of English colonization in America, conceptions of local autonomy had been gradually developing; in 1765 these conceptions overshadowed all other political ideas. Admitting that Grenville failed because his program did not take into account the strength of these conceptions, there is at least a certain rationality about his theory of government. It may be summarized as follows:

There must be obedience to law on the part of all within the British domains. If, as in the case of the trade and navigation laws, particular measures occasionally had borne more heavily upon some than others, it had been inevitable and was truly characteristic of all legislation, although justice, as far as possible, should and would be done to all.[1] Not only must there be general obedience to the law, but a general sharing of the vast expense of the national administration; the old policy of allowing the local, subordinate assemblies to decide how far they were willing and obligated to contribute had not proved satisfactory; there must, in other words, be exercised somewhere a more effective control, without which the empire could never properly function in the interests of all groups within it. Parliament, in the light of its historic position and in the exercise now of so many of the ancient sovereign prerogatives, was the only agency competent to do this work. While it was true that parliamentary representation was not a fully realized thing for all, either in England or elsewhere within the empire, there were vast difficulties in the way of bringing about a representation which would be more satisfactory for America. But, in all fairness, it must be conceded, that, although the colonies had never had members in parliament and had never expressed a desire to assume the expense of sending them, yet for the lack of them they had never been treated oppressively, but, on the other hand, had greatly developed and prospered. This would con-

[1] In speaking to the agents, Grenville, according to Ingersoll, said: "Let us then, instead of predicting the worst, hope that mutual Interest, as well as Duty, will Keep us on both Sides, within the Bounds of Justice— We trust we shall never intentionally, burden you unreasonably—if at any Time we shall happen to do it by Mistake, let us know it, &, I trust, it will be remedied. You find, & I trust, always will find, an easy Access to those, who, from their Office, have the principal Conduct of Revenue Laws." *Ingersoll Stamp Act Corresp.*, p. 27.

tinue in spite of the necessity, for the common welfare, of so reorganizing the colonial administration as to allow America to bear a more just, definite, and responsible part in the general affairs of the empire.

In writing to Governor Fitch regarding the outcome of these conferences, Ingersoll said that "to do Justice to the Minister, Mr. Grenville as to the Comparative few who have interested themselves in the Concerns of America, I beg leave to say that I think no pains have been spared, on the one Side in behalf of America, to make the most ample & strong representation in their favor, & on the other, on the part of the Minister to bear patiently, to listen attentively to the reasonings & to Determin at least seemingly, with coolness & upon principle upon the several Measures which are Resolved on."[1]

Apparently, Ingersoll, in his capacity of Connecticut agent, did his utmost to divert Grenville from this policy and in the last of the interviews, according to Jackson, he took an especially prominent part.[2] However, the more he studied the whole situation and analyzed the motives of the ministry as well as its practical program, the less he saw to fear in the proposed revenue bill, and the more heartily he came to sympathize with the idea of an efficiently organized British administration extending throughout the empire. The phrase, "Taxation of the Colonies," would sound very different to a colonial of broad views, conversing familiarly

[1] Jared Ingersoll to Governor Fitch, March 6, 1765, *Ingersoll Stamp Act Corresp.*, p. 24.

[2] Jackson, writing to Ingersoll the following year, commended him upon his opposition to the Stamp Act, "particularly at the last interview, Mr. Franklin, you & I had with Mr. Grenville over the Subject when he heard us give our reasons against the Bills being brought in for near two hours." Richard Jackson to Jared Ingersoll, March 22, 1766, New Haven Col. Hist. Soc. *Papers*, IX ("Jared Ingersoll Papers"), 383.

each day in the government offices and the halls of
parliament with men of influence in the administration,
some of whom were old acquaintances, who laughed at the
idea that there was the slightest intention on the part of
England to treat America unfairly or to deny to its people the essential rights of Englishmen, from what it
would to the same person living far away from the seats
of power in the atmosphere of a Connecticut seaport. In
like manner, the British constitution would easily come
to mean something quite different to the man listening to
the argument of the head of the ministry and to the
speeches in the House of Commons, from what it would
to the same man deliberating in a New Haven town meeting three thousand miles away from London. "I went
to England last winter," Ingersoll confessed later on to
his friend, William Livingston of New York, "with the
strongest prejudices against the Parliamentary Authority in this Case; & came home, I don't love to say convinced but, confoundedly begad & beswompt as we say in
Connecticut."[1]

In other words, while he disliked to see the colonies
disturbed with additional taxation, while he realized the
possible dangers that lurked in the situation, where the
colonies would be under the full control of parliament,
yet the reasons in favor of such taxation appeared to
outweigh the arguments that could be urged against it.
There seemed to be no other solution of the problem to
one thinking in terms of imperial welfare. "No man sees
in a stronger light than I do," Ingersoll declared upon
his return to America, and when writhing under the lash
of public opinion, "the dangerous tendency of admitting
for a principle that the Parliament of Great Britain may

[1] Jared Ingersoll to William Livingston, October 1, 1765, *The Historical Magazine*, VI, 138-139.

tax us *ad libitum*—I view it as a gulph ready to devour, but when I look around I am at a loss for a plan.'"[1]

After the conferences with the minister had failed, the agents sought to get the issue discussed in an open session of the Commons, in a full debate. But as Ingersoll wrote to Fitch, "The Point of the Authority of Parliament to impose such Tax, I found on my arrival here was so fully and Universally yielded, that there was not the least hopes of making any impressions that way."[2]

If the passage of the measure could not be prevented, the colonial cause, nevertheless, might be served in another way. The bill was still resting at the Treasury, and Ingersoll's friend, Secretary Thomas Whately, was at work on its final revision.[3] If the principle of colonial freedom from parliamentary taxation could not be saved, the same might be applied in such a way as to make the added burden comparatively light and inoffensive. A favorable casting of the measure then became the chief object of Ingersoll's exertions.

It was now that Ingersoll's fundamental honesty of

[1] *The Historical Magazine.*

[2] See Jared Ingersoll to Governor Fitch, February 11, 1765, and Jared Ingersoll to the Connecticut General Assembly, September 18, 1765, *Ingersoll Stamp Act Corresp.*, pp. 12, 29.

[3] Whately was altering the schedule of duties in the draft of the bill as late as the latter part of January. Brit. Mus. Addit. MS. 35,911 (Hardwicke Papers, DLXIII), "American Stamp Office Law Bill." There is preserved a list of "Queries and Remarks on the American Stamp Bill by the Secretaries of the Treasury." *Ibid.*, fo. 15.

It is interesting to note that the bill was not submitted to the inspection of the attorney general before its passage through parliament, as the following makes clear: "Attending Consultations by self and clerk, in Court when Mr. Attorney found great faults with American Bill and of Impropriety in not having same lain before him previous to the passing and when Ordered. Mr. Martin to Consider of Defects therein particularly with respect to the power of Recovering Revenue Debts and to Report same to him." *Ibid.* The cost of "drafting the act, the bonds, etc." was £631.9. *Ibid.*

purpose, sense of fairness, judicial temper, conciliatory attitude, together with his wide knowledge of colonial conditions and grasp of specific American legal practices made him an asset of value to the colonies. For Whately seems to have recognized these qualities and eagerly sought confidential information from him. Ingersoll declared that, as a result of frequent conferences with the secretary, he was able to bring about a material lessening of the duties in general, and in the case of three important instruments—marriage licenses, commissions of the justices of the peace, and notes in hand—he gave the secretary no rest until the latter dropped them from the bill.[1] "Mr. Whately to be sure tells me," wrote Ingersoll, "I may fairly claim the Honour of having occasioned the Duty's being much lower than was intended."[2] When at last the stamp bill was ready for presentation in the Commons, it had been so modified that a careful study of its schedules shows that in the framing of it there was a serious appreciation of the complexities of the economic situation in the colonies. While it was the most compendious and comprehensive taxation measure

[1] "I had frequent Opportunities with that Gentleman. No Article of Duty was added or enhanced after I saw it. But several were taken out. 1, Notes in Hand. 2, Marriage Licenses. 3, Registers of vessels which stood at 10 s. 4, Judge's Salaries." *Ingersoll Stamp Act Corresp.*, p. 3; see also p. 19.

Jared Ingersoll to Governor Fitch, February 11, 1765, *ibid.*, p. 19. Thomas Whately to Robert Temple. Mass. Hist. Soc. *Coll.* (sixth series), IX, 49. In this Whately contends that the duties had been so lowered that as a whole they were much lighter than those imposed on similar documents in England.

[2] *Ingersoll Stamp Act Corresp.*, p. 19. How closely Ingersoll was associated with Whately in the final stages of the bill is shown by the fact that Ingersoll, at Whately's request, consented to draw up an estimate of the probable yearly income from the taxes in Connecticut. The estimate placed the sum between twenty-five hundred and five thousand pounds sterling. The ministry's estimate was four thousand pounds, "about equal to our county penny Rate," according to Ingersoll. *Ibid.*, p. 49.

of its kind that hitherto had issued from the Treasury, it bears every mark of being carefully worked out.

Early in February, the first debate took place in the House of Commons over the bill. Ingersoll said that Grenville, on this occasion, dealt with the proposal ''in a very able and, I think, in a very candid Manner.''[1] The bill passed through its first reading with a ministerial majority of five to one. According to Ingersoll, Colonel Barré, Richard Jackson, and Sir William Meredith were among those who replied to Grenville. Alderman Beckford, a member from London, who was a West India planter, was the only one at that time to deny absolutely the authority of parliament to tax the colonies.[2] At this session Ingersoll was very greatly impressed with the forceful reply that Colonel Barré made to Mr. Townshend, when the latter was urging the ministerial project. Barré was bitterly opposed to the government, which may have added fire to his famous apostrophe beginning: ''They planted by your Care! No! your Oppressions planted 'em in America.''[3] In describing the

[1] Jared Ingersoll to Governor Fitch, February 11, 1765, *Ingersoll Stamp Act Corresp.*, p. 14. ''I shᵈ not do Justice to Mʳ Grenville the Chancellor of the Exchequer, if I did not add that when he opened the design of taxing the Colony, he spoke of the Colonies in general in Terms of great Kindness & Regard & in particular, assured the House there was no Intention to abridge or alter any of their Charters.'' Richard Jackson to Thomas Fitch, February 9, 1765. See *Fitch Papers*.

[2] Beckford's principal fortune lay in Jamaica. In 1759 an attempt had been made to increase the duty on sugar; this put Beckford into strong opposition to plans which would interfere with the colonies. As Horace Walpole said, ''A tax on sugar touched his vitals.'' Horace Walpole, *Memoirs of the Reign of George II*, III, 177; Stephen Dowell, *A History of Taxation and Taxes in England*, II, 137.

[3] *Ingersoll Stamp Act Corresp.*, pp. 15 *et seq*. The speech in full, with variations, is given in Richard Frothingham's *Rise of the Republic*, pp. 175-176. Its authenticity has been questioned. John Adolphus, *History of England*, I, 167; Edward McCrady, *History of South Carolina under the Royal Government, 1719-1776*, p. 579, note 2. In a footnote to his *Correspondence*, which was published in 1766, Ingersoll claimed to be ''the only

speech, Ingersoll wrote: "These Sentiments were thrown out so entirely without premeditation, so forceably and so firmly and the breaking off so beautifully abrupt, that the whole house sat a while as Amazed, intently Looking and without answering a Word. I own that I felt Emotions that I never felt before & went the next Morning & thank'd Coll Barre in behalf of my Country for his noble and spirited Speech."[1]

At the second reading of the bill, an unsuccessful attempt was made, by members of parliament, to present various petitions against it. But all efforts were useless, for the ministerial party urged that there was a long standing rule of parliament against petitions upon revenue bills. It is interesting and important to notice that the opponents of the bill denied that the so-called rule was an order of the house, but on the other hand, merely a practice founded on experience and maintained to prevent inconvenience. The opposition urged that, unreasonable as it would be to admit English subjects, upon every imposition of a tax, to come in and be heard upon

Person by what I can discover, who transmitted Mr. Barré's speech to America." *Ingersoll Stamp Act Corresp.*, p. 16. It appears, however, that Francis Dana, afterward chief justice of Massachusetts, sent home a report of the speech. Cf. J. G. Palfrey, *History of New England*, V, 288.

[1] *Ingersoll Stamp Act Corresp.*, p. 16. Burke, in his speech on American taxation, delivered nine years later, April 19, 1774, says, "Far from anything inflammatory, I never heard a more languid debate in this House." Lord Mahon, *History of England*, V, 86-87.

Richard Jackson, who, as is stated above, participated in the debate, declared that Beckford, Barré, Fuller, Sir William Meredith and "myself spoke against Internal Dutys. I relied on the statute of the 34 & 35 H: 8. c. 13 and 25 Car: 2 c. 9 for giving Members to the Counties & Citys of Chester & Durham, which at the same time they establish the Right of taxing such part of the British Dominions as have no Election of Members shew the sense of the Legislature, that the Right cannot be exercised without great Publick & Private Mischiefs and therefore shod not be, without giving the Right that is given by these Laws." Richard Jackson to Thomas Fitch, February 9, 1765, *Fitch Papers*.

petitions against the same, there were precedents which could be produced to show that when any new species of taxation had been designed, petitions had been admitted against the measure, as in the case of the Funding Bill and on "other particular and extraordinary Occasions formerly; & that this Case, as to America was quite new & particularly hard as they had no Members in the House to speak for them."[1]   However, in spite of a vehement speech by General Conway,[2] the measure was carried smoothly through this and its subsequent reading with overwhelming majorities.

Ingersoll explained this result by reason of the fact that "The Parliament & Even the whole Nation, as far as I could collect their Sense of the matter, seem to be fixt in the following points, viz. first that America is . . . become too important to itself, as well as to the Mother Country & to all foreign powers to be left to that kind of Care & protection that was Exercised heretofore by Each independent Province in the Days of their Infancy: that there must be some one Eye to oversee & some one hand to guide & direct the whole of its Defense & protection. In the Second place that America is able & ought to contribute Something toward this general protection, over & above the Advantages arising from the American trade; the Advantages of trade simply Considered, they say, are mutual.   To give authority to America, to provide for these things, there would be the liability of giving umbrage to the Mother Country and the many jealousies

[1] Jared Ingersoll to Governor Fitch, March 6, 1765, *Ingersoll Stamp Act Corresp.*, p. 21.

[2] In referring to General Conway in his letter to the general assembly, Ingersoll said that he was "a Gentleman who was so displeased with the Ministry, for what he thought were personal Injuries, having been deprived of all his Offices, that he could scarce speak without showing Signs of Anger; & was sure to oppose almost every Thing that was proposed by the Minister." *Ibid.*, p. 30.

that would surely arise among the colonies as to proportioning the parts of this common power. And so, taking everything into consideration, it was generally felt, Parliament should assume the entire responsibility of the protection of British possessions.'"[1]

Speaking of the character of the opposition against the ministerial policy, Ingersoll pointed out that "Except the Gentlemen Interested in the West Indies & a few Members that happen to be Particularly connected with some of the colonies & a few of the heads of the minority who are sure to athwart & oppose the Ministry in Every Measure of what Nature or kind soever, I say, Except those few Persons so Circumstanced, there are Scarce any People here, Either within Doors or Without, but what approve the Measures now taking with Regard America.'"[2]

The ministers had been given a certain discretion as to the particular time the act would go into effect. The agents, defeated in their larger objects, exerted themselves to have the date changed, and it was Ingersoll, apparently, who finally prevailed upon Whately to set the date of enforcement as late as the first of November following.[3] The particular means of enforcement had

[1] *Ingersoll Stamp Act Corresp.* Richard Jackson, in referring to the principles that had previously governed parliament, said, in a letter to Governor Fitch, that "they did not think the County of Durham ought to be free from Taxation because it was unrepresented. They were of opinion that it was represented though it chose no Members & Continued to tax it, but ye House of Commons thought this so good a reason for giving it Members that they passed several Bills for that purpose & at last a Bill passed both houses of Parliament." *Fitch Papers.*

[2] *Ingersoll Stamp Act Corresp.*, p. 22. "And, here, I would remark that in the whole Debate, first & last, Alderman Beckford & G[l]. Conway were the Only Persons who Disputed the right of Parliament to tax us." *Ibid.*

[3] "I have been able from particular Connections and Circumstances to render the Colony more Service than any one Man in it in the Matter of the Stamp Act itself by assisting in getting it modified and getting the

also been left to the ministry. Whately's plan called for two head distributors in each province, one of whom should be the clerk of the provincial council, and the other, an eminent merchant and planter.[1] It was also contemplated to make the governor and council a kind of board of commissioners, to superintend the whole arrangement,[2] but for some reason, probably that of expense, it was finally decided that a prominent colonial in each province should be selected to have charge of the work of enforcement; he would be able to determine "where it pinches & will certainly let us know it, in which Case it shall be Eased."[3]

When the plans were completed for carrying the act into effect, there had been provided an American stamp office in London, with five commissioners of stamps, each drawing £500 apiece, per annum, and with the necessary staff of clerks.[4] Below these were the American inspectors, who were to receive a salary of £100, besides 20 shillings per diem while on their tours of inspection—for purposes of inspection, the colonies were grouped into districts, with Massachusetts Bay, Rhode Island, and Connecticut as one, under Robert Warter.[5] Then came the distributors, who were to be awarded eight pounds for every one hundred pounds worth of stamps that was disposed of within the colony constituting the particular district of each.[6]

Time of its taking Effect put off to a further Period than was first intended." *Ibid.*, p. 2, note.

[1] Brit. Mus. Addit. MS. 35,911 (Hardwicke Papers, DLXIII).

[2] *Ingersoll Stamp Act Corresp.*, p. 28, note.

[3] Jared Ingersoll to Governor Fitch, March 6, 1765. Postscript to letter, written March 9, 1765, *ibid.*, p. 28. Jared Ingersoll to the Connecticut General Assembly, September 18, 1765, *ibid.*, p. 32.

[4] Treasury 1: 442, fo. 34.

[5] *Ibid.*

[6] According to Whately's plan, an allowance of one shilling and six pence on the pound was to be granted to the head distributor and one

It happened that there were only three Americans in
England at that time who appeared to be qualified for so
important a post as that of distributor and who were so
situated as to take the office: Colonel Mercer of Virginia,
George Meserve of New Hampshire, and Jared Ingersoll.[1] All three had gone to England on private business; none of them apparently sought the place,[2] but
each, after being recommended, decided to accept office.
Ingersoll disclaimed any previous thought of obtaining
such a post before his services were solicited by Secretary Whately, after the passage of the act. Franklin, it
would seem, especially urged Ingersoll to assume the
responsibilities of this work.[3] In doing so, little did he,
or Benjamin Franklin, or the other colonials in London,

shilling on the pound to the under distributors. He also added ''perhaps
a clerk and a warehouseman with Salaries will be required for each Head
Distributor.'' Brit. Mus. Addit. MS. 35,910, fo. 310 (Hardwicke Papers,
DLXIII).

[1] Jared Ingersoll to the Connecticut General Assembly, September 18,
1765, *Ingersoll Stamp Act Corresp.*, p. 31.

[2] ''You know also, I believe, that the Office of Distributor was first
mentioned to me by Mr. Whately, without my seeking, or even before I
thought of it.'' Jared Ingersoll to Richard Jackson, November 3, 1765,
ibid., p. 41.

[3] I have not been able to locate the letters that Hollister refers to in
his *History of Connecticut*, II, 130, note. He says, ''These facts are asserted
in one of Ingersoll's letters to Governor Fitch and in a note in one of his
letters to Whately.'' Palfrey, also, apparently had access to these letters,
for he says, ''Franklin advises him [Ingersoll] to accept the office,'' adding,
''Go home and tell your countrymen to get children as fast as they can.''
History of New England, V, 319. See also B. L. Lossing, *Pictorial Field
Book of the Revolution and the War of 1812*, I, 1446. In a letter ''To the
Public,'' Ingersoll, however, declared, ''Again, my accepting the office of
Destributor of Stamps (which was offered to me in the same Manner as to
other Americans in Each Province) was upon the Advice of mine and
Colony's Friends as Supposing it was most probably you would think
there was a Necessity of your submitting to the Act of Parliament, and
that, in that case, I should be able to assist you to the Construction and
Application of the Act; better than a stranger not acquainted with our
Methods of Transacting.'' *Connecticut Gazette*, September 6, 1765.

or the ministry, realize the extent of the storm brewing
in America. In fact, as late as August 9, Franklin had
such a contempt for the radical, anti-ministerial element
in America that he wrote from London, to John Hughes,
who was appointed the Pennsylvania stamp distributor,
"that a firm Loyalty to the Crown and faithful Adher-
ence to the Government of this nation, which is the Safety
as well as the Honour of the Colonies to be connected
with, will always be the wisest course for you and I to
take, whatever, may be the Madness of the Populace or
their blind Leaders, who can only bring themselves and
Country into Trouble, and draw on greater Burdens by
Acts of rebellious Tendency."[1] This view may well be
taken as an epitome of the opinions of moderate Americans generally at this stage of the crisis. They all contemplated that there would be some opposition to enforcement of the Stamp Act, but thought nothing serious
could come out of it. Ingersoll himself saw the solid
advantage of having a strong friend of the colony acting
in the capacity of distributor of stamps. "Upon my
honor, I thought, I should be blamed," he pleaded later
on, "if I did not accept the Appointment."[2]

After accepting office,[3] in order to obtain "a full and
beneficial Construction of the Several Articles of the
Tax," Ingersoll lengthened his stay in England an additional month, which gave him the opportunity to consult
with the board of commissioners and with Doctors' Commons in reference to many of the terms and words used
in the act expressing different ideas in England than in
the colonies.[4] At this time, also, he put up a bond of

[1] Benjamin Franklin to John Hughes, written from London, August 9,
1765. *Writings of Benjamin Franklin* (Smyth), IV, 391-393.

[2] Jared Ingersoll to the Connecticut General Assembly, September 18,
1765, *Ingersoll Stamp Act Corresp.*, p. 32.

[3] Treasury 1: 442, fo. 34; 54: 41, fos. 38-39, 120.

[4] *Ingersoll Stamp Act Corresp.*, p. 32. "Attending Mr. Ingersoll by

£3000 for the faithful performance of his office, getting James Brown of Lombard Street, banker, and his friend, Thomas Life, the Connecticut London solicitor, to join him as bondsmen.[1]

Before leaving England, Ingersoll apparently rendered very valuable service to the colonies in two matters not related to the Stamp Act. One was ''in the matter of the Mutiny Act in preventing the Bill passing, to quarter soldiers in private Houses, as was intended'';[2] the other was, ''in assisting to get passed the Act granting a Bounty on timber'' shipped from America. ''I had the Honor,'' he declared, ''to be often with the Minister and Secretary at War, together with Mr. Franklin and other gentlemen, upon these subjects.''[3]   In May he took passage on a ship bound for the port of Boston.[4]

Order.   15th April at 11 and staid till 2 by self and agent answering divers questions and clearing up his several Doubts Upon the American Law.

''Soll[rs] Answer to Mr. Ingelsols Doubts upon the American Law.'' Brit. Mus. Addit. MS. 35,911, fos. 33 and 36 (Hardwicke Papers, DLXIII. American Stamp Office Law Bill).

[1] The bond covers six folio sheets. It was signed May 1, 1765. Ingersoll Papers. In 1770 the bondsmen memorialized the Lords of the Treasury that the bond be delivered to them and cancelled. It was referred May 9. Treas. 4: 12, p. 169 (Andrews, *Guide*, II, 206). See also Brit. Mus. Addit. MS. 35,911, fo. 33 (Hardwicke Papers, DLXIII). Ingersoll in turn gave to these two sureties his own bond of indemnification. *Ingersoll Stamp Act Corresp.*, p. 36.

[2] *Ibid.*, p. 3, note. In a letter to Governor Fitch, Richard Jackson said in referring to the bill for quartering soldiers in America, then pending in parliament, that great opposition would be made to certain parts of the bill ''such we deem to be a Claim that under the Cloak of the Expression (as has been heretofore practiced) empowers the Civil Magistrate to quarter soldiers in private Houses where barracks are wanting and the Public Houses insufficient.''   Richard Jackson to Thomas Fitch, April 19, 1765, *Fitch Papers.*

[3] *Ingersoll Stamp Act Corresp.*, p. 3, note. On April 7, 1765, Ingersoll wrote an interesting letter to Godfrey Malbone of Newport, Rhode Island, an extract from which follows:

''The Parliament have been and still are very busy with America, laying duties and granting, at least talking about granting bounties—The Spanish trade you may depend is opened as much as the same can be without speaking loud; they say how they intend not to hurt us upon the whole of their regulations but do us good—I wish we may be of that mind—Many things have been said about the molasses duty but, after all, they don't intend to repeal or alter the present Act without at least trying it, tho I believe they think they must by and by.'' Emmet Collection (New York Public Library).

As to the bounty on timber, Jackson, writing April 19, 1765, says, ''However, we have a promise of a Bounty on American Timber imported into England.'' He expresses the hope that this ''may in time prove an Encouragement for the Opening a very beneficial trade and particularly may contribute a little to the facilitating a direct Intercourse between Great Britain and Connecticut.'' Richard Jackson to Thomas Fitch. *Fitch Papers.*

4 Ingersoll, in a postscript to his letter to Governor Fitch, written March 6, 1765, declared that he had taken passage on the *Boscowan*, Captain Jacobsen, bound for Boston, sailing early in April. He, however, did not sign his bond until May 1, 1765.

CHAPTER VI

OPPOSITION TO THE STAMP ACT IN CONNECTICUT

ONE of the most difficult tasks that confronts the student of American colonial history is to approach the study of the Stamp Act agitation and the agitation that followed the passage of the Townshend measures from a viewpoint so thoroughly detached that it is possible to give a sufficiently sympathetic emphasis to the motives and acts of the opposing groups as to do full justice to each. In making an analysis of the Stamp Act crisis, it becomes clear that there were at least three distinct issues involved in the same, and that each of these has had to some extent its counterpart in later American history. There was the constitutional issue, put forward to a place of first prominence. However, in view of the fact that the colonials between 1764 and 1776 felt compelled radically to shift their ground regarding the unconstitutionality of the efforts of the British government in attempting to regulate American affairs,[1] it would hardly

[1] As was brought out in the preceding chapter, Governor Fitch, in 1764, in his "instructions" to the Connecticut agents in London, made clear to them that they were not to deny the constitutional right of parliament to tax the people of Connecticut, but to emphasize the inexpediency of doing so. After the passing of the Stamp Act, as will be seen, a shifting of ground took place; while still accepting the right of parliament to levy American customs duties and to tax American sailors for the support of Greenwich hospital, there was set up the theory that the placing of an "internal" tax upon the colonies by that body was a violation of the constitutional rights of the people of America. This theory was very forcibly set forth by Franklin in his famous "Examination." By 1768 the people

seem that this issue, in truth, can be considered more
fundamental as the real basis for resistance than the constitutional arguments advanced by New England seces-
sionists, previous to and during the War of 1812, against
the "usurpations" of the central government then in the
hands of the "Virginia dynasty"; or those put forward
by that erstwhile ardent nationalist, Calhoun, through the
medium of the South Carolina Ordinance of Nullifica-
tion, against the unconstitutional procedure of Congress
in passing the tariff act of 1828. But once having sought
this means of defense the colonials found it the most
powerful and effective of weapons.

Another issue had to do with the idea which had taken
root in the colonies that, on the one hand, an American
was not an Englishman and, on the other hand, that English institutions were un-American; in other words, that
there were two peoples instead of one, with distinct and
divergent interests. This attitude is clearly presented
in a letter which Jared Ingersoll wrote in 1764 to Thomas
Whately, secretary to the Treasury Board, who had
twitted him about his Puritanism of an "Oliverian descent." In reply, Ingersoll proceeded to make clear that
on the contrary "being so much an Englishman, so much

of Connecticut, and elsewhere in America, had advanced to the point in
their constitutional theorizing that they were now prepared to brush aside
the distinction that they had made between "external" and "internal"
taxation and to deny the right of parliament to secure a revenue from
America by any means whatsoever. Before the outbreak of the Revolution,
so far had American political theory swung from its standpoint of the early
'60's that the doctrine of the coördinate authority of the colonial assemblies with parliament had become the chief reliance of those who were in
opposition to the parliamentary program. Many went still further. "The
idea of inalienable allegiance to any prince or state is an idea to me inad-
missable," declared Samuel Holden Parsons, writing from Connecticut to
Samuel Adams, in 1773, "and I cannot see but that our ancestors when
they first landed in America were as independent of the Crown or King of
Great Britain as if they had never been his subjects." Penn. Soc. of Sons
of the Amer. Rev. *Year Book* (1895), p. 189.

an advocate of you on your side of the water, so unhappily void of all Puritanism . . . I have very much bro't upon me the jealousy of my own countrymen; they suspect me being too much a favorer of court interest.'"[1] This feeling of separateness, as a social group, gave rise in America to the idea that no interests so vital to the people of the colonies as that of taxation and the garrisoning of the frontier forts could be entrusted to the hands of "foreigners," as Englishmen were freely denominated by the American press of 1765.[2] Similar ideas, of course, took root in the South, coming into full bloom during the decade preceding the Civil War; Southerners had become impressed with the notion that they were a distinct people with respect both to constitutional conceptions and social order and possessed of interests which were not to be entrusted to any governmental body that their votes could not control. Both in 1765 and in 1860 one is confronted by certain powerful anti-nationalistic tendencies expressed in the form of the most extreme particularistic theory and in each case this particularism sought shelter behind a wide mantle of sectionalism.

Finally, there was the issue which had to do with the question of increased taxation. This, in itself, coming from whatsoever source, would not have been welcomed

[1] Jared Ingersoll to Thomas Whately, June 6, 1765, *Ingersoll Stamp Act Corresp.*, p. 4.

[2] *Connecticut Gazette*, August 9 and 16, 1765, in letters of "Cato" and "Philopolitus"; see also the number issued on March 29, 1766. In the *New London Gazette*, August 30, 1765, there is reprinted an article from a Boston paper dealing with the contention of the "ministerial writers, and all the great and little tools on this and the other side of the water" that the people of America are British subjects and Englishmen. The reply is made, "Does he think we are to be flatter'd with the mere name of Englishmen?"

In conversing with Grenville regarding the laying of the Stamp Tax, the agents urged that there was "a general want of mutual Knowledge and Acquaintance with each other;—That Want of Connection and Personal Friendship." *Ingersoll Stamp Act Corresp.*, p. 26.

by the colonials. The farmers of Somersetshire and
Devon, it should be kept in mind, resisted in 1763 Lord
Bute's cider tax with almost as much bitterness and violence as the people of the American colonies did the
Stamp Act.[1] Had so sweeping a measure in 1765 emanated from a legislative body made up even of representatives from the different colonies, it would have been
intensely unpopular with those very elements stirred to
violence against the upholders of the Stamp Act. Indeed,
the Whiskey Insurrection in western Pennsylvania in
1794, precipitated by the internal revenue law of 1791,
brought forth a series of denunciations of President
Washington's administration that bear, in many respects,
a remarkable resemblance to the denunciations that filled
the colonial press in 1765 against the Grenville ministry;
both in 1765 and in 1794 unconstitutionality of action and
usurpation of power formed the basis of violent charges
against the central government.[2]

In following the course of the resistance to the act in
Connecticut, it is hardly necessary to point out that lawlessness of the terrorist type was in no way sanctioned
by such intelligent and large-minded opponents of the
Stamp Act as Ezra Stiles, William Samuel Johnson,
Roger Sherman, and probably a majority of educated
people, who preferred to follow the footsteps of these
champions of popular rights that relied strictly upon a
constitutional form of resistance. If, therefore, the
words and actions of the supporters of the Stamp Act
contrast more than favorably with those of the opponents
of the same, it should in all fairness be remembered that

[1] See Stephen Dowell, *History of Taxation in England*, II, 141-144.

[2] See Townsend Ward, *Insurrection of 1794 in the Western Counties of
Pennsylvania* (Pennsylvania Hist. Soc. *Memoirs*, VI) : also H. M. Bracken-
ridge, *History of the Western Insurrection*. This similarity of the form of
protest used in 1765 and in 1791 has not escaped the notice of Professor
J. D. Bassett, *The Federalist System*, p. 106.

the rather slow-moving moderates were pushed aside by radicals who insisted on dealing with the problem in hand according to their own peculiar notions as how best to settle a large question of state.

On July 28, 1765, Jared Ingersoll landed at Boston. He immediately sought the Bernard residence and spent the day closeted with the governor.[1] The conference was undoubtedly held for the purpose of discussing the problems sure to arise in connection with the enforcement of the Stamp Act. According to Ingersoll, everything was quiet in Boston at the time of his arrival, and from information that he then received from Connecticut he "had no Reason to expect any other than a Submission to the Act . . . tho much against the People's Inclinations."[2]

The news of the home-coming of Ingersoll aroused various conflicting emotions in Connecticut, although as early as May 24 information had reached the colony of his appointment as stamp distributor.[3] On the one hand, he was greeted by a crowd of would-be assistant stamp distributors burning with a solicitous desire to supply the people of each community with this novel stamped parchment. Even little Windham, a veritable hotbed of radicalism, furnished her candidate for this somewhat dubious honor in the person of the venerable Nathaniel Wales.[4] Charles Phelps of Stonington, John Coleman of Hartford, Daniel Lathrop of Norwich, and Andrew Adams of Litchfield wrote urgent letters to Ingersoll im-

1 Governor Bernard to Richard Jackson, August 7, 1765, Bernard Letters, IV, 9.

2 Jared Ingersoll to the Commissioners of Stamps, November 2, 1765; also, Jared Ingersoll to Richard Jackson, November 3, 1765, *Ingersoll Stamp Act Corresp.*, pp. 40, 50-51.

3 Ezra Stiles Papers.

4 New Haven Col. Hist. Soc. *Papers,* IX ("Jared Ingersoll Papers"), 325.

pressing him with the fact that nothing would give them greater pleasure than to have the privilege of distributing stamps in their respective townships.[1] Adams's letter was typical. "I should Esteem myself honoured [he wrote] to be thought Worthy your Service; and would Receive the Favour with Gratitude . . . and hope I shall be able to Convince you—as much as the Difference of station will admit,—how much I am your sincere Friend and Obedient Servant."[2]

On the other hand, a feeling of profound indignation was not slow in manifesting itself within the colony, both against the Stamp Act and the Connecticut stamp distributor. Ingersoll attributed this to the excitement caused by the Virginia Resolves, introduced by Patrick Henry in the House of Burgesses, May 30. He declared that Boston, which he had found quiet the latter part of July, was thrown into a flame when these resolves "took air." As a consequence, this intense feeling soon spread to Connecticut.[3] What undoubtedly added acuteness to the situation was the fact that the colony was going through something of an economic crisis. In fact, it was very difficult for the colonial government to collect its taxes, "on account of the poverty of the people."[4] Although many delinquents were committed to jail, the tax

[1] New Haven Col. Hist. Soc. *Papers*, IX, 324-327. In the Ingersoll papers there is a further list of applicants: "Hartford, Capt. [John] Laurence, Mr. Seymour; Windsor, Mr. Henry Allyn; Fairfield, Mr. Rowland," *ibid.*, 327, footnote.

[2] Andrew Adams to Jared Ingersoll, August 15, 1765, *ibid.*, IX, 327. Even so firm an opponent of the Stamp Act as William Samuel Johnson wrote to Ingersoll on June 3, 1765, saying, "If you propose to have a Subaltern in every Town, I shall be at your service for Stratford, if it be agreeable." *Ibid.*, IX, 325.

[3] Jared Ingersoll to the Commissioners of Stamps, November 2, 1765; also Jared Ingersoll to Richard Jackson, November 3, 1765. *Ingersoll Stamp Act Corresp.*, pp. 40, 50-51.

[4] Jared Ingersoll to Thomas Whately. Ingersoll declared, "I informed myself of these matters." *Ingersoll Stamp Act Corresp.*, p. 50.

arrears of the colony, by the end of 1765, amounted to some £80,000 in uncollected rates and taxes laid for calling in and sinking the bills of credit issued as the result of the Seven Years' War.[1] To the debtor class, the thought of being required to assume additional burdens could only seem intolerable. As early as July the question was propounded through the columns of the *Connecticut Gazette,* "whether Americans were going to allow themselves to be bondsmen";[2] for the sad condition of the colonials appealed to writers as strikingly analogous to the Israelites in bondage. "The Egyptians paid dear for their oppression and the Israelites were removed from their government";[3] these and other statements carried with them an almost pungent odor of disloyalty ten years before the actual outbreak of the Revolution. In August, the *Gazette,* which was published in New Haven, in giving the list of persons appointed as distributors of stamps in America, significantly printed beside it certain "extracts of late intelligence from England," which read as follows: "I must take leave positively to declare that all measures prejudicial to the interests of America, ever yet taken, have not only been proposed but even very warmly recommended by mean, mercenary Hirelings, Parricides among yourselves, who for a little filthy Lucre would at any time betray every Right, Liberty and Privilege of their fellow subjects."[4]

1 *Ingersoll Stamp Act Corresp.* The general financial and economic condition of Connecticut during the '60's is treated in Chapter IX of this study.

2 "To the Public of Connecticut. The reigning question now is Whether Americans shall be Freemen or Slaves." *Connecticut Gazette,* July 12, 1765 (special broadside insert).

Even William Samuel Johnson of Stratford, an Anglican, was moved to say, when he heard of the Stamp Act, that "from *this* time date the *Slavery* of the Colonies." *Itineraries of Ezra Stiles,* p. 587.

3 *Ibid.*

4 *Connecticut Gazette,* August 9, 1765, supplement.

To give cohesion, direction, and force to this spirit of resistance, there appeared among the northern colonies in the spring of 1765 a rather loose form of organization under the name of the "Sons of Liberty."[1] It is said to have originated in eastern Connecticut and to have been especially fostered by that fiery agitator, Isaac Sears of New York.[2] There is some irony in the fact that Ingersoll apparently furnished these agitators with their name, in transmitting to Connecticut early in the year his version of Barré's speech in which Americans were lauded as "sons of liberty."[3] The members of the organization were pledged to take any step that might be necessary to prevent the enforcement of the Stamp Act. If the occasion so demanded, even violent means were to be resorted to, for above everything else, the law should be resisted to the last extremity. As a practical program they were not only to see that no stamps were employed, and at the first opportunity to seize and destroy them, but also to compel, by force, if need be, the resignation of all stamp officials. It was this group of Connecticut men,—said to have numbered, before the repeal of the Stamp Act, as many as ten thousand, under the leadership of that romantic character, Colonel Israel Putnam of Pomfret, and possessed of a magazine of arms and ammunition,[4]—

[1] See H. B. Dawson, *The Sons of Liberty in New York*, for a discussion of this.

[2] For Isaac Sears see Carl Becker, *The History of Political Parties in the Province of New York, 1760-1776;* also S. P. Way, "Notes on Isaac Sears," *Sears Genealogy* (1890).

[3] "I believe I may claim the Honour of having been the Author of this Title [Sons of Liberty] however little personal Good I have got by it, having been the only Person, by what I can discover, who transmitted Mr. Barré's speech to America." *Ingersoll Stamp Act Corresp.*, p. 16, footnote.

[4] "By advices from Connecticut, Matters are carried to greater lengths than in any other province having allready provided themselves with a magazine for Arms, Ammunition, etc. and 10,000 men at the shortest warning for opposing the Stamp Act, etc. all under the Command of a Connecti-

which, before many months, was to come into virtual control of the colony.

Dr. Benjamin Gale, a man of patriotic tendencies and yet an acute, frank, and independent critic, in a letter to Jared Ingersoll, written from his home at Killingworth in Windham County, in the heart of the radical section of the colony,[1] declared that the men who were identified with it were the offspring of ''several factions which have subsisted in this Colony, originating with the New London Society,[2]—thence metamorphisd into the Faction for paper Emissions on Loan, thence into the N. Light,[3] into the Susquehannah and Delaware Factions,[4]—into 'Orthodoxy'[5]—now into Stamp Duty opponents.'' The actors, he insisted, were the same, but that they succeeded through each change in drawing in some new members.[6] While it is probably true that the Sons of

cut man called Col. Putnam.'' ''The Journal of Capt. John Montressor,'' N. Y. Hist. Soc. *Coll.* (1881), p. 355.

[1] Dr. Gale was a graduate of Yale College of the class of 1733. In the Revolution he favored the American side.

[2] ''The New London Society of Trade and Commerce'' was established in 1730 for the purpose of promoting direct trade with Great Britain and the development, generally, of the commercial life of the colony, and for the encouragement of the fisheries. In 1732 it was incorporated, by the general assembly, with some eighty members. Loans upon mortgages were obtained from the public treasury and the capital employed in trade. Several vessels were built; to facilitate its work, the society emitted bills of credit or society notes. The government now became alarmed and the new money was denounced by the governor and council. In 1733 the general assembly dissolved the association. *Conn. Col. Rec.*, VII, 390, 420, 449, 508; F. M. Caulkins, *History of New London*, pp. 242-244.

[3] As has been explained in the first chapter, the New Lights were the emotional, evangelical wing of the Congregational communion.

[4] This issue will be treated in Chapter XI.

[5] Dr. Gale, who was a strong opponent of President Clap of Yale, was here making reference to the religious faction in the colony that supported the latter in his efforts to keep the Yale students uncontaminated by the liberal religious views espoused at the New Haven brick meeting house, presided over by Rev. Mr. Noyes.

[6] Benjamin Gale to Jared Ingersoll, *The History Magazine*, VI, 138-139.

Liberty were largely made up of discontented elements always ready to fly in the face of any settled policy and correspondingly quick to embrace new and radical causes; while as a class they could hardly have been called the special guardians of good and stable government, yet there were many men, such as Roger Sherman, who gave the movement their support, at least in the early stages, and who were incontestably devoted to law and order and to sober social control.

Needless to say, Jared Ingersoll was filled with amazement to find himself suddenly enveloped in this bitterly hostile atmosphere. He had anticipated some opposition to the act, but had not expected that he personally would become the object of hostility. He found, early in August, the majority of people in such a tremor of excitement that they could not hear calm, dispassionate statements of fact; and when it was discovered by some ingenious patriot that J. I. were also the initials of Judas Iscariot, the more religiously emotional found gloomy significance in the fact.[1]

The first attack launched against Ingersoll seems without doubt to have come from the pen of Naphtali Daggett, professor of divinity at Yale College.[2] But the basis of this hostility of Professor Daggett toward Inger-

---

[1] One writer, however, claimed to be above such common superstition. "I am not so Foolish as to think that because the first letters of his name are the same with that Traitor of old, Judas Iscariot, therefore, it is Ominous: But suppose Judas had pleaded that 'twas decreed in the Court of Heaven that our Saviour should suffer and that 'twas better for one of his Disciples to betray him than any other that so the Price of his Blood might be sav'd to his Friends; would that at all Expiate his Fault? No, by no means!" *New London Gazette*, September 27, 1765.

[2] In the Ezra Stiles collection of newspapers (Yale University Library) there are opposite the "Cato" signature in the *Connecticut Gazette* the written words, "Professor Daggett." See also the *New London Gazette* in the same collection for a similar statement. Both notations seem to be in the handwriting of President Stiles.

soll probably goes back as far as 1756, when the former, against the bitter opposition of the First Ecclesiastical Society, was appointed the first professor of divinity, as well as college preacher, at Yale College, an appointment which allowed President Clap to withdraw the students from the latitudinarian atmosphere spread by the society's pastor, the Rev. Mr. Noyes.[1] Ingersoll, as was stated in an earlier chapter, was a leader at the brick meeting house and became very active in the controversy. Clap was accused not only of holding New Light views but also of corruption,[2] and in 1763 Jared Ingersoll and William Samuel Johnson appeared before the general assembly in support of a memorial to the effect that the colonial government, as founder of Yale College, should now assume the right to appoint visitors and to reform abuses. The general assembly, however, was in control of the New Light faction and upheld President Clap, who made an able defense of the college administration.[3] Therefore, in attacking Ingersoll, Daggett was settling old scores.[4]

[1] This is given full treatment in Edward E. Atwater's *History of the City of New Haven*, pp. 169-171, 482.

[2] Dr. Benjamin Gale published three pamphlets against President Clap and his supporters, and in a letter to Ingersoll claimed, in 1762, to have convinced the world that Clap was "an Assuming, Arbitrary, Designing Man; who under a Cloak of Zeal for Orthodoxy, design'd to govern both Church & State, & Damn all who would not worship the Beast." Benjamin Gale to Jared Ingersoll, August 9, 1762. New Haven Col. Hist. Soc. *Papers*, IX ("Jared Ingersoll Papers"), 276.

[3] *Ibid.* Also see William L. Kingsley, *Yale College, A Sketch of its History*, I, 90.

[4] Referring to the attack against Ingersoll made by Daggett, the writer "Civis" says, that this "however, well calculated to answer particular personal purposes," appeared to have a tendency only to inflame the public mind and not to enlighten. *Connecticut Gazette*, August 16, 1765.

That the spirit of faction was running high in Yale College circles in 1765 seems to be shown by the records of a trial which took place in New Haven on August 27, before the superior court. On this occasion Elihu Hall, king's attorney, presented "William Nickells, Ralph Romnay, William

The Connecticut stamp master, according to Professor Daggett's implication, had asked his indignant neighbors, "But had you not rather these duties should be collected by your brethren than by foreigners?"[1] To which Daggett, sheltering himself behind the nom de plume, "Cato," replied, in the columns of the *Connecticut Gazette:* "No, vile miscreant! Indeed, we had not. That same rapacious and base spirit which prompted you to undertake the ignominious Task will urge you on to every Cruel and oppressive Measure. . . ."

But Jared Ingersoll was not without loyal friends. The gauntlet was hardly thrown down when it was snatched up by one who, under the name "Philopolitus," rivaled "Cato" in the violence of his language. "Cato's face," he wrote, "appeared through his veil and *he,* was the real enemy of his country in desiring a foreigner, rather than a brother, to execute the laws. But as either the Love or Hatred of such a conceited Upstart is not worth the Notice of any but his Fellow Fools, I shall say no more."[2]

Adams of Stratford, Gershom Burr of Fairfield, Richard Olcock of New York and Ralph Isaacs of New Haven, together with Thomas Kimberly and Simon Woodruff.'' They were charged with acting in a riotous manner ''in the night season'' of July 30, when they made an attack against ''the College Mansion where the President and fellows lived.'' According to the records, they ''with Evil Intent did with Strong hand burst and take off the gates of the yard of the mansion house and Carry away and with Screaming and Shouting did in furious Violence throw into said House Numbers of large small stones with Cattles Horns into the windows of said House.'' The young men pleaded guilty and were fined amounts ranging from £8 to £10 apiece. Records of the Superior Court, vol. XV, New Haven session, under date August 27, 1765. In fact, President Clap so lost control of the situation that he was led to resign the presidency of the college.

1 *Connecticut Gazette,* August 9, 1765.

2 *Ibid.,* August 16, 1765. ''That piece . . . signed Cato seems to be wrote,'' declared ''Seneca,'' also through the *Gazette,* ''with the haughtiest airs, the greatest bitterness of temper, Baseness of Ill-Manners, and Opposition of the Christian spirit of Any that has come to my Observation,

"Civis," in the same issue of the local paper, with a fine dignity remonstrated with "Cato." "I would ask the favour of the letter-writer to lay his hand on his heart, and ask himself whether the personal abuses he has dealt out so freely and so bitterly are becoming a Christian or Gentleman; whether he has any Evidence to warrant such gross imputations to particular characters?" He proceeded in justification of the Stamp Act to point out that Great Britain felt obliged to maintain along the frontier some seven thousand men to protect American interests from the lately subdued French. The cost of this would be over £300,000, and, including the West Indies, America was expected to raise only £100,000 of this sum by stamps and other duties. On this basis it would take from Connecticut only about three or four thousand pounds. "Civis" then made clear that there would be no drainage of currency from America, that all sums raised in the colonies would be spent in the defense of America, besides the annual sum of £200,000 coming from England, which would be a benefit.[1] It must not be

which at best is but a mere heap of Bombast of swelling blustering Nonsense. By which the Author—if he were known, would be rendered infamous and would become the Detestation of all serious People." As to Ingersoll, "Seneca" asserted that he was "a Gentleman of known and real merits—a fine Patriot and Friend to his Country." *Ibid.*, August 30, 1765.

[1] The money, however, was, through orders issued from the Treasury Board, to be paid by the different distributors into the hands of the deputy-paymaster, who, in turn, would pay out the same, to the army. The reason for this procedure, according to Ingersoll, was that it was thought to be unconstitutional to make any grants to the Crown payable anywhere "but in the Course of the Exchequer." *Ingersoll Stamp Act Corresp.*, p. 18, note.

That which adds significance to this statement of "Civis" is the fact that he, according to the evidence presented below, was none other than Jared Ingersoll himself, who was probably the best informed man in America regarding the plans of the Treasury Board with respect to America.

Chauncey Whittelsey, a shrewd business man, in writing to Ezra Stiles, April 16, 1765, expressed his fear, which seems to have been commonly held and which Ingersoll combated, that the specie would be drained from the

forgotten that Great Britain was also burdening herself
in carrying out a program of American defense. Englishmen claimed that this program, when taken together
"with the enormous expence which the mother country is
at in the General Defence of the Kingdom occasions a
taxation of themselves at least ten fold beyond what will
fall on America and for that reason, if for no other,
colonials would not with any colour of Reason be against
bearing a small Part of the Common Burdens of the
State." Moreover, there was a conviction regarding this
matter of defense that the colonies, "if left to themselves, will not exert themselves in an Equal and Proportionate manner, but while some (as appears from Experience in the late war) are ready and willing to do Much,
others will do little or Nothing; and that no power but

country. He, however, added a most significant statement in remarking
that in such a contingency the specie would not return unless there was
"another American war." *Itineraries of Ezra Stiles*, p. 587. It may be
asked what would bring the specie back in case of "another American
war," unless it were the coming of the regular troops? The Grenville
program provided for this.

Under title of "American Expedition," which is undated, Fane drew
up a memorandum relating to the contract with Messrs. Thomlinson and
Hanbury, financial agents for the Treasury. The question involved was
whether or not to send money to America to provide for the expenses of
four regiments, estimated at £103,701. "The Money, they think," said
Fane, "may be procured there, but lest they should be disappointed they
propose to send over in specie ———— Months Subsistence, which they must
buy up here. . . . If they give here 4 s 9 d a Dollar and can buy it there
at 4 s 6 d the gain will be . . . 5 P ct. . . . This is according to the present Exchange, a War may alter the Exchange and then it will be more or
less as Money is plenty or scarce. And even in that case Mr. Hanbury
seems to think there will be no need to send any more Money over for the
Troops, because as they make returns home from thence in specie, the
merchants will much rather give their Money for good Bills of Exchange
than run the Hazard of the Money and pay Freight and Insurance."
Brit. Mus. Addit. MS. 33,030, fo. 334. This is very important as it shows
that, at the time Fane prepared his memorandum, it cost 3d. less to buy a
Spanish dollar in America than in London. The presence of the regiments
would hardly do otherwise than benefit the American money market.

that of Parliament can enforce such Equitable and fair contribution of the whole; this, they say, the Stamp Act will do, and, at the same time will lay the burden principally upon Luxury, Law-Suits, etc. where it ought to fall.''[1]

The ''Civis'' replies written at this period in defense of the Stamp Act and those that later appeared in the *Pennsylvania Journal* in defense of the special and newly created vice-admiralty courts seem to have been inspired by Ingersoll, if not actually written by him. The sentiments expressed, the air of authoritativeness with which information regarding Great Britain is presented, and the striking similarity of style with his acknowledged writings creates a very strong presumption, in itself, that they came from Ingersoll's own pen.[2]

The reply of ''Civis'' had the effect of chastening ''Cato's'' spirit. Apologizing for his previous violence, Cato now made a restatement of his position against the Connecticut stamp master. ''If every American bravely refused to become instrumental in enslaving his country, it would have given all sensible and Free Britains an exalted Idea of our Patriotism and so would have been the most effective Means to influence them in our Favour. But, on the Contrary, when the Ministry saw how greedily *some* of those who has sustained the highest Character in the Colonies catched at the Bait, what must have been

[1] *Connecticut Gazette,* August 16, 1765.

[2] Ingersoll's authorship of the ''Civis'' letters of this period is practically advertised by the editor of the *Connecticut Gazette,* who made the following statement in his issue of August 23. ''The Printer of this Paper begs Leave to pospone a Critical Production signed 'Philologus,' written against 'Philopolitus' who lately appeared as a Defender of 'Civis.' '' The articles of ''Civis'' and ''Philopolitus'' were in the same issue, which shows that the printer was not referring to the defense of the sentiments expressed in the ''Civis'' article but had in mind the author of the latter. The entire ''Philopolitus'' communication was, in fact, a strong pro-Ingersoll retort.

their Sentiments? . . . However, neither the Sum to be raised nor the Pay of the Officers give us so much Uneasiness as the Manner of laying this Tax and the strange Design *they say* it is to support; namely, '*to Keep a Body of Troops, viz., about 7000 Men upon the frontier of America to preserve the People from the Violence of the bordering Indians.*' Truly, Mr. 'Civis,' we tremble at the Prospect of this.' "[1]

"Civis," not to be outdone, again came to the defense of the measure. First of all, turning his attention to "Cato," he declared, "I would have his Heart warm so long as his Head is cool, on a subject so important as the Stamp Act. He supposes the Act being unconstitutional as a Matter determined . . . 'Tis doubtless a Principle of the English Constitution that the People are not to be taxed but by their Representatives in Parliament; 'tis also as much a Principle that the People are not bound by any laws but such as are made by their Consent in the same Manner. Perhaps we shall find, upon these Principles, that the Parliament has no Authority over us in any Case. This, I believe, would be proving a little too much. . . . The favourite Col. Barré in that speech of his, delivered with so much Warmth in our Favour, said expressly that no man in his senses would deny the Authority of Parliament to tax America, and he was pleased to add that he did not believe the more sensible People of America thought otherwise." Then, taking up the general situation, "Civis" deprecatingly remarked, "Alas a perfect Frenzy seems to have seized the Mind of the People and renders them deaf to all Reason and Consideration. . . . I wish we may not by our Imprudence precipitate ourselves into greater Troubles than that which the Stamp Act would occasion.' "[2]

[1] *Connecticut Gazette*, August 23, 1765.

[2] *Ibid.*, August 30, 1765. In August, likewise, Ingersoll, under his own

A "frenzy" had, in fact, taken possession of rich and poor people of almost every type and description, not only in Connecticut, but elsewhere in America. The existence by August, 1765, of what psychologists might call a "mental wave of high tension," extending along the whole Atlantic seaboard and into the back country, is a fact that offers a field of study for the student of mass psychology, as interesting as that wave, which, under the name of the Great Awakening, had swept, in the form of religious emotionalism of an extreme type, through the colonies three decades before.[1] The press, of course, took a most active part in stirring up resentment of an unthinking sort by giving greatest prominence to inflammatory denunciations and thus engulfing the more thoughtful contributions that came to them.[2] In

name, addressed the "Good People of Connecticut," assuring them that he did not intend to oppress them. This is printed in John Almon, *Prior Documents*, p. 12.

Compare the language used above with reference to Colonel Barré with the statement in Ingersoll's letter to the general assembly which he wrote September 18. "Even Col. Barry who spoke so warmly in our favour said in his first general speech that he believed no man in that house would Deny the Authority of Parliament to tax America, and he was pleased to add, that he did not think the more sensible people in America would deny it." In other words, the connection between the "Civis" and the Ingersoll letters is not to be mistaken.

[1] "The whole country was thunderstruck. All Faces gather'd Paleness, an unusual Panic seized the land at the gloomy Prospect of their destined Slavery. No particular Colony could know at first, how the neighboring ones would act; whether they would assert their Rights, or submit in Despair to the grievous Yoke. Business stagnated and the Courts were shut up, But presently the British (no, the American) Spirit of Liberty was aroused; it catched from Breast to Breast, it ran; it flew thro' all the Colonies, like a Stream of Light from Heaven, surprising, uniting them in a most determined Opposition to the Stamp Act and that wretched State of Vassalage to which it was designed to reduce us." *Connecticut Gazette*, March 29, 1766.

[2] John Hughes, in a letter to the commissioners of stamps, has the following to say: "But as a prelude to the destruction and disorder made by these mobs, the printers in each Colony, almost without exception,

an open letter to the public, Ingersoll dealt with this situation. "And here," he said, "I cannot but take notice
how unwilling some News Writers seem to be to publish
any thing that serves to inform the minds of the people
of any matters which tend to abate their Prejudices.
They even make use of some kind of Caution, I observe,
to prevent the people from listening to any such cool and
dispassionate dissertations and remarks which at any
time they happen to publish, and, at the same time deal
out their personal abuses in the most unrestrained manner, repeating, with pleasure, the accounts of the most
extraordinary libellous exhibitions and practices."[1]

The results of this steady feeding of the flames of pas-
sion were not slow in appearing. On August 15, 1765,
Andrew Oliver, the Massachusetts stamp distributor,
was forced to resign.[2] In a letter to Ingersoll he said
that after having stood the attack thirty-six hours, "a
single man against a whole People," he had been forced
to yield.[3] James McEvers of New York, who seems to
have been a leading merchant, received and accepted the
appointment as distributor for that province. McEvers,

stuffed their papers weekly for some time before with the most inflammatory pieces they could procure and excluded everything that tended to cool
the minds of the people; these measures they pursued until the Presby-
terians in particular, in every colony began to threaten the Stamp officers."
John Hughes to the Commissioners of Stamps, October 12, 1766. *Pennsylvania Journal.*

[1] *Connecticut Gazette,* September 13, 1765. Previous to this, on August
24, Ingersoll had sent to the editor of the *Gazette* an "Advertisement . . .
To the good People of Connecticut," in which he declared that he would
in no wise force the stamps upon the public. "I cannot but wish you
could think more how to get rid of the Stamp Act than of the Officers who
are to supply you with the Paper and that you had learned more of the
Nature of the Office before you had undertaken to be so very anxious
at it." *Ibid.,* August 30, 1765.

[2] Ezra Stiles Papers.

[3] Andrew Oliver to Jared Ingersoll, August 26, 1765, New Haven Col.
Hist. Soc. *Papers,* IX ("Jared Ingersoll Papers"), 308.

however, was forced out of office August 22.[1] He informed Ingersoll that when he accepted the post there
was little or no clamor about it; but when the news spread
of Oliver's treatment at Boston and the "Cato" letter
from New Haven had been published in the *New York
Gazette*,[2] the agitation commenced. He was threatened,
he said, with a fate worse than Oliver's, and therefore
wrote out his resignation "& have Been Inform'd you
have Done the Same; . . . if you have not should be Glad
to Know how you Purpose to Act, as it may be some
Government to me in Case I Can't Procure a Release."[3]
Soon after Ingersoll had received this letter, there came
the news also of the resignation of Augustus Johnson,
the Rhode Island distributor.[4]

Ingersoll now realized how uncomfortable his situation
was. Although he had experienced no violence, as yet,
nevertheless the temper of the radical group was reaching a high pitch. "A Friend of the Public and no Enemy
of the Stamp Act," through the columns of the *Gazette*,
predicted that "if the Assembly shall think it necessary
and prudent . . . to submit to it [the Stamp Act] and to
practice upon it, I conclude every Member of the House
who is of that Sentiment will be voted an Enemy of his
Country by the Mob, be burnt in Effigy and stowed away
with the Stamp Officers."[5] Terror, in fact, struck into
the hearts of timid supporters of the home government.
Nathaniel Wales of Windham, who had solicited from

1 Ezra Stiles Papers; *Connecticut Gazette*, August 30, 1765.

2 The "Cato" article appeared in the August 22 issue of the *New
York Gazette*.

3 James McEvers to Jared Ingersoll, August 26, 1765, New Haven Col.
Hist. Soc. *Papers*, IX ("Jared Ingersoll Papers"), 328-329.

4 On August 27 Johnston was burned in effigy at Newport and on the
thirtieth he resigned. Ezra Stiles Papers; *Connecticut Gazette*, September
6, 1765. Regarding the significance of the violence at Newport see *Itineraries of Ezra Stiles*, p. 588.

5 *Connecticut Gazette*, August 23, 1765.

Ingersoll the office of assistant distributor of stamps, wrote to the stamp master, August 19, to the effect that he had first written "without much Consideration and while matters were much indigested," both in his own and other people's minds. He asserted that a thousand pounds annexed to the trust would not tempt him to act as assistant stamp distributor.[1]

There was every reason why Wales should feel as he did, for on August 21 Ingersoll was burned in effigy at Norwich, and the following day the proceeding was repeated at New London.[2] The ceremony at the latter place was elaborate and carried out with great care for all details. At six o'clock in the evening there was exhibited on a gallows erected in the most public part of the town, the effigy of the stamp master, "with a Boot placed a little back of his right shoulder wherein was concealed a young Imp of the D——l peeping out of the same in order to whisper in his ear."[3] On the breast of

[1] Nathaniel Wales to Jared Ingersoll, August 19, 1765. New Haven Hist. Soc. *Papers,* IX ("Jared Ingersoll Papers"), 325-326. It appears, according to Almon, that Ingersoll had designated Wales as one of the assistant distributors and requested him to come to New Haven to get his commission. The inhabitants of Windham, hearing of the letter, surrounded his house, and not only demanded the letter, but warned him not to accept office, "which so terrified him that the very same post he sent back an absolute refusal of taking the charge upon him." *Prior Documents,* p. 12.

[2] The *Boston Post* expressed it rather ambiguously in saying that on August 22, the stamp master both at Norwich and at New London "was hung in effigy and afterwards burnt amidst the shouts and acclamations of a great number of persons." *Connecticut Gazette,* August 30, 1765; F. M. Caulkins, *History of Norwich,* p. 365.

[3] It is interesting to notice that the New London radicals, as in many other ways, imitated the performances of the Boston agitators by employing the device of the boot and the whispering imp. This emphasizes the contagious character of the movement, the contagious effect of example, which tended to exclude a rational basis for action.

General Conway, who had spoken against the Stamp Act in parliament, early in 1765, and who entered the ministry, as reorganized during the summer, in a letter to the governor and company of the Colony of Connecti-

the effigy was a copy of the Stamp Act and an inscription in praise of liberty. When the crowd had assembled, the effigy was pulled from the gallows, mounted on a pole and carried through the main street, ''attended by the people of all Professions and Denominations,'' with music, the firing of guns, the beating of drums, and the acclamations of the crowd. After ''arriving at the place of Assignation, a Halter was placed around the neck of the Effigy which was again suspended in the air, on a gallows, and a bonfire being erected under it, the same was consumed. During this exhibition the guns on the Battery were repeatedly discharged, and even the children cried, 'THERE HANGS A TRAITOR, THERE'S AN ENEMY OF HIS COUNTRY,' etc., after which the Mobility, Gentry, etc. dispersed to different Taverns, and after drinking some royal Toasts, the whole was concluded with great Decorum.'''[1]

In a discourse delivered at the gallows, the speaker ''kept alluding to Pitt as the Moses and the St—pm—n as the Beast that Lord Bute set up in this Colony to be worshipped.'' He went on to declare, ''Go, one and all, go to such a man, and make him sensible of his error . . . and if he is in any post that unjustly grinds the face of the poor or that contributes to your slavery ask him peaceably to resign it, and if he refuses to, use him in such a manner, that he will be glad to do anything for a quiet life. For Britons never must be slaves. And, as we read that 'he which being often reproved, hardeneth

cut, said, ''It is hoped and expected that this want of confidence in the Justice and Tenderness of the Mother Country and this open Resistance to its Authority can only have found Place among the lower and more ignorant of the People.'' Dated October 24, 1765. *Fitch Papers*. While Conway was mistaken regarding the character of the opposition, it may, nevertheless, be suggested that such an exhibition as that at Lyme would make its appeal fundamentally to that element of the population.

1 *Connecticut Gazette,* August 30, 1765.

his neck shall suddenly be destroyed, and that without remedy!' Therefore take care of Mr. St—pm—n, alias the molten calf.' "[1]

On August 26, both at Windham and at Lebanon, the effigy ceremony was reënacted.[2] At Lebanon, the home of Jonathan Trumbull, effigies of Ingersoll and the Devil were bundled into a cart, taken to trial, found guilty and "miserably executed," amidst the wild plaudits of the onlookers.[3] On that same day a Boston mob wrecked the home of Lieutenant Governor Hutchinson and destroyed other property. The proceedings at Lyme, Connecticut, on the twenty-ninth, were characterized by such studied efforts to work the people into a state of blind fury that it will be necessary to give some account of them, in order to show the character of the forces that were arrayed against the Connecticut stamp distributor.

These proceedings were called the "Tryal of J—d Stampman, Esq., before the Proctors of Liberty." The accusations against him were, "That not having the fear of God before his eyes, but being moved thereto by the instigation of the Devil, he did, on the 29th of Sept., 1764, Kill and murther one of his own Bretheren, of the same family to which he belonged; and that still further pursuing his wicked designs, he did, on the first of June, 1765, enter into a Confederacy with some other evil minded, wicked, and malicious persons, to kill and destroy his own mother, Americana, . . . And urged on by Satan with the warmest Zeal to perpetrate this wicked Crime, he by the help of those designing Persons, in Confederacy with him, obtained a weapon wherewith to commit the horrid Fact. The Weapon he obtain'd was called a

[1] See anonymous pamphlet, *Liberty and Property Vindicated and the St—pm—n burnt* (1765), which is ascribed to Benjamin Church.

[2] Ezra Stiles Papers; *Connecticut Gazette*, August 30, 1765; *New London Gazette*, August 30, 1765.

[3] *Ibid.*

Stamp, which came from an ancient and lately Bute-fied Seat in Europe: With this Weapon his intent was on the 1st of Nov. following, to have Stamp'd his languishing Mother till she becoming unable to resist, and incapable of supporting the Grievous Burthen; should expire.'' The counsel for the defense, which was ''Scroggs and Jeffries,'' urged that the person murdered September 29, 1764, was not his brother ''but a Servant of his Father's Family, and that the pride of his Heart had prompted him to take many unjust Measures to raise his Fortune above the proper bounds of his station in Life.'' As to the part of the indictment charging him with a design against his mother, Americana, it was urged in defense that ''as her fate was absolutely determin'd, and could not possibly be avoided, he had good right himself to be the Executioner, since he should by that means save 8 per c't out of her Estate, to himself, (which probably would be a living worth 5 or 600 per ann.) which might as well be put into his Pocket as another's.'' Upon mature deliberation the court found the prisoner guilty, and gave sentence against him, ''That he should be forthwith tied to the tail of a Cart, and drawn thro' all the principal streets in Town, and at every Corner and before every House should be publicly Whip'd; and should be then drawn to a Gallows erected at least 50 feet high, and be there hanged till he should be dead, and then cut down by the common Hangman, and buried at the meeting of three Roads and a Monument erected over him, shewing the Cause of his ignominious Death, that the infamy of his Crime might be perpetuated to after Generations.'' The sentence was thereupon put into execution.[1]

Such demonstrations as these cannot but impress one with the feeling that the people concerned in them, prob-

[1] *New London Gazette*, September 6, 1765.

ably kindly and generous-hearted enough under ordinary
conditions, were so caught in the swirl of this tidal wave
of apprehension and resentment sweeping the country,
that they lost the power of using rational means in defense of their cause, and sank back to the mental levels
of the emotional primitive.

On the tenth of September George Meserve, the New
Hampshire distributor, was frightened into a resignation. Jeremiah Miller of New London wrote a letter of
warning to Ingersoll, also on the tenth. "I really believe,"
he said, "that your Person and Estate will be greatly
endangered if you continue in this office"; Miller also
informed him that the people were in a great rage against
the governor for not calling the assembly, and he hoped
that Ingersoll would use his interest that it might be
done.[1]

While no effigy was prepared by New Haven people, it
would appear from the *New London Gazette*[2] that one
evening a crowd gathered about Ingersoll's home, and
demanded that he should resign, threatening to tear
down the building should he attempt to act. He told
them of his inability to resign until the colonial government had taken some stand in the matter, and promised
either to keep the stamps out of the colony or, should
the parchments be sent to his home, to throw open the
doors to the public so that the people might make a bonfire of them, if that continued to be their demand. This
promise seems to have satisfied them.

However, at West Haven, on the night of the tenth,
there appeared "a horrible Monster, or Male Giant,
twelve Feet high, whose terrible Head was internally

[1] Jeremiah Miller to Jared Ingersoll, September 10, 1765, New Haven
Col. Hist. Soc. *Papers*, IX ("Jared Ingersoll Papers"), 330-331.

[2] *New London Gazette*, September 6, 1765; John Almon, *Prior Documents*, p. 13.

illuminated. He was mounted on a generous Horse groaning under the enormous Weight. This Giant seemed to threaten Destruction to every Person or Thing around him, which raised the resentment of a Number of stout Fellows, who constantly pelted him with Stones till he fled. The Assailants pursued and soon took him Captive, and triumphantly drove him about a Mile in the Town, attended with the discordant Noise of Drums, Fiddles, and taunting Huzzas. The People then directed their Course toward a Hill called Mount Misery. There the Giant was accused, fairly tried and Condemned by a special Jury and Impartial Judge as an unjust Intruder, a Patron of Ignorance, a Foe of English Freedom, etc. and was sentenced to be burnt. The Sentence was accordingly executed, amidst the joyful Acclamations, of near three Hundred *Libertines,* Men, Women and Children. It should be mentioned that, through the whole of this Raree show, no unlawful Disorder happened, as was the Case in the last truly deplorable and truly detestable Riot in Boston.'"[1]

For months Governor Fitch had resisted the demands of the radicals that a special session of the general assembly be called in order to decide whether or not Connecticut should send delegates to the Stamp Act congress, which was to assemble in October in New York. Fitch, unable longer to delay matters with safety to himself and property, now gave way and issued an order for a gathering of deputies at Hartford on September 19. Ingersoll personally was gratified to hear of the special session, for he felt, as things became more and more critical, that it was imperative for him to find out, as soon as possible, the attitude of the Connecticut government toward the enforcement of the Stamp Act. However, until there was a decision in favor of the act, he was not

[1] *Connecticut Gazette,* September 13, 1765.

at all disposed to admit into the colony for bonfire purposes any of the stamped parchments. He therefore
wrote to Lieutenant Governor Colden[1] of New York,
requesting him to hold in New York, until further notice,
all stamped paper designed for Connecticut.[2] He also,
once again, appealed to the people of the colony, through
the *Gazette,* to be calm; they could be assured, he wrote,
that he would not serve against their wishes; the assembly should decide whether or not the act was to be
obeyed; in closing this exhortation, he declared with
fervor, "I believe you will have very different Sentiments a few Months hence of who are the true Friends
and who the Enemies of their Country."[3] But, in spite
of this conciliatory statement, he did not hesitate, a week
later, to come strongly to the defense of the unfortunate
McEvers of New York, who had been appointed distributor of stamps without his own knowledge, through
the recommendation of Alderman Barlow Trecothick of
London, who was the leader of the London merchants in
opposition to the passage of the Stamp Act.[4] Also, at

[1] Colden was in charge until November 14, when Governor Moore
arrived from England.

[2] Governor Fitch also advised Ingersoll not to bring the stamps into
the colony because there was no "strong place." *Ingersoll Stamp Act
Corresp.,* p. 58.

[3] *Connecticut Gazette,* September 6, 1765. In the issue of August 30,
Ingersoll had appealed to "the Good People of Connecticut." A writer
in the *New London Gazette* replied to Ingersoll's published statements.
"Mr. Ingersoll in his Letter . . . with an Air of Insult seems to signify
that 'tis thro' Ignorance the people of this Colony have made such a Stir
at the Appearance of the *Stamp Act.* If the Gentleman had charged his
Country with Ignorance and Folly for the Trust they reposed in him to
Act on their Behalf at the Court of Great Britain, I should have readily
joined with him." See the issue of September 27; also the reply by Tom
Touchit, "a Friend of Liberty," in the *New York Gazette,* September 19,
1765. A correspondent of the *New York Gazette,* in the same issue, denominated Ingersoll's contributions to the newspapers as "all fallacious, insidious, and deserving the highest resentment of his country."

[4] *Connecticut Gazette,* September 13, 1765.

a meeting of freemen held at New Haven, on September 17, he showed his courage. When called upon to resign immediately, he refused and defended his position in a vigorous speech, in which he emphasized the fact that the general assembly of the colony at its May session had not been averse to the enforcement of the Stamp Act,[1] and for that reason, it was quite necessary for him, before deciding upon any course of action, to ascertain the will of the approaching assembly, which was called to meet in special session at Hartford. His position upon this point was sound, especially in the light of the conservative tendencies displayed by the Connecticut government during the summer months, when the Massachusetts assembly, through a circular letter of June 8, to all the colonial governments, was striving for the calling of a colonial congress.[2] The freemen, it appears, subdued by Ingersoll's logic, eloquence, and determination, adjourned without taking any further steps against him, after having appointed Roger Sherman and Samuel Bishop as deputies to the general assembly.[3]

For some unknown reason, the Connecticut Sons of Liberty were slow in attempting to carry out the plan

[1] Jared Ingersoll to Thomas Whately, November 2, 1765, *Ingersoll Stamp Act Corresp.*, p. 45. ''In May, 1765, the Assembly was not disposed to refuse to sanction the operation of the Stamp Act in Connecticut but a new election taking place about one-half of the members of the October session were new members and generally such as were warm against the Stamp Act.''

[2] *Boston Evening Post*, August 26, 1765, for a copy of the letter.

[3] The *Connecticut Gazette* of September 20, in its account of this meeting, says, ''The Stamp Master General of this Colony was at the said meeting where these words were read aloud, 'Likewise voted, that the Freemen present earnestly desire Mr. Ingersoll to resign his Stamp Office immediately.' Numerous were the signs of Consent to this vote, when a Gentleman condemned it as needless and inconsistent after their former Proceedings. The Stamp Officer then arose and declared in the strongest terms that he would NOT resign till he discovered how the General Assembly was inclined in that respect.''

they seem to have devised in August for putting an end to the office of stamp distributor for the colony. However, the news of the special session seems to have brought them to a resolve to compel Ingersoll to follow in the footsteps of Oliver, McEvers, Johnston, and Meserve, in resigning, thus relieving the general assembly of the weighty responsibility of taking any official step against the act. By the middle of September well-confirmed reports came to Ingersoll that there were gathering in eastern Connecticut at certain points bands of men who were making ready to march upon New Haven. It would appear that this news brought about a decided reaction in the town in favor of the stout-hearted stamp master. His position on the matter of enforcement had been such as to do away with considerable prejudice. Moreover, the more law-abiding elements resented the idea of having the town invaded by men ''from the eastern parts,'' with lawless designs. The more ''loyal'' people even began gathering arms in the determination that their fellow townsmen should be defended. The local militia also seemed disposed to put down any attempts at disorder.[1] New Haven, in spite of the previous gathering about Ingersoll's home, was in a conservative mood, and it is not unlikely that there would

[1] *Ingersoll Stamp Act Corresp.*, p. 62. Ingersoll declared that ''there would be most likely opposition to their Design and probably by the militia.'' *Connecticut Gazette*, September 27, 1765.

In fact, as early as September 6 ''the civil Authority, Select Men, and a Considerable Number of the principal Gentlemen and Inhabitants of the Town of New Haven, being occasionally met at the Court House'' were informed that a considerable number of persons ''from some of the Neighboring Towns'' were expected to gather there and in conjunction with some of the inhabitants show their resentment against Ingersoll. ''Whereupon the Gentlemen present unanimously declared their dislike and disapprobation of any such Proceedings, as being of dangerous Tendency; and resolved to use their Endeavors to discourage and prevent any such Riotous Assemblys, and would advise the People of this Town not to be concern'd therein.'' *Ibid.*, September 13, 1765.

have been bloodshed if any such violent measures had been attempted in New Haven as were carried out in Boston.

On the seventeenth of September, Governor Fitch arrived in New Haven on his way to the general assembly, which was to sit in Hartford. Ingersoll thereupon not only delivered to him written information which acquainted him with the intelligence just received from the eastern part of the colony, but also requested his aid in as far as the emergency demanded it. The two men were firm friends, and it is unnecessary to say that Fitch felt disposed to do everything within his power to aid Ingersoll at this juncture. Yet there was very little that Fitch could do, for a Connecticut colonial governor had scant power except as the instrument for putting into effect the will of the general assembly.[1] It was agreed, however, that the bands must be diverted from their purpose of entering New Haven, and there was no better way to accomplish this than for the stamp master to go to Hartford, where he would be able to meet the assembly.[2]

On the morning of the eighteenth, Ingersoll set out with Fitch and certain members of the assembly. For eighteen miles the group rode along the Hartford road without disturbance. There then appeared two horsemen "with pretty long and large new made white Staves in their Hands." These proved to be the advanced guard

[1] "A Governor in this Colony, you know, has no Negative to any Act of the Assembly, nor can he exercise scarce any Power, but as the Assembly gives him Leave." Jared Ingersoll to Thomas Whately, November 2, 1765, *Ingersoll Stamp Act Corresp.*, p. 46.

[2] There was a general impression abroad that Ingersoll was afraid to trust himself outside of the limits of New Haven, as the following published item shows: "But we are credibly informed that the said stampman is not now so entirely void of remorse of Conscience as has been Reported; and that he now thinks proper to keep a bright look-out, not choosing to go out of Town on any Account, notwithstanding some late Assertions to the Contrary." *New London Gazette,* September 6, 1765.

for one of the main bands of the Sons of Liberty, sent out to reconnoiter and see who would join them. While the remainder of the party rode on to Bishop's tavern "at the Stone House [Meriden]," Ingersoll stopped short to ask the strangers if he were not the man they were "in pursuit of." When they answered in the affirmative, he told them that he was not disposed to avoid a meeting with "the People." Nevertheless, he asked the riders to accompany him to the tavern in order that they might together confer with the governor. One of the two consented to do so, while the other went on about his mission of beating up recruits.[1]

In the conference that ensued at the tavern, the stranger frankly informed the governor as to the purpose of this march upon New Haven. When the latter solemnly charged him to go back to his fellows with a message to disperse immediately and return home, the bold spirit replied to this mandate by saying that the project was looked upon as the cause of the people, and he further assured his excellency that "they did not intend to take Directions about it from any Body."[2] He was not, however, averse to disclosing the fact that the Sons of Liberty were coming from the eastern parts in three divisions with eight days' rations in their saddlebags. One of these, starting from Windham, was approaching by way of Hartford, gathering recruits along the way; to

[1] *Connecticut Gazette,* September 27, 1765; *Ingersoll Stamp Act Corresp.,* pp. 61-62. "The direct road from New Haven to Hartford (a part of what was known as the Old Colony Road to Boston) passed through Meriden, Berlin, and the western part of Wethersfield (now Newington); and what was universally known as 'the Old Stone House' was on the Belcher Farm in the present city of Meriden." New Haven Col. Hist. Soc. *Papers,* IX, 344, footnote.

[2] "The Governor did all he could to prevent the extremes that have happened, but you know he has little power as Governor." Jared Ingersoll to Richard Jackson, November 3, 1765, *Ingersoll Stamp Act Corresp.,* p. 44.

this band he himself belonged; another division, starting from Norwich, was approaching New Haven by way
of Haddam; while a third, from New London, was moving
westward through the towns along the Sound.   Branford was to be the general rendezvous, whence on the
morning of the twentieth it was planned that the force
should enter New Haven, which was close at hand.[1]

When Ingersoll understood that two other bodies of
riders, besides the one approaching from Hartford, were
moving toward New Haven, he immediately wrote to each
a letter for the purpose of checking them, in which he declared that he would certainly give up his office if he
found it generally disagreeable to the people; he also
agreed to meet them in Hartford, if this promise did not
satisfy them.   After dispatching a Son of Liberty
with these messages, he took the precaution to send the
proprietor of the tavern posthaste to New Haven with a
letter to his family "that they and my house might be put
in a proper state of defence and security, in case the people should persist in their first design."[2]   When those
labors were finished, it was so late that he determined to
tarry for the night at the tavern.   Meanwhile, the governor, bearing a letter which Ingersoll had addressed to
the general assembly, rode on with the assemblymen, in
order to be at Hartford at the time set for the opening
of the general assembly the next day.

The Windham-Hartford band soon received the intelligence that Ingersoll was on the way to Hartford "to
apply to the Assembly for their protection,"[3] and the
determination was reached that he should not be allowed
to appear before that body until the Sons of Liberty had

[1] Hartford correspondence of September 23, to the *New York Gazette*,
September 26, 1765.

[2] *Connecticut Gazette*, September 27, 1765.

[3] Hartford correspondence of September 23, to the *New York Gazette*,
September 26, 1765.

settled with him. As a precaution, one guard was placed around the state house at Hartford, where the legislature was to meet, and another stood in front of Ingersoll's "usual lodgings," when in that town. The stone bridge on the road from Wethersfield and the approaches by way of the road from Farmington were also made secure. With this accomplished, early on the morning of the nineteenth, the main body of Windham-Hartford men rode forward in search of their victim.

About seven o'clock Ingersoll, accompanied by Bishop, the tavern keeper, started for Hartford. The two soon overtook Major Elihu Hall of Wallingford, who was on his way to the assembly, as one of the deputies.[1] The three rode without incident until, within two or three miles of the town of Wethersfield, they perceived four advancing horsemen. When Ingersoll acknowledged his identity, they wheeled about and attached themselves to the stamp master and his acquaintances. About half a mile farther on there appeared a group of some thirty riders, who likewise fell in behind the Hartford party, and shortly after this the main body of the Sons of Liberty were seen advancing in a truly imposing array.[2] Three trumpeters were in the lead; then came two dignitaries of military rank dressed in red, and wearing "laced hats," and behind them a cavalcade of about five hundred moving along two abreast, each carrying in military fashion a "stout clean-shaven, willow wand." The uniforms of some betrayed the fact that they were militia officers.

Without uttering a word, the squadron wheeled about and just as silently escorted Ingersoll to an immense elm

[1] Major Hall had preceded Ingersoll as king's attorney of New Haven County, and was at this time acting in that capacity. See Chapter II.

[2] According to the Hartford correspondent to the *New York Gazette* the main body met Ingersoll "at the lower end of Wethersfield." *New York Gazette,* September 26, 1765.

at the lower end of Wethersfield which stood in front of the mansion of Colonel Chester.[1] The plan, apparently, was to take him into a house and there come to an understanding agreeable to the Sons of Liberty. Objection was raised to this, with the result that a great circle was formed with Ingersoll, Major Hall, Bishop, and two or three of the leaders in the center. Ingersoll started to address his audience, but stopped, declaring that he did not know why he should say anything, for he was not certain what they wanted of him. They then told him that they wanted his resignation. He replied that he had already declared that he would not exercise the office against the general inclination of the people, and that he had given orders to have the stamped paper held at New York, where it should remain until he was able to learn from the assembly that it was their desire to have it come. He reminded them that he was under bonds to the stamp office in England and he therefore did not think it either safe or proper to resign the office "to every one that should ask it" and that he only wished to get the sense of the government whether or not to conform to the act in order to get dismissed from his office properly. It had been asserted that the assembly would say nothing about the matter; in that case, the speaker said, he would hardly think it safe to suffer stamps to come into the colony or to take any steps in his office. Moreover, as to resignation, the governor had the power to appoint another distributor.

[1] Henry R. Stiles, *The History of Ancient Wethersfield, Connecticut,* I, 416. "Mr. Ingersoll's escort appears to have turned to the right hand after leaving Berlin (to give time for the Assembly to convene), and passed through Wethersfield village, halting to carry out their design on the west side of Broad Street, in front of Colonel John Chester's house under an elm tree which has disappeared only within the last half-century." New Haven Col. Hist. Soc. *Papers,* IX ("Jared Ingersoll Papers"), 344-345, footnote.

In reply to this expressed desire of Ingersoll to gather the sense of the government came the answer, ''Here is the sense of the government, and no man shall exercise that office.'' Ingersoll thereupon asked if they thought it was fair that the counties of Windham and New London should dictate to all the rest of the colony. Upon this one of the band said, ''It don't signify to parly—here is a great many People waiting and you must resign.'' Ingersoll retorted that he didn't think it proper to resign until he met one authorized to ask it of him, and then added: ''What if I won't resign? what will be the Consequence?'' Some one said, *''Your Fate.''* Ingersoll turned upon him, looked him full in the face and said, with some warmth, ''My FATE, you say.'' Upon which a person just behind said, *''The Fate of your Office.''* Ingersoll was in a fighting mood and answered that he could die and perhaps as well now as another time; that he could die but once.

At this point, the commandant, who was Major John Durkee of Bean Hill, near Norwich, a veteran of the French and Indian War,[1] suggested that the matter would be concluded at a near-by tavern a few rods north of the Chester home. The crowd then moved along until opposite the hostelry and the riders began to dismount. Ingersoll thereupon declared to them, ''You can soon tell what you intend to—my business is at Hartford—may I go there or Home?'' and made a motion to go. The reply was, ''You shan't go two Rods from this Spot, before you have resigned,'' and his bridle was seized. Seeing that nothing could be accomplished by remaining in the

[1] According to David Humphrey, Colonel Israel Putnam was to have had command of this expedition, but owing to an accident his place was taken by Captain Durkee. See his *Life of Israel Putnam.* The latter later participated in the battles of Long Island, Harlem Heights, White Plains, Trenton, and Monmouth; he also was in Wyoming Valley and served under General Sullivan against the Iroquois.

saddle, Ingersoll dismounted and went into the tavern, accompanied by the ''committee'' of the Sons of Liberty, who were—besides Major Durkee—John Burrows and Jonathan Sturgis of Fairfield and Captain Hugh Ledlie of Windham.

It was possible now for Ingersoll to talk over matters generally with these representatives of the popular side. First of all, he disabused their minds of the idea that he was in England when the first leading vote of parliament was passed regarding the Stamp Act and failed to advise the governor regarding the same.[1] The strength of character displayed by the stamp master evidently overawed these men, who treated him not only with ''moderation and civility,'' but were even inclined to accept certain proposals which he made. When these, however, were referred to the people who crowded the streets, they were rejected—nothing would do but an absolute resignation.

While Ingersoll was being detained in the tavern, several members of the general assembly happened to pass by on their way to Hartford. Ingersoll saw them from the window and hailed them, calling out that he was being held a prisoner and asked their assistance and that of the assembly to effect his release. The assemblymen halted and began to remonstrate with the Sons of Liberty, who treated them with as scant respect as they had treated the governor the day before, telling these lawmakers that they had better go along to the assembly ''where they might possibly be wanted.'' As there was nothing to be done, the assemblymen took the hint and were accompanied to Hartford by Ingersoll's companions, Major Elihu Hall and the tavern keeper. The latter carried a message at the stamp master's request to the governor and assembly.

[1] Ingersoll, of course, was in Connecticut at the time, waiting for the mast ship which was to convey his white pine masts to England.

Ingersoll now made other fruitless proposals. The committee then informed him that he must bring the matter to a conclusion, threatening to carry him to Windham as a prisoner. In reply, the stamp distributor expressed his willingness to go. As this was not what they wanted, they resorted to other tactics. He was warned to keep away from the front window, as the sight of him enraged the people; now and again the populace would even burst into the tavern room in great numbers, "look pretty fierce" at him, and upon the desire of the committee withdraw. This sort of thing went on for three hours. The committee then frankly informed Ingersoll that certain of their sympathizers in the general assembly had told them that the matter must be concluded before the assembly could take any action; they accused him of artifice and of wheedling so as to get the assembly ensnared. At that stage of the discussion, Major Durkee entered the room and with much concern told him that he was unable longer to keep the people from him, and that, if they once began, he could not promise where they would end. It was high time to submit, and Ingersoll, thereupon, went to the front window and made known to the crowd below that he would comply with their desires and would sign whatever paper was drawn up. He then set to work and drafted a statement regarding his resignation, but this was rejected in favor of one prepared by the committee, which, when completed, Ingersoll signed.[1] He was then informed that the people insisted on his swearing never to execute the duties connected with the office. This Ingersoll peremptorily refused to submit to on the ground that it would be a profanation of an oath and, before the

[1] The resignation declaration reads as follows:

"I do hereby promise that I never will receive any stamped Paper which may arrive from Europe in Consequence of an Act lately passed in the Parliament of Great Britain; nor officiate as Stamp Master or Distributor

people could come to a decision in the matter, he left the tavern and entered the street in the midst of them. Mounting a chair, removing his hat and beckoning silence, Ingersoll then read the signed declaration and after- wards addressed them in a short speech in which he told them that in some measure he could excuse them, for he believed they were actuated by a real, though, he feared, a misguided zeal for the good of their country. He added that he wished the transactions of that day might prove happy for the colony, though he confessed that he very much feared the contrary. Then, upon being requested, he gave "Liberty and Property, with three cheers," throwing his hat into the air in the conventional man- ner,—all of which was greeted with loud huzzas; many now crowded about the chair to grasp the hand of the ex-distributor of stamps and to tell him that he was re- stored to their friendship. These protestations were cemented at a dinner in a near-by house.

Meanwhile, the general assembly had been notified of the riotous proceedings at Wethersfield. A discussion at once took place as to the best policy to pursue under the circumstances. The lower house came to the conclusion that it would do more harm than good to send a force to the relief of the stamp distributor. At last it was decided that a group of influential men should go to Wethersfield and try the power of persuasion. This easy solution was accepted by the upper house and the delegation was about to set out when the news arrived that "the matter" had been amicably settled.

of Stamps within the Colony of Connecticut either directly or indirectly. And I do hereby notify to all the inhabitants of his Majesty's Colony of Connecticut (notwithstanding that the same office or trust has been com- mitted to me) not to apply to me ever after for any stamped Paper, hereby declaring that I do resign the said office and execute these presents of my own free will and accord without any equivocation or mental reservation." This is printed in the *Connecticut Gazette,* September 27, 1765.

But the incident was not ended. Ingersoll was informed, when he had dined, that the Sons of Liberty
would accompany him to Hartford in order to be present
when he read his declaration before the general assembly. By this time, it would appear that the Norwich and
New London bands had joined the Windham-Hartford
band at Wethersfield, for the number of horsemen
which started for Hartford was estimated at about a
thousand.[1] This journey seems to have been a good
deal of a frolic. The story has been handed down that
the ex-distributor of stamps, who was riding in advance
on a white horse, cleverly retorted, when asked how he
felt to find himself attended by such a retinue, "that he
had now a clearer idea than ever he had before conceived
of that passage in Revelations which described Death on
a pale horse and Hell following him."[2]

When the company reached Hartford, they boldly came
within some twenty yards of the state house,[3] where the
legislature was sitting, and thereupon dismounted. While
Ingersoll was escorted to a near-by tavern, the Sons of
Liberty, four abreast, in military formation and preceded
by the three resounding trumpets, brazenly marched
around the state house. This, it is presumed, had the
effect of clearing that building of its occupants. After
the march, a great semi-circle was formed about the
tavern and Ingersoll was then called upon to reread the
Wethersfield declaration, to cheer again for liberty and
property, and, according to the Rev. Samuel Peters, to
throw into the air not only his hat, but also his wig.[4]

[1] This estimate appeared in the Connecticut papers. In the *New York
Gazette* (September 26, 1765) the number is put at five hundred.

[2] David Humphrey, *Life of Israel Putnam*, p. 94.

[3] The old state house was a wooden structure built in 1720, on the
second floor of which were the rooms for the assembly. Its site is in front
of the second or Bulfinch state house, which is still standing.

[4] Rev. Samuel Peters, *History of Connecticut*, p. 233.

The Sons of Liberty had now fulfilled their mission. They therefore turned their backs upon Hartford and took the road to the eastern counties. At Windham they spent an evening of great hilarity. A fire was kindled on the village green and the boisterous crowd could not refrain from burning again the hapless Ingersoll in effigy.[1]

After quiet had been restored in Hartford, and the sitting of the assembly resumed, Jared Ingersoll appeared before the united membership of both houses and, in an address of some length, made clear the history of his relations to the passing and enforcement of the Stamp Act. Ingersoll was, of course, a powerful speaker and his record was clear; moreover, he was heartily supported by Governor Fitch. Probably by reason of the address the assembly was brought into such an attitude of mind that it was disposed to take cognizance of the riotous actions of the Sons of Liberty, which, indeed, had put the loyalty of the colonial government in a bad light. It seems that, as a body, the deputies favored an opposition to the Stamp Act along lines that were strictly constitutional and, as men of property, were not a little concerned with these lawless manifestations within the colonies. As a result of this reaction, the general assembly, cautiously waiting until the eastern bands had dispersed, repudiated the recent coercive act of the populace and authorized the governor to issue a "proclamation" calling upon the officers, civil and military, to suppress all riotous proceedings, which he proceeded to do.[2] This placed Ingersoll in such a predicament that, viewing things from his legal standpoint, he felt obliged to with-

[1] An account of this is given in the *Windham Bicentennial Publications* (1893).

[2] This will be found in the *Connecticut Gazette*, September 27, 1765; see also the *Connecticut Courant*, September 21, 1765.

draw his resignation extorted by force, justifying himself upon the ground that his bond, under the circumstances, would be forfeited.[1]

The special session of the general assembly had been called to decide whether the colony was to be represented at the approaching Stamp Act congress. While Eliphalet Dyer, William Samuel Johnson, and David Rowland were appointed commissioners to the congress, the conservative element in the assembly was so far in control that these commissioners were not allowed in any manner to bind the colony. "In your proceedings, you are to take care that you form no such juncture with the other Commissioners as will subject you to the major vote of the Commissioners present." The Connecticut delegation, therefore, was unable to sign the petition to the crown adopted by the congress. The general assembly, however, drew up a memorial in which it endorsed the principles laid down in the petition.[2]

Although Ingersoll was now allowed to remain in New Haven without being subjected to physical violence, it may be surmised that this ordinarily genial man was far from happy. He seems to have been oppressed with a sense of isolation. A letter which he wrote to his friend, William Livingston of New York, at this period, shows his state of mind. "It is much if you dont by this time paint me out in imagination as a kind of fiend with a cloven foot and fiery-forked tongue—a Court Parasite and a Lover of the Stamp Act; and yet, the truth is that I love the

[1] *Ingersoll Stamp Act Corresp.*, p. 38.

[2] Fitch later on was obliged to defend himself against the charge that he purposely delayed the forwarding of the Connecticut memorial so that it did not reach England until after the repeal of the Stamp Act. His defense may be found in the *Connecticut Courant*, August 25, 1766. There is documentary evidence in the Trumbull Papers that Fitch sent to Jackson on November 13, 1765, the assembly's endorsement of the Stamp Act Congress petition. Thomas Fitch to Richard Jackson, Trumbull Papers.

Stamp Act about as little as you do and remonstrated to the late Minister against it, all in my power.—What! and Accept of the Office of Distributor of Stamps when you have done? impossible!'"[1]

The way in which he was regarded at New Haven and elsewhere in western Connecticut is probably reflected pretty faithfully in a communication to the *Gazette* by a local correspondent who wrote, September 27, that "Patriotic writers in the Boston and other News Papers still propagate their Abhorrence of a late Stamp-Master in this Town. They call him a Dictator, a Negrosoul, a voracious, mad Creature, a Hero and a G——n. They treat him and his Writings with the utmost Contempt and Detestation, it seems, chiefly owing to the Weakness of his Cause, and because he seem'd and still seems to think that a tame Obedience to the oppressive Stamp-Act would benefit this Country. . . . It ought to be mentioned that the intelligent Freemen of this Town, almost unanimously contemplate with Horror, the dreadful Consequences of being (internally) taxed by any other Power than that which is given to their own undoubted Representatives." If Ingersoll thought, the writer went on to say, that in accepting office he did the colony a service, he must now be sensible of the contrary. "If he did really abandon the Cause of his Country, and do any Things towards encouraging, wilfully, the late destructive Measures, I wish it may be proved. In the Mean Time, I think it cannot serve the Common Cause to treat him with scurrility; for there are a great many brave Hearts in this Colony that hate a stamp-man, but love Mr. Ingersoll.'"[2]

[1] Jared Ingersoll to William Livingston, October 1, 1765. *The Historical Magazine,* VI, 138-139. New Haven Col. Hist. Soc. *Papers,* IX ("Jared Ingersoll Papers"), 349.

[2] *Connecticut Gazette,* September 27, 1765.

The general assembly met for its regular fall session at New Haven, October 10. Governor Fitch was fast losing in popularity, but was still influential. Ezra Stiles declares that the first thing which "really lost him with the people" was his urging the assembly to prosecute as rioters the five hundred that coerced Ingersoll at Wethersfield. Stiles affirms that the people could have forgotten this had not Fitch, in the October session, held back when it came to passing resolves and "talked of the public spirit in the Language of Enemies, said that the Act must go down, that forty men, regulars, could guard the stamp papers and that the American conduct would bring violent measures from the home government & particularly the loss of the Charter."[1] Fitch, under the terms of the instructions he had received from the home government, was obliged to take an oath, before November 1, that he would uphold the Stamp Act. Had he refused to do so, he would have been liable to the loss of £1000 sterling and his office, and would have put the colony in danger.[2] The governor delayed taking any action until the very last. He appeared before the lower house of the assembly and sought its advice, but it was disinclined to commit itself. Therefore, in light of this undecided attitude on the part of the deputies, he felt constrained, on the last day of October, to call together the assistants in order that the oath should be administered in their presence. A long debate ensued among them, with the result that "finally the Gentlemen on the East side of the River refused and withdrew,"[3] declaring that in conscience they could not be present since they

---

[1] Ezra Stiles Papers.

[2] Jared Ingersoll to Thomas Whately, November 2, 1765, *Ingersoll Stamp Act Corresp.*, p. 48.

[3] Dr. Leverett Hubbard to Rev. Ezra Stiles, November 1, 1765, *Itineraries of Ezra Stiles*, pp. 512-513.

esteemed the oath unconstitutional, together with the provisional oath that the governor had taken. Elisha Sheldon, another assistant, "twisted and nestled about but finally staid in the Council Chamber."[1] The oath was administered by Assistants Silliman, Hamilton, Chester, and Hall. Some of the assistants from the eastern parts, according to Ingersoll, took the ground that they should not scruple as judges, which all assistants were, "to declare the act of Parliament, ipso facto void."[2] When the news spread that the oath had been administered, the four assistants, who were present at the time, together with the governor, were "threatened in the highest manner with political Death."[3]

On that very day a ludicrous incident took place. While the governor and the assistants were debating the question of the propriety of administering the oath, Ingersoll received a letter from Lieutenant Governor Colden of New York. In this, the latter desired him most earnestly to take care of the stamps which he had received and which were for distribution in Connecticut. Ingersoll thought it proper to inform the assembly of the situation; but, according to Dr. Leverett Hubbard, a prominent citizen of New Haven, when that august body heard that he was approaching, they shut the door and the

[1] *Itineraries of Ezra Stiles.*

[2] Jared Ingersoll to Thomas Whately, November 2, 1765, *Ingersoll Stamp Act Corresp.*, p. 46.

The governor was obliged to swear ''That he will do his utmost, that all, and every the Clauses contained in said Act, be punctually and Bona fide observed, according to the true Intent and Meaning thereof, so far as appertains to him as Governor.'' The oath is printed in a pamphlet which is entitled, *Some Reasons that Influenced the Governor to take, and the Councillors to administer the Oath, required by Act of Parliament, Commonly called the Stamp Act. Humbly submitted to the Consideration of the Publick.* MDCCLXVI, Hartford.

[3] Jared Ingersoll to Richard Jackson, November 3, 1765, *Ingersoll Stamp Act Corresp.*, pp. 40-41.

"East side of the Upper House run away which made Mr. Ingersol Laugh very Hartily."[1] The morning of November 1, 1765, the bells of New Haven, in the belfries of the State House, Center Church, and Yale College "continued tolling and mournfully saluting each other at suitable intervals and a fast was proclaimed in all the churches": this was the day when the Stamp Act was legally to take effect.[2] On this day, at New Haven, it is also related, a large number of the "lower sort of people—Captain Wolcott at the head"— made a coffin about two feet long, put a copy of the Stamp Act in it, and then buried the same, leaving the king's colors flying over the grave.[3] At Hartford, it is said that the Sons of Liberty not only buried the Stamp Act "but the governor also."[4] The following day Ingersoll wrote to Thomas Whately and made clear the formidable aspect of the opposition to

[1] Dr. Leverett Hubbard to Rev. Ezra Stiles, November 1, 1765, *Itineraries of Ezra Stiles*, pp. 512-513.

[2] *Connecticut Gazette*, November 1, 1765.

[3] Dr. Leverett Hubbard to Rev. Ezra Stiles, November 1, 1765, *Itineraries of Ezra Stiles*, p. 513.

[4] *Ibid.* The *Connecticut Gazette* of November 15, 1765, contains an account of the celebration held at Middletown on November 1. According to the writer, the bell at the meeting house was tolled all day with tongue muffled; minute guns were discharged, a pennant was hoisted "half-staff high before the town house," and all the vessels in the harbor had their flags at half-mast. In the evening the young people prepared three images, two of which were dressed "very grand"; one was seated in an armchair; the other was waiting upon him in a private conference, holding up a piece of parchment, with the words written upon it in large characters, "Lets Inslave America with Stamps." Behind these grandees was a figure representing "the D———." In large letters there was emblazoned the sentiment, "Confusion on Lord B——, G——, the D——l and Company. God bless King George, Pitt, Conway, Barre and Patriots to Liberty." The song of the evening, according to the *Gazette*, was far from puritanical, for it ran as follows:

"This is the D——l, is known full well,
He's come to Kick Lord B—— to he—."

the act. He suggested that in case parliament could be
brought to modify the measure, it would be advisable to
free all probate-testamentary matters from the tax, a
modification which would take away "the Cry of the
Widows and the Fatherless"; he also suggested that the
tax on the registry of deeds should be given up, as it would
amount to but little and yet be burdensome, for it was
customary to register them in books; and lastly, that
processes before single justices to the amount of forty
shillings, should be freed, as they generally were concerned with debt and would fall principally upon the
poor.[1] However disposed Whately might have been to
aid in the modification of the act, he was now without
influence or standing in the ministry, which had been
reorganized in July under the young Marquis of Rockingham. It is doubtful, moreover, if any such concessions would have reconciled Connecticut to the Stamp
Act. The assembly endorsed petitions of the Stamp Act
congress and the lower house, with only five dissenting
voices,[2] voted the act of parliament unprecedented and
unconstitutional and resolved to let the ensuing winter
pass without transacting any business requiring the use
of stamped paper.[3] "You will easily see," wrote Ingersoll to Richard Jackson, "by everything we say and do on
this side the water that our notions of our Constitution
and rights are such as I suspect you on your side will call
notions of independence."[4]

[1] Jared Ingersoll to Thomas Whately, November 2, 1765, *Ingersoll
Stamp Act Corresp.*, p. 41.

[2] The five out of a total of one hundred and thirty who voted against
the resolutions were Dr. Benjamin Gale, Thomas Fitch, Jr., Seth Wetmore,
Joseph Platt, and Henry Glover. *Itineraries of Ezra Stiles*, p. 221.

[3] Jared Ingersoll to the Commissioners of Stamps, November 2, 1765,
Ingersoll Stamp Act Corresp., p. 51.

[4] Jared Ingersoll to Richard Jackson, November 3, 1765, *ibid.*, p. 42.
Ezra Stiles recorded, in his notes, December 19, 1766, that those who advo-
cated the Stamp Act in Massachusetts were, among others, "militia offi-

cers for perh. 40 Reg^{ts} Episc^s''; in New Hampshire among others, ''Epis-copalians, 100 fam''; in Pennsylvania, ''Quakers & 1/3 Episc^s'' and in South Carolina, ''Scots Presb. Scots Episc^s.'' *Itineraries of Ezra Stiles,* pp. 227-228. For Connecticut, he mentions as advocates, ''Ingersoll, Har-rison, Chh. Clergy, Chew, Miller,'' and opposite this list he recorded the chief opponents, ''Major Durkee & 500, Devotion, Alex. Wolcott, Col. Trumble, Col. Huntington, G. D. Pitkin, Col. Pitkin, Putnam, Johnson, Dr. Johnson, Daggett, Hilhouse, Col. Saltonstal.'' Ezra Stiles Papers.

CHAPTER VII

THE SONS OF LIBERTY AND THE CONNECTI-
CUT GOVERNMENT

AFTER November 1, 1765, the date set for the Stamp Act
to go into effect, the government of Connecticut virtually
passed out of the hands of the legally constituted authorities; in place of these was substituted a species of
control in public affairs essentially revolutionary in character.[1] This was made possible by the general "uneasiness and resentment" aroused by the attitude of Governor Thomas Fitch and his supporters in the council
toward the enforcement of the Stamp Act. In attempting to explain to Thomas Whately the gravity of the situation, Jared Ingersoll affirmed that "no one dares, and
few in power are disposed to punish any violences that
are offered to the Authority of the Act—In short, all the
springs of Government are broken and nothing but
Anarchy and Confusion appear in Prospect."[2]   The

[1] The activities of the Sons of Liberty were not limited to opposing the
measures of parliament, for the following shows that they assumed general
police powers within the colony: "We hear the Sons of Liberty at New
London, have taken such methods with the Rogerenes, that they are prevented from disturbing the worshiping assemblies in that neighborhood on
Lord's days; a practice they have followed more or less for many years
past; and which all the laws made in that government, and executed in the
most judicious manner could not put a stop to." Boston correspondence
of March 27, in the *Connecticut Gazette*, April 5, 1766. The Ku Klux
Klan of Southern reconstruction days was also involved in other matters
than the suppression of negro political activities, which was the purpose of
its establishment.

[2] Jared Ingersoll to Thomas Whately, November 2, 1765, *Ingersoll Stamp
Act Corresp.*, pp. 46-47.

utter helplessness of the Connecticut governor to perform his constitutional functions is clearly shown in the
account given by a close friend of Israel Putnam of a
famous interview between Fitch and that doughty leader.
Putnam, it seems, went to the governor, and threatened
that, unless the stamp paper, which might be entrusted to
the latter's safekeeping, were locked in a room and the
key turned over to the Sons of Liberty, his house would
be "levelled with the dust in five minutes."[1]

On November 11 there was convened at Windham a
meeting of the Sons of Liberty, who, from this time on,
saw fit to refer to themselves as the "Respectable Populace of the Colony." At this gathering resolves were
voted and plans for future gatherings were made. The
significance of all this is such as to call for a careful
examination of the proceedings of the assemblage. In
turning to the resolutions, the first thing that attracts
attention is the statement, "We now, as the representatives of the people of the several towns to which we belong, recommend union, harmony and good Agreement in
and Among us." In other words, those who came together at Windham at this time did so in a representative capacity and we have here, it would appear, a Stamp
Act congress in miniature. There then followed in the
resolutions the announcement that "We hereby do declare and publish this, as our settled and deliberate purpose as a free people, that we will, by all due and effectual
means, prevent the use, distribution, or receiving of said
papers stamped according to said act, in any branch of
business or trade, either foreign or domestic by any member or members of this colony." However commendable
the impelling motive, this was, of course, nothing else
than a challenge thrown down to the regularly estab-

[1] David Humphreys, "Life of Israel Putnam," *Miscellaneous Works*,
pp. 285-286.

lished colonial authority when taken in connection with
the governor's oath to uphold the act. In the concluding
resolution, which presented a plan of organization, the
determination of the Sons of Liberty to be in thorough
control of every portion of the colony was set forth in
the following words: "We, further, recommend it to the
several towns in this colony that they meet by their representatives chosen for this purpose once in every month or
oftener, if need be, until we have intelligence whether
the united request of the united provinces on the Continent, at the Court of Great Britain be granted, and that
the method of meeting be for each County to Associate
and each immediately to send a Report and a copy of
their Conclusions to the other counties and, if thought
proper, at any time, the counties agreeing, to have a
general meeting."[1]

These resolutions were "signed in behalf of the respectable populace of this Colony," by "Philo Patria"
and were subsequently published in the *New London
Gazette,* which now became the official organ of the Connecticut Sons of Liberty. Before the meeting adjourned,
it was voted that in the county of New London there
would be a meeting at the court house in Norwich on
Tuesday, the nineteenth of November, at which time and

[1] An account of these proceedings will be found in the *Connecticut
Gazette,* December 6, 1765. The western section of the colony was very
cautious in following the example of the towns to the east. There is evidence to show that a systematic campaign was entered upon by the Sons
of Liberty during the late fall and winter of 1765 to excite the people
of the western communities. At Fairfield, on November 12, the Lebanon
performance of August 26 was reënacted with but minor changes. A large
number of the Sons of Liberty having assembled, placed an "image" in
a cart, which the common hangman drove through the town amidst cries
of "Liberty and Property." A gallows was erected; the effigy was set
on fire after suspension in the air; but, instead of being consumed to ashes
in the conventional manner, a charge of powder concealed within it suddenly blew the dummy "Limb from Limb." *Connecticut Gazette,* November 15, 1765.

place "deputies" from each town of this county were desired to meet and afterwards to publish the proceedings of the gathering in the *Gazette;* the deputies in Windham county were to meet on Tuesday the twenty-sixth of November, at the Windham court house; they also were to publish their proceedings in the *Gazette.* The Windham meeting of November 11 must have been limited almost entirely to "the representatives" from communities in these two eastern counties, in light of the fact that no definite steps were then taken to attempt to organize the western counties. There is further indication of the inability of the Sons of Liberty up to that time to swing the western section of the colony into line with their purposes; for, appended to the published report of the gathering, was a statement to the effect that the inhabitants of any town in any county would be welcomed at either of the meetings "as they in all the counties in this colony have not yet commenced; but it is undoubted, that when the general principles of these proceedings are fully known the same measures will be adhered to through the whole colony and there will be a connection and correspondence between the meetings of the several counties and their constituents."[1] Only grad-

[1] *Connecticut Gazette.*   Eastern Connecticut earned the reputation of being more radical than western Connecticut. The following reasons for this may be suggested: (1) The old controversy regarding the Winthrop appeal against the Intestacy Law had created a spirit of opposition to the home government, especially in that region where the Winthrop lands lay.   (2) More important still, there was the pending Mohegan appeal involving the title to eight hundred square miles of land and the rights of no less than six hundred families within and about Windham and New London counties. (3) Largely by reason of geographical factors, eastern Connecticut had a degree of solidarity lacking in western Connecticut with its isolated communities.   As a result, in the former, the people had learned to follow leaders in seeking to get things accomplished; it now happened that these leaders were radical.   See *The Present State of the Colony of Connecticut* (1755), p. 19.   (4) Eastern Connecticut was under the influence of Massachusetts and Rhode Island culture and politics just as it was commercially

ually were the people living in the remaining counties drawn into the movement, and from beginning to end it was those living in "the eastern parts" who formed the dominating and aggressive element.

For months, following the first of November, no courts of justice sat in Connecticut except for criminal matters, since, according to the law, no civil case could be settled in court without the use of stamps. Naturally, the man, symbolizing in his empty office the obnoxious legislation, did not escape abuse. Writing to his friend, William Samuel Johnson, at this period, Ingersoll declared that mankind seemed to think it had the right not only to shoot at him with the arrow that flies by day but to assassinate him in the dark.[1] His every act was watched with suspicion and he suspected that his mail was tampered with,[2] although this was not true. It was ascertained that he

bound up with these colonies, while western Connecticut had shown itself receptive to Anglicanism and to other conservative tendencies by reason of its contact with New York.

[1] Jared Ingersoll to William Samuel Johnson, December 2, 1765, Johnson Papers.

[2] Ingersoll sent certain letters to New York in the special care of one John Bay. The latter stopped, on his journey, at the home of John Chandler of Stratford, and soon afterwards reports began to spread that these letters contained special information to be transmitted to England. On hearing the reports Ingersoll naturally supposed that his letters had been tampered with, and in a letter to William Samuel Johnson of Stratford, accused Chandler of breaking the seals of the particular letters that Bay was carrying. He also wrote to Chandler in a threatening tone, claiming that it was he who had carried information to Colonel Putnam, leader of the Sons of Liberty. In a letter written December 15, Chandler denied these charges and informed Ingersoll that one of his reputed friends had gone to Colonel Putnam with the complaint. Ingersoll was not satisfied and wrote to his agent, Richard Ray of New York, with whom John Bay had left the letters, accusing him of meddling with them, instead of forwarding them immediately to England. To prove his innocence Ray returned the letters. When Ingersoll found the seals untouched he realized, of course, that all his suspicions had been unfounded. Jared Ingersoll to William Samuel Johnson, December 2, 1765; Richard Ray to Jared Ingersoll, December 12, 1765; John Chandler to Jared Ingersoll, December 15,

was carrying on a correspondence with England and the report spread in this connection that among other things he had advised the British government to take away the admiralty courts and to alter in one or two respects the Stamp Act, by way of concession, after which it should be "crammed down."[1] As a result, Colonel Israel Putnam of Pomfret, acting as head of the Connecticut Sons of Liberty, called for a gathering at Windham late in November. Evidently between three and four thousand men answered the summons.[2] Perhaps by reason of the governor's proclamation no effort was made to go in force against Ingersoll as was previously done; instead, the much more rational plan was followed of sending a committee of three of the leaders, Captains Hugh Ledlie, Aaron Cleaveland, and Asel Fitch, to wait upon the stamp master for the purpose of demanding an explanation regarding the rumors.[3] The committee came to New Haven, and, in its meeting with Ingersoll, informed him that it had with considerable difficulty obtained leave to give him a chance of clearing up the charges.[4] The latter, while admitting that he had written letters to England, not only denied the accusations that he had been acting unpatriotically but, feeling that the fullest possible publicity would only vindicate him, allowed the committee to read copies of the letters he had sent abroad, as well as the letters he had received. The men were friendly, behaved with candor, and declared themselves satisfied with

1765, New Haven Col. Hist. Soc. *Papers*, IX ("Jared Ingersoll Papers"), 361-367.

[1] *Ingersoll Stamp Act Corresp.*, p. 1.

[2] In writing to William Samuel Johnson at this period, Ingersoll referred to the "Deputation of a Comte. from a Body of People Consisting of not less than three or four thousd. men to come to me" to demand a look at the letters. Jared Ingersoll to William Samuel Johnson, December 2, 1765, Johnson Papers.

[3] *Ibid.*

[4] *Ingersoll Stamp Act Corresp.*, p. 1.

what Ingersoll had written.[1] They, however, asked permission to take the entire correspondence back to Windham, which was granted. There, at a later meeting of
the Sons of Liberty, the letters were repeatedly read.
Unfortunately for Ingersoll, some of the statements, after
being twisted and distorted, were printed in the *New London Gazette*.[2] This had the effect of inflaming further

[1] Jared Ingersoll to William Samuel Johnson, December 2, 1765, Johnson Papers.

[2] A New London correspondent claimed that Ingersoll delivered up the
letters with tears, *Connecticut Gazette*, December 27, 1765. Ingersoll wrote
that these letters were made known to many thousands and that there were
"certain pretended Extracts taken upon Memory . . . so different from the
true meaning of the original Letters themselves, that I found myself under
the Necessity of promising the Publick, that as soon as I should recover
the Letters, I would publish the whole." Upon the advice of one of the
leaders in the popular movement, he delayed doing this until June, 1766.
Ingersoll Stamp Act Corresp., pp. i and ii.

General Silliman, writing to Ingersoll from Fairfield, on March 1, 1766,
shed light upon the cause of the reluctance of the radicals to have the
correspondence published at any early date. In urging an early publication of the letters he said that "it seems not right that a small number of
zealous People in the Colony should have them as long as they please and
publish such parts of them as they think proper with their own Comments
on them, and that a full Publication of them should be suppressed by means
of those very People or rather only one of their number. Now pray, S[r].,
what is the Language of this their Conduct? is it not this? that they know
they have published such things of your Letters, that their own Conscience
tell them your Letters will, when published, shew them to have no other
real Foundation than Malevolence? if this is a Cause of their desireing a
Suppression of them, I think it is & ought to be the strongest Reason for
publishing them." Gold Selleck Silliman to Jared Ingersoll, March 1, 1766,
New Haven Col. Hist. Soc. *Papers*, IX ("Jared Ingersoll Papers"), 379-
380.

"I have one piece of news from the East," wrote Roger Sherman,
"which a little surprises me, that is, the publication of some exceptionable
passages extracted from Mr. Ingersoll's letters after all the pains taken
by the Sons of Liberty to prevent them being sent home to England."
Roger Sherman to Matthew Griswold, January 11, 1766, printed by L. H.
Boutell in his *Life of Roger Sherman*, p. 52. Joseph Chew, writing from
New London to Benjamin Franklin, after speaking of the increased confusion of the times, declared that Ingersoll was so far intimidated as to
give up his letters, public and private. Chew confessed that he himself

the public mind against him and he was compelled to promise not to write anything in the future to England without express permission of those in authority among the Sons of Liberty.[1]

Jared Ingersoll, however, was not the only one to be visited at this time. Chauncey Whittelsey, writing from New Haven, the latter part of December, to Ezra Stiles, said: "Political affairs with us are still unsettled. Mr. Ingersoll has been visitted by committee after com^tee from the Eastern uneasy part of the colony and they have the Assurance (or may I not say, Impudence) to go and catechise Mr. Silliman and even the Govern^r. I am much concerned about the state and issue of public affairs, especially on Acc^t the Vileness committed among ourselves; but I hope for Light to arise out of darkness."[2] How estranged Governor Fitch was from this rebellious attitude of mind within the colony, is revealed by a letter written by him at this period to Charles Lowndes, secretary to the Treasury Board, in reply to circular instructions which that board had sent to the colonial governors in September, and which had to do with the enforcement of the Stamp Act: "In answer I must request you to acquaint their Lordships that at present there is no one

"disapproved in the most modest manner of the Stamp Act," and was looked upon with disfavor by the advocates of extreme methods. *Calendar of Franklin Papers* (Hays), I, 54.

[1] His declaration was printed in the *Connecticut Gazette*, January 10, 1766. "I am glad these letters were recalled and that Mr. Ingersoll was free to retract all those passages which were thought to be of disservice to the government and to agree for the future not to write home anything but what should be inspected and approved by persons that the government could confide in; but by means of the publication of those passages in the newspapers they will likely arrive in England near as soon as if the original letters had been sent and perhaps will not appear in more favorable coat of light." Roger Sherman to Matthew Griswold, January 11, 1766. L. H. Boutell, *Roger Sherman*, p. 53.

[2] Chauncey Whittelsey to Ezra Stiles, December 24, 1765, *Itineraries of Ezra Stiles*, pp. 588-589.

exercising that office within the colony. The Person who was appointed to that office and gave security for it hath publicly declared his Resignation of his office and that he will not officiate therein. . . . If the Distributor had Received and Undertaken to Distribute the Stamps and had accordingly executed that office, I should have carefully attended to the Practice under the Act and in Every Particular endeavored to Discharge the Duty which appertains to me agreeable to the Intentions of the Act of Parliament, and this I shall endeavor whenever there shall be opportunity and occasion for it.'"[1]

How far from unanimous was the dislike and suspicion manifested against Ingersoll, during this period, is evidenced by a letter which he wrote to Thomas Whately. He was not only able to declare that ''the governor is my fast Friend, as I am his, and can only wish he had that countenance and Approbation which his Conduct and Behaviour upon all occasions well deserves,'' but could assert that his friends in Connecticut were those that Whately could consider ''the better people of the colony.''[2] His philosophical attitude of mind is better brought out in a letter to Richard Jackson, the Connecti-

[1] Governor Thomas Fitch to Secretary Charles Lowndes, December 24, 1765, Trumbull Papers, II, 71. Fitch, in this letter, sees fit, for very obvious reasons, to ignore the fact that after he had taken the oath to uphold the Stamp Act in Connecticut, Ingersoll had felt compelled to recall his resignation. Each of these men was not only sympathetically inclined toward the home government but also was a shrewd lawyer who took every step with great regard for legal consequences. Both were liable to forfeit large sums of money if convicted of neglect of duty.

[2] Jared Ingersoll to Thomas Whately, November 2, 1765, *Ingersoll Stamp Act Corresp.*, p. 48. In a footnote prepared at the time of the publication of the letters written and received by him during this period, Ingersoll explained the meaning of the latter passage to be, ''those who are opposed to violence and disposed to pay more deference to Parliament.'' *Ibid.* The student, however, must draw his conclusions irrespective of this formal explanation as to what Ingersoll implied in his letter to Whately.

cut agent in London, to whom he wrote from a lofty view: "I hope you will be the Colony's friend whatever some people may think of me. . . . Whatever errors I have committed in public life, I have always loved my country. . . . Whatever usage, I have received from my country, it shall never make me break with her. . . . I have received much undeserved favor and good at the hands of my country and shall I not bear with a little abuse, especially, upon so irritating an occasion as the Stamp Act.'"[1]

The Connecticut general assembly, as has been stated, voted, at its October session, that no business requiring the use of stamps should be transacted in the colony during the following winter. This was a legitimate and constitutional method of protest against the actions of the home government. The Sons of Liberty of eastern Connecticut, however, had gone so far that they were disposed to ignore not only the laws of parliament but also the measures of their own colonial assembly.

At "a large Assembly of the respectable Populace" at New London, December 10, 1765, resolutions were passed to the following effect:

"That every officer in the Colony duly execute the Trust reposed in him, agreeable to the true Spirit of the English Constitution, and the Laws of this Colony.

"That every Officer neglecting the Exercise of his Office may justly expect the Resentment of the People, and those who proceed may depend on their Protection.

"It is presumed that no Person will publicly, in the Pulpit, or otherwise, inculcate the Doctrine of passive Obedience, or any other Doctrine tending to quiet the

[1] Jared Ingersoll to Richard Jackson, December 19, 1765, *Ingersoll Stamp Act Corresp.*, p. 44. Ingersoll did not lay claim to the original composition of this extract, although fully sympathizing with its point of view.

Minds of the People, in a tame Submission to any unjust Propositions.'"[1]

This program comprehended, of course, not only the repudiation of the authoritative action of the general assembly, but the open violation of the Stamp Act as well, since the colony was still provided with a stamp distributor and could readily obtain a supply of stamps. The people of Connecticut, as a whole, were not as yet prepared for any such advanced step as this.

The next important gathering of the Sons of Liberty occurred at Pomfret, on Christmas Day. The resolutions which were there adopted were even more extraordinary than those of the New London meeting. After affirming their loyalty to the king and stating that they would "bear the highest Indignation to any that shall take Advantage of our present situation to oppose the lawful Authority of this colony, to obstruct . . . justice, or to injure any man in Person or Property," they went on to proclaim "that God and Nature brought us into the World Freemen, and by solemn Charter Compact and Agreement we came into the English Constitutions." They then asserted "that we have ever unmolestedly enjoyed (except some grievous Acts of Trade, etc.) our just Rights and Privileges, as the true born Sons of Liberty, until the oppressive and detestable Stamp Act was deeply formed and fatally levelled at the very Root and Foundation of our dearest Rights and enjoyments in Life, that's worth living for," and that "all those who were accessory in framing said Act are unfriendly to the Constitution." Then they began formal indictment of Jared Ingersoll.

"That, whereas, our stamp master was appointed Agent for this Colony . . . nevertheless he returned the executioner of those Evils he was sent to defend us from, And, notwithstanding his solemn Resignation . . . still

[1] *Connecticut Gazette,* December 27, 1765.

obstinately Persists to plot the ruin and total overthrow of his native Country by all the ways and means his Malice and Craft suggests or his unbridled Audacity can attempt. And thereby has . . . forfeited all privileges in and protection from the same; is no longer to be believed, his Friendship no more to be trusted, nor his malignant Designs any longer to be endured; and that assuredly, unless he instantly desist plotting our ruin, writing anything prejudicial to the Government, or even relative to the same, he shall forthwith feel the weight of his Injured Country's righteous indignation and know by sad Experience all the Horrors of falling a defenceless Prey into the Hands of a free and enraged Populace. As to the matters of charge . . . we challenge him to deny and vindicate himself against them in any of our public meetings.''

Moreover, they resolved: ''That Mr. Ingersoll's Letters be read publicly in Every County in the Colony in their public Meetings, if they see fit; That copies of Mr. Ingersoll's Letters be given out to some one Person in each County to be by him kept for the benefit and use of the People in the same.''

Then after announcing ''That we will most critically inspect every avenue by which the Stamp Papers may be introduced into the Colony,'' they recommended that the colony ''proceed in business as usual as our cessation of Business will be construed an implicit acknowledgment of the validity of the Stamp Act,'' and to that purpose they gave their endorsement of an article advocating such a step, written by a ''Friend of Liberty'' in Pennsylvania, which had been published in the last number of the *New London Gazette*.[1]

---

[1] *Boston Post-Boy and Advertiser*, January 6, 1766. These Pomfret resolves were sent to England by Governor Bernard, and subsequently went to the House of Lords. See *Lords' Journal*, XXXI, 300.

Dr. Benjamin Gale wrote to Ingersoll soon afterward regarding this meeting, which he called the "Babel Convention." He assured Ingersoll that he had done what he could, by sending "Messengers" to it, "to Mitigate their Rage and Folly. . . . A more wicked sceem, I think, never was on foot in this Colony to destroy us."[1] Even such a sturdy opponent of the Stamp Act as Roger Sherman became alarmed at the ominous character of the political activities in eastern Connecticut. His apprehensions were expressed in a very cautiously framed letter which he addressed to Matthew Griswold early in January. Sherman said that there were taking place "some things which appear to me a little Extraordinary and which I fear (if persisted in) may be prejudicial to the interests of the Colony—more especially the late practice of great numbers of people Assembling and assuming a Kind of legislative authority, passing and publishing resolves, etc." Then with manifest deep anxiety, he asked, "Will not the frequent Assembling such large bodies of people without any laws to regulate or govern their proceedings tend to weaken the authority of the government and . . . tend to such disorders and confusions as will not be easily suppressed or reformed?"

In spite of the undoubted sympathy that many in the colony had for Ingersoll, it is not surprising that at last the strain of bearing so great a weight of odium and positive hatred became too great for even so determined a

[1] Dr. Benjamin Gale to Jared Ingersoll, January 13, 1766, New Haven Col. Hist. Soc. *Papers*, IX ("Jared Ingersoll Papers"), 372-373. What Gale had in mind in referring to the "wicked sceem" was of course the plan of the Sons of Liberty to defy openly the British government by the conducting of legal business while ignoring the distributor of stamps and the stamped parchments held at New York for Connecticut whenever she was ready to use them. It is interesting to note that in writing to Ezra Stiles in 1767 Gale declared that the Stamp Act had laid the foundations for an independent state for America. *Itineraries of Ezra Stiles*, p. 494.

man. Early in January he received two letters, both anonymous, but supposed to have been sent from "A Considerable Number of People in the Colony," which "threatened very high" in case he would not take an oath to give up the empty office.[1] No longer willing to risk his property, not to speak of his life and the safety of his family, and convinced that it was folly for one man, as it were, to attempt to stand out against so decided a public sentiment, he took an oath before a local justice of the peace never to exercise his stamp office, forwarded his resignation to the stamp commissioners in London,[2] and made public these facts in the columns of the *Gazette*.[3] In this manner, there was terminated a truly memorable struggle between Ingersoll and the Connecticut Sons of Liberty, which Alexander Johnston likened to the striking of flint against steel.[4]

At a meeting of the "respectable Populace," held at

[1] *Ingersoll Stamp Act Corresp.*, p. 59. "I hope," wrote Ingersoll, in a footnote to the printed letters, "that the authors of them whoever they were are convinced by this time that this step of theirs under all circumstances was rather too rash." *Ibid.*

[2] Jared Ingersoll to the Stamp Commissioners, January 10, 1766, *Ingersoll Stamp Act Corresp.*, pp. 3-9.

[3] *Connecticut Gazette*, January 10, 1766; *Connecticut Courant*, January 20, 1766. The renouncement was made and the oath taken January 8, 1766. He declared:

1. "I never was nor am I now desirous, or even willing, to hold or exercise the aforesaid Office, contrary to the Mind and Inclinations of the General Body of People in this Colony.

2. "I have for some Time been . . . persuaded that it is the general Opinion . . . of the People . . . that the Stamp Act is an Infringement of their Rights and dangerous to their Liberties; and therefore I am not willing nor will I, for that and other good and sufficient Reasons . . . exercise the said Office. . . .

"New Haven, January 8, 1766. Then personally appeared Jared Ingersoll Esq., and made Oath to the Truth of the foregoing Declaration by him subscribed. Danuel Lyman, Justice of the Peace." *Ibid.*

[4] Alexander Johnston, *Connecticut: A Study of a Commonwealth-Democracy*, p. 287.

Lyme, in New London County, on the second Tuesday of January, the reconciliation of the radicals with Ingersoll was confirmed by a resolution to the effect that ''tho' we had reason heretofore to distrust his veracity yet we do rely on his said oath.''[1] It was then voted that the papers and letters which Ingersoll had been compelled to deliver over should be returned after copies were made of the same. That the resignation of the Connecticut distributor, however, had not quieted the fears of the Sons of Liberty lest some attempt should be made to enforce the Stamp Act, is shown by a further resolve passed at this time.

''Whereas, it is believed that the Stamp Papers for this Colony are hovering about on our coast on board the *Cygnet* man-of-war stationed at this colony, it is resolved that the Sons of Liberty keep a vigilant watch and in any attempt to land the same, we engage our united assistance to take and secure them for his Majesty's use.''[2] Nevertheless, it is clear that the Sons of Liberty, after Ingersoll's oath of resignation, became slightly more temperate in their position. This is indicated by the following final resolution adopted at Lyme, which, while similar to the Pomfret resolution, shows a disposition to get results by petitioning, rather than through the defiance or coercion of the authorities within the colony. ''Whereas, the adjacent colonies proceed in business without regard to the Stamp Act, 'tis earnestly desired that the civil authority in this colony do follow their laudable example, as the delay of business will be construed an implicit acknowledgement of the validity of the Stamp Act and a

[1] *Connecticut Courant,* January 27, 1766.

[2] Regarding the rumor that the *Cygnet,* stationed in Connecticut waters, had on board the stamps for the colony, Ingersoll said, in a footnote to his published correspondence, that this was not true, ''Nor have any of those Papers ever, I believe, been in any Part of the Colony.'' *Ingersoll Stamp Act Corresp.,* p. 53.

practical contradiction of the principal arguments urged in our petitions at home for the repeal of the same, and for that purpose the eyes of all are on the Superior Court of this colony, to give the example to the Subordinate Authority.'"[1]

By January, western Connecticut, through persistent propaganda from the east, was also becoming "organized" in the popular cause. At Wallingford, in a meeting of the "inhabitants," on January 13, 1766, at which Elihu Hall, king's attorney for the county, acted as moderator, resolutions of a most unusual character were passed; in these the authority of the town meeting was actually made to transcend the authority of parliament; they read as follows:

"Whereas, it appears from antient Records and other Memorials of Incontestible Validity, that our Ancestors with a great Sum Purchased said Township, at their only Expence Planted, with great Peril possessed, and Defended the same, we are Born free (having never been in bondage to any) an Inheritance of Inestimable Value. Voted and Agreed that if any of the said Inhabitants, shall Introduce Use or Improve any Stampt Vellum Parchment or paper, for which tax or Tribute is or may be Demandable, such Person or Persons shall Incurr the Penaltie of 20s. to be recovered by the Select men of said Town for the Time being for the Use of the Poor of the said Town. This order to continue in force until the next meeting of said Inhabitants in Town Meeting.''[2]

There was also, during the evening of the thirteenth, a meeting at Wallingford "of a number of the true Sons of

[1] *Connecticut Courant,* January 27, 1766.

[2] C. H. S. Davis, *History of Wallingford,* p. 356; *Connecticut Gazette,* February 2, 1766. Compare also the petition sent by the first society of Wallingford to "the Inhabitants of the Society of Wells assembled in Society Meeting, Dec. 1st, Tuesday, A. D. 1766.'' Davis, as above.

Liberty.'' They were clearly ready for a rebellion, according to their recorded attitude. The resolutions which they passed rivaled anything that emanated from the eastern communities, and are as illuminating as those of the town meeting. These resolutions propounded:

''1. That the late Act of Parliament called the Stamp Act, is unconstitutional and intended to enslave the true subjects of America.

''2. That we will oppose the same to the last extremity, even to take the field.

''3. That we will meet at the Court House in New Haven on the third Tuesday of February next; And we desire all the Sons of Liberty in the County would meet then by themselves or representatives. There to consult what is best to be done in order to defend our liberties and properties and break up the stop to Public Affairs.'''¹

There is something significant in the fact that the general meeting for New Haven County was announced so far in advance. For it would argue that certain communities in the county had not, as yet, absorbed the ideas laid down in the Windham program of November 11, and, therefore, needed to be put through a preliminary course of instruction. What is still more significant is that the Wallingford resolves apparently were so coldly received in other portions of the county that no general meeting was ever held.² John Hubbard, who for years had been

¹ *Connecticut Gazette*, February 2, 1766. Apparently, it was not until March 6, 1766, that the movement got sufficient hold of the popular element at Stratford to lead to resolves on the part of the Sons of Liberty. It was, however, then asserted by them ''that although we are thus late in publishing, yet these have been our real sentiments ever since we saw the said pernicious Act and in the sincerest Manner return our most hearty Thanks to our Brethren in all Parts of America for the ready and laudable Zeal they on every Occasion have shewn.'' *Ibid.*, March 15, 1766.

² Ezra Stiles, in his ''Notes on the Stamp Act Occurrences,'' took great pains to record the leading facts, and especially the different meetings of

chosen a deputy for New Haven to the general assembly, wrote to Ezra Stiles in no uncertain manner regarding his attitude toward this outburst of radicalism. "The Stamp Act," he said, "has drawn a gloom over every Face, and sowered the Temper of not a few, and all that don't run the extravagant Length of a giddy and distracted Mob are looked upon as Enemies to their Country and Betrayers of its Liberties. Among other fine Devices to set People together by the ears a Man's religious Principles are made the Test, or shall I rather say the badge of his political Creed. An Arminian, and a Favourer of the Stamp Act signify the same Man; think then in what a Situation some of your friends are.'"[1] Indeed, there were to be found in New Haven County, at this time, even those who openly supported the Stamp Act.[2] Deacon Jonathan Mansfield had the courage to

the Sons of Liberty. He mentions the Wallingford meeting but has no record of one at New Haven. Neither was any mention made of a New Haven meeting in the local paper. Ezra Stiles Papers.

[1] *Itineraries of Ezra Stiles*, pp. 509-510. The letter was written January 2, 1766.

[2] The following item, published in the *Gazette*, shows the anxiety of some regarding this disposition to defend publicly the Stamp Act, and to oppose the plans of the Sons of Liberty.

"Mr. Printer. Since a curious Dissertation in Favour of the Stamp-Act, and against our Courts immediately proceeding in the Trial of Civil Causes, publicly appeared (and which had *so* exhausted the Subject) I did not imagine that any Body would think it needful to add upon that side of the question; and yet I saw no less than two Pieces in your last Paper, on the same subject, and to the same Purport, in Part at least." *Connecticut Gazette*, February 28, 1766.

A man living at Mount Carmel was accused by the grand jurors of fornication. A writ was issued against him which he at first refused to recognize on the grounds that it was illegal because it was not stamped. "He was soon convinced that the Stamp-Act did not include such Papers, and then confessed its Lawfulness and made no further Resistance." *Ibid.*, January 31, 1766.

"We hear that a person in a neighboring government lately refusing to pay a debt for which he was attached because the writ was not on stamped paper; the populace immediately upon hearing thereof assembled, and

insert the following defense of that measure in the local New Haven paper:

"Now concerning the Stamp Act, if it was well known and Considered by the Husbanman and Comon People they would approve of itt and not side with the Mob, it doth not touch theire Interist the seafaring business is Delt faeorly favorably with the Taxes Laid upon Atturnies and Corts Affares is high and by that means itt is likely we shall have feuer Lawers and les busines at Courts which will be a Publick Advantage the Tax runs high on Tavern Keepers and Retailes of Lickers and this may be a mens to lesser their number and prevent Intemperance which will be a great favour, the taxis upon Scollars in taking their Degree. Theire being so many scollars is thought to be a Disadvantag. . . . Conserning the Mobing partey in the Land they are Justly stiled Riators.'"[1]

In fact, it would appear that, at a town meeting, held at New Haven, February 3,[2] a battle royal took place be-

having the fellow before them, passed the three following votes: 1. 'That this man is not a Christian; 2. That he ought to be of some Religion. 3. Voted that he be a Jew. Whereupon, Resolved, That he be circumcised.' This resolution so terrified the poor creature that he begged forgiveness of his imprudence and promised to behave better for the future. He was permitted to make a confession of his faith; upon which the sentence was remitted, and he was dismissed." Boston intelligence of March 27, *ibid.,* April 5, 1766.

[1] The printer inserted the following comment as a preface to Mansfield's communication. "The following piece in Favour of the British-American Stamp Act is undoubtedly the genuine Production of a well-meaning old Gentleman, who paid the Printer handsomely for publishing it; and that he now does with particular Pleasure, because he is fully persuaded it is well-calculated to weaken the sinking Cause which the Deacon seriously attempts to strengthen—The Publick and the Writer will excuse the Printer for sending it abroad exactly as it came to Hand, because any ill-advised Alterations might exclude it from Number One, and render it less singular and forcible." *Connecticut Gazette,* February 14, 1766.

[2] The *Connecticut Gazette* of January 31, has a call for the meeting which is signed by a majority of the selectmen.

tween the conservatives and the radicals over the following resolutions submitted for approval or rejection:

"Taking into Consideration . . . that for several Months past there has been a total Suspension of the Execution of the Laws in Civil and Probate Matters in this Colony, the Courts, Magistrates, justices of the peace and other Officers in their respective Departments having (for some reason) wholly declined proceeding therein which Obstruction of Business has been attended with Considerable Inconveniences and if much longer continued ('tis apprehended) will involve the people in great difficulties prejudicial to their interest and be attended with very bad and dangerous Consequences.

"Therefore, voted, that the said respective Courts, Magistrates and Justices (particularly the Hon[ble] Superior Court by Way of Example to the others) be desired and they are thereby humbly requested to proceed in and transact the usual Business. . . . Agreeable to the Laws of this Colony.'"[1]

The opponents of the resolution attacked it from four angles. First, "they apprehended that the courts proceeding to do Business, at present, in opposition to the Stamp Act, was not consistent with the humble Petition of the Colonies to King and Parliament, for Relief under their present Grievances"; second, "that a Cessation of Law-Suits, for a while, would greatly conduce to People's working themselves out of Debt, and so be a public Benefit"; third, "that, lands will be greatly undersold, for want of a certain and indisputable title, by legal Convey-

[1] See the New Haven Town Records, IV, 489, for the original, which in some respects is less precise than the copy prepared by the town clerk for publication in the *Gazette*.

The *Gazette* of January 31 printed an extensive address to the inferior court of common pleas of Providence, Rhode Island, by an attorney of that court in which the latter urged the legality of resuming the civil business of the court without the use of stamps.

ance on Stampt Paper"; fourth, "that when Persons
come to feel themselves crowded and pinched by Executions, they will be exacting, apt to *squirm* in every possible Method, to be likely to object against the Legality of
the Process, that 'tis not on Stampt Paper, and so, in
Hopes of a temporary Relief will become Friends of the
Stamp Act which may tend to introduce the use of the
Paper.'"[1] These arguments, however, could not prevent
the passage of the resolutions; but out of the two hundred and seventy-four "voters" present, forty-eight arrayed themselves against the same.

In spite of this declaration of New Haven, coupled with
similar requests from other towns, the superior court
could not be brought to endorse a position having so
many elements of danger, especially for a colony which
so often had been threatened with the loss of its charter.[2] After holding a three days' session at New Haven
"for the trial of criminal causes only," the court adjourned on February 27, until the last Tuesday in
August.[3] Yet a correspondent to the *Connecticut Gazette,*

[1] *Connecticut Gazette,* February 14, 1766. Surprisingly enough, Ingersoll
not only participated in the town meeting but actually voted for the resolution, since the people had "thought best to risque the Consequences of a
non Submission & as the Emergencies of Govt absolutely require the Administration of Justice to and among the people." MS. in Emmet Collection
(New York Public Library). "Your Friends this way of the Steady thinking Sort," wrote Gold Selleck Silliman from western Connecticut in astonishment, " . . . are more at a loss to account for your being in your Town
Vote & being to all Appearance in Earnest to go on with Business than
anything in your Conduct before, because say they, Mr. Ingersoll knows
that such a measure would most certainly be a Cause of the Forfeiture of
the Charter, etc." New Haven Col. Hist. Soc. *Papers,* IX ("Jared Ingersoll Papers"), 380-381. Ingersoll may have sought to reëstablish himself
with the people.

[2] See the *Connecticut Gazette,* February 21 and March 15, 1766; *Itineraries of Ezra Stiles,* pp. 212, 213, 425 and 463.

[3] *Connecticut Gazette,* February 28, 1766. No stamps were required in
court proceedings involving criminal matters. According to the records of
the court a session was held earlier in February at Fairfield.

writing as early as December 30, declared "that the Custom House in New London was opened last week, and that vessels are cleared out there as usual without *Stamps*—and that the Justices and Lawyers in the County go on with Business in the old way."[1] While the New Haven custom house began granting clearances to vessels as early as the beginning of January,[2] the officials of the town and the county scrupulously refrained from carrying on any business that required the use of stamps.[3]

At a meeting of the county court, the second Tuesday of November, 1765, with Roger Newton as judge and John Hubbard, Thomas Darling, and Roger Sherman, justices of the quorum, it was voted that the court, without transacting any business, should adjourn to the third Tuesday of March, 1766.[4] At this adjourned meeting the court readjourned "without day,"[5] but reassembled the first Tuesday of April, when, after inflicting punishment

[1] *Connecticut Gazette,* January 17, 1766. "We have the Georgia papers to the 21st of November, by which we find that they had no stamped paper there, and that business went on as usual." *Ibid.* Some stamps, however, were sold in Georgia. See Professor Schlesinger's *The Colonial Merchants and the American Revolution, 1763-1776,* p. 75. "We hear some vessels from St Kitt's, Antigua, and Barbadoes cleared out there since the first of November, without stamps, which our Collector will not yet admit to enter. There hath been no attempt to seize them, neither do I think there will." Correspondence from South Carolina dated December 3, *Connecticut Gazette,* February 25, 1766.

[2] *Ibid.,* January 31, 1766.

[3] It is curious that Atwater should have written the following with the county court and probate court records at hand: "After the first day of November no Courts of Justice sat in New Haven for several months; but as spring approached, the inhabitants in town meeting signified their desire that the Courts, would sit as formerly for the administration of justice. The Courts accordingly resumed their functions not only before tidings arrived of the repeal, but before the repeal itself." Edward E. Atwater, *History of the City of New Haven,* p. 38.

[4] New Haven County Court Records, VI, 151, 152.

[5] *Ibid.*

upon nine people convicted of immorality,[1] again adjourned to the third Tuesday of June; and then by a series of adjournments held off the transaction of business, for reasons that are not clear, until the first Tuesday in July. The first civil action in the court came in its July session.[2] The court of probate for the district of New Haven met on the third Monday of November, 1765;[3] at this session Joshua Munson of Wallingford, executor of the estate of the late Caleb Munson, was allowed to add certain items to the inventory of the estate of the deceased and Ezra Ives of New Haven also was permitted to appear in order to petition that he be relieved of the guardianship of Samuel Hitchcock.[4] The next meeting of the court was the third Monday of February, when matters relating to the division of four different estates came before the court.[5] Nevertheless, it was apparent that there was little desire on the part of the people of this section to make efforts to proceed with probate matters; but one case for settlement came before the court at its session held the first Monday of April and this case also was the sole subject for consideration at the session of April 9,[6] while on April 14 there was but one application for the settlement of an estate. There was no meeting of the court then, until the third Monday

[1] Three of these cases involved married couples who were convicted of pre-marital relations.

[2] This involved a book debt between Sidney Breese of New York, plaintiff, and Ralph Isaacs of New Haven, defendant, for £100. Judgment was given in favor of the plaintiff. *Ibid.*

[3] The colony was divided into eighteen probate districts. John Whiting was judge of the court for the district of New Haven. *Conn. Col. Rec.,* XIV, 500, 503.

[4] New Haven Probate Court Records, X, 326, 327.

[5] *Ibid.,* X, 327-330. These estates were those of Ebenezer Smith of Milford, David Brooks of Wallingford, and John Bay and David Tuttle of New Haven.

[6] *Ibid.,* X, 330, 331.

of May. In the court records between these two latter dates the following comment was inserted:

"N. B. No Business having been done at this Court or any other Court, since the last day of October last that required Stamp'd Paper and having now the news that the Stamp Act was repealed by Parliament on the 18 day of March last—Business goes on again as formerly."[1]

An examination of the New Haven land records, which were kept by the town clerk, who also attested all deeds, shows that the last deed recorded in 1765 was on October 31, and that it was not until July 23, 1766, that the next transfer of real estate was recorded, involving the exchange by Joshua Chandler, of five and three-fourths acres for £80 lawful money, paid by Hezekiah Sabin.[2]

This repudiation of the demands of the Sons of Liberty represents a substantial victory of the conservative forces within the colony and especially within New Haven County. Of course this did not necessarily mean an endorsement of the policies of the British ministry, but rather a manifest determination on the part of those in control of affairs to protect themselves, as well as others, by confining their opposition to the Stamp Act to methods not inconsistent with the policy formulated by the general assembly the preceding November. In fact, the popular element seems to have been apprehensive lest the conservatives should be left in control of the government as the result of the approaching May election. For on March 25, a "General meeting of the Delegates of the Sons of Liberty, from a great majority of the Towns," was held at Hartford. Their proceedings have an extraordinary interest for the student of American

[1] New Haven Probate Court Records, X, 331.

[2] New Haven Land Records, XXVII, 159, 160. During the month of October and especially the last week of that month the town clerk was kept busy recording land deeds.

political institutions. In accordance with the desire of the New York Sons of Liberty, expressed through the agitator, Lamb, they adopted a declaration in favor of keeping up a friendly correspondence with the Sons of Liberty in the neighboring colonies ''for the purpose of perpetuating Union and Harmony so happily established and maintaining common Liberty.''[1] A committee of correspondence was thereupon established, consisting of Colonel Israel Putnam, Major John Durkee, Captain Hugh Ledlie, Thaddeus Burr, John Sturgis, Samuel Bradley, Jr., John Brooks, and LeGrand Cannon.[2] Yet, what is most noteworthy in connection with the proceedings is the fact that soon after the meeting was called to order and business of a general nature had been transacted, the delegates went into secret session, the spectators having been requested to withdraw. Upon a motion inquiring the purpose of this, the reply was made that ''as there was a Dissatisfaction in the Colony, it was proposed whether a Change in the 'Ministry,' as it was termed, might not be necessary among us.'' Those in charge then explained that they ''ment to collect the Minds of the People, for Unity, and by that Means be able to give the Freemen a Lead in the ensuing election, since, should they run upon different Men, the Persons desired might not be elected, by the Freemen.''[3]

[1] *Connecticut Courant*, March 3, 1766. C. L. Becker, *Political Parties in New York, 1760-1776*, p. 46.

[2] Putnam and Ledlie were from Windham County, Durkee from New London County, Burr, Sturgis, Bradley, and Brooks from Fairfield, and Cannon from Stratford. The clerk of the meeting was William Pitkin, Jr., of Hartford County.

[3] *Connecticut Courant*, March 31, 1766. For a statement regarding the peculiar method that Connecticut had adopted for the filling of the chief offices of the colony, see Chapter I; see also the letter of Benjamin Gale, written to Jared Ingersoll, February 8, 1766, warning the latter that it was the plan of the Sons of Liberty ''to unite in Men.'' New Haven Col. Hist. Soc. *Papers*, IX (''Jared Ingersoll Papers''), 374.

The idea of turning this meeting of delegates of the Sons of Liberty into a nominating convention was received with amazement by some, who were completely taken off their feet. A lively debate ensued. The opponents of this scheme urged that no such plan was comprehended in the public warning of the meeting, that, as delegates, they were not properly instructed to proceed in this matter, and that such a procedure would be highly unconstitutional, since it would in an undue manner influence the minds of the freemen and be "fraught with the worst of Mischiefs, as it would tend to produce infinite Disquietude among the People, and lay a Foundation for perpetual Feuds and Animosities in every future Election; especially as a Step of this Kind would . . . be establishing a pernicious precedent, unknown to and unpracticed by the virtuous Founders and supporters of the Colony"; finally, it was represented that the meeting was "but a partial, or rather, no just Representation of the Freemen."

The promoters of the nominating convention plan, according to the *Connecticut Courant,* made no solid answer to these arguments. The meeting was adjourned until the next day. It was soon apparent that those in favor of the innovation were in control of the situation. Without renewing the discussion the delegates divided into groups according to counties, and went into deliberation. The contemporary account of the meeting says that as a result it was "agreed that most of the Freemen would— vote for —— to be Governor, and for —— to be Deputy Governor." The county of Litchfield dissented from this procedure by a vote of nine against four; the Hartford County delegation was also divided. After the question had been settled regarding the two leading offices within the gift of the people, the filling of the governor's council was then taken up for consideration. But the propo-

sal to nominate men for the council met with such opposition that it was finally deemed imprudent "to make too
great an Alteration in the Body Politick at once." From
beginning to end the gathering was apparently controlled by the men from the eastern section, for the "two
Eastern Counties were much more generally attended
than any other part of the government."[1]

The results of this nominating convention—doubtless
the first political party nominating convention held in
Connecticut—were all that the heartiest Son of Liberty
could desire. When the general assembly met at Hartford the second Thursday in May, and the votes of the
freemen were counted, it was found that William Pitkin
was chosen governor and Jonathan Trumbull, deputy
governor.[2]

Fortunately for the colonies, during the period of the
Stamp Act crisis the Rockingham ministry was weak and
half-hearted in all its efforts, for it had come into power
upon a program of opposition to the work of the previous
ministry.[3] The news of the tumultuous condition of
affairs in America served only to widen the breach between the different parliamentary factions. The Grenville group favored a strong policy in dealing with the
lawless manifestations in the colonies, and secured one
hundred and thirty-four votes as against two hundred
and seventy-four,[4] on Grenville's motion made December 17, "to express our just Resentment and Indignation
at the outrageous Tumults and Insurrections which have
been excited and carried on in North America, and at the
Resistance given, by open and rebellious Force, to the

[1] *Connecticut Courant*, March 31, 1766.

[2] *Conn. Col. Rec.*, XII, 453.

[3] For an excellent characterization of the Rockingham ministry, see
Alvord's *Mississippi Valley in British Politics*, I, 233-241.

[4] London correspondence in the *Connecticut Gazette*, May 3, 1766.

Execution of the Laws in that Part of His Majesty's Dominions,'' and ''to assure His Majesty that His faithful Commons . . . will firmly and effectually support His Majesty in all such Measures as shall be necessary for preserving and securing the legal Dependence of the colonies upon this their Mother Country; for enforcing their due Obedience to the Laws, for maintaining the Dignity of the Crown, and asserting the indubitable and fundamental Rights of the Legislature of Great Britain.'"[1]

Persistent rumors spread through London of the fitting out of ships of war and the gathering of soldiers for the purpose of upholding the authority of the government.[2] On March 3 Charles Antrobus, who was in charge of his majesty's sea forces stationed upon the coast of New England, wrote to Governor Fitch, from on board the *Maidstone,* in Rhode Island waters, that, according to the king's command, ''in case the exigency of affairs should make it necessary for His Excellency to procure the aid of the military in support of the Civil,'' he should apply to the commanders of the British land and sea forces respectively, as the occasion might require. Antrobus then went on to say: ''I am to acquaint you that His Majesty's Sea Forces stationed upon the Coasts of New England under my Command will at all times concur and assist you to the utmost of their power for the Support, Honor & Safety of Government and for the Preservation of Peace and good Order in His Majesty's Colony under your command, for which purpose I have dispatched an Order to Captain Durell, Commander of H. M. Frigate, the *Sygnet,* stationed at New London, but

[1] *The Commons Journal*, XXX, 437-438; *Parliamentary History of England*, XVI, 89-90.

[2] London correspondence of November 9, 1765, in the *Connecticut Gazette*, January 31, 1766.

should the exigency of affairs make a further aid necessary on Application to me at Rhode Island, I shall dis-
patch such additional Assistance as the nature of the
Affair may require and His Majesty's other services
shall admit.'"[1]

The ministry, however, was in a state of hopeless indecision. Much as it asserted its dislike of the Grenville
policies, it did not want to be convicted by the country
of timidity and weakness. Friends of the colonies emphasized the fact that, under the most favorable conditions, the duties provided for in the Stamp Act could not
be collected without the greatest hardship. "So great
is the scarcity of cash in the colonies," they declared,
"that we are assured taking all the Plantations together,
they could not raise three hundred thousand Pounds."[2]
A proposal, it was reported, was made that the sums provided for in the act should be paid in produce.[3] On January 11 Richard Jackson, the London agent of Connecticut, wrote to Governor Fitch, telling of his efforts to get
a repeal of the measure. "I am informed," he said, "by
the best Intelligence I can procure that the Stamp Act
will not be repealed; every other Relief may be, I think,
expected & even this Law will probably be reduced to
nothing more than a Proof of the Power of Parliament to
impose Taxes as well as make other Laws for America.
Something to assert this Power is judged necessary by
leading men in both Houses."[4] On January 17 the London merchants trading in America presented their famous petition asking for a repeal of the troublesome law;

[1] Charles Antrobus to Governor Thomas Fitch, March 3, 1766, Trumbull Papers.

[2] London correspondence of November 9, in the *Connecticut Gazette*,
January 13, 1766.

[3] *Ibid.*

[4] Richard Jackson to Governor Fitch, January 11, 1766, Trumbull
Papers.

their efforts were seconded by the English mechanics and resident Americans.[1] In March came the repeal and the Declaratory Act.[2] On the thirty-first Secretary Conway, in a circular letter sent from St. James to the colonial governors, recommended that they should exert themselves to make full and ample compensation to those who "from the Madness of the People have suffered for their Deference to Acts of the British Legislature." At the same time, he transmitted copies of the two acts.[3]

Early on the morning of the nineteenth of May an express arrived at New Haven "with the charming news that the obnoxious Stamp Act had been repealed by Parliament." The inhabitants were soon awakened with the banging of flintlocks throughout the town, bells rang madly, cannon volleyed; in the afternoon the people gathered in their churches where the clergy returned thanks for the blessing, after which the militia, under the command of Colonel Wooster, appeared on dress parade; in the evening the rejoicing was concluded with illumina-

[1] *Commons Journal*, XXX, 462; *Parliamentary History of England*, XVI, 138. Bristol and Glasgow sent in petitions to the House of Lords also.

Phineas Lyman to Governor Fitch, February 20, 1766. Lyman tells of writing forty pages on the subject of the repeal for the consideration of the ministry. He informed Fitch "how Mr. Harrison who lives with the Marquis of Rockingham, the First Lord of the Treasury, has great opportunity and improves it." Trumbull Papers. The Harrison referred to may have been Joseph Harrison, who had acted as collector of customs for the port of New Haven and who went to England in the fall of 1764. See the *Connecticut Courant*, October 29, 1764. In a letter dated April 12, 1766, the Commissioners of Customs informed Governor Fitch that they had issued a deputation to Peter Harrison to be collector of the revenues of customs at New Haven "in room of Joseph Harrison, who has resigned that employment." Trumbull Papers.

[2] The bill to repeal the Stamp Act was presented and read February 26, committed on the twenty-seventh, considered on the twenty-eighth and reported. On March 3 it passed the Commons; on the fourth it was agreed to by the Lords and on the eighteenth received the royal assent. *Commons Journal*, XXX, 609, 615, 620, 621.

[3] Secretary Conway to Governor Fitch, March 31, 1766, Trumbull Papers.

tions, bonfires, and dances—all, as the chronicler care-fully recorded, "without any remarkable indecency or disorder."[1] The celebration at Hartford, on the twenty-third, if more dramatic, was less happy in its termina-tion. According to the account left by Ezra Stiles, "the large Brick School house was blown up with twenty-four white persons, two molattos, & two negro Boys. There were 22 of the Persons aforesaid in the Chamber, two of which were blown out of the window."[2]

While these events, during the fall and winter of 1765 and the spring of 1766, were transpiring in Connecticut, one may ask what was happening to the parchments which the American Stamp Office had forwarded for the use of the people of that colony.

There were five separate consignments of stamps to Ingersoll. The first was sent the twenty-ninth of July, in care of Captain William Davis, commander of the *Edward;*[3] on August 5 Captain Joseph Haveland sailed in the *Polly,* with the second allotment; the third left Eng-land August 15, on the *Minerva,* Captain Thomas Tillet; the fourth, instead of being sent by way of New York, as was the case with the three preceding consignments, was placed on board the *John and Sukey,* Captain James Bruce, on September 18, and was carried to Boston; the fifth was entrusted to the care of Captain James Cham-bers, in charge of the *Waddel,* which cleared for New York October 22.[4] The reason why no further shipment

1 *Connecticut Gazette,* May 24, 1766.

2 Ezra Stiles Papers.

3 Treasury 1: 442, fo. 59. Jared Ingersoll to the Stamp Commissioners, January 4, 1766, *Ingersoll Stamp Act Corresp.,* p. 58. This letter also gives information regarding the sending of the subsequent consignments.

4 It does not appear that every captain was willing to accept the respon-sibility offered him of bringing the parchments to America. A London correspondent, writing to Connecticut, November 1, said: "Last Friday a Captain Refused to take on board his ship two cart loads of Stampt Paper for America, declaring he could not land them when he arrived there with-

of stamps was made to Connecticut probably lies in the fact that on October 22 the news reached London of the resignation of Ingersoll.[1]

On October 22 the *Edward* reached New York with ten packages of stamps, a part of which were intended for the province of New York. Previous to the arrival of the *Edward,* Ingersoll had written to Lieutenant Governor Colden not to forward any of the Connecticut stamps until conditions were more settled. Although Colden thought that it was best to have the consignment for that colony on board a man-of-war ready to proceed to New Haven, on receiving Ingersoll's request he lodged them in the fort,[2] together with the New York stamps. The Sons of Liberty at that port took such violent measures as not only to intimidate Colden but also to alarm the conservative elements.[3] The result was that the lieutenant governor, with the advice of General Gage, turned over the New York stamps to the city council, by whom they were lodged in the city hall. Whether the Connecticut stamps also were transferred to that place, left in the fort, or returned to the *Edward* is not clear.[4] Governor Moore arrived in New York in November,

out great Danger of having his Ship burnt.'' *Connecticut Courant,* January 13, 1766.

[1] ''Events in Connection with the Stamp Act.'' Ezra Stiles Papers.

[2] Jared Ingersoll to the Stamp Commissioners, November 2, 1765, *Ingersoll Stamp Act Corresp.,* p. 52. In the *Connecticut Gazette* of January 24 is found a large advertisement by John McCrackan who ''hath lately imported in the *Edward,* Capt. Davis from London . . . an assortment of European and East-India Goods suitable for the Season.''

[3] See Becker, *The History of Political Parties in the Province of New York, 1760-1776,* pp. 28 *et seq.*

[4] Professor Becker suggests that the Connecticut stamps were the three packages left on board the *Edward* after the seven packages had been transferred to the city hall, November 5. *Ibid.,* p. 34, note. On the other hand, Fitch, writing to Governor Moore regarding Ingersoll and the stamp paper, said, ''yet on his Resignation and Situation Judged he could not with truth and safety Receive them, therefore informed Lt. Gov. Colden thereof

superseding Colden. He at once proceeded to write to Governor Fitch requesting him to take charge of the Connecticut stamps. Fitch replied late in December: "I need not, I suppose, acquaint you that the gentleman appointed Distributor of Stamps for this Colony hath been, as well as those in the other governments, compelled to Resign and that he was the proper and only Person to Receive those papers."[1]

When the *Polly,* under Captáin Haveland, put in her appearance at New York, it was decided to leave the stamps on board. However, early in January, at midnight, a number of armed men boarded her and, having overawed the crew, secured the keys to the lockers, searched the vessel, and carried away to the shipyards ten bales of parchment designed for New York and Connecticut, and then made a patriotic bonfire of them.[2] Also, on the night of the eleventh, armed men boarded Captain Tillet's vessel, the *Minerva,* lying off Rotten Row, in the same harbor, and demanded the stamps which Tillet had brought for Connecticut. But this time they were disappointed; they were assured by those on the vessel that the stamps that same day had been deposited in Fort George.[3]

The Connecticut stamps, sent by way of New York, had been consigned to Theophylact Bache, a leading New

and desired him to permit those Papers to lye in the fort where they were lodged till further orders." Governor Fitch to Governor Moore, December 20, 1765, Trumbull Papers.

[1] *Ibid.* On January 3, Ingersoll wrote to Governor Moore requesting him to receive into the fort at New York all stamped paper consigned to him. Brit. Mus. Addit. MS., 22,679, fo. 8.

[2] "The Narration of Ebenezer Hazard" (Library of Congress MS., "Revolutionary Miscellany, The American Stamp Act," Vol. I); *New York Gazette,* January 13, 1766. It would appear that this took place on the evening of the tenth because of the transfer the next day of the stamps from the *Minerva* to the fort.

[3] *Connecticut Courant,* January 13, 1766.

York merchant, to be sent on by him to Connecticut. After these episodes, Bache wrote to Ingersoll requesting that no more stamps be entrusted to him.[1] When Captain Chambers of the *Waddel* arrived in New York, late in the winter, the Connecticut parchments which he carried were taken without delay to the fort;[2] there they reposed until the summer of 1766, when Governor Moore, at the request of Ingersoll, placed on a ship of war all of the stamped paper designed for Connecticut that had been deposited in this stronghold, and sent it back to England.[3]

[1] Jared Ingersoll to the Stamp Commissioners, March 5, 1766, *Ingersoll Stamp Act Corresp.*, p. 60. It does not appear that Bache at any time attempted to act as intermediary. In 1770 he was a member of the committee of inspection but sided with the conservative Friends of Liberty and Trade.

[2] *Ibid.* It seems that no attempt was made to land the Connecticut stamps sent by way of Boston on board the *John and Sukey*, Captain Bruce. The only reference to them made by Ingersoll is in a letter written on the fourth of January to the Commissioners of Stamps, in which he says that the parcel of stamps sent by Captain Bruce had not yet arrived. *Ibid.*, p. 58.

[3] Jared Ingersoll to Governor Sir Henry Moore, July 14, 1766. Brit. Mus. Addit. MS., 22,679, fo. 21. In the ''General Account of Duties'' arising on stamped vellum, etc., made December 23, 1774, by the comptroller general before the chancellor of the exchequer, it is stated that there was due from Jared Ingersoll, receiver of stamps for Connecticut, the sum of £1909 10s. 11d. This sum probably represents the value of the parchments which were taken from the *Polly* and burned. Audit Office, Declared Accounts, 2192: 207 (Andrews, *Guide*, II, 102).

CHAPTER VIII

A NEW HAVEN COUNTY JUSTICE OF THE PEACE. THE PASSING OF THE TOWNSHEND ACT

At its May session in 1765 the general assembly appointed Jared Ingersoll, together with thirty-three others, a justice of the peace in and for the county of New Haven, for the year ensuing.[1] This was done before the receipt of the news of his acceptance of the post of Connecticut stamp distributor. During the month of August he does not appear to have attended to this office. However, on September 16, just two days previous to starting on his memorable journey to Hartford, he issued a summons requiring the sheriff of New Haven County to bring one John Smith, who "had made an assault upon the body of Edward Allen, June 20, 1764," before the general assembly to show reason why the judgment of the superior court should not be set aside and a new trial awarded.[2]

The chief business of a Connecticut justice of the peace was to give judgment in civil cases involving such matters as debts of small amounts, etc., and to take cognizance of breaches of private conduct, in the interests of public morals and public order generally. He might do this upon his own initiative or upon information that was furnished to him, either by the grand jury of the county or by a constable. The less serious misdemeanors he

[1] *Conn. Col. Rec.*, XII, 346.
[2] Conn. Archives, Crimes and Misdemeanors, XV, 239.

was competent to determine definitively; in the case of grave offenses the parties were bound over on a recognizance to appear before the judge and justices of the quorum in the county court. An examination of the record book kept by Ingersoll while justice of the peace shows that when acting in this capacity he was chiefly occupied in drawing up acknowledgments of judgments for debt and with cases involving violations of the ancient ecclesiastical code of the colony.[1] The most common of these violations was neglect of public worship; fines of three shillings—which went to the town—and costs, amounting to six shillings, were levied against those with godless tendencies. The "profane swearer" was also constantly falling under Justice Ingersoll's censure; as may be suspected, the profane swearer was apt to be the chronic Sabbath breaker. The following entry in Ingersoll's record book shows the patriarchal character of his office:

"Joe Potter, fined March 21, for profane swearing, on March 24 was brought before Jared Ingersoll on charge of neglecting to attend public worship. Pleaded not guilty, urging for reasons of neglect a wound and lameness in one of his legs, which is judged sufficient reason by the Court."[2]

It often happened, of course, that these petty offenders were without means. When, therefore, the fines could not be collected, other penalties were applied. On one occasion, for example, Curtiss Clemens, "a transient person," was unable to pay the six shillings levied against him for profane swearing, and the eight shillings for drunkenness, plus the eleven shillings, the cost of prosecution; as a result, he was sentenced to sit in the public stocks "by the space of one hour for each of said

---

[1] The Ingersoll Record Books are in the Yale University archives.
[2] Jared Ingersoll Record Book, II, March 27, 1766.

crimes.'"[1]   However, offenders were not always given the option of paying a fine. Where questions of private morality were involved, the suspect was bound over to appear before the county court, as was shown in a previous chapter;[2] in cases of petty larceny, the guilty party was sent to the whipping post. Isaac Tomlinson, a free negro, charged before Ingersoll with stealing a pair of silver shoe buckles, even after making restoration, was mulcted £1 19s. 2d. for damages, 6s. 2d. for costs and 5s. for a fine, and was in addition given ten stripes on the naked body at the whipping post. Failing to pay these fines, he was then given four months' imprisonment.[3]

[1] Jared Ingersoll Record Book.

[2] See Chapter II of this study.

[3] Jared Ingersoll Record Book, II. While the sentence that Tomlinson received seems extraordinarily harsh to the sense of the present humanitarian age, it did not equal the punishment inflicted in 1768 upon Benjamin James of New Haven, who plead guilty to stealing from Ralph Isaacs, one of Ingersoll's friends, a number of miscellaneous articles including six half-shillings, two shirts, two pair of stockings, one glass bottle, forty ounces of ''cotton-wool,'' and ten ounces of whalebone. He was proceeded against by Ingersoll, as king's attorney, and was sentenced by the county court to be whipped on the naked body ten stripes and to pay Ralph Isaacs treble damages estimated at £82 17s. 6d., besides the cost of prosecution, amounting to £2 16s. 9d. Having no estate, the wretched James was assigned to Isaacs by the court for the space of ten years. The New Haven County Court Records, VII, 122. James pleaded guilty May 28, 1768. His servitude was to be dated from April 8. More barbarous than the above, however, was the punishment meted out by the superior court of the colony to James Haning, in 1767, who had been convicted of burglary. He was not only whipped fifteen stripes and had his right ear cut off but was also branded with the letter ''B'' on his forehead. Connecticut Journal, October 23, 1767. That little sentiment was allowed to enter into the legal proceedings of the pre-Revolutionary Connecticut authorities against those guilty of theft is also indicated by numerous other cases on record. For examples, see the case of John Wilson alias John Grant (New Haven County Court Records, VII, 197) and that of one Collins (Connecticut Gazette, February 28, 1766). In 1763 David Shister of East Haven and James Darly, a transient person, were found guilty of stealing merchandise from a shop; they were sentenced to be branded on the forehead. Each was to have an ear nailed to a post and then cut off, and each was to be whipped

It must not be supposed that Ingersoll, during the
years that he acted as a justice of the peace, gave his
entire time to that work. As will be noticed in the progress of this chapter and the following, he was engaged
in a variety of activities and especially was occupied in
taking care of the interests of numerous clients.[1] For

fifteen stripes and to pay £36.3.7. Records of the Connecticut Superior
Court, XIV, under date of February 22, 1763.

   Even these atrocious penalties, according to some, appeared to be too
mild, for in 1768 the *Connecticut Journal*, when referring to the crime of
burglary, complained about the ''lenitive law of this colony only punishing
for first and second offenses by whipping, cropping and branding.'' *Connecticut Journal*, September 9, 1768.

   [1] During the years that immediately followed the giving up of the stamp
mastership, Ingersoll was interested in many things besides his work as a
justice of the peace and king's attorney. His record books show that he
was engaged in numerous business transactions. On one occasion he wrote
to Andrew Oliver of Boston, who was acting in behalf of one Thompson,
owner of certain Guilford lands, offering £2000 for the same (Jared Ingersoll to Andrew Oliver, February 7, 1771. Ingersoll Papers). He was the
agent for Lord Stirling's settlement project embracing one hundred thousand acres east of the Penobscot River (Ingersoll Papers). In 1766 he
received from the crown an appointment on the New York-New Jersey
boundary commission, together with Benjamin Franklin, Peyton Randolph,
Andrew Oliver, and nine others (*Acts of the Privy Council, Col., 1745-1766*,
pp. 686-687; C. O. 5: 1101, fo. 61; New Jersey *Archives* (first series), IX,
XXVI; *New York Gazette*, October 9, 1769; *Connecticut Courant*, October
14, 1769). In 1767 Bartlett Brundidge of Danbury, guardian for
Daniel Ninham, Indian chief of the tribe of Wappinger Indians on the
Hudson, sought his legal aid in a complaint on behalf of the tribe laid before Governor Moore of New York, declaring in his letter that the Indian
commissioner, Sir William Johnson, had recommended him as ''a worthy
gentleman endowed with parts capable to act in an affair of so great
concern'' (Bartlett Brundidge to Jared Ingersoll, February 2, 1767, Ingersoll Papers).

   It is also of interest to note that in 1767 he was called upon to draw up
an indenture between one ''Bernard Lintot, Attorney for certain London
merchants,'' and Benedict Arnold, for the conveyance of the latter's sloop,
Sally, and her cargo, to the merchants, for the security and payment ''of
the one half of the demands of the said merchants of London against the
said Arnold being £850 12s. 8d.'' Ingersoll and Jonathan Mix of New
Haven acted as witnesses to this indenture, and according to the terms of
the same, it was left to Ingersoll to approve the security that Arnold was to

little as most Connecticut people appreciated Ingersoll in his attempted rôle as stamp master, they nevertheless still eagerly sought him whenever they felt in need of legal assistance of a high order—and could pay for it. So early as February, 1766, while still under the fire of the agitators, he became identified with a case which clearly shows some of the direct results flowing from the attempt on the part of the Sons of Liberty to override their legally constituted authority. This was the notorious Peter Boles incident.

Benedict Arnold, during this period, was not only the proprietor of an apothecary shop in New Haven but also had gone rather extensively into the business of trading with the West Indies as well as with Newfoundland. He exported a good many "large, genteel, fat horses," also pork, oats, and hay. Besides the products of the West Indies, he imported salt and cotton.[1] It seems apparent that he was accustomed to smuggle. For some unknown reason, Boles, who had been one of his sailors, determined to lodge information against him with the local customs official and in fact went to the customs house but did not find the collector in.[2] Arnold was apprised of his intention, chastised the man, and threatened him with

furnish "in case his trip is not sufficiently successful and he desires to make another." Arnold was to have "a reasonable time" to convert the cargo into cash, the length of time also to be decided by Ingersoll. A copy of this indenture, which was signed May 9, 1767, is in the Ingersoll Collection; see also a letter written by Lintot to Ingersoll, August 11, 1767, regarding the same transactions. New Haven Col. Hist. Soc. *Papers,* IX ("Jared Ingersoll Papers"), 412. In 1770 Ingersoll again seems to have been brought into Arnold's affairs in a legal capacity. January 3 he received a communication from David Landon, asking him to sue David Goodrich for £1000 damages for slander. "The like affair you have in hand, I understand with Mr. Arnold and Capt. Fobes" (Ingersoll Collection).

1 See the *Connecticut Gazette,* February 14, 1766.

2 Boles approached one of the tide waiters by name of Sanford and desired to know what share of forfeited goods would belong to an informer.

dire calamity should he persist in his design. Boles, according to the testimony, then left town as ordered, but, it would seem, thirsting to get even with his master, returned; whereupon he was immediately seized at one of the taverns and compelled to sign an oath to the effect that "being instigated by the Devil" he attempted to give information against Arnold for importing contraband goods, and he even acknowledged that he "Justly deserved a halter."[1]   Again, he was ordered to leave town; he failed, however, to do so and remained such a source of uneasiness to Arnold and his friends that, on January 29, they broke into a dwelling house where the hapless Boles was stopping, fell upon the man, stripped him of his clothing, dragged him to the whipping post on the green, and, having bound him to the same, in the presence of the spectators gave him forty lashes, "in a shocking, cruel and dangerous manner." He was then chased out of town.[2]

The conservative element in New Haven, which had been pretty thoroughly cowed for some time by the prevailing mob rule in the colony, now took alarm at the growing contempt of law and order. At a town meeting, held February 3, this element took control and passed the following resolution:

"Whereas, the growing disorder and violence and breaches of law in this town are become very threatening to the public peace and even dangerous to civil society and at which we are justly alarmed,

"Therefore, voted, that the informing officers and Civil Authority in this town be desired . . . to be espe-

As the waiter could not tell him, he would not make an information, but promised to return when the collector was in. *Ibid.*, February 21, 1766.

[1] *Ibid.*, February 14, 1766.

[2] See L. H. Boutell, *Life of Roger Sherman*, p. 44; also the *Connecticut Gazette*, February 14, 1766.

cially watchful and painful in bringing to proper punishment all such disorders, and we do hereby declare as we think it our duty so we will mutually assist one another and particularly the Civil Authority in the due execution of their office.'"[1]

But the aroused conservatives did not stop with words. The grand jurors made an investigation, filed a complaint with Roger Sherman, who, like Ingersoll, was a justice of the peace. Sherman issued a warrant for the arrest of the offenders, who were brought before him and bound over for trial.[2] As was stated, Ingersoll took an active part in the judicial proceeding, apparently in Arnold's behalf.[3] The unsettled condition of the community is shown by the fact that a mob, on the thirtieth of January, made "two certain Images or Figures habited with Cloathes" representing the two most aggressive of the grand jurymen, Tilley Blakeslee and John Wise, which "said Images or Figures did hang upon a gallows with a Rope by the Neck and the mob then burnt the same, and all in open view of the People thereby openly casting contempt upon . . . the good and wholesome Laws of the Colony.'"[4]

As for Benedict Arnold, this adventurous gentleman took the position publicly that he was being persecuted by his misguided neighbors for performing a patriotic act. In a protest published in the local paper he spoke

[1] New Haven Town Records, IV, pp. 489-490.

[2] L. H. Boutell, *Life of Roger Sherman*, p. 44.

[3] The entry in his record book reads as follows: "Benedict Arnold. 1766, Feb. To my fee Rex ag^t you & the sailors £7.5 putting a Rapalle affair." Jared Ingersoll Record Book, II, 89. See also the *Connecticut Gazette*, February 7, 1766. It would appear that Arnold engaged him as his attorney to file an appeal. In fact it seems, according to the information at hand, that Arnold was accustomed to employ Ingersoll. (See footnote, p. 233.)

[4] New Haven County Court Records, VI, 81.

rather scornfully of the law-abiding tendencies of New Haven. ''Is it good policy,'' he asked, ''or would so great a number of People in any trading Town on the Continent (New Haven excepted) vindicate, protect and caress an informer—a character, particularly at this alarming time, so justly odious to the Public?''[1]

Such an open statement placed the local customs house in a very bad light and its officials felt called upon to make a reply to Arnold. ''It might have been imagined,'' they declared, ''that private resentment had urged the man on to seek revenge by informing of trifling things had not Mr. Arnold's publication given reason to think differently. As he suggests, there is a beneficial illicit trade carried on, contrary to what we really imagined to be done, in any considerable degree. . . . We think ourselves in honor bound to acquaint the publick, that we require an oath of every master or other person having charge of a vessel, to the truth of his manifest at entry. . . . When any vessel enters from a foreign port with goods subject to duties, a waiter is sent on board to see that the cargo agrees with the manifest, to attend the unloading and see the weight and gauge of sugar and molasses.''[2]

How near to anarchy the radicals had plunged the colony in working up a spirit of resistance to the Stamp Act, is evident from an attempt made, on June 14, 1766, to terrify the judges of the county court, by Wallingford men, ''who having not the fear of God before their eyes and with intent to disturb the Peace and prevent the execution of the good and wholesome Laws of the Colony . . . made and subscribed a Certain Scandalous and menacing writing, and on the 17th day of June did

[1] *Connecticut Gazette,* February 7, 1766.

[2] This statement was signed by N. Whiting, Geo. Mills, and J. Fitch, *ibid.,* February 21, 1766.

cause the same to be forwarded and published in the County Court then setting.'"[1]

In fact, it was not until November of 1766 that the reaction was strong enough to give the conservative group the courage to take things in hand. Early in that month, James A. Hillhouse, who had succeeded Major Elihu Hall as king's attorney of the county,[2] arraigned eleven of these Wallingford men before the county court. The defendants pleaded not guilty; the case was then submitted to a jury, which also returned a verdict of not guilty; the court, not to be defeated, penalized them to the extent of £58 19s. 3d. as "cost of prosecution.'"[3] For some reason, upon this action, Hillhouse saw fit to withdraw from the not too comfortable responsibility of acting as county prosecutor. At the next meeting of the county court, held the second Tuesday of November, Jared Ingersoll was again back at his old post of king's attorney,[4] and his first act was to arraign the leading New Haven rioters who the preceding January had burned in effigy the grand jury men. One may imagine, by reason of his own late experiences, that he took a certain grim satisfaction in doing so. The case appears on

[1] New Haven County Court Records, VI, 180.

[2] See footnote, Chapter II, p. 51.

[3] These men were bound over upon a recognition of £1000 to appear at the court. New Haven County Court Records, VI, 180.

[4] How Ingersoll combined his duties as king's attorney with those pertaining to his justiceship is shown by the following document:

"To the Hon. County Court now sitting at New Haven.

"Jared Ingersoll, Attorney for our Lord the King for the County of New Haven presents to said court and informs against Jonathan Gilbert. April 1, 1758."

Endorsed "Information against Jonathan Gilbert by Jared Ingersoll."
Attached to this information is the following:

"In his Majesty's name you are hereby requested to make your appearance before the Superior Court. August 26, 1767. Jared Ingersoll, Justice of the Peace." Ingersoll Collection; New Haven County Court Records, VI, 181.

the records as "Our Sovereign Lord the King by Jared Ingersoll, Esq. his Attorney vs. Lyman Hitchcock, Robert Townsend, Samuel Center, Thomas Levoke, Stephen Bradly, Stephen Gorham and Caleb Ford." The defendants pleaded not guilty; the jury returned an equivocal verdict to the effect that Levoke and Ford were not guilty. The two were dismissed upon paying the cost of prosecution. At the January, 1767, session of the court, the five others pleaded guilty, and for some reason the court let them off with fines of but five shillings apiece and costs.[1]

This effort to restore to the county an orderly and legal procedure in the conduct of affairs is also illustrated by the case of Thomas Strong of Durham. On February 3, 1767, the grand jurors of the county made a presentment against him "for putting in more than one vote at a time for choosing Town officers, etc." Strong was bound over with a surety of £30 to appear before the county court. When the case came up for trial, Ingersoll prosecuted him and he was found guilty and was fined £30 plus £2 6s. 10d. as costs.[2] In 1768 the case was taken on appeal to the superior court under title of "John Whiting, Esq. vs. Thomas Strong, et al,"[3] with Ingersoll and Hillhouse representing the county.[4] Failing to secure proper settlement there, Whiting, who, as county treasurer, appeared in behalf of the county as plaintiff, petitioned the general assembly.[5]

While things were thus moving along smoothly enough for Jared Ingersoll,[6] the same could not be said for his

---

[1] New Haven County Court Records, VI, 242.

[2] *Ibid.*, VII, 68.

[3] Conn. Archives, Crimes and Misdemeanors, XV, 295-296.

[4] *Ibid.*

[5] *Ibid.*

[6] It is interesting to note that at a meeting of the Yale Corporation in 1766, two of the members, Elnathan Whitman and Solomon Williams,

friend, Augustus Johnston of Newport, who, unfortunately, had accepted the appointment of stamp distributor for Rhode Island. During the summer of 1767, this
gentleman wrote a letter to Ingersoll which was full of
discouragement. He complained that the rage of the
people of Rhode Island against him on account of this
acceptance still continued and he had become convinced
that it would never end. He therefore declared his intention of moving to England at the earliest possible
moment.[1]

In Connecticut, as has been noticed, the repeal of the
Stamp Act brought about a sharp reaction against the
anarchic tendencies of the Sons of Liberty.[2] There appeared to be a disposition, especially on the part of those
in authority, to show to the British ministry, under the
nominal leadership of the invalid Earl of Chatham, that
Connecticut had not been surrendered to the rule of the
mob but was loyal to the empire. For example, early in
January, 1767, General Gage, in charge of his majesty's

seemed agreeably disposed towards the election of Ingersoll to succeed
Thomas Clap, who retired from the presidency of the college at this period.
This, of course, testifies to the fact that Ingersoll, in spite of all the abuse
that had been heaped upon him, was not without friends and champions.
Itineraries of Ezra Stiles, p. 5.

[1] Augustus Johnston to Jared Ingersoll, August 13, 1767, New Haven
Col. Hist. Soc. *Papers,* IX (''Jared Ingersoll Papers''), 413. Johnston
continued to reside at Newport until his removal, in 1769, to Charleston,
South Carolina, where he was judge of the court of vice-admiralty for the
Southern District.

[2] In the election of 1767 ex-Governor Thomas Fitch secured 3481 votes
as against William Pitkin, who as the choice of the popular element received
4777 votes. The western part of the colony went for Fitch, but the minority
there, combining with the eastern radicals, returned Pitkin. ''After all our
paper War, Squibs, Curses, Rhimes, etc. I am not yet satisfied Govr Fitch
will be chose, however, he has a large Majority on the West side C———t
River. Even N Haven have done it,'' wrote Benjamin Gale to Ezra Stiles,
April 17, 1767. *Itineraries of Ezra Stiles,* p. 492. See also letter of Titus
Hosmer to Jared Ingersoll, written from Hartford, on April 14, 1767.
New Haven Col. Hist. Soc. *Papers,* IX (''Jared Ingersoll Papers''), 404.

forces in America, wrote to Governor Pitkin requesting him to make provision, under the terms of the quartering act, passed by parliament in April, 1765,[1] for two officers and one hundred and thirty-four German recruits who were unable, on account of the winter weather, to reach the battalions to which they had been assigned and which were located, one at Quebec and the other in the Great Lakes country. Pitkin proceeded to call, first, a meeting of the council for January 20, and then a special session of the general assembly, which convened January 29, and passed, apparently without much opposition, the legislation necessary for making suitable provision for the soldiers.[2] However, instead of quartering the troops at Stamford, Norwalk, and Fairfield, as Gage had desired, it was decided since these towns had been "heretofore burthened with a great number of his Majesty's forces quartered and billeted on them during two winter

[1] 3 George III, c. 33; Pickering, *Statutes at Large*, XXVI, 305-318.

[2] Gage had expected that his aid-de-camp, Captain Kemble, who brought from New York this requisition for quarters, would be able to make all necessary arrangements with Governor Pitkin. The result was that when Kemble arrived from Hartford on the twenty-fifth of January with Pitkin's reply, to the effect that the assembly must be consulted, he was very much irritated. "Captain Kemble has delivered me your letter of the 20th instant," Gage wrote to the governor, "and I can't help expressing my surprise at the contents of it, and the delays given to his Majesty's service— I had the honor to make application to you, as the executive part of government, for the due execution of a law in your colony, in the same manner as the said law is daily put in execution by every justice of the peace, constable, headborough, or tythingman, throughout the Kingdom of England. I cannot comprehend that your Colony is affected by my requisition in any shape, as to expense, there being no barracks in the Colony, therefore there is no expense to be incurred for bedding, fuel, utensils, etc., but the troops to be quartered in public houses, in the same manner as in England; and as the public houses in the places mentioned in my letter of the 8th instant are more than sufficient to quarter the few troops that are to be sent into them, the further provision required by law, of fitting up outhouses, barns, etc., in case there should not be sufficient room in said public houses to quarter the troops, is out of the question." Major General Gage to Governor Pitkin, January 25, 1767, in J. Almon, *Prior Documents*, p. 131.

seasons," that they should be provided for with quarters at New Haven, Wallingford, and Branford.[1] At the same time, while complying with this request, the assembly called upon the governor to ask General Gage to issue orders to the soldiers against carrying their arms at any time except on duty, since it had been found by experience that this "hath been the occasion of notorious breaches of the peace, to the terror and disquiet of his Majesty's good subjects."[2]

There were, however, those who felt that this billeting of soldiers in time of peace was an ill omen. "Our Assembly have agreed to billet 136 of the Troops," wrote John Devotion of Saybrook. "The Wedge has entered, and I expect Glut upon Glut."[3] Yet, to most men in Connecticut, there had come a feeling of confidence, it seems, that the period of strained relations with the mother country was becoming a thing of the past. But Connecticut's neighbors—Massachusetts and New York—failed at this period to show the tactful spirit of compliance which she herself displayed. In the former colony the struggle went on between the governor and the house of representatives and, what is more, an act of general pardon and indemnity was passed in connection with the measure, to grant compensation to the sufferers in the late Stamp Act riots.[4] The New York assembly, when re-

[1] *Conn. Col. Rec.*, XII, 541-543. It was provided that any person or persons on whom these soldiers were quartered should be paid out of the treasury of the colony "so much more than is allowed by his Majesty for their subsistence as to make the same equal to five shillings lawful money, per week, for each soldier so quartered."

[2] *Ibid.* See also Governor Pitkin to Major General Gage, January 13, 1767, J. Almon, *Prior Documents*, p. 131.

[3] John Devotion to Ezra Stiles, February 6, 1767, *Itineraries of Ezra Stiles*, p. 460.

[4] Governor Bernard to the Earl of Shelburne, November 14, 1766, J. Almon, *Prior Documents*, pp. 113-115; Mass. Hist. Soc. *Coll.* (fifth series), IX, 224-225.

quested in June, 1766, to make provision for troops, adopted, instead, a set of resolutions declaring that the character of the request was "unprecedented"; and though it later was brought to approve a plan which would at least partially meet the requirements of the Quartering Act, there was a feeling in the province that the people had already been to greater expense, in supporting regular troops, than any other colony, and that the charges were bound to become "ruinous and unsupportable."[1]

The news of this recalcitrant attitude on the part of two of the most important colonies had a very disturbing effect upon England. In the House of Lords, speeches were delivered dealing with the ingratitude of the American provinces;[2] many of those who, during the Stamp Act crisis, had opposed Grenville, now spoke severely against the colonies in general; and especially against New York.[3] "The spirit is greatly changed with respect to America," wrote the Connecticut agent, William

---

[1] It should, of course, be remembered that these troops, which stopped in New York en route to the upper country, were an invaluable protection to her great fur trading interests. The famous Book of Reasons issued by the Connecticut general assembly in 1764 shows the feeling of the colony regarding the question of paying for the support of troops on the frontier: "If the Expence arises in defending and securing the Fur Trade and the Out-Posts requisite for carrying on the same, to oblige these Colonies which receive no immediate Advantage by it, to bear a Proportionate Part of the Burden, will also be hard and unequal, and especially if that Trade is sufficiently profitable to support itself, if otherwise, why is there so much Care and mighty Attention constantly exercised toward it?" Reprinted in *Conn. Col. Rec.*, XII, appendix, p. 669.

For the New York controversy see J. Almon, *Prior Documents*, pp. 94, 95, 97, 119, 120, 240; C. L. Becker, *Political Parties*, 1760-1776, p. 53, *passim*.

[2] William Samuel Johnson to Governor Pitkin, April 11, 1767, Mass. Hist. Soc. *Coll.* (fifth series), IX, 224.

[3] William Samuel Johnson to Samuel Johnson, April 4, 1767, E. E. Beardsley, *Life and Times of William Samuel Johnson*, p. 38.

Samuel Johnson, "last year they were all for favoring and relieving us; now they are as much engaged to lay burdens upon us, and reduce us to subjection."[1] George Grenville, from his seat in the House of Commons, demanded that all Americans, before they would be allowed to sit in their local assemblies, or to exercise office, should give a political test in the shape of a declaration acknowledging the sovereignty of Great Britain and the right of parliament to tax America. Although this was lost by a vote of forty-three to one hundred and forty-six, through the exertions of the Chathamites and the other opponents of Grenville, yet the ministry was becoming more and more impressed with the fact that a firm hand should be placed upon the colonies and that they should be required to share in the expense of the imperial upkeep.

Pitt, undoubtedly a great war minister and a man who could incite others to action, was, irrespective of his physical disabilities, not so well qualified for the solution of the tremendous financial problems which confronted parliament. He had brought to a successful conclusion the Seven Years' War, but in doing this he had spent with a lavish hand; how the nation's obligations were to be met, he seemed disposed to leave to others to suggest. Even the Rockingham Whigs, who had joined with him in opposing the Stamp Act, now upbraided him with great warmth for his "profusion of the public treasure and disregard to the means necessary to increase the reve-

[1] William Samuel Johnson to his father, Samuel Johnson, *ibid.*, p. 44. "The Lords were alarmed at the independent ways of America. With regard to the Massachusetts Act of General Pardon and Indemnity, the same was denounced as an insult upon Parliament and a high encroachment upon the King's prerogative, who alone could grant a pardon, for the Massachusetts Assembly had done something that the British Parliament could not do unless the Act was originated by the Crown and was passed in the very language and extent proposed by the King." William Samuel Johnson to Governor Pitkin, April 11, 1767, Mass. Hist. Soc. *Coll.* (fifth series), IX, 225.

nue.'"[1]   The war had cost, over and above the amount
necessary to maintain the military and naval peace establishment, about eighty-two million pounds, and left Great
Britain with a debt of more than one hundred and thirty
millions.   Over one hundred and twenty-four millions
of this had accrued during the series of wars with France
and Spain, which the nation had fought for the preservation and building up of the growing empire, and for the
securing of the right to navigate freely the highways of
the great seas.[2]   Even before the Seven Years' War, the
interest charges on the debt, including the terminable
annuities, amounted to over two and one-half million
pounds.   Not including the civil list, there was an annual
cost of over two million pounds for the maintenance of
a military and naval establishment sufficient to insure
all parts of the empire proper protection.   Not only the
prosperity but the very existence of the American colonies, it must be borne in mind, had depended upon the
successful outcome of this struggle, which had lasted for
almost a hundred years.   Subsidy upon subsidy was piled
on the shoulders of the English people and, while they
had long been accustomed to heavy taxation, the feeling
had spread among them that their brothers, who had
slipped over to the colonies by the tens of thousands, were
unfairly leaving those who stayed at home to groan under

    [1] William Samuel Johnson to Governor Pitkin, February 12, 1767, *ibid.*,
IX, 416.   This waning of Pitt's popularity has an echo in Connecticut.   "I
would let you know that I am not in the spirit of Torey Sentiment, & I
believe not the Atmosphere of their Influence; I have ever and still retain
the highest Opinion of Mr Pitt as a politician & Patriot—but saw some
Hints of his *Insanity & Lost Influence*, which with Affirmations from private Letters made me fear, and therefore asked for Light supposing you
might have better knowledge in the Matter.   Pray in your next tell why the
Officers of the Crown dont Love him as well as Fear him."   John Devotion
to Ezra Stiles, October 15, 1767, *Itineraries of Ezra Stiles*, p. 469.

    [2] Stephen Dowell, *A History of Taxation and Taxes in England*, II, 130-
131, appendix, tables No. 1 and No. 2.

the weight of crushing national obligations and were not doing their share.[1] "I have been alarmed," wrote William Samuel Johnson to the governor of Connecticut, "with assurances that something very striking must be and will be done, and that the anxious spirits of this country can no longer brook the impositions upon them without some similar impositions upon America."[2] When Hillsborough, in speaking to Johnson regarding the situation of the colonials, said that, as to taxes, they were infinitely better off than any of their fellow subjects in Europe, the latter made no attempt to deny it, but answered in a way that had become characteristic of Americans and that carried a warning. "I replied," wrote Johnson concerning the interview, "that if we paid less, we had less ability, and fewer advantages; and, all circumstances considered, our burdens were truly very great, and even more than we knew how to bear, and I hoped that this country would

[1] Lady Lugard in her article on the British Empire in the *Encyclopedia Britannica* (eleventh ed., IV, 611) says: "The struggle which developed itself between the American colonies and the British parliament was in fact a struggle on the part of the people and taxpayers of one portion of the empire to resist the domination of the people and taxpayers of another portion."

Writers have been too prone to overemphasize the exclusive benefits that accrued to Great Britain under the highly protective navigation and trade acts. Walpole and others thought of the colonial trade in terms of exclusive benefits to Great Britain; this also lay at the root of Burke's reasoning in approaching the question of the indirect taxation of America through trade. The truth is that the benefits were largely mutual. If Great Britain had prospered by the raw products of America, the colonies had not less prospered by receiving the manufactures of the mother country. Whenever the operation of the trade and navigation acts bore heavily upon the colonies, it to that degree reduced their capacity to consume British manufactures and tended to depress British industry. But as is now well recognized, from many angles, especially with regard to the building up of colonial shipping, the navigation acts operated most beneficially for America.

[2] William Samuel Johnson to William Pitkin, March 19, 1767, Mass. Hist. Soc. *Coll.* (fifth series), IX, 218.

not add to them, as they would certainly find it would eventually redound to their own prejudice, at the same time that it effectually ruined us.'"[1] However, the following year in referring to those burdens which were more than his fellow countrymen "knew how to bear," Johnson declared in a confidential communication: "I am glad to find the colony is so nearly out of debt. . . . You are aware that our being so little in debt is earnestly urged here as a reason why we should acquiesce in the impositions laid upon us by Parliament; for which reason, as well as others, I wish them to know as little as possible of our internal circumstances and policies, especially in point of taxation, which they will never clearly understand and which may be liable to misconstruction.'"[2]

Regarding the question of taxation in Connecticut the writer "Civis," in the *Connecticut Gazette* of August 16, 1765, who manifestly was none other than Jared Ingersoll,[3] quoted with approval the estimates made in England that, should the colonial pay the stamp duty, his contribution would not be more than one-tenth of that paid by his brother in England "in the general defence of the Kingdom." In the "Answers to the Board of Trade," made in 1756, Governor Fitch stated that the revenue by direct taxation—practically the only revenue the colony had—amounted to about £4000 sterling;[4] in 1764 it was estimated that a tax of one penny on the pound would produce £5000.[5] In 1774 Governor Trumbull, in his "Answers to the Board," stated that "the ordinary annual Expenses are near four thousand

---

[1] Johnson to Pitkin, February 13, 1768, *ibid.*, IX, 262.

[2] Johnson to Joseph Trumbull, April 15, 1769, *ibid.*, IX, 333, 334.

[3] For a discussion of this point see Chapter VI of this study.

[4] *Conn. Col. Rec.*, X, appendix, p. 624.

[5] *Ibid.* See also Henry Bronson, *A Historical Account of Connecticut Currency, Continental Money and the Finances of the Revolution*, p. 77, note.

Pounds Sterling, exclusive of the schools: there hath been
no extraordinary expenses since the last war & the Burden of that is felt to this day.'"¹ As to this "burden," it
is by no means certain that Trumbull stated the matter
with frankness. On October 25, 1769, the auditor for the
colony reported that the preceding May £45,369.7.10 was
due from the "collectors of the Colony Taxes," and that
"there was in the Hands of the late Treasurer Talcott
£21,995.19.11.3 not accounted for, which made in the
whole the Sum of £67,365.7.10¼ in favor of the Colony.²
As to what was then due from the Colony it was reported
to be viz. £31,713.8.¾ in Bills of Credit outstanding,
interest thereon added made the Debt due from the Colony on outstanding bills about £39,641.15.¾.'"³ Thus the
assets of the colony without resort to additional taxation
were, in 1769, more than sufficient to meet its obligations,
which certainly rested lightly upon the shoulders of the
people. In fact, it seems to be true, as was commonly
boasted, that between the years 1766 and 1770 no colony
taxes were collected,⁴ which accounts for the large sum

¹ *Conn. Col. Rec.*, XIV, appendix, p. 500. In 1756 about £490 sterling
was appropriated for school purposes; in 1774 more than £2000 was appropriated for the education of ''children and youth'' in the several towns.

² The Talcott accounts were never completely straightened out, for they
were left in a state of hopeless confusion. However, no charges of dis-
honesty were ever preferred against the treasurer.

³ Connecticut Archives, Finances and Currency, V, No. 26.

⁴ An illuminating article on Connecticut taxation is to be found in the
Connecticut Journal, August 31, 1770. In that year the assembly voted to
raise a tax. The writer is considering why. ''When I ask the members
of the General Assembly the reason—by some I am told the colony has paid
no taxes since the year 1766, and those monies appropriated to the sinking
the bills [of credit] have been applied to the support of government ever
since that time—I well know some have been so daring as to say no taxes
have been insisted upon, in order to establish the reputation of those gentlemen, who were elected when those changes in the government took place.
But I can never be persuaded they would run counter to a plain act of
parliament, as well as our own laws and thereby violate the public faith of

of £45,369.7.10 due from the collectors of the rates. Indeed, through the aid of the large sums of money received from England for reimbursement for expenditures during the late war,[1] Connecticut had practically freed herself from debt by 1770 and the late emissions of bills of credit from May, 1770, to October, 1774, can hardly be regarded in any other light than an effort to meet the demands of the Connecticut inflationists.

In other words, the situation of the people of Connecticut, with reference to public burdens, was, in reality, in spite of their customary complaints, vastly different from that of the masses in England. Connecticut naturally appreciated her advantages, and it is not strange that she was extremely anxious to preserve them, and as Hillsborough in 1768 pointed out to Johnson, the colony kept herself in the dark; her correspondence with the home government was very deficient, and whenever it took place, a very incomplete idea of the state of affairs was rendered.

It should be observed in this connection that although Governor Fitch had instructed the London agents of Connecticut, in 1764, not to deny the constitutional right of parliament to tax America, but to plead rather its inexpediency, the colony, in order to maintain its privileged situation regarding the national burdens, felt

the government to answer such mean and low purposes, that would be to suppose them to be very wicked.'' The writer of course has reference to the act of parliament relating to bills of credit, which was passed in 1751 and is cited as 24 George II, c. 53.

1 From March 15, 1759, to July 28, 1765, Governor Fitch had drawn upon the Connecticut agents in London in bills of exchange up to the amount of £173,467.10.8. See ''An Account of the Sum Total of the Bills of Exchange Drawn by Governor Fitch on the Colony's Agent or Agents in England Agreeable to Acts of Assembly.'' (Wolcott Papers, I, 191. This is to be printed in the forthcoming Volume II of the *Fitch Papers*.) December 14, 1765, Richard Jackson wrote to Governor Fitch, stating that he still held as a balance in London £9263.4.9.

obliged to repudiate this position and to take advanced grounds with reference to the legal competency of parliament to make revenue plans that would comprehend and bind the colonies.

Faced by this general situation, what was left for any British ministry to do? National repudiation of the great debt with its interest charges was not to be considered and yet it seemed as though something must be done to give relief to the English people. To lower the prices on food, the exportation of corn was prohibited and the protection of the British farmers against the cheaper wheat and Indian corn from America was swept away. To Johnson, who had been raised in the midst of the rude plenty of the little agricultural community of Stratford, Connecticut, the sight of the misery he found in England was shocking. "Notwithstanding all they have done," he wrote in 1767, "the distress of the poor for want of bread is terrible and affecting."[1] In 1768, in a letter to his father, Dr. Samuel Johnson of New York, he said: "we seem here to be almost in a state of anarchy, there being beside this of Wilkes's five other mobs assembled, viz., the sailors (who in a body of six or eight thousand went down on Wednesday and delivered a petition to Parliament, but behaved with much decency), the coalheavers, sawyers, journeymen hatters, and weavers, all complaining of the excessive price of provisions, and insisting upon an advancement of their wages. By this rising of the seamen, the maritime trade of London has been several days totally stopped, and no ship can go down the river. These several mobs are yet independent of each other, but a general discontent is visible among the people, and if government cannot discover some

[1] William Samuel Johnson to Governor Pitkin, December 26, 1767, Mass. Hist. Soc. *Coll.* (fifth series), IX, 250.

method to quiet them before they unite, the most fatal consequences may be apprehended.'"[1]

It was in the midst of this situation in England that Charles Townshend, chancellor of the exchequer in the Pitt-Grafton ministry, early in 1767, gave expression to the almost universal demand in England, that a means should yet be found whereby the people of the colonies be brought to contribute a more reasonable share toward the maintenance of troops along the American frontier,— a measure of precaution and an aid to the rapid settlement of the hinterland which every conception of statesmanship pointed to as wise and necessary. Townshend declared, in a speech delivered January 26, that this could be done without disturbing the sensibilities of the colonies regarding what they claimed to be their right of "internal" taxation, little as that right was admitted by the government.[2] As a result, on June 29 an American revenue act was passed, providing for certain import duties on glass, lead, painted colors, tea, and paper.[3] The proceeds, however, arising from this act, estimated at some £40,000, were to be applied, not to the upkeep of an

---

[1] William Samuel Johnson to Samuel Johnson, May 14, 1768, in E. E. Beardsley's *Life and Times of William Samuel Johnson*, pp. 61-62. "We imagine we are very near the crisis of some considerable political revolutions, but it may nevertheless be some time, perhaps, before anything very decisive takes place." William Samuel Johnson to Samuel Johnson, November 2, 1769, *ibid.*, p. 72.

[2] "Mr. Townsend, Chancellor of the Exchequer, a few days past, upon an accidental mention of America, said in the House, 'I do not know any distinction between internal and external taxes; it is a distinction without a difference, it is nonsense; if we have a right to impose one, we have the other.'" William Samuel Johnson to Governor William Pitkin, February 12, 1767, Mass. Hist. Soc. *Coll.* (fifth series), IX, 215-216. See also Johnson to Pitkin, May 16, 1767, *ibid.*, IX, 229.

[3] 7 George III, c. 46; Pickering, *Statutes at Large*, XXVII, 505-512. Regarding the tea schedule, the student should consult the article by Professor Farrand, entitled, "The Taxation of Tea, 1763-1773," *Amer. Hist. Rev.*, IV, 226-269.

American military establishment, the support of which had been the first objective of the ministry earlier in the year,[1] but to "defraying the charges of the administration of justice, and the support of the civil government, within all or any of the said colonies or plantations." An act was also passed for establishing an American board of customs commissioners.[2] This clearly showed the determination of parliament to get control of the American situation before taking up the question of the military establishment. For in spite of the fact that that body was cut up into "bitter political factions," "all were agreed in having an ill opinion of the Colonies and in a Resolution to assert the supremacy of this country."[3]

[1] "Before the act was passed, there were meetings of the agents and the London merchants who waited upon Townshend. At one of these interviews Townshend was told that the army perhaps might with safety be withdrawn from America, in which case the expense would cease and there would be no further occasion for a revenue. He replied that he would resign his office rather than withdraw the army." William Samuel Johnson to Governor William Pitkin, Mass. Hist. Soc. *Coll.* (fifth series), IX, 229.

[2] George III, c. 41, Pickering, *Statutes at Large*, XXVII, 447-449.

[3] William Samuel Johnson to Jared Ingersoll, from London, June 9, 1767, New Haven Col. Hist. Soc. *Papers*, IX ("Jared Ingersoll Papers"), 408-410. Two weeks previous to the passing of the revenue act, parliament had passed an act suspending the New York assembly "until provision shall have been made for furnishing the King's troops with all the necessaries required by law." 7 George III, c. 59, Pickering, *Statutes at Large*, XXVII, 609, 610. There was a general feeling in parliament that the colonies were ungrateful, that they had little regard for the mother country, and had cultivated views of independence. William Samuel Johnson to Governor William Pitkin, April 11, 1767, Mass. Hist. Soc. *Coll.* (fifth series), IX, 224.

CHAPTER IX

CONNECTICUT HARD TIMES; NON-IMPORTA-TION; THE TRIUMPH OF RADICALISM

It is undeniable that the American colonies were con-fronted, during the '60's and '70's, with a long period of financial stringency accompanied by an economic crisis.[1] Lands that had sold in Connecticut in the '50's for £30 an acre old tenor, in 1762 were selling at £19; and other lands that had sold for £4 proclamation money, were only bringing £3.[2] ''This colony is Eighty Thousand Pounds in Debt, Arrears of Taxes, that Cannot be collected, by Reason of the Poverty of those on whom they are laid,'' wrote Jared Ingersoll to Richard Jackson, in November, 1765.[3] In the April session of the New Haven County Court, in 1761, there were two hundred and sixty-five suits, mostly for book debts.[4] During the year 1761

---

[1] C. M. Andrews, *The Boston Merchants and the Non-Importation Move-ment*, pp. 180-191; see also A. M. Schlesinger, *The Colonial Merchants and the American Revolution, 1763-1776*, p. 56, *passim;* and C. L. Becker, *Political Parties in New York, 1760-1776*, p. 65, *passim.*

[2] *Itineraries of Ezra Stiles*, pp. 50-51.

[3] *Ingersoll Stamp Act Corresp.*, p. 44.

[4] Book debts refer to credit accounts. In these actions it is interesting to note that parties residing in New Haven, which, in 1774, numbered 8022, were mentioned one hundred and twenty-nine times as either plaintiff or defendant, while those hailing from Wallingford, with only 4777 population, in that same year, were mentioned one hundred and seventy-five times. New Haven County Court Records, V, 326-359. Wallingford was very much more radical in temper than New Haven and very early cultivated strong anti-British feelings. There seems to have been at this period a very intimate connection between the growth of radicalism and the existence of a large debtor class in any community.

twenty suits were brought by New York parties, four by
Massachusetts parties, and one each by Pennsylvania
and New Jersey parties, against inhabitants of the
county;[1] in the November session of the court in 1766,
John Hotchkiss of New Haven was plaintiff in no less
than twenty-six suits;[2] one is amazed at the amount of
litigation in which the people were involved.   Such
prominent men in the colony as Jonathan Trumbull of
Lebanon, Benedict Arnold of New Haven, Benjamin Gale
of Killingworth, and Joseph Chew of New London were
loaded with debts in the late '60's.   In 1771 Chew petitioned the assembly, stating that from prosperity he had
been reduced to poverty ''by reasons of many misfortunes
sustained in the course of . . . trade and business:''[3] he
had accumulated debts amounting to £15,406.   The assembly, after ordering him to turn over his remaining property, freed him from arrests.   In 1769 Gale, who, among
other activities, was interested in manufacturing steel,
wrote to Ingersoll about his vain efforts to pay a certain
debt; he had a negro couple, he admitted, but they were
lawfully married, and he did not want to separate them
through a sale.[4]   Benedict Arnold, in 1767, was owing
London merchants over £1700 and was compelled to make
a conveyance to them in that year of his sloop, *Sally,* and
her cargo.[5]   Jonathan Trumbull, in 1766, found himself,
upon the failure of the partnership of Trumbull, Fitch,
and Trumbull, with debts that must have totaled between
ten and fifteen thousand pounds, most of which was owing

[1] New Haven County Court Records, V, 326-359.

[2] *Ibid.,* VI, 182-199.

[3] *Conn. Col. Rec.,* VI, 182-199.

[4] Benjamin Gale to Jared Ingersoll, December, 1769, Ingersoll Papers.

[5] The indenture, signed May 9, 1767, is among the Ingersoll Papers; see
also New Haven Col. Hist. Soc. *Papers,* IX (''Jared Ingersoll Papers''),
p. 412 and note.

to British merchants.[1] In a letter to Ingersoll, Trumbull described his pecuniary embarrassments as "shocking."[2] In 1768 a London gentleman directed inquiries to be made regarding the possibilities of opening up certain business relations with the colony. He received the following reply from his friend: "Without mentioning names, I have consulted Mr. —— about the American affair, who says it will not do: he says he would not give £800 for the whole Province; that he has been all over it at New Haven and New London; that they are all mortgaged to the full to the Bostonians and New Yorkers; that they have all their goods from those two places, and import very little; very few merchants, chiefly farmers, all upon a level, labor very dear, spirit Oliverian, but very great rogues, no money amongst them, and nobody would live amongst them that could possibly live anywhere else!"[3] "Cash is so very scarce," wrote Trumbull to Lane, Son and Frozier of London, to whom was owing a debt of over £3000, "that it is almost impossible to collect it for outstanding debts, or by sale of lands."[4] To soothe his anxious creditors, his son Joseph went to England, carrying with him "Kind letters from Jared Ingersoll, whose acquaintanceship in England . . . was quite

[1] I. W. Stuart, *Life of Jonathan Trumbull*, pp. 119-124.

[2] *Ibid.*, p. 123.

[3] E. E. Beardsley, *Life and Times of William Samuel Johnson*, p. 60. This outcry against the good people of Connecticut finds an echo in the will of Judge Lewis Morris of New York. "It is my wish," declared Morris, "that my son Gouverneur shall have the best education that can be furnished him in England or America but my express will and directions are that under no circumstances shall he be sent to the Colony of Connecticut for that purpose, lest his youth should imbibe that low craft and cunning so incident to the people of that country and which are so interwoven in their constitution that they cannot conceal it from the world, although many of them, under the sanctified garb of religion, have attempted to impose themselves upon the world as honest men." *American Historical Magazine* (1906), p. 36.

[4] I. W. Stuart, *Life of Jonathan Trumbull*, p. 120.

extensive, and who cheerfully endorsed all the statements of Trumbull, and employed his influence in soothing his Creditors to lenity.'"[1]

The reasons for this period of general financial embarrassment still await investigation before other than tentative conclusions can be drawn. Trumbull was convinced that, if parliament would grant leave for the colonies to enjoy a good paper currency, thus affording relief to specie, Connecticut merchants might easily pay their debts to England. Undoubtedly scarcity of specie was a very important factor. As Professor Andrews has pointed out, the movement of specie was prevailingly toward England, so that the colonies were kept pretty well drained of hard money.[2] There were times, of course, when that was not true. During the latter years of the late war, the price of bullion (that is, the value of an ounce of silver) was so enhanced in London as compared with its value in America, that the colonies found it to their advantage not to ship the money paid for reimbursement, as had been the practice, but to sell it to those desiring London bills of exchange.[3] It is undeniable that the rapid increase of population in the colo-

[1] *Life of Jonathan Trumbull*, p. 122.

[2] See also C. L. Becker, *History of Political Parties in the Province of New York, 1760-1776*, p. 65, *passim*. ''The readiness of the Colonists to buy goods from England, even beyond their ability to pay for them, resulted in a steady drain of the silver specie to Europe.''

[3] ''This Assembly, considering the extraordinary price foreign coins now bear in England, and also that the demand for and value of bills of exchange have of late greatly increased here, find it will be more for the interest and advantage of this Colony that the whole of the Money granted and that is or may be paid this Colony on account of the services done in the year 1759, be lodged in some secure bank in London, to be drawn out by bills of exchange, than that part thereof should be sent over in specie pursuant to the directions contained in a resolve of the General Assembly of this Colony held in October last.'' *Conn. Col. Rec.*, XI, 489, 490.

In October, 1760, William Pitkin, John Chester, and George Wyllys were appointed a committee ''to sell seventeen thousand pounds sterling of the

nies required, for the best interests of business, a stable currency, which, at the same time, should be capable of expansion according to the needs of commerce. From 1756 to 1762 the population of Connecticut, according to the "Answers to the Board of Trade," was increased only about eleven thousand, on account of "losses sustained during the War and frequent and numerous emigrations from hence to his Majesty's newly conquered or evacuated countries in America";[1] but from 1762 to 1774 there was an increase of over fifty-two thousand, although "within this Time, there have been frequent and numerous Emigrations from hence, to settle on new Lands in His Majesty's other colonies in America.'"[2] To meet the enlarged demands for money, there was issued, after 1770, for circulating purposes, £10,000 in bills of credit, bearing two and a half per cent interest, and £39,000 without interest. But this paper money was only adapted, naturally, to meet the local requirements. The result was that hard money, by reason of the growing demand for it in the colonies, as the only medium for international exchange, and for carrying on business with the mother country, was driven as completely from circulation as was gold during the economic crisis of the '70's and '90's of the following century. This was unfavorable to a developing international trade.

But there were other causes for the economic depression of the colonies during the decade preceding the

money granted for the services aforesaid for the full value thereof in silver, gold, or bills of credit of this Colony emitted by Act of Assembly in March, 1759, to any person or persons that should appear to pay the value thereof as aforesaid into the treasury of this Colony." The governor was empowered "to draw proper bills of exchange on the said agents, or either of them, in favour of such purchaser or purchasers, for such sum or sums purchased as aforesaid accordingly." *Ibid.*, 490, 491.

[1] *Conn. Col. Rec.*, XI, appendix, p. 630.
[2] *Ibid.*, XIV, appendix, p. 499.

Revolution, which rightly called for measures of economy. There are evidences that the earlier habits of frugality and conscientious meeting of obligations had been gradually cast aside by too many of the people living in the colony. "The great folly that the Americas are running into is luxury," declared "Common Sense," in the *London Chronicle*.[1] William Samuel Johnson, writing to Governor Pitkin in 1767, regarding the purchasing of English manufactures by America, referred to the colonists' "natural propensity to luxury."[2] In 1769 Johnson declared that the non-intercourse agreements might be effective were "the prudent spirit of frugality and industry once diffused through the bulk of the people of America."[3] "Natural Wealth increases in our Land greatly," asserted John Devotion of Saybrook, in 1767, though it is important to notice that he went on to say that "Luxury & Pride eternally cry Poverty & bad Times."[4]

This tendency to live above one's means, so characteristic of America of this period, was aided by the general practice of extending credit for long periods of time. Everybody sought to buy on credit, and, on the other hand, when it came to meeting these obligations, it was done, as a rule, in a most unwilling spirit. In going over the county court records for this period, one is led to wonder, in view of the astounding number of cases of book debts that came before the tribunal at each session, whether men, as a rule, would pay any indebtedness without taking a chance of relief through the technicalities of the law. In 1769 Green and Watson, editors of the *Con-*

[1] *London Chronicle*, April 15, 1774.

[2] William Samuel Johnson to Governor Pitkin, December 26, 1767, Mass. Hist. Soc. *Coll.* (fifth series), IX, 249.

[3] William Samuel Johnson to Governor Pitkin, February 6, 1769, *ibid.*, p. 319.

[4] John Devotion to Ezra Stiles, April 22, 1767, *Itineraries of Ezra Stiles*, p. 462.

necticut Courant, printed at Hartford, addressed the public through the columns of the paper, declaring that upon an average they had not received, since beginning their partnership, two shillings out of every six shillings due for the yearly subscription of the paper. "We beg leave," they wrote, "to address our delinquent Customers in the Language of Civility and with a Deference due to the Character of Persons, either of Probity, Honesty and Verasity, or of Humanity, Honor, and Ingenuity; in either of which, we are assured they will take no Offense at our once more calling upon them for a settlement." They announced that by reason of the "unexpected & Perservering Negligence of far the greater Part" of their customers, they were obliged to think of discontinuing the paper.[1] The *Connecticut Journal* of New Haven was apparently no more fairly treated by the public. There was something that almost approached eloquence in the announcement made by this paper early in 1773. "The printers are sorry, they can with truth inform the public, that they have not for this year past received from all the customers for this journal so much money as they have expended for the blank paper on which it is printed."[2] "Gentlemen and Ladies," wrote Leverett Hubbard of New Haven, in an open advertisement in the local paper in 1774, "you may remember, I have several times desired in this paper that you would settle accounts with me. I suppose . . . you thought I was in jest. I have you now take me in earnest. I have a large number to settle with. . . . I shall employ an attorney."[3] Yet a writer in the *Journal,* in 1770, spoke of "lately walking thro the Town, & Contemplating its great Increase, within those few Years past, by the many new and Ele-

[1] *Connecticut Courant,* November 6, 1789.

[2] *Connecticut Journal,* April 2, 1773.

[3] *Ibid.,* March 4, 1774.

gant Buildings erected in it'';[1] while Hugh Finlay, who traveled through the northern colonies in 1773, and stopped at New Haven, was impressed with the fact that this was a ''flourishing sea Port Town.''[2]

If the means for investigation were at hand, it would doubtless be found that a large part of the difficulty which merchants and others experienced in coming to settlements with English creditors was due to an over-willingness to allow great numbers of people with careless habits, which had dulled the keen ethical edge of their Puritanism, to run up bills which they either could not settle or would not, without the burdensome expense of a lawsuit.[3]

The litigious spirit which ran riot among the people of Connecticut at this period[4] gave the appearance of dis-

[1] *Connecticut Journal*, December 7, 1770.

[2] *Journal Kept by Hugh Finlay, surveyor of the post roads on the Continent of North America . . . begun 13th of September 1772 and ended 26th June, 1774* (1867).

[3] In this connection it should not be forgotten that many colonial merchants were inclined to operate upon what would be called by business men of the present day a dangerous speculative basis. Jonathan Trumbull, Benedict Arnold, Joseph Chew, and Benjamin Gale were, it appears, men who became involved financially in what now would be called ''plunging.'' The long-time credit system encouraged speculative undertakings.

[4] The pastors set an example of dragging people into court in order to compel them to make a suitable settlement. The Reverend Joseph Noyes, of the Old Light meeting house, in the April term of the county court, sued Stephen Smith of Goshen on a note for £8. At the same session of the court Rev. Samuel Bird, the pastor of the New Lights, sued both Stephen Frischild of Kent and Jedediah Gregory of Stratford, on a note for £60, and Drayton Johnson of Wallingford on a note for £12. New Haven County Court Records, V, 197, 349, 356.

The most noted litigation, involving a New Haven minister, occurred in 1759, when Rev. Mr. Noyes sued his ecclesiastical society, which was controlled by his opponents, the New Lights of the White Haven congregation, who outnumbered those remaining at the regularly established First Society meeting house. In his plea Noyes demanded £150 lawful money damage because the society had failed to give him proper financial support. The case came before the county court at an adjourned session

tress and brought upon many great misfortunes. One writer, under the name "Lazarus," in the *Connecticut Courant,* in the spring of 1769, said, "I have taken much pains to find out the foundation of our growing poverty; and among the many conjectures (so many as are about perpetual motion) I fix it upon litigation; . . . only to maintain a suit of but 5 s., consequence, thus men act, to gain this world, and conscientiously lose their souls—I say litigation is the cause of our growing poverty, nakedness and frigid confinement." The writer had come to the conclusion that "upon the whole this destructive method is peculiar to this colony, whose inhabitants justly boast the highest privileges, who sing the song of liberty and property, and whose practices are most abusive and fatal to all expected happiness."[1]

in January of that year under title of "Rev. Noyes v. Samuel Bishop and the rest of the Inhabitants of said First Society." The court ruled in favor of the plaintiff; the defendants, thereupon, asked for a review of the case upon a bond for £150 furnished by Phinehas Bradley. At the April session the case was reviewed and again damages were awarded to the plaintiff. Not to be outdone, the defendants furnished bond for costs and appealed to the superior court, which at its August session "gave judgment in Favr of Father Noyes, granting him for the last Year's Salary and Wood, £130.0.0. Lawfull Money, at which Mr Bird's People were not a little disgusted." *Itineraries of Ezra Stiles,* p. 582; New Haven County Court Records, V, 207, 219, 349. See also the New Haven Hist. Soc. *Papers,* IX ("Jared Ingersoll Papers"), 392-393, for an account of the extraordinary suit that the Reverend Nehemiah Strong instituted against the estate of Andrew Burr, Jr.

[1] *Connecticut Courant,* April 17, 1769. "Lazarus," who was writing from Hartford County, went on to say that "in this County we have twenty ministers of the law or lawyers. I viewed the docket, I found 77 actions for the superior court last fall term, the county and jury fees in each action 46/6, total £1790.6; [with] 4 lawyers to each action, and 6 dollars to each lawyer, £380; allow 6 evidences to each action makes 462 witnesses, each upon a medium cost £2., total £924—Plaintiffs and Defendants 154, cost £308—77 copies from the county clerk £23.2/0 and many other trifles, total £1742.2/6." "Lazarus" then illustrated the trials of a litigant. "The defendant appealed to the superior court, where were 119 actions to be tried in ten days, when all parties attended out that session, and then 'twas

Moreover, it should be borne in mind that the decline of land values in Connecticut in the early '60's was probably due not so much to the poverty of the people as to the excessive appreciation of money, brought about, among other causes, by the desire of large numbers of the inhabitants at that time to sell their property in Connecticut immediately in order to settle upon the new lands opened up by New Hampshire on the upper Connecticut.[1]

It appears to be a fact that the people of Connecticut were living in the midst of abundance. A Boston correspondent to a London paper, writing early in 1769, declared that he was surprised when he went westward the preceding fall, as far as Connecticut, and rode one hundred miles up the banks of "the river," to find that the people were increasing as rapidly to the westward as they were to the eastward. He found that many of the towns had two, three, four, and some five parish churches. Most couples, he stated, after they had been married from sixteen to twenty years, had from eight to twelve children, who in turn married, as a rule, when twenty-one years of age, and "almost all before they are 25." The parents were able to make provision for them by purchase or grants from the government, and in addition to the land, started them out with a cow or two, a horse, a yoke of oxen, and some swine. "It is remarked

continued to the next when all parties appeared as before, and then 'twas again continued with 77 other suits and then came to a trial, and upon a demurer the plaintiff lost his cause. The defendant's bill amounted to £64.0/9 being not half the cost he had been out, but also the plaintiff has money yet. He petitions for another trial—'twas granted. To court all parties come as before. It was continued by reason of a number of actions, from court to court, and accounting from the beginning the 9th court gave judgment in favor of the plaintiff that he should recover 200 acres of wood land and his costs."

[1] *Itineraries of Ezra Stiles*, pp. 50-51.

that those who are industrious, provide themselves with provisions after the first year.''[1]

What has been said goes to show that in 1767 the people of Connecticut, in spite of appearances to the contrary, were comparatively free from burdens other than those they had, as individuals, placed upon their own shoulders. The opposition, therefore, that developed against the Townshend Acts in the colony was fomented by those who, as a body, were most happily situated, in comparison with the majority of their kinsmen in England.

In fact, it is not at all certain—putting aside for the moment the political phase—that the payment of the Townshend duties would have seriously and permanently affected the prosperity of America.[2] Dr. Benjamin Gale took the view that "the Dutys laid on Paper may be justly reputed a premium upon the very branch of Manufacture in the Country. I am amazed," he added, in referring to the ministry, "at their Stupidity, when I reflect.''[3] In October, 1767, Ezra Stiles was informed that the "Paper Mill at Norwich is plentifully supplied with

[1] *Connecticut Courant,* September 4, 1769.

[2] ''Besides, the other duties (perhaps all of them), in several respects, are advantageous to the Colonies, or certainly may be so, because they must operate by way of premium upon American productions, will encourage the people to extend and increase their manufactures of every species, and especially those of the particular articles so taxed, and are a powerful discouragement to unnecessary consumption and luxury of every kind. So that, were it not for the precedent established by the act, as being an actual exercise of the power of taxation, one might very safely pronounce this to be the most beneficial act of Parliament, in its operation, that ever was contrived for the Colonies. . . . A partial repeal of the Act, or a modification of it, is therefore not to be wished for by the Colonies, since they must lose by it the manufactures they have already established, with the prospect of all future ones, and in point of right or precedent will have gained nothing.'' William Samuel Johnson to Governor William Pitkin, May 25, 1769, Mass. Hist. Soc. *Coll.* (fifth series), IX, 350, 351.

[3] Benjamin Gale to Ezra Stiles, October 15, 1767, *Itineraries of Ezra Stiles,* p. 493.

Rags and has full Demand for its Paper. . . . The Duties on Paper will give it Advantage, I imagine. They have two other Manufactories there, one in the Cutlery Way, the other what is usually called Stone Ware.'"[1] "There has lately been discovered within three Miles of this Town," announced the *Connecticut Journal,* in its issue of July 22, 1768, "a prodigious quantity of a brown Species of Paint. It is nearest the Colour of a dark Spanish-Brown, and may with a little Preparation, answer all the Purposes of common Painting—and is as yet entirely unpolluted with any Duty. A sample of the above Paint may be seen at the Printing Office in New Haven." Connecticut, moreover, was beginning to produce other articles previously entirely imported. "We carry on our Steel Manufacture very Brisk, have made six Tons of good steel since the 25 May last; it is now in high reputation in New York, will sell preferable to English Steel No. 3," Gale had written to a friend in 1766.[2]

[1] John Devotion to Ezra Stiles, October 15, 1767, *ibid.,* p. 470. "Our common artists improve greatly since Stamp Act has half removed the Lethargy. I saw Cloth sold in this Town, for 61 pr y^d two yards of wh^h equal one of Broad Cloth, which had it been in Broad Cloth width and in the Merch^ts Shop, I should readily have bot at 18/ pr yd." Devotion to Stiles, April 22, 1767, *ibid.,* 463. "This paper I write on is better than British gilt," wrote Jonathan Trumbull in 1770. "It is the manufacture of your own Colony." Mass. Hist. Soc. *Coll.* (fifth series), IX, 420. In reviewing the New England situation, in a letter to William Samuel Johnson, Trumbull was able to say, in January of the same year, "The principal people in Boston, and the landholders and most substantial people in the neighborhood and through the country, stand firm to the agreement, and manufactures appear to increase and flourish." *Ibid.,* IX, 403.

[2] Benjamin Gale to Ezra Stiles, July 8, 1766, *Itineraries of Ezra Stiles,* p. 490. The colonials of course were restricted in the manufacture of steel by 23 George II, c. 29, sec. 11. In this connection the student should consult Beer's *British Colonial Policy, 1754-1765,* p. 198.

"As our steel furnace was erected before the act made in the 23rd year of the late king took place, we concluded ourselves safe, although I was conscious that some concerned in that manufacture looked upon it with an evil eye. Having lately made great improvements in that manufacture

"I am sorry," declared John Devotion, in 1768, "that Boston & other Places vapour so much about their *posse*. Should be much more pleased if they and all others would be content with *agendo* and Reflection upon it—privately, or without Noise increase our own Manufactories. . . . Had once the Fav'r of Conversation with Dr. Franklin upon this Topic. Manufacture as much as possible, but say Nothing—was his Remark."[1] William Hart of Saybrook was impressed with the fact that the proposal to garrison the frontier with regular soldiers would benefit America rather than England. "If the Ministry continue sending and stationing their troops in our Provinces," he wrote in 1769, "our Country will fill up very fast; they will increase and improve our Manufactures, and help to ruin their own; and their wealthy people growing poorer, will come over by and by. If they dont alter their measures they will defeat their own designs, and in the end make America great and Britain small."[2]

The people of the colony, it is hardly necessary to say, were not disposed to think of the opportunities now afforded America to establish manufacturing, for they gradually fell under the spell of those who appealed to their apprehensions. "They are ever jealous of their liberty, and fear every innovation," wrote Jonathan Trumbull of them in 1768.[3] This revenue measure by the central authority was pictured to them as the be-

and since last May actually manufactured 20 tons of excellent steel, we should very unwillingly give it up or have the same obstructed by the interposition of the British Parliament." Benjamin Gale to Samuel Johnson, February 20, 1767, Bancroft Manuscripts, Connecticut Papers.

[1] John Devotion to Ezra Stiles, February 8, 1768, *Itineraries of Ezra Stiles*, p. 471.

[2] William Hart to Ezra Stiles, March 14, 1769, *ibid.*, 498.

[3] Jonathan Trumbull to an unknown party, July 1, 1768, I. W. Stuart, *Life of Jonathan Trumbull*, p. 96.

ginning of their bondage. It was novel, and they were devoted to the old method of contributing to the needs of the central government; in fact, it took them twenty years to realize what the ministry, by 1765, had come thoroughly to appreciate: that the requisition system was a broken reed for any government to be obliged to rely upon. "Have there not been methods and ways of treatment from the Crown by the way of requisitions made many times in consequence of addresses from Parliament, which always succeeded and answered the ends of government, and the Colonies were thereby treated as children, and not as slaves? Why is the method changed?" asked Trumbull.[1] "I think," he declared at another time, in pointing out what was a tender spot with the colonial, "it may be truly said there is no disposition in the Colonies to contend with Great Britain but for what they look upon to be their sacred Constitutional rights and privileges. . . . The keeping on foot a body of troops in the Old Colonies, where they serve no other utility but only to overawe the inhabitants into compliance with something they think grievous and burdensome, is what they are uneasy with."[2] One may be sure, in this connection, that the sensational and almost fanatical attacks of Wilkes and others against the government did not aid in reassuring Americans, for the colonial papers were filled with the inflammatory articles that had been published in the *North Briton* and other papers of that type. "The Americans are now groaning under all the horrors of a military government," declared the *North Briton;* "and nothing but the terrors of such a government could oblige them to submit to the unconstitutional taxes we have imposed upon them. And to talk

[1] Jonathan Trumbull to William Samuel Johnson, January 24, 1769, *ibid.,* p. 101.

[2] *Ibid.*

of tranquility being restored in America is just as good sense as it would be to talk of an angry man's being pacified, when his mouth was gagged, and his feet and hands shackled.'"[1] The psychological effects of this ardent sympathy, expressed by the followers of Wilkes, must have effectively nursed the conviction that the mother country was engaged in the insidious design of subjecting the colonials to a species of servitude.

When the news arrived in Connecticut that the revenue bill had become a law, there took place among leading men considerable discussion as to how the measure would be applied to the colony. The latter part of July, 1767, Jared Ingersoll addressed a letter of inquiry to Johnson, asking, among other things, "whether the Parliament means to pay salaries to *our* governor and the *Judges* and let *us* choose them at the same time?'"[2] Letters from London to people in the colony bore the information that the home government would appoint a Connecticut superior court.[3] This was in line with the warning that Richard Jackson, the London agent of Connecticut, had privately sent to Governor Pitkin, the preceding autumn, apprising him of the fact that the colony had many enemies to her charter privileges, and that they were not only men living in England, but among those who had come to America; it was very unfortunate, he considered, that the charter of the colony was so similar to that of Rhode Island, where the people had made them-

[1] Reprint from the *North Briton,* No. 58, March 20, 1769, in the *Connecticut Courant,* September 4, 1769.

[2] Jared Ingersoll to William Samuel Johnson, July 23, 1767, Johnson Papers.

[3] "Mr. Dorr says there are Accounts in private Letters that they are about appointing us a Superior Court from Home; whenever this happens Farewell the Spirit of Charter. They intend to leave the Parchment in our Hands saying 'tis the Kings Prerogative to appoint Officers, etc.'" John Devotion to Ezra Stiles, October 15, 1767, *Itineraries of Ezra Stiles,* pp. 469-470.

selves more obnoxious to the home government than Connecticut people were ever likely to become.[1] William Samuel Johnson, writing to Governor Pitkin from London, in July, 1767, said that although the act in question was penned in general terms and equally included all the colonies, yet he could not find that any use was intended to be made of the power of appointment with respect to the charter colonies. They, however, would be subjected to pay their full proportion of those duties by which the civil establishments of the other colonies would be supported, while maintaining their own officers, "which, in event, amounts to the payment of a tax to the other Colonies."[2]

There was at first, it appears, little excitement regard-

[1] John Devotion to Ezra Stiles, April 22, 1767, *ibid.*, p. 463. "There is no doubt," wrote William Samuel Johnson, in May, 1767, "that the charter of Connecticut has its enemies both in the neighboring governments and here; but upon the most minute urging, I do not find that there is at present any design to attack that in particular, or to infringe in any respect upon the special privileges of the Colony. The danger seems to be, rather, that by general regulations the universal liberties of America may be endangered, and by degrees the charters and Assemblies in general, in effect and Consequence, be superseded and rendered useless, rather than taken away or abolished. The sentiments of people in general are indeed unhappily very unfavorable to the Colonies. But (so far as one may be allowed to compare) Connecticut is at present rather a favorite Colony, and I flatter myself will meet with no particular marks of resentment." Mass. Hist. Soc. *Coll.* (fifth series), IX, 235.

[2] William Samuel Johnson to Governor William Pitkin, July 13, 1767, *ibid.*, IX, 240. Johnson went on to say: "To avoid this inequality, some think it would be advisable for them to apply that their proportion of the duties may be appropriated to the support of their own officers; but this subject is so delicate, and the consequences that might follow from a step of this Kind are of so dangerous a nature, that I think it would be by no means prudent to attempt it. Would it not rather endanger their Constitutions? Would it not be said, in Answer to such an application that the King cannot support (with propriety) officers whom he does not appoint? And that this inequality would therefore be better remedied by putting all the governments upon the same footing, etc.?" See also Jonathan Trumbull to Richard Jackson, July, 1768, printed in I. W. Stuart, *Life of Jonathan Trumbull*, p. 98.

ing the act, as far as Connecticut was concerned. "It
seems to me," wrote Ingersoll, during the summer of
1767, "the Duties intended to be levied are as well chosen
as any could be—what effect they will have I cannot say—
I don't hear of any grumbling about the matter as yet.'"[1]
But, as in the movement against the Stamp Act, Boston
took the lead in stirring up the rest of New England
through an aggressive committee of correspondence. In
October, 1767, her people in town meeting entered into
a non-consumption agreement with regard to a large
number of articles of luxury, as well as certain products
that could be produced in America, but which, as was
the case of the luxuries, were drawn from abroad; they
also passed resolutions in favor of non-importation and
the encouragement of American manufactures.[2]

As would be expected, the eastern Connecticut towns
were the first in this colony to fall into line with the
Boston merchants. Windham held a meeting as early as
December 7 to consider the proposal. But it was not
until February 8 that the friends of this movement were
able to get the New Haven authorities to call a meeting
of the inhabitants to determine whether or not the town
was disposed to adopt similar measures. At this gathering, called to consider an urgent communication from
"the selectmen of Boston, respecting some measures of
economy," the whole matter was referred to the civil

[1] Jared Ingersoll to William Samuel Johnson, July 23, 1767, Johnson
Papers.

[2] *Boston Gazette*, November 2, 1767. Two studies of great importance
have recently been published which throw much light upon the whole question of the non-importation movement. The first, by Professor C. M. Andrews, is "The Boston Merchants and the Non-Importation Movement"
(*The Publications of the Colonial Society of Massachusetts, XIX*), the second, by Professor A. M. Schlesinger, is *The Colonial Merchants and the
American Revolution, 1763-1776*. The latter work is larger and more elaborate than that by Professor Andrews, but in matters common to both much
the same conclusions are reached.

authority and the selectmen, who were asked to bring in a report. After deliberating two weeks, a second meeting was called, by the selectmen, on February 22; it was not, however, until March 4 that the inhabitants were disposed to fling aside their conservatism and to vote that, beginning with March 31, there would be no purchasing of the "enumerated Articles, imported from abroad."[1]

The news of the activities of the Boston agitators at first caused great indignation in England. Friends of the colonies attempted to put the whole matter in a favorable light, urging that this non-consumption movement was founded simply upon the necessities of the people, the want of trade, scarcity of specie, and the inability to pay debts without greater frugality than formerly. To the criticism that the agreement was entered into with other motives, especially to show resentment against England and the laws and regulations of parliament, colonial supporters replied, it is to be feared not very ingenuously, "that there is no clear ground for this position and that it is a harsh, uncandid construction, which ought not to be made."[2] Johnson, writing to Pitkin in December, regarding the activity of Boston, laid bare his

[1] The report that was "Passed by a full vote" reads as follows: "To encourage the produce and manufactures of this Colony and to lessen the use of superfluities, and especially the use of the following importations:

"Carriages, Horse furniture, Hats, Ready Made Apparel, House furniture, shoes, laces, articles of jewelry, Clocks, furs, broadcloth costing above 10s per yard, liquirs.

"That a subscription is recommended for the Inhabitants whereby they agree after the 31st day of March next not to purchase any of the above articles imported after said 31st of March, and will promote saving of linen rags for manufacture of paper."

The New Haven Town Records, IV, under date of February 28 and March 4, 1768; *Connecticut Journal*, February 12 and March 4, 1768.

[2] William Samuel Johnson to Governor William Pitkin, December 26, 1767, Mass. Hist. Soc. *Coll.* (fifth series), IX, 248-249.

real feelings. "I must own, indeed, that our best friends do rather condemn the time and manner of doing it, and hope the example will not be followed in other towns and Colonies."[1]

As was stated above, the resistance against the Townshend Act, starting from Boston, spread from town to town in New England and southward. In other words, it was essentially, although not exclusively, a town movement and was promoted in the official gatherings of the inhabitants. The report of the American Board of Customs Commissioners sent to the Treasury Board from Boston early in February, 1768, was not such as to reassure the ministry regarding the official activities of the New England towns. In these popular governments, they declared, there were frequent assemblies of the people at large under the name of "town meetings," which were originally instituted to regulate the prudential concerns of the towns, but had been converted to answer political purposes. "At these meetings the lowest Mechanics discuss upon the most important points of government, with the utmost freedom, which being guided by a few hot and designing men become a constant source of sedition. Men of character avoid these Meetings and the strongest have generally the best of the argument, and they could not oppose any popular measure without being exposed to insult and resentment."[2]

There is little doubt that a change was taking place in New England, which warrants much that the commissioners had to charge against this section. The conservative group was slowly losing its grasp. Opposed to changes as New Haven had been, even she was now under the domination of that religio-politicio, radically inclined

[1] Mass. Hist. Soc. *Coll.*

[2] American Board of Customs Commissioners to the Lords Commissioners of His Majesty's Treasury, February 12, 1768, C. O. 5: 226, fo. 192 a.

faction known as the New Lights.[1] Such an unusually able and solid man as Judge Ebenezer Silliman of Fairfield, Connecticut, was retired from public life for a time for opposing the appointment to a town office of one of the local Sons of Liberty, "which raised great indignation."[2] "Political Orthodoxy, I think is dying in this Government," lamented John Devotion, "could we but recover Gov'r Fitch & the Old Senators, methinks there might be better times."[3] The change was, of course, reflected in the attitude of the men who were now sent to the general assembly. At the May session of 1768, that body passed the famous Connecticut Import Duty Act, which levied a duty of £5 for every £100 worth of goods, wares, and merchandise, except lumber, brought into the colony by all those who were not inhabitants therein. This struck at English importers as well as those of New York, Massachusetts, and Rhode Island.[4] Furthermore, the assembly came to the resolution to petition, from now on, only the king, "because to petition Parliament would be a tacit confession of its right to lay impositions upon us; which right and authority we publicly disavow."[5] Acting upon this, a petition to the king against the taxation by parliament was drawn up and signed by Governor Pitkin, June 10, 1768.[6]

The superior court of the colony, which in 1766 showed its independence of the radicals, now, with Jonathan Trumbull as chief justice, threw its influence into the balance of the popular cause. Both in March, 1768, and in April, 1769, Duncan Stewart, collector for the port of

[1] John Hubbard to Ezra Stiles, September 21, 1766, *Itineraries of Ezra Stiles*, p. 511.

[2] John Devotion to Ezra Stiles, October 15, 1767, *ibid.*, p. 470.

[3] John Devotion to Ezra Stiles, February 6, 1767, *ibid.*, p. 462.

[4] *Conn. Col. Rec.*, XIII, 72.

[5] I. W. Stuart, *Life of Trumbull*, p. 100, note.

[6] *Conn. Col. Rec.*, XIII, 86-88.

New London, applied to this court for writs of assistance. The court submitted the matter to the general assembly at its May session in 1769; the assembly appointed a committee to consider the issue, and this committee advised the assembly to take no notice of the affair one way or the other, and also *"as individuals,* not as members of the assembly, they advised the court *not to grant* such Warrants, which seemed to be the universal opinion."[1] Trumbull, writing to Johnson, June 14, informed him of the determination of the court to grant only such warrants as were "at the same time consistent with the liberty and privilege of the subject, and made returnable to the Court."[2]

Indeed, affairs in the corporate colonies by 1768—according to a memorial of the American Board of Customs Commissioners—had taken on a very discouraging aspect for those endeavoring to uphold the king's authority. "Though smuggling has been carried to very great height, yet six seizures only have been made in New England provinces within the course of two years and a half, & only one prosecuted to effect, the second was rescued out of the custody of our officers at Falmouth, who were at the same time attacked by a mob, a third was carried off clandestinely at New London while under prosecution, the fifth and sixth were acquitted at Rhode Island through the Combination and influence of the people."[3] William Hart, writing from Saybrook, Connecticut, Au-

1 Jonathan Trumbull to William Samuel Johnson, June 14, 1769, I. W. Stuart, *Life of Trumbull,* p. 81. "I have taken care to find what the courts in the other Colonies have done, and find no such Writs have been given by any of the Courts Except in Massachusetts and New Hampshire, where they were given as soon as asked for. I believe the Courts in all the other Colonies will be well united, and as firm in this Matter, as in anything that has yet happened between us and Great Britain." *Ibid.*

2 *Ibid.*

3 American Board of Customs Commissioners to the Lords Commissioners of His Majesty's Treasury, February 12, 1768, C. O. 5: 226, fo. 192 a.

gust 12, 1768, and in touch with the situation, was filled
with foreboding. "We are in a strange, dangerous, unsettled disposition, meditating great changes in all respects, in America and in Brittain. I suspect things are
ripening for some great revolution."[1] "It seems pretty
probable," said William Samuel Johnson gloomily, in a
letter from London to Dr. Gale, the following year, "that
we shall go on contending and fretting each other till
your prophesy shall, as it certainly will be, fulfilled, and
we become separate and independent empires. . . . If we
were wise and could form some system of free government upon just principles, we might be very happy without any connection with this country. But should we
ever agree upon anything of this nature? Should we not
more properly fall into factions and parties among ourselves, destroy each other and become at length an easy
prey of the first invader?"[2]

That the attitude of the colonies was giving the Grafton
ministry no little concern is shown by the creation, in
1768, of the office of secretary of state for the colonies,
and the appointment of the energetic, well-meaning, but
tactless Earl of Hillsborough to this post. Hillsborough
sought to get control of the situation. As for Connecticut, he was convinced that the colony was "in danger of
being too much a separate, independent state, and of
having too little subordination" for the mother country.[3]
The treatment at this time accorded to Connecticut com-
municants of the Church of England was one, among
many things that may be cited, which, in the minds of
contemporaries, justified this attitude.[4]

[1] William Hart to Ezra Stiles, *Itineraries of Ezra Stiles*, p. 496.

[2] William Samuel Johnson to Benjamin Gale, April, 1769, E. E. Beardsley, *Life of William Samuel Johnson*, p. 65.

[3] William Samuel Johnson to Governor Pitkin, February 13, 1768, Mass.
Hist. Soc. *Coll.* (fifth series), IX, 261.

[4] *Connecticut Courant*, June 12, 1769. Rev. Samuel Peters of Hebron in

Not many weeks after taking office Hillsborough had a memorable interview with William Samuel Johnson, who was still serving the colony as its London agent. He complained to Johnson that Connecticut had been negligent about sending over her laws. He declared that he had requested a copy of them and "had known the like demand made when he was at the Board of Trade, and had been informed that it had been repeatedly made long before that, but he could not find that any obedience had been paid to the requisition."[1] Johnson replied that he believed the colony had several times sent over copies of the printed law books; and that he thought there was one or more of these at the Plantation Office.[2] The secretary, however, went on to state that, as his was a new office, it would be necessary to lodge a copy of the laws with him; he also thought it was the duty of the colony to transmit, from time to time, not only the laws that should pass, but all the minutes of the proceedings of the governor's council and the general assembly, that it might be known what lines the colony was pursuing and how the government was administered, in order that whatsoever was amiss might be rectified.

The Connecticut agent did not hesitate to reply to this sweeping request that "if his Lordship meant to have

an open letter of protest, in the *Connecticut Courant* of May 26, 1769, made clear the situation of the Anglicans. "The Rubrick of the Church of England confirmed by act of Parliament," he declared, "enjoins me to rejoice and be exceeding glad upon Sundays, Christmas and Easter Holydays—But the Governor's Proclamation enjoins all to fast upon Easter holydays. I cannot serve two masters; of the twain whom shall I obey?" What led the rector to make this public appeal was that eight of his parishioners were, according to him, unjustifiably fined for breach of the public fast at Easter time.

[1] William Samuel Johnson to Governor Pitkin, February 13, 1768, Mass. Hist. Soc. *Coll.* (fifth series), IX, 255.

[2] Johnson was correct. See the introduction, written by Professor Andrews, to *Fane's Reports on the Laws of Connecticut*, p. 10, *passim*.

the laws now in force there and those which should here-after pass, transmitted (as from the Colonies imme-diately under the Crown) for the inspection of the Min-istry, as such, and for the purpose of approbation or disapprobation by his Majesty in Council (which I saw very plainly was what he was driving at), it was what the Colony had never done, nor thought themselves obliged to do, and I was persuaded would never submit to.''

Hillsborough informed Johnson that he had read with some attention the charter, and knew what powers had been exercised under it. There were, however, he in-sisted, such things as extravagant grants, which were, therefore, void; there were many things which the king could not grant as the inseparable incidents of the crown and it might deserve consideration whether some things which King Charles had pretended to grant to the Colony of Connecticut were not of that nature, particularly the power of absolute legislation, ''which tended to the ab-surdity of introducing *imperium in imperio,* and to create an independent state.'' The laws of the colony, he con-cluded, ought, therefore, to be regularly transmitted for the inspection of the Privy Council, ''and for *disappro-bation,* if found within the saving of the charter, *repug-nant to the laws of England.*'' Johnson, however, boldly retorted ''that the Colony did not apprehend that any extra judicial opinion of his Majesty's Ministers, or even of the King's Privy Council, could determine whether any particular act was within that proviso or not; that this only could be decided by a court of law; having jurisdiction of the matter about which the law in question was conversant . . . that this might be done in the courts of law in the Colony, and . . . very fairly decided there, and have no room for an application here.'' It is need-less to say that Hillsborough was given the impression that this little Puritan colony had cultivated a very inde-

pendent frame of mind and was disposed to stand firmly
for the retention of every special exemption and privilege.

In entering into the non-consumption agreement, the
Connecticut townsmen had been led to believe that by this
means so many interests in the mother country would be
injured that sufficient pressure could be brought to bear
upon the ministry, as was the case in the Stamp Act
crisis, to result in the repeal of the Townshend revenue
measure, which they now had come to consider a distinct
violation of charter privileges. Undoubtedly the majority of the freemen in the town subscribed to the agreement in good faith. As the weeks and months passed
by, however, the loyalty of many to the plan seems to
have been badly shaken, especially when brought face to
face with personal interest. Local merchants kept stock-
ing up with supplies of the prohibited articles. A Son
of Liberty, early in 1769, lamented the visible failure in
Connecticut of this method of opposition against the
distasteful acts of parliament. "Notwithstanding all
the Talk, and the Resolves upon the Subject, 'tis an in-
contestable Fact," he declared, "that all our Trading
Seaport Towns are stored full as ever with British
goods."[1] Clearly non-consumption of enumerated im-
ports could not stand without the aid of a non-importation agreement. As early as March 1, 1768, the Boston
merchants came to a realization of the necessity for this
step;[2] the New York merchants, in April, arrived at a
similar decision,[3] and in the latter part of August adopted
certain resolves which New Haven was ultimately pre-

[1] *Connecticut Journal*, January 6, 1769.

[2] C. M. Andrews, *The Boston Merchants and the Non-Importation Movement*, pp. 201 et seq.

[3] *New York Gazette and the Weekly Mercury*, April 18, 1768. For the
general progress of the non-importation movement, see A. M. Schlesinger,
The Colonial Merchants and the American Revolution.

vailed upon to accept, without much modification, but not, however, until the month of July, 1769.[1]

Officially New Haven remained cautious and conservative in action. However, as time went on, the temper of many of the people, and especially the mercantile element, in their opposition to parliamentary control, rose to a new level. This is evidenced by the punishment inflicted upon a fellow townsman, Nathan Smith, late in the summer of 1769. It seems that Smith lodged with the customs officials information against one of the ''first merchants'' of New Haven, whom he accused of smuggling rum into the colony by landing it at a cove some distance away from the city. The customs officials went to the designated spot but failed to find there the vessel that Smith alleged was used for this illicit traffic. The merchant in question asserted that she was at that time in the West Indies and was not taking rum on board.

The wrath of the community now descended upon the head of the unfortunate Nathan. ''Being caught he was advanced to the command of a cart, suitably dressed out for the voyage, on whose deck no one except himself and his musicians appeared, and thus equipped he took his land tacks on board and made the most public ports of the town, proclaiming himself a liar, an informer and a pest to society, until he got safe moored on a stand in the market place. When, on assuming those ludicrous and opprobrious attitudes suited to his character for a proper space, he was conducted down and pay'd well with so much tar, feathers and infamy as he could wag home.''[2] The writer of this narrative was careful to mention the fact before concluding that ''the whole being conducted by the principal merchants not the least violence or dis-

---

[1] *Connecticut Courant,* November 6, 1769.

[2] *Connecticut Journal,* September 15, 1769.

order was committed, but after the bonfire of a tar barrel, suitably elevated, all was quiet.''

The pronounced determination to terrorize those who might be disposed to assist in the enforcement of the trade laws by reporting smugglers to the customs officials was also manifested the following week, when a crowd set upon Adonijah Thomas, another resident of the town. ''In the Presence of the Gentlemen Merchants, and Inhabitants'' he was compelled to declare, ''I have attempted to inform against Mr. Timothy Jones, Jun[r], for running of Goods, for which I humbly beg the pardon of the whole inhabitants of this Colony, and this Town in particular and hope the said Inhabitants will receive me into their former Favor and Esteem: And acknowledge that my Punishment is far less than the Demerit of my heinous Crime deserves.''[1] After this confession had been publicly read, the frightened man was forgiven and the crowd dispersed, but not before declaring ''that whosoever attempts to do the like, or to support or encourage any of those mean Wretches, who may be hardy enough to attempt any Thing of the like Nature, that they may expect to receive a Reward adequate to their Crime.''[2] It is easy to perceive that New Haven, by 1769, had become, as a community, much more radical than it was in 1766, when, in the affair of the informer, Peter Boles, the leading townsmen turned sternly against mob rule and terrorism.[3] This attitude, which appears to have been generally manifested throughout the colony, placed the people in a most contradictory position. On the one hand, through their agents, they were demanding a most punctilious observance on the part of the central

[1] *Connecticut Journal*, September 22, 1769. It should be noticed that there was no attempt made to deny that Timothy Jones, Jr., had been ''running goods.''

[2] *Ibid.*

[3] See the preceding chapter for an account of this.

government of every established legal relation between themselves and the mother country; they insisted that harmony and happiness alone could come through the careful respecting of every customary right. On the other hand, the inhabitants of one of the soberest and best regulated towns of the colony were most flagrantly repudiating this very position by sternly suppressing those who were disposed to help in the maintenance of the trade and navigation acts, which, it must be remembered, had long been accepted as binding.

To maintain the non-importation agreement meant no little sacrifice on the part of the people. But even this willingness to dispense with English products was not considered to be sufficient; manufactures, within the colony, and elsewhere in America, must be promoted. The latter part of February, 1770, a meeting was called at Middletown, which was attended by the principal merchants and traders of the colony; it was presided over by Gurdon Saltonstall, with Silas Deane acting as clerk. The list of articles that might be imported into the colony was increased over the list published by New Haven, July 10 of the preceding year, but it is to be noted that these additions included such things as powder, shot, saltpetre, brimstone, and bar lead; all of which gave an ominous appearance to the proceedings of this meeting. Articles necessary to promote fisheries, and the manufacture of paper, shoes, clothes and hats were also to be allowed ready entrance into the colony. It was voted, also, that no dealings should be had with inhabitants of neighboring colonies who did not adhere strictly to the non-importation agreements of their respective colonies. For the encouragement of "Arts, agriculture, manufactures, trade and commerce," it was further recommended that the people of the colony form themselves into a "resultary society," and that a committee be appointed to take

the subscriptions of such as should think proper to join
the same and to receive donations, with the understanding that those who contributed twenty shillings should be
admitted to vote in the society at all times thereafter. To
further this end, there was collected among those present over £100 lawful money, and a meeting of the society was called for May 22, at which premiums of various
kinds for the promotion of industry were to be agreed
upon and published.

Before the adjournment of the Middletown meeting,
four additional resolutions were adopted. One, to the
effect that a committee, appointed for the purpose, should
propose to the general assembly at the May session that
a bounty of six pence per hundred be given on all flour
manufactured in the colony, and exported out of the same
in bottoms belonging to the colony, to any market south
of Pennsylvania and east of Connecticut; and that to
raise a fund to provide the bounty there should be levied
a duty of six pence a pound on all tea to be consumed in
the colony. Again, in order to bring ''great and extensive benefits'' to the colony, by developing the cod and
whale fishery, the same committee was also to petition
the assembly that all vessels owned in the colony and
employed in the cod and whale fishery for the space of
four months in any year should be free from any tax and
left out of the ratable list, and that the persons likewise employed in this enterprise should be exempt from
a poll tax, and from working on the highways for the
year in which they should be so employed. Further, in
consideration of the extreme scarcity of cash in the colony and the many frauds and the inconveniences arising
out of the fact that notes in hand were not negotiable in
the colony, as they were in Great Britain and in some of
the other colonies, it was voted that all present should
use every proper means to obtain an act making notes in

hand negotiable. Lastly, the gathering pledged itself to obtain, if it could, proper encouragement for the erecting within the colony of works for the making of window glass.[1]

It would appear that an attempt was made, in a more or less tumultuous way, to carry the above proposals through the general assembly in May, but that body, representing especially agricultural interests, was not disposed to yield to all of the demands of the trading and commercial elements even in such a crisis. Instead of providing for bounties and exemptions, it passed a ringing resolution that ''for the future no petition brought to the assembly and to be heard upon the merits of the cause . . . shall have a public hearing of the parties before the assembly, *viva voce;* but every petition . . . shall be determined upon the pleas and exhibits made in writing only . . . any law, usage, or custom to the contrary, notwithstanding.''[2] Unwilling as it was to burden the people of the colony with a tea tax to encourage the exportation of flour, the assembly, however, at its October session, extended the desired encouragement to those who would engage in the cod and whale fisheries.[3]

That there was much genuine determination on the part of the people of New Haven, in common with other American seaports, to make effective the non-intercourse measures against England was shown when, on June 12, 1770, it was resolved, on a meeting of traders and tradesmen, held at the state house in that town, that all commercial intercourse with the inhabitants of Rhode Island, ''who have most unaccountably violated their Non-Importation agreement,'' should be discontinued, until they

[1] *Connecticut Journal,* March 2, 1770, supplement; see also the *New London Gazette,* June 15, 1770.

[2] *Conn. Col. Rec.,* XIII, 301.

[3] *Ibid.,* XIII, 365.

returned to their duty. More than that, a committee was appointed to wait upon the captain of a trading vessel from Rhode Island, which had arrived in Stratford River, and to desire him to depart from the colony immediately. This was done, and the captain gave his promise to leave as soon as he had cleared his vessel at the custom house.[1]

There were, of course, many living in this community who could not easily sacrifice personal comforts to promote the general cause. Great pressure was brought to bear upon local traders to violate the agreement, especially with reference to such highly desired articles as tea. One skipper claimed that he was beset by ladies to furnish them with "that expensive herb called Bohea tea." When he urged that the duties were not taken off, the ladies, according to his statement, answered that they would keep the matter secret or lay those whom they told of their good fortune under obligation not to tell.[2] It was charged in the papers that a quantity of tea and sundry other things had been spirited into the colony from Boston, and that there was such a longing for these things that there was little real opposition against the bringing of them in, in spite of the agreements and the fact that the Sons of Liberty took the matter of these violations in hand and "partly made the importers promise not to sell, which sufficed." But sales apparently went on.[3] Indeed, some of these very Sons of Liberty

[1] *Connecticut Journal*, June 15, 1770.

[2] *Ibid.*, January 22, 1770.

[3] *Ibid.*, February 3, 1770. Professor Schlesinger considers that all evidence would indicate that New Jersey, the Delaware Counties, and Connecticut "were true to their professions of non-importation and non-consumption." *The Colonial Merchants and the American Revolution*, p. 196. In support of his position he cites, "A Freeman of Connecticut," who affirmed, in the July 30 issue of the *Connecticut Courant*, that the town agreements had been kept "save in three or four trivial instances, inadvertently and inconsiderately done; and in every instance, one excepted, public satisfaction has been given and the goods stored."

were accused of buying the prohibited articles, which
brought forth a stinging rebuke from a correspondent to
the local paper, who declared that "a snake in the grass
had a better advantage to bite than in a plain open field.'"[1]
It is not, of course, surprising that some of those who
had, for the sake of self-interest, been violating the trade
laws of the nation, failed to find it any easier to abstain
from violating the non-importation agreement made with
their fellow townsmen, when they found that this, likewise, conflicted with notions of personal benefit; it was
all, largely, a habit of mind with them. What undoubtedly encouraged this practice was the assurance received from England that the ministry had decided to
give up and to bring about the repeal of the Townshend
Act.

The ministry, in fact, was sailing through rough
waters, in the warring of the parliamentary factions.
Whichever way it proceeded, it was sure to be bitterly
assailed by those within and without parliament. The
Grenville faction took no little satisfaction in the writhing of those former opponents of the Stamp Act who
had started out so confidently to prove how it was possible to equalize, in a measure, the crushing burdens of the
state, due largely to the national debt and the cost of the
necessary military and naval protection; but Grenville
would not vote to repeal the revenue act. The opponents
of the act, however, were gaining in strength day by day,
as the realization came home to members that nothing
was being accomplished by the measure, except the further irritation of the colonies. On April 19, 1769, ex-
Governor Pownall moved the repeal of the act, offering
as the basis for this his reasons that it was universally
held to be anti-commercial, prejudicial to the manufac-

[1] *Connecticut Journal,* January 22, 1770.

tures of Great Britain, and even unjust, as it imposed
duties for the support of government equally upon those
who had and those who had not provided funds for that
purpose. In the same debate Burke vigorously declared
that he believed all parties were now pretty well agreed
that it was in vain to think further of any real practical
plan of raising a revenue in America, and he hoped that
it would never again be attempted; the money of the
colonies must be drawn from them in another way, and
that was by commerce alone. On the other hand, Lord
North pointed out that for parliament to give way upon
this issue would be practically to signify to the colonies
their independence of the mother country; that members
would find in the future whenever any act of parliament
was made not perfectly agreeable to the Americans, they
would again go into the same measures to obtain a repeal, and, in the end, get rid of all acts of parliament,
"Even that essential one, the Act of Navigation, the
basis of the wealth and power of Great Britain."[1] After
several meetings, the English merchants agreed to apply
to parliament for a total repeal of the act, although there
was no such anxiety displayed as during the Stamp Act
crisis.[2] At length, on March 3, 1770, by a vote of 244 to
142, the ministry carried a motion through the House of
Commons that all dutiable articles in the Revenue Act
should be withdrawn from the schedule with the exception of tea. When the news of this reached America, it
had a decisive influence in breaking down the non-importation agreements. New York, up to that time, had shown
a most enviable determination to refrain from importing
until the total repeal of the act. From December 25,

[1] William Samuel Johnson to Governor Pitkin, April 26, 1769, Mass.
Hist. Soc. *Coll.* (fifth series), IX, 335-338.
[2] William Samuel Johnson to Jonathan Trumbull, February 3, 1770, *ibid.*,
IX, 406.

1767, to December 25, 1768, the value of goods that she had received from England had amounted, according to the custom house entries, to £48̇2,000; between 1768 and 1769, the total dropped to £74,000.[1] ''How forcible would the commercial agreement have appeared, had all the colonies abated in the proportion New York has done, who seems to have imported only the articles by the agreements,'' wrote William Samuel Johnson from London, to Jonathan Trumbull, early in March, 1770.[2] Her spirit, however, had been greatly weakened as the reports came in from the North and the South about the breaking of the agreement, and it was, at last, decided, at a merchants' meeting, held in June, to take the sense of the city whether it was in favor of holding out or of modifying the agreement. After two canvasses were made, which seemed to show the community in favor of modification, the merchants gave their orders for British goods, with the exception of tea.[3] ''I cannot express to you with what astonishment and confusion, on the one hand, and with what exultation and triumph on the other, the news that the merchants of New York have agreed to open trade has been received here,''[4] wrote Johnson to Governor Trumbull from his London lodgings. In Connecticut, great bitterness of feeling immediately manifested itself against New York. A New Haven meeting of merchants, traders, and other inhabitants was called

---

[1] Among the Trumbull Papers, which are printed in the Massachusetts Historical Society *Collections* (fifth series), IX, 424, there is presented a table showing the values of these importations into the various colonies.

[2] *Ibid.*

[3] For the collapse of non-importation, see A. M. Schlesinger, *The Colonial Merchants and the American Revolution, 1763-1776*, pp. 217-227; also, C. M. Andrews, *The Boston Merchants and the Non-Importation Movement*, pp. 236-259; C. L. Becker, *Political Parties in New York, 1760-1776*, pp. 88-94.

[4] William Samuel Johnson to Governor Trumbull, August 20, 1770, Mass. Hist. Soc. *Coll.* (fifth series), IX, 450.

on July 26, at which Roger Sherman presided. There was laid before the gathering a letter from the merchants of New York to those in Philadelphia, acquainting them with their plan to import. The New Haven assemblage thereupon expressed its "surprise and astonishment at the defection of New York. Is it possible? She who made the greatest professions of patriotism, and stood foremost in the glorious cause of American liberty, should suddenly break that very agreement she so zealously affected to accomplish! . . . Is it for a few months' commerce, for which they . . . sacrifice liberty, not only theirs, and their posterities', but of their countrymen in general; and give them over to vassalage and slavery?"[1] It was thereupon resolved to withdraw the New Haven trade—"so far as not to purchase any goods imported from Great Britain"—from such persons in New York who should import goods contrary to the agreement, even though the act should be repealed, unless these individuals would speedily return to their agreement.

In a letter addressed to the merchants of other towns in Connecticut, the feelings of the New Haven traders and merchants were even more freely expressed. "The time is now come for us to determine whether we will be freemen or slaves: . . . whether we will tamely coalesce with the measures of our backsliding brethren of New York, who by resolving on importation at this Juncture have meanly prostituted the common cause to the present sordid prospect of a little pelf. . . . There is no time to lose and can we hesitate a moment in choosing whether we will continue our connection with those degenerate imposters, and with the prospect of a little temporary wealth bequeath infamy, poverty and slavery to our posterity?"[2]

[1] *Connecticut Journal*, August 3, 1770.
[2] This is printed in L. H. Boutell's *Life of Roger Sherman*, pp. 58-59.

Similar indignation meetings to that at New Haven were held at Hartford on August 13, at Norwich on August 23, at Farmington and Middletown on August 30. In fact, "a great Majority of the Towns" of the colony held gatherings of a similar type. In the August 17 issue of the *Connecticut Journal,* published at New Haven, there appeared an announcement on the part of the "Merchants and Traders of the Colony of Connecticut," calling upon the New York importers "to draw out their accounts immediately," as they were determined to have no further dealings with them. Those who had balances in their favor with Connecticut merchants were desired to apply personally in order that an opportunity might be given "to show them every mark of respect which their late patriotic conduct entitles them to"—for this reason no money would be paid to their attorneys. The same issue of the *Journal* also conveyed the news that "The tavern keepers throughout Connecticut, it is said, have posted up a list of names of New York importers and have determined not to give them shelter or entertainment." What is more, by concerted action the different towns selected representatives to go to New Haven for a meeting on September 17, and it is important to notice that these delegations were made up of both the mercantile and the landed interests. The meeting was held as scheduled and again Gurdon Saltonstall presided and Silas Deane acted as clerk, as was the case at the Middletown gathering in February. The "Middletown Agreement" was reaffirmed as "founded on free, virtuous, peaceable, manly and patriotic principles," and it was voted that by action of New York, "the union of Colonies . . . is greatly weakened, our enemies abroad rather animated against us, and our friends in a degree discouraged," and it was therefore decided not to purchase from New York merchants any merchandise imported from Great Britain directly or indirectly.[1]

It is interesting to note that, in spite of this developing hostility to the mother country, Jared Ingersoll appeared to have grown in favor with the people of his community and the colony generally. In September, 1768, he was recompensed, rather tardily, it is true, to the amount of fifty pounds for his special exertions as colonial agent in England at the time of the passing of the Stamp Act,[2] and in addition received the thanks of the general assembly for making the colony a present of some £110 sterling still due for past services.[3] In 1770 the selectmen of Wallingford, the center of radicalism within the county, employed him as special counsel,[4] and on September 18, the day after the general meeting of the mercantile interests of the colony, he was delegated at a town meeting to act as one of a committee "to take into consideration the present state of the commercial interests of this place."[5] It is significant that Ralph Isaacs, who was also identified with the most conservative group of the town, and who later became a pronounced Tory, was likewise on the committee. This shows that either there had taken place a reaction in New Haven in the direction of its earlier conservatism, or that the non-trading, agricultural element, which was opposed to the extreme position of the traders, was powerful enough to dictate the personnel of the committee. Nothing apparently came of its activities, unless it was that the report which it made tended to discourage the maintenance of the non-importation

[1] *Connecticut Journal*, September 21, 1770.

[2] His original charge of £100 was reduced to £50, Ingersoll Record Book, vol. II.

[3] *Connecticut Journal*, February 17, 1769.

[4] Ingersoll Papers, loose-leaf memorandum.

[5] New Haven Town Records, V, 6.

agreement. The year 1771 was destined to witness the collapse of the non-importation program in Connecticut.[1]

Early in 1771 there began to appear in Connecticut papers attacks against this program, which was now held up to be an imprudent and injurious measure. It was freely asserted that if all who had signed the subscription had religiously adhered to it, bankruptcy would have faced every merchant in New Haven who was not independently rich, and the distress which came to the poor, now deprived of cheap clothing, was emphasized.

"But, alas!" mournfully wrote one townsman, "we see no more patriotic resolves of our merchants in the papers since the arrival of the ships at New York with goods. Our towns are already filled with the manufactures of Great Britain—how cheap they are sold and how much preferred to our own manufactures I will leave the purchaser of experience to say."[2] By May every pretense of maintaining non-importation seems to have disappeared. The whole first page of the May 31 issue of the *Connecticut Journal* was taken up with an elaborate advertisement by John and James Morton, New York merchants, who had just imported from London quantities of the very goods barred by the Middletown and New Haven agreements. "Altho the perfidious and avaricious conduct of New York" was not forgotten entirely by the people, yet in their weakness, "like sheep led to the slaughter," they fell to buying the coveted articles.[3] But, broken as the agreement was, Connecticut had now learned to walk in the ways of radicalism and those ways led straight to political revolution.

[1] However, New York, Philadelphia, and Boston gave up the agreements in 1770. A. M. Schlesinger, *The Colonial Merchants and the American Revolution, 1763-1776*, pp. 233-236.

[2] "A Farmer," in the *Connecticut Journal*, February 22, 1771.

[3] *Ibid.*, October 11, 1771.

CHAPTER X

THE SEARCH FOR PREFERMENT. JUDGE OF
THE COURT OF VICE-ADMIRALTY FOR
THE MIDDLE COLONIES

JARED INGERSOLL became a place hunter. In fact, soon
after the excitement had died down over the attempt to
enforce the Stamp Act, not to be discouraged, he sought
to secure some new appointment in connection with the
British administrative system in the colonies, through
the influence of his friends, Richard Jackson, the Connecticut agent in London, and Thomas Whately, the ex-
secretary to the Treasury Board, whose efforts were
supplemented by those of William Samuel Johnson of
Stratford, Connecticut, who was sent to England in 1766
in connection with the Mason appeal regarding the
Mohegan Indian lands. Ingersoll had certainly suffered
financial loss and the loss of prestige by assuming the
post of stamp distributor for Connecticut in 1765, and
it is clear that he felt that the home government was
under certain obligations to those who had supported
it during the late crisis. And he was not alone in that
opinion.

In February, 1767, Jackson wrote to Ingersoll, "I
heartily wish you may meet with a proper token of regard
from the Government here"; although on friendly terms
with almost all those in the administration, Jackson confessed that he had not been able to discover what plan
would be adopted in America "that will open you a
Door." He had already, he said, proposed something of

benefit for ex-Governor Fitch of Connecticut, who, with
Ingersoll, had been, as it were, a victim of Stamp Act
agitation, with the request that if Fitch did not accept it,
the same should go to Ingersoll; but he went on to remark that if Grenville should come back into power, he
would not ask him for anything, "but," he declared to
Ingersoll, "you have an Interest with him through
Whately, who, I believe, sincerely wishes to serve
you. . . . "[1] For a time, however, nothing came of these
efforts.

During the spring of 1767 Grenville made a speech in
parliament defending the right of that body both to legis-
late for and to tax the colonies, and in this connection
offered two resolutions, one of which demanded that all
the officers of the colonial governments, before entering
upon their duties, should take an oath in which they
should acknowledge the full supremacy of parliament
over the colonies. Although this resolution was lost by
a large majority, Grenville then moved that those in
America who stood by the government during the late
events should be mentioned for favor in a humble address
to be presented to the king. This was passed.[2] Johnson,

[1] Richard Jackson to Jared Ingersoll, February 20, 1767, New Haven
Col. Hist. Soc. *Papers*, IX ("Jared Ingersoll Papers"), 402-403.

On February 8, 1766, Dr. Benjamin Gale wrote to Ingersoll: "I hear
you are appointed Judge of Admiralty for Connecticut & £800 Sallary if
true I Heartily Congratulate you." *Ibid.*, IX, 374. It would be of interest to know the source of this report.

[2] Whately, writing to Grenville, in October, said: "Mr. Ingersol has
heard of the motion made by you in Parliament for marks of favor to the
sufferers, and of your reference in particular to him, for which he desires
me to present to you his most humble acknowledgements, and to let you
know that he has a most grateful sense of your disinterested and truly
friendly goodness to him, who has it not in his power to reward it otherwise than [by] sentiments of unfeigned goodness." Thomas Whately to
George Grenville, October 5, 1767. *The Grenville Correspondence*, VI, 170.
If there seems to be a slight touch of obsequiousness about this, one need
only compare it with a letter that one John Lane wrote to Ingersoll from

writing to Ingersoll in May, said regarding this note, "You have only to regret that it came from Mr. Grenville and proceeded from his Motion, which must be very odious in Amᵃ and may seem to be the immediate reward of supporting his measures, which produced so much Indignⁿ in that Country."[1] There was certainly a feeling within the administration that something should be done for Ingersoll, who had shown the greatest courage in his efforts to give force to the Stamp Act in Connecticut. This is evident from the fact that Whately made known to Johnson that there was talk of giving the ex-distributor of stamps the chief justiceship of New York, "if it can be genteel'y disengaged from another person. . . ."[2]

Ingersoll's receptivity to any good offer is indicated in a communication that he wrote to Johnson the latter part of July. He referred to the fact that parliament had mentioned him as one particularly deserving of recognition and reward and said that he had to thank Whately for that. Turning to the suggestions that had been made in his favor, he then declared, "I will form no objections to the Chief Justiceship of N. York, if obtainable, nor to a Seat at the New Board of Revenues, nor to any other that you shall approve of, as I still have a full confidence

Boston: "I do not purpose to see Connecticut till the latter end of the year when I intend myself the pleasure of kissing your hands. Till then I beg leave to remain, your most humble servant, John Lane. Boston, May 9, 1767." Ingersoll Papers.

[1] William Samuél Johnson to Jared Ingersoll, May 16, 1767, Johnson Papers.

[2] *Ibid.* "In 1698 the chief justice received £100; in 1702 he received £300 and a fee of ten shillings on the first motion in every cause; the second Judge £150; the associate £50; in 1765 the chief justice was allowed £300 and the associates £200 for holding the circuits; in 1774 the chief justice received from the crown £500 sterling and £300, New York currency, from the province." E. A. Werner, *Civil List and Constitutional History of the City and State of New York,* p. 376.

both in your Judgment & friendship.'"¹ The new board of revenues here mentioned was of course the new American Board of Customs Commissioners provided for, in June, by the Townshend Acts, which was to sit in Boston. Jackson, writing in September, assured Ingersoll that he would not forget to further his interests whenever possible. "I think you will not want much Assistance, but will infallibly sometime or other be somehow remembered to your advantage." He further declared that he had recommended both Fitch and Ingersoll for places on the American customs board, but had been met by the objection that the measure, which provided for these commissioners, might be rendered obnoxious if "unpopular People" were named; this, he thought, was "the ostensible Reason only."² Johnson, in a letter to Ingersoll, the middle of November, said that it was confidently expected that both he and Fitch would be appointed to the board of customs; he was sorry to announce, however, to his friend that these lucrative places were filled without paying regard to the address to the crown in favor of the Stamp Act sufferers. As to the chief justiceship of New York, it had been hinted that it also had now been "reserv'd for a certain Gentⁿ now in Amᵃ & to a particular purpose which I durst not mention unless I could whisper it in yʳ Ear.'"³

¹ Jared Ingersoll to William Samuel Johnson, July 23, 1767, Johnson Papers. Ingersoll told Johnson in the same letter that Whately had given proofs of his friendship. He also stated that he had written to Fitch "to learn his intentions."

² Richard Jackson to Jared Ingersoll, September 8, 1767, New Haven Col. Hist. Soc. *Papers*, IX ("Jared Ingersoll Papers"), 413-414. Later in September, Oliver sent Ingersoll an enclosure "from our mutual friend, Mr. Whately," which showed the determination of the government "to support its friends." Oliver had heard that Fitch was to be one of the board of customs. Andrew Oliver to Jared Ingersoll, September 22, 1767, Ingersoll Papers.

³ William Samuel Johnson to Jared Ingersoll, November 12, 1767, New Haven Col. Hist. Soc. *Papers*, IX ("Jared Ingersoll Papers"), 415-417.

Ingersoll's disappointment in thus being passed over must soon have disappeared; for, not long after receiving Johnson's discouraging letter, there came the news of his appointment as judge of one of the four special courts of vice-admiralty that had been created by letters patent under the great seal in 1768. The district within which the jurisdiction of this new court ran embraced the colonies of New York, New Jersey, Pennsylvania, the lower counties on the Delaware, Maryland, and Virginia.

It seems that Lord North, who was now a leading member of the Grafton ministry, had made up his mind, apparently uninfluenced by anyone, that Ingersoll, whose great abilities as a lawyer were appreciated in England, should be given the refusal of one of these important judgeships. Knowing of Whately's intimacy with the latter, he sought information from him as to whether such an appointment with a salary of £400 per annum and a residence at either Philadelphia or Virginia or South Carolina would be agreeable to him. Whately immediately sought Johnson, and after the two had discussed the matter, the former waited upon Lord North and accepted for Ingersoll, under the condition that he should not be sent to South Carolina, which was considered to be too far south "for a Northern Constitution."[1] In congratulating him upon this appointment, Johnson wrote, "The office is Honorᵉ, & lucrative & I hope will be agreeable to you"; he also took occasion to emphasize the fact that since Ingersoll had a large district, in time of war, especially, he might find it more lucrative than a chief justiceship at common law even

[1] William Samuel Johnson to Jared Ingersoll, November 30, 1767. Printed in the "Jared Ingersoll Papers," in vol. IX of the New Haven Col. Hist. Soc. *Papers.* Johnson here confessed to Ingersoll that he had begun to despair of anything being done for the American supporters of the crown during the late crisis, but was agreeably disappointed.

with its proposed salary of £500, and also "from the diffe of Fees in these two kinds of Courts, probably not inferior in time of Peace.'"[1]

As Whately informed Johnson that he did not choose "to be seen in the affair," the latter took charge of the work of suing out Ingersoll's commission, settling the fees, which amounted to £5 7s. 6d., at the Admiralty, and £12 9s. 4d. at Doctors' Commons.[2] The commission reached New Haven early in 1769.[3]

For some unaccountable reason it was over two years before Ingersoll took up his residence at Philadelphia and actually entered upon the duties of his office. That his continued residence in Connecticut became indeed the subject of adverse comment in England, is evidenced by a letter which Johnson wrote to him early in December, 1769. He declared that there was some surprise in London that the latter was still in Connecticut and also that Mr. Sewall, appointed judge of the Halifax court, was still in Boston; there was still more surprise to hear that Ingersoll was yet in the practice of the law. "Do those Gentn Imagine, say they, that this Office is to be a sine Cure, Are they to be Non resident Judges, or is it

[1] New Haven Col. Hist. Soc. *Papers.* In his statement regarding fees, Johnson has reference to the fact that the collections of vice-admiralty court fees were more certain than those in the common law court. "No man can more sincerely rejoice at yr succeeding in your wishes than I do," Jackson wrote the following March. He declared that he was not sure that Ingersoll would relish the offer made him of "a seat on the Bench of Admiralty Jurisdiction." Richard Jackson to Jared Ingersoll, March 12, 1768, New Haven Col. Hist. Soc. *Papers,* IX ("Jared Ingersoll Papers"), 421-423.

[2] William Samuel Johnson to Jared Ingersoll, January 2, 1768, and September 30, 1768. The first of these is printed in the New Haven Col. Hist. Soc. *Papers,* IX ("Jared Ingersoll Papers"), 419-421; the other is in manuscript among the Johnson Papers.

[3] Captain Rowland, who had been entrusted with the commissions, landed at Boston, January 19, 1769. *New Jersey Archives* (first series), XXVI, under date 1769.

Consistent with the Dignity of a Judge to Cont⁰ in the Practᵉ of the Law?'"¹ In reply to a suggestion from Ingersoll in a previous letter that he also might secure certain good things from the home government, Johnson now took occasion to say that he did not expect any of the good things mentioned "if indeed they are good things," but would return to the practice of law. Even this rather cutting communication from a friend so thoroughly respected did not lead Ingersoll into any precipitate closing up of his law practice. "I am very glad to find," wrote Whately to Judge Ingersoll, the following year, in October, "that you are at last determined to settle at Philadelphia; it was a necessary Precaution; tho' at present I do not hear any Talk of the Admiralty Courts; & I suppose we have too much Business on our hands to take them into consideration.''²

¹ William Samuel Johnson to Jared Ingersoll, December 9, 1769, New Haven Col. Hist. Soc. *Papers*, IX (''Jared Ingersoll Papers''), 426-428. Johnson went on to say: ''Those things I should not trouble you with did they not come from En[gland]. They have dropped from your Friend, & you will pardon my mentᵍ them, merely that you may make such use of them as you think best. I do by you as I wish every Friend to do by me. You will I am sure pardon me if you do not approve such liberty.''

² Thomas Whately to Jared Ingersoll, October 11, 1770, New Haven Col. Hist. Soc. *Papers*, IX (''Jared Ingersoll Papers''), 434. In February, 1770, Andrew Oliver wrote from Boston to Ingersoll, ''I hope you have received a warrant for your pay from the admiralty, as I hear that Judge Auchmuty has received one for his.'' He went on to declare that Fitch had been promoted to the advocate-generalship of the vice-admiralty court of Massachusetts Bay. Ingersoll Papers. On March 12 he replied to a letter of inquiry that Ingersoll had sent to him: ''I cannot find that any Gentⁿ has as yet recᵈ a warrant for his Pay besides Judge Auchmuty and I find that there is some 'demurrer' upon that, but what it is I cannot inform you. I imagine his warrant was obtained by Mr. Hallowell's solicitation. Perhaps you may wait for your agent to apply for it?'' *Ibid.*

Ingersoll congratulated him on his new post. Oliver, in answer to this, said: ''I wish I may enjoy this new appointment with more ease and quiet than the other some years past . . . your friends here wonder at your not having taken the previous measures requisite in order to receive the benefit of your appointment.''

This unaccountable delay in setting up the court may possibly be explained upon the grounds that the home government delayed taking certain necessary steps; it may also be that Ingersoll was indisposed to suffer financial losses by precipitately closing up his law practice. It is interesting and surprising, and in a sense represents a serious indictment of the efficiency of the British colonial administration, to know that he later received his salary for this period of sojourn in Connecticut, which was between October, 1768, and the spring of 1771. Whether or not he sought payment for this period is not known. The fact that it was granted in 1772 was probably due to a desire on the part of the ministry to compensate in some tangible way one who sacrificed not a little to support the home government during the Stamp Act crisis.[1] But it does not alter the fact that for a time the ex-stamp distributor *did* enjoy a sinecure.

By the spring of 1771 Ingersoll was prepared to take

[1] In "An Account of the Application of the Monies arising from the Duties collected and received in America by Act of Parliament as far as the Accounts have been received complete"—which was the period from September 8, 1767, to January 5, 1771—£124,758 17s. 3d. was collected. Out of this sum there was applied to "Jared Ingersoll Esq. Judge of Vice Admiralty; in part of his Salry of £600 up to 17. Oct. 1769, £361. 3s. 3½d." and up "to 17. Oct. 1770, £403. 8s. 6½d." Treasury 1: 514, fo. 226. On April 16, 1772, there was entered at the audit office a warrant allowing "J. Ingersoll, Judge of Vice Admiralty in America £238. 16s. 8½d. Out of Old Stores to Complete One year's Salary to 17th October, 1769." Audit Office 15: 60, p. 352. This warrant was given at the Treasury office November 7, 1771, as was also one for the amount of £196 11s. 5½d. "due on £403. 8s. 6½d. year ending 17 Oct. 1770." *Ibid.*, vol. 60, p. 353.

For the benefit of those students who may desire to use the records of the audit office, it may be stated that since the publication of Professor Andrews's *Guide*, the cataloguing of the documents has been changed. The *Guide* reference for the above is A. O. 1609-1667.

"When I was in Boston last October," wrote Judge Augustus Johnston of the Southern District, "Mr Auchmuty showed me a Letter he had recd from Mr Hallowell in London enclosing him a copy of the minutes of the Treasury Board wherein it was determined, that we should be allowed our

up his new duties. Leaving his son Jared, who had grad-uated from Yale College in 1766, to settle up his remain-ing accounts at New Haven, he and Mrs. Ingersoll sailed for Philadelphia. Soon after his arrival, he set up his court of vice-admiralty for the middle colonies and there-upon, it seems, settled down to a very comfortable, enjoy-able and not exceedingly strenuous routine of life. For Ingersoll was well and favorably known in the American metropolis of that day,[1] and among other old friends he found there was the delightful and fashionable James Hamilton of Bush Hill, who had twice acted as governor of the provinces and who enjoyed considerable popular-ity, especially among the leading people of the city.[2] In-deed, Ingersoll, from a hard-working lawyer in a small Connecticut town, became now one of the leading digni-taries of this aristocratic center. His salary of £600 per annum looked impressive beside the £200 granted to the chief justice of the province of Pennsylvania, and the £100 which the assistant judges of the superior court

Salaries from the dates of our Commissions, provided we entered upon the Execution of our Offices in six months from the date.'' Augustus Johnston to Jared Ingersoll, August 21, 1770. New Haven Col. Hist. Soc. Papers, IX ("Jared Ingersoll Papers"), 432-433.

[1] In 1768 Ozwell Ive of Philadelphia wrote to Ingersoll and among other things he mentioned the fact that the latter was well known in Philadelphia. Ive expressed himself as most fortunate to have his business in such hands. Ingersoll Papers.

[2] In a letter to Ingersoll, written in 1762, Hamilton made clear the basis of the bond between them. ''I reflect with great pleasure on the many happy hours we have passed together on the other side, in such company and conversations as alas! are not to be had on this side of the world and it would afford me a particular satisfaction to have an opportunity of talk-ing over with you some of those agreeable scenes. . . . Your friend, Mr. Franklin and mine if he pleases; for it will much depend on himself, is daly expected from England.'' James Hamilton to Jared Ingersoll, July 8, 1762, Ingersoll Papers. As to the popularity that Governor Hamilton had enjoyed, see J. F. Watson, Annals of Philadelphia and Pennsylvania, II, 276; see also ibid., II, 274, concerning Hamilton's liberality.

were paid.[1] The mere fact that his jurisdiction included both the ports of Philadelphia and New York may be said to have made his district perhaps the most important of the four that had been established. It is unfortunate that the records of the tribunal over which he presided until the outbreak of the American Revolution have disappeared. Yet there is every indication that he was fairly busy with judicial duties. Not only did the new court immediately absorb practically all of the business which previously had gone to the Pennsylvania provincial vice-admiralty court, but it must have drawn to itself either through appeals or through the exercise of original jurisdiction many of the vice-admiralty cases arising in other parts of the district.[2] "I am at present pretty full of business at my Court," wrote Ingersoll, in 1773, to his brother Jonathan, who was pastor of the church at Ridgefield, Connecticut.[3] However, this did not prevent the judge from maintaining the closest connections with New Haven, where his extensive law practice was being continued by his nephew, Jonathan Ingersoll; he made extended visits in Connecticut during the sum-

[1] *Penn. Archives*, IV, 591-600. At first it was planned to give these special judges £400 per annum but the sum was raised to £600.

[2] Laurence Lewis, *Life of Edward Shippen*, p. 19. In a report made to the Earl of Dartmouth from the governor of Pennsylvania, January 20, 1775, the statement was made with reference to the provincial court of admiralty for Pennsylvania, "Of little or no annual value since the establishment of the preceding Court." *Penn. Archives*, IV, 591-600.

[3] Jared Ingersoll to Jonathan Ingersoll, May, 1773. This letter is in the possession of Mr. George Pratt Ingersoll of Ridgefield, Connecticut. In 1770 Augustus Johnston, judge of the admiralty court for the southern district, wrote to Ingersoll from Newport, where he was spending the summer. Referring to his office, he says: "I have not done any Business in the Office myself yet. I left Carolina the 6th of May, & a few days after I left it, there were two Seizures made, which have been tryed by my Deputy in my absence. I propose to set off for Charlestown the beginning of November again, & shall stay the Winter there." Augustus Johnston to Jared Ingersoll, August 21, 1770, New Haven Col. Hist. Soc. *Papers*, IX ("Jared Ingersoll Papers"), 433.

mer vacation of the court, and his continued influence in the affairs of the colony was more than once displayed after taking up his residence in Philadelphia; for the conservative element had not ceased to look to him for leadership. The character of his popularity at New Haven is shown by the fact that in the summer of 1772 the New Haven county court gave a dinner at which Judge and Mrs. Ingersoll were the guests of honor. It apparently was somewhat of an event, for a gentleman by the name of Wylly Elliot besought Ingersoll to use his influence that his son might be one of the speakers on that occasion.[1] It is, indeed, most curious to find this high official of the British government in such favor in a community that, together with the other towns of the colony, was slowly drifting in the direction of open revolt against the authority of the mother country.

As has been evidenced in so many ways, Jared Ingersoll's attachment to Great Britain was not limited, by any means, to a formal and official loyalty to the crown; it was something deep and sincere. His experience in England had been, on the whole, of a most delightful character; he highly esteemed the English people and this was reciprocated by those with whom he had become acquainted during those years of his residence in the mother country.[2] This probably had much to do with the

[1] Wylly Elliot to Jared Ingersoll, August 6, 1772, Ingersoll Papers.

[2] As an example of this mutual regard, Thomas Bridges, whose brother was a member of parliament, wrote to Ingersoll from Hedley, November 8, 1763, a letter expressing affectionate good will. After apologizing for the delay in answering Ingersoll's last letter, he went on to say: ''I will assure you that it did not proceed from forgetfulness, for you are often in our thoughts, the agreeable days we have spent together both at Hedley and in Cavendish Square is often the topic of Mrs. Bridges and my Conversation. . . . It gave Mrs. Bridges and myself great pleasure to find you, Mrs. Ingersoll & your son enjoyed your health; it gives us no small satisfaction, particularly Mrs. Bridges, to find that you did allow Old England to have the preference to North America, which she thinks a great point

decision to send his son to London, where he would be able to complete his legal studies and at the same time be removed from influences in America which warred against a hearty loyalty to the British administration. As a result, early in 1773, Jared, Jr., who was now twenty-four years of age, took passage for Europe; but not before successfully passing his bar examinations and securing admission to practice in the supreme court of the province of Pennsylvania.[1] It may here be added that after traveling on the Continent for a short time, the young man settled down to study at the Inns of Court in London and not until 1779, toward the latter end of the Revolutionary War, did he return to America. Yet, as will be seen, the experience in England did not have the effect of uprooting certain ardent American sentiments which probably had taken root long before his journey abroad.

Comfortably situated as he was in Philadelphia, Ingersoll was made to feel, as time went on, that there were troubled waters ahead. On November 23, 1771, not many months after the opening of the new court of vice-admiralty, there occurred an incident which must have impressed him with the seriousness of the task that confronted him in judicially enforcing the trade and navigation acts within his district. It seems that the collector of customs at the port of Philadelphia, John Swift, had been provided with a schooner, which, under the command of Thomas Musket, coasted for smugglers,

gained, tho you would not allow it when here. & she says she makes no doubt but we shall soon have you again amongst us and begs me to tell you, that she shall most readily execute any commission you will employ her in, such as taking a House, Buying furniture, hiring servants, as against your arrival.'' Ingersoll Papers.

[1] Jared Ingersoll to Jonathan Ingersoll, May 3, 1773. This letter is also in the possession of Mr. George Pratt Ingersoll of Ridgefield, Connecticut.

much as our present revenue cutters are accustomed to do. One night the schooner overhauled a pilot boat which was moving up the Delaware. When ordered to open the hatches the crew of the boat refused. The result was that this vessel, which was found to contain a cargo of wine and thirty-six boxes of tea, was seized and conveyed by the captain of the schooner up the river some distance, whereupon the anchors were cast. While the ships were thus resting, a second pilot boat appeared, containing thirty men, all with blackened faces and "disguised in sailors' dresses," who sprang aboard the schooner with clubs, muskets, and cutlasses, "most cruelly and inhumanely beat, cut and wounded" Musket and two of his assistants, overwhelmed the crew and threw its members into the hold of the ship; the schooner was then run on a bar and left to its fate after the sails and rigging had been cut up. While the perpetrators of this bold act must have been known to many of the people of Philadelphia, it was impossible to secure an information· against them, although Lieutenant Governor Penn offered a reward of £200 for their apprehension and conviction.[1]

The year following the incident just described, there came the news of the burning of the *Gaspee* and the futile appointment of the commission of inquiry regarding this incident; and in 1773 there appeared in the Philadelphia papers accounts of the Virginia Resolves and of the destruction of the tea at Boston. Ingersoll's growing apprehensions regarding the general situation are shown in a letter written at this time to his brother. He begged that "if anything . . . remarkable should turn up in the political world, I must desire speedy information; for

[1] "A Proclamation," by the Honorable Richard Penn, Esq., *Pennsylvania Journal*, December 12, 1771; *Pennsylvania Gazette,* December 12, 1771; E. P. Oberholtzer, *History of Philadelphia*, I, 222.

you must know that I have as much and as anxious care about the state, upon me, as by your letter to son, it appears you have.'"[1] Things, however, moved along quite smoothly for the new court of vice-admiralty until early in the year 1774, when a series of burning attacks were commenced against Judge Ingersoll in the Philadelphia papers. These and the replies made to them, irrespective of the personalities involved, throw such a flood of light upon the peculiar position that the new vice-admiralty courts occupied in the developing issue between the colonies and the mother country that an analysis of the arguments employed by the writers cannot be neglected.

The occasion of the attacks, it seems, was the seizure of a shallop owned by one David Van Dyke, who had attempted to carry a cargo from Philadelphia to Newcastle County on the lower Delaware, without securing clearance papers at the Philadelphia customs house. The case came up in Ingersoll's Court.[2]

[1] Jared Ingersoll to Jonathan Ingersoll, May 3, 1773. This letter is referred to above.

[2] It was claimed and not denied that the owner failed to secure the permit costing three shillings for a bill of lading of goods for use in trading on the river; he also failed to give a bond for goods. *Pennsylvania Journal*, February 9, 1774. The requirements were inconvenient and the charges also annoying. ''Mercator,'' in writing about this matter, made the issue plain. The shallop men of the lower Delaware, he declared, would refuse to pay the required three shillings and would transfer their trade to Wilmington, which was situated in the lower counties, much to the loss of Philadelphia. For, instead of being able to discharge her cargo upon arriving and thus loading up immediately and proceeding on her way, the shallop must, according to ''Mercator,'' await office hours of the customs to make a regular entry. After securing her discharge, she must obtain a sufferance to take in and then her skipper must obtain certificates that the goods he is to take on board have been legally imported and take them to the customs. ''Mercator'' claimed he was acquainted with the owner of a shallop who was obliged to wait upon the officers of the customs not less than twenty-four times to obtain sufferances and clearances for one trip. See ''Mercator's'' protest in the *Pennsylvania Journal*. *Ibid*. Also Professor An-

It is interesting to note that the first writer to assail Ingersoll was one who signed himself "Cato," just as was the case when, nine years earlier, he was first assailed for accepting a commission as stamp distributor. In each case the language was highly inflammatory.

"Ever since the arrival of our Commissioner at Boston,"[1] declared "Cato," "these lawless vultures placed over us in an unconstitutional manner have been giving us renewed instances of their designs by throwing every possible obstacle in the way of trade, leaving no device untried to distress us. The more effectually to succeed in these enterprises, they first sought out men to place under them who had given to the world sufficient proofs of their being enemies to their country."[2]

The following week there appeared in the *Journal* another arraignment of the new vice-admiralty court by one signing himself "Russel," but who, according to Ingersoll, was none other than Jacob Rush, a brilliant young Philadelphia lawyer, who was a brother of Dr. Benjamin Rush, and who later became chief justice of the state.[3] "Russel" came forward to prove that the pow-

drews, "The Boston Merchants and the Non-Importation Movement," in Col. Soc. Mass. *Publications*, XIX, 170-172.

"The Collector awhile ago made a Seizure of one of the river Vessels called a Shallop for a Cause that is very interesting to the people in trade. Great preparations have been making and the Cause is expected to come on in about a fortnight," wrote Ingersoll, on March 12, 1774, to his nephew Jonathan. New Haven Col. Hist. Soc. *Papers*, IX ("Jared Ingersoll Papers"), 446-447.

1 This refers to the reorganization of the customs service for America, which was one of the Townshend measures.

2 "Cato" to the Freemen of Philadelphia. *Pennsylvania Journal*, January 19, 1774. Robert Temple, writing to William Samuel Johnson, at this period, says that "a true son of liberty is the only true friend of good government. Not the sly, designing crew who are the reputed friends of government whose object is power and money." See E. E. Beardsley, *Life and Times of William Samuel Johnson*, pp. 90-91, for this letter.

3 "Russell proves to be a Mr Jacob Rush, a young Gentleman of the Law

ers Judge Ingersoll exercised in his court "vastly exceed those of the Grand Court of Admiralty in England." In this connection he cited Coke and Blackstone[1] to support his contention that the English High Court of Admiralty could have no jurisdiction in cases arising over bills of exchange, bills of lading, bottomry bonds, charter parties, policies of insurance, freights of ships, or any contract or any other thing done within the body of any English county, nor concerning any wreck—all of which matters, however, were given over to the jurisdiction of the American vice-admiralty courts. "Russel" further insisted that in England cases of mayhem happening in rivers and ports were under the jurisdiction of the coroner,[2] while in America the new courts were given power "to search and enquire of and concerning the bodies of persons drowned, killed or by any other means coming to their death" in the seas, ports, or rivers. Then in personally addressing Ingersoll, "Russel" declared: "I cannot help thinking and I hope you will excuse me from telling you so, that the execution of the office *you* hold must wound every feeling of honor and delicacy. You know what I mean. Your salary of £600 a year is to be paid, in the first place, out of the moiety of money arising

and with whom Jerry [Jared Ingersoll, Jr.] had some little Acquaintance. This Mr Rush by all accounts is not wanting in his Understanding, but is so overloaded with a family disorder . . . called Vanity & Self Conceit, that he is seeking every opportunity of rendring himself famous, but hitherto without Effect. He had heard so much in News papers about the Extension of the powers of Admiralty Courts that he thought there must needs be something in it, & so went gravely to work to show his profound Learning in evincing it. This gave me an opportunity, under the signature of Civis, of showing his Mistake, and I am credibly informed that Mr Rush's own friends advised him to drop the Controversy." Jared Ingersoll to his nephew, Jonathan Ingersoll, March 12, 1774. New Haven Col. Hist. Soc. *Papers*, IX ("Jared Ingersoll Papers"), 447.

[1] 4 Inst. 137, 139, 141, 142; Book 3, Comment 106 (1768).
[2] 4 Inst. 137, 140.

from condemnations made by yourself as a Judge. This, sir, people will think looks too much like being party, judge and jury. The administration of justice should not only be pure, but like Cæsar's wife, should be above suspicion.'"[1]

A reply to "Russel" was not long forthcoming, by one employing the pseudonym, "Civis." The latter came to the defense of the British administration of colonial affairs in the same measured language and judicial temper that had characterized the utterances of "Civis," who in 1765 endeavored, in the *Connecticut Gazette,* to vindicate the propriety of the Stamp Act in replying to "Cato." In fact, as was pointed out in the chapter on the Stamp Act, the similarity of these "Civis" writings of both periods with the publicly acknowledged work of Ingersoll is so very striking that were other evidence lacking one would still be justified in attributing these productions to this source. However, in the case of the letters of 1774, Ingersoll privately acknowledged his authorship, which, of course, gives a special significance and interest to this controversy.

"Civis" began the defense of the new American vice-admiralty courts by denying that they had jurisdiction over treason, robbery, and murder committed on the high seas; he also denied that British vice-admiralty courts did not have authority over bills of exchange and like matters "of a maritime nature"; he called "Russel's" attention to the fact that in every case where a power had been granted to the new American courts it had been qualified by the words "according to the civil and mari-

[1] *Pennsylvania Journal,* January 26, 1774. As the writer "Veritas" pointed out, there were only two sources of revenue for supplying Ingersoll's salary; one was the fines and mulcts in vice-admiralty cases, and the other, the sale of naval stores. "If both should fail, what then? The judge, therefore was personally interested that there be no failure in the payment of his salary." *Ibid.,* February 2, 1774.

time laws and customs of our High Court of Admiralty in England''; finally, with reference to the question of the salary he pointed out the fact that it was an advantage to everyone concerned that the judge should have a definite, guaranteed salary for he "neither adds to his salary by condemning nor lessens it by acquitting." He moreover pointed out that it was "no uncommon thing for the common law judges to be paid out of the gross sums arising in part from fines and mulcts of their own imposing.'"[1]

When "Russel" returned to the attack he boldly accused Judge Ingersoll of writing the defense by "Civis." "There is no occasion," he said, "to make any apology for considering you as the writer of a piece published in the *Pennsylvania Journal* last week under the signature of 'Civis,' in which an attempt is made to vindicate your commission . . . the stile and matter as effectually betrays the author to the public as if his name had been subscribed to it.'"[2]

Again taking up the salary question, "Russel" pointed out that the old naval stores did not constitute a dependable fund. "I have been well informed," he declared, "that it has already failed more than once." The judge, therefore, must make sure of his salary by way of penalties and forfeitures. A more serious thing than the salary situation, however, according to "Russel," was the power of the new court to summon those accused, together with witnesses from the farthest parts of New York, New Jersey, Pennsylvania, the lower counties in Delaware, Maryland, and Virginia, with authority to fine, imprison, and strip them of their estates for want of

[1] *Pennsylvania Journal*, February 2, 1774.

[2] *Ibid.*, February 9, 1774. In a letter to his nephew Jonathan, Ingersoll acknowledged the authorship of these letters. See page 304, note 3, of this chapter.

obedience. "You may harass the whole country at your pleasure. . . . It is impossible, we can ever be a free people while such a Commission as yours is held over our heads, which alone with the Stamp Act or Revenue Act is sufficient to prostrate all the liberties of America at your feet.''[1]

When "Civis" made his second reply to "Russel," naturally enough he did not attempt to clear himself of the charge of being the judge of the very court then under fire. However, he did his best to refute the other charges. As to the old naval stores, he had never known of an instance where they had failed as a source of revenue for the payment of judges' salaries; in fact, he was able to state that for several years past the judge in question had received a great part of his salary from that source and he denied that the salary of the judge could be affected by failure of both sources.[2] As to the size of the judicial district of the particular court under discussion, he maintained that it was not so large as the district of the High Court of Admiralty in England, and also that if experience should prove the new court "either inconvenient or useless, it was to be hoped that

[1] *Pennsylvania Journal*, February 9, 1774. This attack of "Russel" against Ingersoll was printed as a broadside and probably distributed widely. A mutilated copy of the broadside is in the possession of the American Antiquarian Society.

[2] See page 297, note 1, of this chapter. On October 17, 1776, there was granted to Ingersoll "out of such Monies as are in or shall come . . . by the Sale of Old Naval Stores . . . the sum One thousand two hundred pounds without deduction and without account in full satisfaction and discharge of his salary in respect of the said office for two years ending the seventeenth day of October, 1776." Audit Office, 15: 64, p. 51. See the table reproduced in Professor Channing's *The United States*, III, 154, which sets forth that Ingersoll, between the dates June, 1768, and July 5, 1776, was paid out of the American customs revenue the sum of £3164; Auchmuty received £3968; Sewall, as judge of the Halifax court, £1657, besides £375 as attorney general of Massachusetts Bay; while Augustus Johnston received £88 from these funds.

the same power that created it would abolish it."
"Civis" then declared that "notwithstanding all the
town meetings have voted or other persons have said or
wrote to the contrary, the commissions of the Courts of
Admiralty in America of one kind or another were the
same as they had always been from the time of their first
establishment in America and were not furnished with
any new or unusual powers.'"[1] The clamor against the
vice-admiralty courts that had lately been created in
America, he claimed, proceeded from hostility to certain
acts of parliament which were very obnoxious to the people, who would avoid them, if possible. There was a
popular feeling, in other words, that if the prosecution
for breaches of these unpopular laws took place in courts
of common law there would be a better chance of evading
them, "the reason for their thinking so may easily be
guessed." If the offenders were sure that the prosecutions would be carried through in the common law court,
they would not be very anxious to which of the courts
they were brought. While trials by jury were an eligible
mode of trial, yet "Civis" desired to point out that the
people were not necessarily devoted to them; for there
had never been any objections to having captures in time
of war determined in a court of admiralty.[2]

But "Russel" was not to be outdone or driven from
his ground. In a third attack he maintained steadily the
proposition that Judge Ingersoll had jurisdiction to try

[1] "Civis" was clearly wrong in making this statement. While the
jurisdiction of the English High Court of Admiralty had been progressively
weakened by parliamentary enactment, the jurisdiction of the American
vice-admiralty courts had, on the other hand, been progressively enlarged.
In other words, the form of the judge's commission in this particular
instance was no proper test of the scope of the jurisdiction of the American
vice-admiralty court in comparison with that of the admiralty court in
England.

[2] *Pennsylvania Journal*, February 16, 1774.

persons and causes which in England would be tried in a court of common law and further that there was no power in the province to stay proceedings in a court of admiralty. That the jurisdiction of the court of admiralty in England was as extensive as that of the new courts in America even Ingersoll, himself, according to "Russel," could no longer assert. From this judge's own confession, under signature of "Civis," the courts of vice-admiralty were created to enforce certain obnoxious acts of parliament. "Are you not," the writer then asked, "a mere creature of the Crown appointed to execute the laws that your country is anxiously struggling to get rid of? Nothing can be more absurd," he continued, "than the supposition that a man has any real love for his country who accepts a place which lays him under the official obligation of acting contrary to its interests. . . . Are you not, therefore, a dangerous judge? . . . Will it not do you honor to throw up your commission immediately?"[1]

This series of attacks and replies was concluded by a semi-editorial reply to "Russel" in the March 30 edition of the *Pennsylvania Journal*. In a review of the arguments pro and con it is clear that the main criticisms of "Russel" against the court of vice-admiralty remained unshaken throughout the controversy. That Ingersoll was a dependent judge; that his salary, when regular sources would not suffice, must be supplied by the crown; that the home government, under the circumstances, would be likely to support him in any interpretation that he might be disposed to put upon the limits of his jurisdiction; that he certainly could determine causes that in England were always decided in courts of common law; were contentions that "Civis" did not succeed in

[1] *Pennsylvania Journal*, March 16, 1774.

overturning, although with great skill he attempted to shift the basis of controversy. However, there were not lacking those in America who were disposed to justify the British government in the measures that it had taken to develop the jurisdiction of the vice-admiralty courts in America to the widest limits. The situation was succinctly summed up by Joseph Reed, a leading Philadelphia lawyer possessed of a large point of view, who later became president of the provincial council of Pennsylvania. Writing to the Earl of Dartmouth, who was secretary for the colonies,[1] Reed declared, ''It is to be wished that the mode of trying revenue causes in this country were more agreeable to the English practice and the English Constitution, but at the same time, I acknowledge that, at present, there seems little probability of justice being done to the Crown by an American jury.'' Although devoted to American interests, he could not but admit that ''the due observation of the laws of trade is so essential to the interests of the mother country that nothing tending to weaken or enforce them is beneath notice.''[2] He was convinced that a project was unfolding to distress and harass the vice-admiralty courts so as to make all the offices in them ''odious and disgraceful''; the attacks, moreover, were leveled against the new courts, while the old courts of vice-admiralty passed unnoticed ''though there is no difference as to the objects of their jurisdiction and the extent of it is not novel.'' The reason for this, according to Reed, was on account of the personnel of the officers of these courts. The judges had made themselves obnoxious by their conduct at the time of the

[1] He succeeded the Earl of Hillsborough in August, 1772, and remained in office until November, 1775.

[2] Joseph Reed to the Earl of Dartmouth, April 4, 1774. This letter is printed in W. B. Reed, *Life of President Reed*, I, 657. Even Pitt was firm upon this point.

Stamp Act. As to the under officers of these courts, "absurd conduct" had been shown in their appointment; for the holders of these posts were allowed to live in England and the commissioners of customs at Boston appointed their deputies. As a result, when Judge Ingersoll opened his court every officer in it was some "underling" of the custom house: the register of the court was customs gauger and surveyor, and the court marshal was one of the principal tide waiters.[1] This could only have one effect upon the public mind, for these vice-admiralty officials were frequently interested as customs officials, by reason of their fees, in cases which were carried before the court. Indeed, Reed asserts that Ingersoll had in his presence lamented his "unfortunate situation" in this respect.[2]

The confirmed attitude of mind of a majority of Americans in 1774 regarding the existence of the vice-admiralty courts was without doubt expressed by "America Solon," who, in a communication to the *Connecticut Gazette and Universal Intelligencer,* published in New London, wrote: "I could at this time call the attention of my countrymen to a most glaring and capital instance of tyranny which ought to make every villain blush and every free mind kindle with indignation against the abandoned herd of tyrants and their Tools, viz. the *hydra* Courts of Admiralty. By the commission of a judge of one of these courts . . . it appears they were calculated not only to annul the American charter, but *Magna Charta,* and to overturn the whole constitution of the nation. . . . These unconstitutional and most abominable Courts of Admiralty, are a clear demonstration, that a

---

[1] *Life of President Reed.* James Biddle was deputy commissary; Philip How, register; John Smith, deputy register, and Arodi Thayer, marshal and sergeant-at-arms. *Pennsylvania Archives,* IV, 591-600.

[2] *Pennsylvania Archives,* IV, 600.

system of tyranny has been formed to enslave the Americans.'"[1]

Extremely unpopular as was undoubtedly the tribunal over which Ingersoll presided, it yet managed to survive after a fashion, in the midst of this hostility, until the outbreak of the Revolution. The presence of these special courts of vice-admiralty was held to be, it is clear, one of the most glaring evidences, presented to the excited imagination of people, of an intention on the part of the home government to rule the colonies, if need be, through a highly developed system of administrative coercion.

[1] *Connecticut Gazette and Universal Intelligencer,* March 4, 1774.

CHAPTER XI

INGERSOLL AND THE SUSQUEHANNA DIS-
PUTE. THE SUBMERGING OF THE
INGERSOLL GROUP AT NEW
HAVEN

CONSERVATIVE New Haven, as was previously pointed out, had learned the ways of radicalism. This had come hand in hand with the growing importance of the mercantile and shipping interests dominated by those, among whom was Benedict Arnold, who were known among the ancient settler families as the "interlopers." From 1764 on this group had so thoroughly inculcated among the people hostility against those new measures of the British government which had to do with the colonies, that it found itself in the possession of a dangerous weapon which it used on more than one occasion. That weapon was the mob spirit.

How far the contempt of law and order had gone among the "liberty" element in this community, before the outbreak of the Revolution, is evidenced by a report of Hugh Finlay, made in connection with his official survey of the post roads in North America. In November, 1773, he went to New Haven to investigate conditions, and put the deputy of the local post office, Christopher Kirby, under a sharp examination. Kirby especially lamented the fact that he could not enforce the acts of parliament. He declared that if every vessel arriving at the port were to send the mail which it carried to the office, the income would be doubled and the revenue increased in other respects. But he affirmed that when he sent to the ship-masters for the letters, the latter were accustomed "to insult and threaten his messengers"; he also complained that the "portmanteau" containing the mail seldom came locked, with the consequence that the post riders "stuff them with bundles of shoes, stockings, canisters, money, or anything they get to carry, which tears the Portman-teau and rubs the letters to pieces." Moreover, Kirby said that these postmen were accustomed to "ride off the road to deliver summons and buy oxen on commission and drive them while they have his Majesty's mail under their care."[1]

However, it should be kept in mind that the majority of the enfranchised group—a decided minority of the inhabitants of the town—and especially those who domi-nated the freemen's meetings and the meetings of the town were of a decidedly cautious and slow-moving tem-per, as men of landed property are always apt to be; and it was with this group that Jared Ingersoll, as the old recognized leader of the conservatives, although officially and professionally identified with Philadelphia after the spring of 1771, continued, until the outbreak of hostili-ties with the mother country, to exercise a powerful influ-ence. This was made possible by reason of the pro-tracted visits he made each year to New Haven during the summer recess of the court over which he presided. In fact, he was fated to be intimately involved as a fore-most figure in practically every crisis that confronted Connecticut from 1760 down to the date of his death in 1781.

Hardly had the excitement caused by the Townshend revenue acts died down than Connecticut was thrown

[1] *Journal kept by Hugh Finlay, surveyor of the post road on the Con-tinent of North America . . . begun 13th of September, 1773, and ended the 26th of June, 1774* (1867).

into a perfect whirlwind of controversy over the Susquehanna question. This had arisen out of the organization in 1753 of the famous Susquehanna Company by
parties living in and about Windham, for the purpose of
occupying lands in the Wyoming Valley country in northern Pennsylvania.[1] The enterprise, in itself, would have
been of the most laudable character had it not as its leading motive the design of taking from out of the jurisdiction of the government of Pennsylvania these lands
and of denying the proprietary claims to them of the
Penn family, in spite of the fact that they were clearly
included within the bounds of Pennsylvania by the royal
patent granted to William Penn in the year 1681. But
the Susquehanna Company proceeded to put forward the
charter of 1662 with its indefinite sea-to-sea grant, contending that no later royal patent could in any way im-
pair the validity of that document. As one writer expressed it, the territory lying within the bounds of the
charter claims was "a very fine Tract of Land, comprehending the present inhabited Part of Connecticut, a
great Part of the Province of New York, the whole of the
Province of East and West Jersies; the greater part of
the Province of Pennsylvania! . . . being above a degree
in width North and South in the West part and about
5000 miles in Length, East and West."[2]

The weakness of the Connecticut claim manifestly lay
in the fact that the Connecticut authorities acquiesced,
at the time, in the establishment by royal authority of
those governments within what it later claimed were the
limits of its western extension; in 1680, in answer to the

[1] The minutes of the Susquehanna Company are printed in W. H. Egle's
Documents Relating to the Connecticut Settlement in the Wyoming Valley;
which is published as Volume XVIII of the *Pennsylvania Archives* (second
series).

[2] Article signed by B. Schemer in the *Connecticut Gazette,* April 13, 1774.

THE SUSQUEHANNA DISPUTE 317

queries of the Board of Trade, the statement was returned by the colony that it was bounded on the west by
the province of New York;[1] no one in Connecticut in 1681
dreamed of questioning the validity of the grant of Pennsylvania to William Penn and his heirs. The claim also
displayed a fatal inconsistency in that while it was made
for the northern two-fifths of Pennsylvania, there was
no demand for any part of the province of New York that
intervened between Pennsylvania and Connecticut. The
movement grew out of the unsatisfied land hunger of the
population of Connecticut and is a striking episode in the
truly romantic history of the exploitation of the domain
of the North American continent; a history unfortunately
replete with acts transcending, or in overt defiance of,
laws, treaties, and prescriptive rights.

In 1755 the Susquehanna Company, with a membership of eight hundred and fifty, succeeded in getting the
endorsement of their enterprise by the governor and
assembly, in a formal resolution.[2] In 1758 Ingersoll, in
accepting the London agency, was called upon by the
company to exert himself in its behalf. He carried to
England a copy of the resolution of the assembly, canvassed the views of those in authority with regard to
the possibility of vitalizing the dormant claims of Connecticut to the Pennsylvania lands, and in 1761, upon his
return to America, wrote to the officers of the company
fully and frankly regarding the issue. As everything he

[1] W. H. Egle's *Documents Relating to the Connecticut Settlement in Wyoming Valley*, p. 492.

[2] *Conn. Col. Rec.*, X, 378; C. O. 5: 1276, X 27. The company also secured a title from the Iroquois to the land, upon which the members desired to settle, by the payment of £2000, although in doing so the adven-
turers ignored the fact that the Delaware Indians were in possession of the tract. "Anything more worthless in law or equity than the Iroquois title to this land cannot be imagined." Forrest Morgan, *Connecticut as a Colony and as a State*, I, 452.

had to communicate "wore a discouraging aspect," he advised them to give up a project "which in the end must prove abortive."[1]

Not discouraged by this report or by the proclamation of Lieutenant Governor Hamilton of Pennsylvania of February 20, 1761, warning "the persons settled at Wyoming off the Lands,"[2] the company, which had rapidly increased its membership, determined to send to England as its special agent, Eliphalet Dyer; and at a meeting in Hartford, held early in 1762, it is interesting to note that Jared Ingersoll was asked to serve as a member of the committee to draw up the case which Dyer was to present.[3] It would appear that Ingersoll, on that occasion, counseled strongly against the prosecution of this endeavor. Joseph Chew of New London, in writing to him later, could not refrain from saying: "Your Behaviour at Hartford has answered my Expectations. I have on all occasions asserted you were two Honnest and had two great a regard for truth than to say one thing and mean another—in short that you would not Cringe, Twist and Turn Twenty ways to get into any post the Colony had to give."[4] That Ingersoll's position on the matter won adherents among those more conservative people of the colony who feared the consequence of this daring attempt to overthrow the Pennsylvania patent of over eighty years' standing, is shown by the fact that on June 8 Governor Fitch issued a proclamation against the Susquehanna Company, "warning all Persons, Inhabitants of this Colony to forbear making entries on

[1] *Connecticut Journal*, March 18, 1774.

[2] C. O. 5: 1276, X 31.

[3] "Minutes of the Susquehanna Company," in the *Pennsylvania Archives* (second series), XVIII, 87, 89.

[4] Joseph Chew to Jared Ingersoll, June 8, 1763, New Haven Col. Hist. Soc. *Papers*, IX ("Jared Ingersoll Papers"), 281.

said Lands.'"[1] Soon after the Fitch proclamation, Lieutenant Governor Hamilton wrote to Ingersoll, expressing
his pleasure at the action of the Connecticut government
and pointing out how it would be necessary to oppose the
attempt of forcible settlement by all the means within
his power.[2] Moreover, the following January, the Earl
of Egremont, secretary of state for the southern department, who had been informed of the proceedings of the
company, wrote to the Connecticut governor, saying that
''the King has commanded me to express to you His
surprise at this Behaviour as well as His Displeasure to
find that any of his subjects . . . should persist in an
undertaking of this Nature.'"[3]

The Dyer mission to England was without results. In
fact, during the next four years the Wyoming Valley
project, while by no means dead, was subordinated to
the issues that arose out of the Sugar Act of 1764, and the
Stamp Act of 1765. It was not until 1768 that the company was prepared to push aggressively its plans, in the
face of all opposition.[4] In that year a small body of set-

[1] C. O. 5: 1276, X 29.

[2] James Hamilton to Jared Ingersoll, July 8, 1762, Ingersoll Papers.

[3] Earl of Egremont to Governor Fitch, C. O. 5: 1276, X 35. The Susquehanna adventurers were relying upon the support of Franklin, who had
been sent to England by the lower house of the Pennsylvania legislature to
combat the proprietors and to petition the crown to assume all governmental powers within that colony. While, according to Colonel Dyer, who
talked with him, Franklin was ''Extremely friendly and very much approved of the Settlement''; according to Joseph Chew, who also talked
with him, Franklin thought that it was ''Idle and Ridiculous'' to set up a
claim to all the lands to the ''West Seas'' and that ''no person could
pretend to think it Consistant with Common Sense to have a Governm^t 60
miles wide & 3000 miles Long.'' Joseph Chew to Jared Ingersoll, August
10, 1763, New Haven Col. Hist. Soc. *Papers,* IX (''Jared Ingersoll
Papers''), 286-287.

[4] During this period the most active Connecticut assailant of the Susquehanna Company's policy seems to have been Dr. Benjamin Gale of
Killingsworth. In 1769 he wrote to Ingersoll asserting that the enterprise

tlers was sent to the lands in question, under Captain
Zebalon Butler and the famous Major Durkee, who led
the five hundred Sons of Liberty against Ingersoll in
1765. The proprietors, in turn, sent men to resist the
intruders and after some fighting of rather a bloodless
kind, known as the first Pennamite War, in which an old
four-pounder cannon played a decisive rôle, the "Yan-
kees" were expelled; in fact, the Connecticut men were
driven from the country six times by Ogden, Penn's
lieutenant. In June, 1769, Governor Pitkin of Connecticut published a proclamation warning the people of the
colony against participating in these attempts at settlements. Nothing daunted at this, in support of the movement Dyer and his associates went into that county in
July, actually stopping at Philadelphia on the way, and
in September great efforts were made to sell the lands;
John Parker, Jr., of East Windsor offering for sale
20,000 acres, through the columns of the *Connecticut
Courant*. In fact, such an impetus was given to the
enterprise that by 1770 the company had succeeded in
erecting forts and in repelling the forces which the proprietary government sent against them. This encouraged the Connecticut general assembly, which was under
the influence of the company stockholders, who by this
time numbered about twelve hundred, to assert vigorously the claims of the colony "to its Charter limits west
of the Delaware."[1] However, Richard Jackson, the Con-

was "Col¹ Dyers Hobby Horse by which he has rose & as he has been
unmercifull to Govᵣ Fitch & Yourself I never design to Give him rest untill
I make his Hobby Horse throw him into the Dirt." In the same letter he
promised Ingersoll not to mention the latter's name in connection with the
pamphlets he was publishing against the company. Benjamin Gale to
Jared Ingersoll, December 29, 1769, New Haven Col. Hist. Soc. *Papers*, IX
("Jared Ingersoll Papers"), 428-429. See especially Gale's *Observations
on a Pamphlet entitled Remarks on Dr. Gale's letter to J. W. Esq., signed
E. D. etc.*, Hartford, 1770.

[1] See the *Connecticut Courant*, issues of June 12, July 10, September 11,

necticut agent in London, wrote to Governor Trumbull about this time, strongly advising against the colony appearing before the Privy Council with a demand for these lands, as he was of the opinion that the establishment of the New York line would be considered a "derelection" of the Connecticut western claims.[1]

The attitude of the home government, while these things were transpiring, was one of uncertainty. But on June 7, 1771, the Privy Council approved a report of its committee, which had taken into consideration a petition of Thomas and Richard Penn against the forcible seizure of their lands by the inhabitants of Connecticut; this report was to the effect that "this forceable intrusion is a matter entirely within the jurisdiction of that province and that it is unnecessary and improper for your Majesty to interpose your authority therein."[2]

and November 8, for the year 1769; *Conn. Col. Rec.*, XIII, 427. Governor Pitkin died in October, 1769, and was succeeded by Jonathan Trumbull, who was asked to join with William Samuel Johnson, George Wyllis, and Colonel John Chester in collecting all the evidence relating to the present title of the colony and to transmit it to Connecticut agents in Great Britain. It is interesting to note in this connection that Johnson was personally opposed to the claims, although it is probable that his views were not generally known in Connecticut. Writing to Jackson, in 1773, he said: "I own I was not in the vote [in favor of the western claims] having never altered the opinion I settled when I had the happiness to serve with you upon the subject. I am not satisfied that it would be of any use to us to have these lands if we could obtain them, nor can bring myself to believe that we stand much chance, all circumstances considered, of recovering them." William Samuel Johnson to Richard Jackson, November 5, 1773. "Correspondence of Samuel and William Samuel Johnson" (Bancroft Transcripts).

[1] Richard Jackson to Governor Trumbull. This letter is quoted in the *Pennsylvania Gazette* of May 25, 1774.

[2] C. O. 5: 1278, Z 35. In a letter to William Samuel Johnson, Jackson makes clear the position assumed by the law officers of the crown. "The Sollicitor General," he declared, "always inclined against the Colony's title at several meetings; the Attorney at the first strongly in their favor afterwards came over to the Sollicitor's opinion, which was that the possession of a foreign State did not only defeat the grant to the Colony as far as that

In 1774 Connecticut took the next step in asserting its jurisdiction over the western lands by erecting the Susquehanna district into a Connecticut township under the name of Westmorland and deputies from it were invited to take seats in the assembly.[1] In turn, the Pennsylvania House of Assembly passed resolutions that the province use all of its power ''to suppress acts of violence and illegal attempts to dispersing the peaceful inhabitants of this province.''[2] The indignant assembly went on to relate ''that a number of persons emigrating from the Colony of Connecticut have, under a pretense of right to lands within the limits and boundaries of the royal grant to the proprietors of this province, without prosecuting their claim before His Majesty in Council, the only proper place of decision, in a riotous and tumultuous manner taken possession of a tract of country within the said known limits and boundaries and have held and still retain their said possession in a hostile manner to the great disturbance of the peace of the province.''[3]

possession actually existed, but totally stopped the grant on that side, as if the grant had said, westward until it meets with the possession of some foreign state.'' Richard Jackson to William Samuel Johnson, April 5, 1774, ''Correspondence of Samuel and William Samuel Johnson'' (Bancroft Transcripts).

[1] *Conn. Col. Rec.,* XIV, 217, 218. It was annexed to Litchfield County, Alexander Johnston, *Connecticut. A Study of a Commonwealth Democracy,* pp. 273-284. ''I cannot but think the Assembly of your Colony were guilty of an imprudence little short of madness, when they passed the Votes of last Jany making & planting a Town in this Province, and I think it is a great Chance if you dont live to see much greater Consequences flow from it than most people are aware of.'' Jared Ingersoll to Jonathan Ingersoll, Philadelphia, March 12, 1774. New Haven Col. Hist. Soc. *Papers,* IX (''Jared Ingersoll Papers''), 446.

[2] This is printed in the *Pennsylvania Journal,* January 19, 1779.

[3] *Ibid.* ''The people here,'' wrote Ingersoll from Philadelphia, ''begin to Consider the Northern New England men as a Set of Goths & Vandals who may one day overun these Southern Colonies unless thoroughly opposed, and to this End they will naturally Court the friendship of the Mother

It was at this critical juncture that Ingersoll became the storm center of the controversy. During the summer of 1773, while he was at New Haven, there happened to fall into his hands a pamphlet which strongly favored the Connecticut claims. In this, he found mention of certain "ancient memorials" respecting the history and titles of the colony, "some of which were quite new" to him. This led him to investigate with great thoroughness the whole subject. As a result, he seems to have become more convinced than ever of the groundlessness of the Connecticut pretensions. The results of this investigation he drew up in the shape of a survey of the subject, a copy of which he handed to a member of the Susquehanna Company. However, as it was not his idea to become once again personally involved in the quarrel between the two colonies, he refrained from publishing broadcast his views.

Although Ingersoll claimed to have said nothing to anyone in Pennsylvania about this work in which he had been engaged, the report spread abroad that he had written a treatise favorable to the Penns. Thereupon Provost Smith of the College of Pennsylvania, and others, waited upon him with a request to see the manuscript. "I was told," he declared, "that the Colony's claim to the western lands was now become a serious affair to this province—that every material paper of a public nature ought to be known to both parties and that I ought to consider myself in my present situation as equally the friend of both.'"[1] As a result, he was led, after declining at first to do so, to deliver over for publication not only the survey but also the corroborative documents which he had collected in Connecticut. By means of this material,

Country." Jared Ingersoll to Jonathan Ingersoll, March 12, 1774, New Haven Col. Hist. Soc. *Papers*, IX ("Jared Ingersoll Papers"), 446.

[1] *Connecticut Journal*, March 18, 1774.

Provost Smith prepared and published anonymously, in January, 1774, his pamphlet, *An Examination of the Connecticut claim to Lands in Pennsylvania*,[1] in connection with which he printed as an appendix the body of papers, twenty-seven in all, that Ingersoll had collected. His dependence upon these documents for presenting the Pennsylvania case is shown by the fact that every important assertion he made in the text was reënforced by a sidenote reference to them. This pamphlet was distributed broadcast, especially in Connecticut, and was undoubtedly one of the most decisive factors in the ultimate vindication of the rights of Pennsylvania to the limits provided in her patent.[2]

The appearance of this crushing reply to the Connecticut pretensions raised a storm of denunciation against Ingersoll, who was accused of being the author. One of the most bitter of the attacks against him was from the pen of an anonymous writer signing himself "Brutus Americanus," in the local New London paper. He rather inconsistently accused Ingersoll of cowardly conduct for fearing to publish under his own name the article in question that Provost Smith, as a matter of fact, had prepared. "Now I am not about to blame you," he wrote with biting sarcasm, "for writing or acting on the side inimical to this Colony—were it the first instance I might possibly expostulate with you, but somehow it is not very strange nor very disagreeable to see men act with uniformity of character. Though I confess, I could not so easily pass over your thus acting under cover were it not that I know you to be one of the most timorous men alive and from the remembrance of past scenes, and at

[1] For a reprint of this see the *Pennsylvania Archives* (second series), XVIII.

[2] See *ibid.* for an estimate of the importance of the pamphlet.

least a possible anticipation of future, may often be and are I am told 'most tremblingly alive all o'er.' "[1]

As an answer to this, Ingersoll made a dignified statement of his position, setting forth at length the history of his connection with the dispute; this he published in the *Connecticut Journal* at New Haven. "I will leave time to discover," he declared, "who have been the Colony's best friends, those who have urged or those who have disuaded from these measures. A defeat would be very detrimental but a victory must be absolute ruin to the Colony, at least I think so." To the charge of working in the interest of Pennsylvania, he answered, "I am not in the secret of the Council of this province nor am I actuated by any lucrative or sinister views." He then skillfully turned the tables upon those who were upbraiding him for furnishing all possible light upon this serious matter. "And will any of these people openly avow to the world that they would willingly, if they could, attain a cause of this magnitude and complexion by the suppression of records which from the circumstances their antagonists could not come at?"[2]

This reply called forth a retort from Ingersoll's old New Haven acquaintance, Roger Sherman. He took up Ingersoll's statement, "A defeat will be very detrimental but a victory must be absolute ruin." "But he gives no reason," declared Sherman, "for his opinions and can his bare assertions make the people of this Colony who are a company of farmers believe that to be quieted in their claims to a large tract of land would ruin them? I know some gentlemen," he continued in a satirical vein, "who love to monopolize wealth and power, think it best for lands to be in a few hands and that the common people should be their tenants, but it will not be easy to persuade

1 *Connecticut Gazette,* February 25, 1774.

2 *Connecticut Journal,* March 18, 1774.

the people of this colony who knew the value of freedom and of enjoying fee-simple estates that it would be
best for them to give up the lands acquired for them by
their ancestors for the privilege of enjoying the same
lands as tenants, under the proprietors of Pennsylvania.''[1]

However, the conviction seems to have taken hold of
the majority of the conservatively inclined Connecticut
people, who paid attention to the discussions of such men
as Ingersoll and Provost Smith, that the colony was com-
mitting itself to a policy which could not succeed and that
would, as a result, unhappily and deeply involve not only
the Susquehanna speculators but the generality of the
people in Connecticut also. Not long after the publication of Ingersoll's reply to ''Brutus'' the New Haven
town meeting appointed a committee to meet with other
towns to be similarly represented at Middletown for the
purpose of drawing up a remonstrance against the prosecution of the claims to the western lands. The meeting
was held, and, on its return, the committee reported that
twenty-two towns were represented at the gathering and
that as a result of their deliberations a petition had been
prepared in remonstrance ''against certain doings of the
late Assembly and measures taken in favor of the Susquehanna Company.''[2] When the question came before the

[1] *Connecticut Journal*, April 8, 1774.

[2] New Haven Town Records, V, entries for March 20 and April 11, 1774.
The measures of the general assembly referred to were, as has been stated,
the erection of the Susquehanna district into the town of Westmorland and
the admission of deputies from there to seats in the Connecticut assembly.

The petition recited the fact that the general assembly had been brought
to act in favor of the western claims through the influence of deputies who
were heavily involved financially in the success of the enterprise. It was
apprehended that great numbers of the people of the colony, ''taught as
they are from their youth to place the highest Confidence in the Legislature
will be by the Acts of the last Assembly tempted to transport themselves
and their effects and settle on said Lands, pending the Controversy about

town meeting whether or not New Haven should indorse or reject the remonstrances there were polled one hundred and two votes in favor of it as against ninety-nine votes cast by the Sherman group. This is interesting testimony as to the comparative strength of the conservative and radical elements in community at this time, for, as Dr. Benjamin Gale pointed out to Ingersoll, it seems to have been true that the Susquehanna faction in the colony was almost identical with the "liberty" group.[1]

In spite of the Middletown remonstrances, the general assembly, still dominated by the Susquehanna interests, maintained the western claims; in 1775 the district of Westmorland was established and was provided with a court of probate. Over three thousand people migrated to this region, the men were enrolled as members of the Twenty-fourth Connecticut regiment; a powder mill was authorized by the assembly to be established there, and it appeared as though the settlement were permanently established. However, in 1778 there took place the Wyoming Valley massacre and "the Connecticut pos-

the Title, and will waste their personal estate in Improvements of said Lands; and in case the Title of the Colony should finally fail, they would be reduced to abject Wretchedness, Dependence and Poverty there, or fall back on this Colony by thousands in extreme Penury, to waste the Residue of their Lives, a burden to themselves and an expense and dead Weight upon the Community; by which Means the support of the *Poor*, already a heavy burden, will become intolerable." The petition ended by calling on the Assembly to exclude the proprietors of the company from voting on these matters. *Pennsylvania Gazette*, April 27, 1774.

[1] It is of interest to notice that at the freemen's meeting, held previous to the town meeting on April 11, there were five hundred and fourteen freemen present. Why only two hundred and one votes were cast at the town meeting on this important subject is accounted for by a writer in the local paper by reason of the fact that it was nine o'clock in the evening before the final vote was taken and in the meantime those living some distance from the center of town had been obliged to return home. See the *Connecticut Journal*, April 22, 1774; New Haven Col. Hist. Soc. *Papers*, IX ("Jared Ingersoll Papers"), 373.

sessions vanished into thin air.'' In 1782 a court of arbitration, under the confederation, was appointed to settle the dispute between the two states. After a hearing covering forty-two days, a unanimous decision was rendered in favor of the contentions of Pennsylvania.[1]

While the conservatives and radicals of Connecticut were contending in the spring of 1774 over the Susquehanna policy, there arrived the news that the British ministry, in order to bring Massachusetts to submission, on account of the tea riot of December 16, 1773, had closed the port of Boston. The Massachusetts committee of correspondence, hastily summoned together, addressed a letter to the different colonies, calling upon them to suspend all trade with Great Britain, on the ground that Boston was suffering for the common cause; the next day the Boston town meeting addressed a similar appeal to the other colonial ports and assured them that if by a policy of non-intercourse, ''the Act for Blocking up this Harbor be repealed, the same will prove the salvation of North America and her Liberties.''

A town meeting was called at New Haven, May 23, to consider the Boston letter. As a result, it was voted to defend to the utmost ''the liberty and immunities of British America.''[2] A standing committee was also appointed to keep up a correspondence with other towns. However, it should be noted as a significant fact that the one named chairman of the committee was none other than Ingersoll's friend and supporter, Joshua Chandler, an ultra-conservative, who at the outbreak of the war became one of the most uncompromising Tories in Connecti-

[1] It is of interest to note that William Samuel Johnson, in spite of his views about the legitimacy of the Connecticut claims, was the leading counsel upholding the colony's side in the court of arbitration.

[2] New Haven Town Records, V, 42.

cut.[1] New Haven also sent him to the general assembly, both in 1774 and in 1775, and in December, 1774, installed him as a selectman of the town. In fact, it was not until November, 1775, that public sentiment finally forced the town authorities to place him under arrest and in confinement on parole at his home in North Haven.

On May 27, the Virginia House of Burgesses, meeting unofficially at the Raleigh Tavern, adopted resolutions in favor of an annual congress of all the colonies. By June 20 New Haven was ready to take action regarding this proposal and gave it a hearty endorsement. As during the Stamp Act crisis, the controlling authority of the colony was fast passing into the hands of an extra-constitutional organ of government; in place of the officers of the Sons of Liberty of the '60's, it was now the central committee of correspondence. Not only was it to this body that the New Haven town meeting reported its approval of the plan for a congress, but it was to this body that the Connecticut deputies deferred when finally the colony come to the question of choosing the delegates.

Ingersoll apparently exerted himself both in New Haven and in New York, as well as in Philadelphia, to prevent the sending of delegates to the congress. A New York correspondent to the *Pennsylvania Journal* has the following to say about his activities: ''It will no doubt give you pleasure to be assured that this city will be firm in the cause of liberty and will be ready to come into any measure the colonies in general shall adopt. J. In——l from your place has taken great pains here to prevent anything being done, by asserting to all with whom he conversed that they might be assured Philadelphia would do nothing and in Connecticut he has been doing the same.''[2]

1 New Haven Town Records.
2 *Pennsylvania Journal*, June 29, 1774. William Samuel Johnson looked

In fact, at the very time that the above item was printed, Ingersoll was in New Haven trying to enhearten the ranks of the conservatives. The news of this reached the eastern section of the colony, with the result that early in July he received from New London a most ominous and menacing letter. "After your solemn assurance in Sept. 1765," declared the unknown writer, "confirmed by oath that you would no more take any Post inimical to the country which gave you birth, which nourished you, and raised you by her favors to undeserved honours, we had right to expect you would at least not have taken an active part in the ruin of your country and its Liberties; but when we find you openly avowing and publishing principles subversive of our rights and vindicating the arbitrary measures of a corrupt British Ministry we conclude honor and conscience have left your breast and you are become a determined enemy to your country and as such ought to be cast out from among us.

"We inform you that you have only ten days from the receipt of this to put your house in order and if you do not leave this Colony by that time depend proper care will be taken to remove you to a place fitted for your reception where all such villains and traitors ought to be.

"This is the voice of multitudes who will not suffer the free air of this Colony to be polluted by your poisonous breath—to prevent trouble you'l notice your departure in the N. Haven paper—you may depend if you do

upon the proposed congress in no very friendly light. "I was called upon to attend the proposed Congress as one of the Delegates from the Colony, my previous engagements were such as to render it highly inconvenient for me to undertake it and I declined the office, *inter nos,* I did not think it advisable either on my own acct or, on account of the Colony to make one of that Assembly, though it is very unpopular at present to doubt in any measure either the legality, or, expediency of the measure." William Samuel Johnson to Richard Jackson, August 30, 1774 (Bancroft Transcripts).

not comply directly, you will hear from the enraged Inhabitants.'"[1]

Instead, however, of taking fright and leaving the colony as ordered, Ingersoll, upon receipt of the letter, made a copy of it, which he enclosed in a letter to Governor Trumbull.[2] He well knew that the colony could ill afford to allow an outrage to be committed upon one who stood so high in the British colonial administrative system and apparently paid little attention to the threat, for he continued in residence at New Haven until early in the fall.

Although, as it has been stated, Ingersoll was unable to keep New Haven from taking a stand in favor of a Continental Congress, it seems that his presence there during the summer of 1774 prevented any display of radicalism on the part of the people. Indeed, it is singular how powerful an influence he seems to have had in the affairs of this community during this period. This is particularly well illustrated by the control that he and his friends exercised over the people on August 16,

[1] This letter was without date. It was addressed to "Jared Ingersoll Esq. at New Haven," and was signed by "Multitudes." Ingersoll Papers.

[2] The letter reads as follows:

"To Jonathan Trumbull
        New Haven, July 9, 1774.
Sir:
I send you inclosed a copy of an anonymous letter which I received this day by the Post from the office at N. London.

As the contents of this Letter carry with them a high handed threat and breach of the peace toward me, and which if executed might be very prejudicial to the interests of this Colony, I thought it my duty to make known the same to your Honor that you may take such steps thereon as you shall think best for the public good.
                    I am
                Your honorable, most Obedient,
                            Jared Ingersoll.
Gov. Trumbull."
Ingersoll Papers.

when the Boston delegates to the congress arrived in the town en route to Philadelphia. They were met at North Haven "by a grand parade" and escorted into New Haven in the midst of the firing of cannon and the ringing of bells. John Adams, however, writing about the incident, declared that he found out from his landlord while at New Haven, that the parade "was a sudden proposal in order to divert the populace from erecting a liberty pole," and that "Ingersoll's friends were at the bottom of it."[1] Adams also has left testimony as to the hospitable attitude of the Ingersoll group. "Nothing shows to me the spirit of the town of New Haven in a stronger light," he wrote, "than the politeness of Mr. Ingersoll, Judge of Admiralty for the Pennsylvania Middle District, who came over with his neighbors this evening and made his compliments very respectfully to Tom. Cushing, Sam. Adams, John Adams and Bob Paine."[2]

In spite of the fact that Ingersoll had been the recipient of a threatening letter just referred to, no attempt seems ever to have been made during the revolutionary crisis to subject him to personal violence. It is really surprising, considering all the circumstances, that he was able to escape, during the troublous times that now came to America, with so little molestation on the part of the radical element, when other loyalists in Connecticut en-

[1] C. F. Adams, *Works of John Adams, with a Life of the Author, Notes and Illustrations,* II, 343. The plan for a liberty pole seems to have been carried out in September, according to Rev. Ezra Stiles. Under date of September 14 he wrote in his Itineraries: "Great Tumults about Liberty. A Liberty Mast erected this Day here." *Literary Diary of Ezra Stiles* (edited by Dr. F. B. Dexter), II, 456, note 3. Writing October 24, from Philadelphia, to Jonathan Ingersoll, the judge inquired: "Pray tell me where abouts on the Green Liberty Pole stands and who are the principal members of the Patriotic Club which meet at Steph. Munson's in order to take care of the N. Haven Tories?" New Haven Col. Hist. Soc. *Papers,* IX ("Jared Ingersoll Papers"), 449.

[2] C. F. Adams, *Works of John Adams,* II, 343.

joyed no such immunity.[1] For the days of real persecution had come, and the truth of this must have been
deeply impressed upon him in the light, especially, of the
treatment meted out to his cousin, David Ingersoll, a
graduate of Yale College in the class of 1761, who had
settled at Great Barrington in Berkshire County, Massachusetts, as a lawyer, and who, from 1770 to 1774, had
represented his town in the general assembly.   The
Berkshire mob, after driving the judges of the court of
common pleas from their seats and after having shut up
the court house in 1774, turned upon Ingersoll, who had
signed the complimentary address to Governor Hutchinson early in that year. Not only was his property laid
waste but he himself was seized and carried over into
Litchfield County in Connecticut, where, among other
outrages inflicted upon him, before his release, not the
least was a coat of tar and feathers. The hounded man
thereupon determined to move to England.[2] In sailing
for there, late in 1774, he carried with him an interesting
letter of introduction written by Captain Evelyn of the
Kings Own Regiment, stationed in Massachusetts, who,
while referring to the actions of the mob within that
colony, gave his opinion of the populace in no uncertain
terms. ''I firmly believe,'' he wrote, ''that so execrable a
set of sanctified villains never before disgraced the hu-
man species.''[3] As for the wretched David Ingersoll, in
April, 1776, the British government came to his assist-

[1] For proceedings against Rev. James Nichols, Rev. Smalley, and Rev.
Samuel Peters see the *Connecticut Courant* for September 19, September 26,
and October 17, 1774. I. W. Stuart, *Life of Jonathan Trumbull*, pp. 158-
160; Lorenzo Sabine, *American Loyalists*, under heading ''Samuel Peters.''

[2] See Dr. Dexter's *Biographical Sketches of Yale Graduates* (Class of
1761), pp. 698-699.

[3] *Memoirs and Letters of Captain A. G. Evelyn of the Fourth Regiment*
(*the Kings Own*), edited by G. D. Scull. The editor thought that David
Ingersoll and Jared Ingersoll were one and the same. See index to third
edition.

ance with a grant of £100 in compensation of the losses that he had sustained, "on account of his Majesty's government."[1]

Upon his return to Philadelphia early in the fall of 1774, Jared Ingersoll found the Continental Congress in session. While it is not probable that he made any further open attempts to work against the forces of radicalism, yet the attitude he had been displaying down to that time toward public issues did not escape unfavorable comment; this feeling against him on the part of political opponents found an echo in a letter penned by Silas Deane of Wethersfield, one of the Connecticut delegates. "In conversation last evening at the coffee house," he wrote, "with gentlemen of the first character in the province and of Mr. Ingersoll's acquaintance, I find his conduct very much condemned in this city even by Prerogative men themselves or those who might be titled such."[2]

One of the principal achievements of the congress was the famous "Association," according to which, among other things, it was agreed that after December 1, 1774, nothing should be imported from Great Britain; that after March 1, 1775, no East India tea should be purchased, and no article should be used which was on the prohibited list; that after September 10, 1775, no goods should be exported to Great Britain. The Association was ratified at the October session of the Connecticut

[1] Stevens, *Facsimiles of Manuscript in European Archives Relative to America* (1773-1783), XXIV, No. 2024[18], under date April 6, 1776.

[2] *Deane Papers* (edited by Charles Osborn), I, 16. Writing to his nephew, Jonathan, at this period, Ingersoll shows that the Connecticut radicals at least did not scorn his hospitality. "Present my Comp° to Mr Chandler & tell him that if you forgot to acquaint me with his being chosen Deputy, Mr Shipman did not—and that I had the pleasure to acquaint Mr Sherman with it. By the way Co^l Dyer & Mr Dean & I, have smoakt the pipe together at my house." New Haven Col. Hist. Soc. *Papers*, IX ("Jared Ingersoll Papers"), 448.

general assembly and on November 14 New Haven, in conformity with the general practice in the colony, as well as elsewhere, selected a committee of thirty-one to see that no one should violate the terms of the agreement.[1] On account of dissatisfaction with the unequal distribution of the membership of the committee among the different parishes, it was enlarged to include fifty-one members.[2] Radicalism was clearly on top. In January, 1775, a new military organization was established; in February, as a token of her sympathy, the town loaded a ship with all manner of supplies for the needy at Boston, and in the following month a still more advanced step was taken by voting in town meeting that "It is the opinion of this Town that if any Inhabitant thereof shall Entertain any inhabitant of the towns of Ridgefield and Newtown, that opposed the acceptance of the doings of the Continental Congress he will be guilty of a Breach of the Association of said Congress."[3] By April, according to one writer, the New Haven committee of inspection had "proceeded to very unwarrantable limits." "What! do you drink tea?" demanded one of its members of a non-conformer, who was probably Joshua Chandler, an ardent loyalist. "Take care what you do,

[1] New Haven Town Records, V, 45.

[2] Ibid.

[3] Ibid., entry for February 27, 1775. Ridgefield, it will be borne in mind, was the home pastoral field of Ingersoll's brother, Jonathan, who seems to have exercised a restraining influence upon the people of that little town. "Ridgefield, I find," wrote Jared Ingersoll, early in 1775, "speak their mind plainly and not in parables." Jared Ingersoll to Jonathan Ingersoll, February 11, 1775, New Haven Col. Hist. Soc. Papers, IX ("Jared Ingersoll Papers"), 452. Both Ridgefield and Newtown repudiated the Association all but unanimously at their respective town meetings. Not until late in 1775 could Ridgefield be brought into line, while Newtown remained firm in her position. G. A. Gilbert, "The Connecticut Loyalists," Amer. Hist. Rev., IV, 273-281, and especially, A. M. Schlesinger, The Colonial Merchants and the American Revolution, pp. 445-447.

Mr. C—, for you are to know the committee commands the mob and can in an instance let them loose upon any man, who opposes their decree, and complete his destruction.'"[1]

What now had become of the Ingersoll group, so powerful the previous year in the councils of New Haven?

[1] New Haven Correspondence of April 9, 1775, in the *New York Gazette.*

CHAPTER XII

OUTBREAK OF HOSTILITIES, NEW HAVEN PATRIOTS AND LOYALISTS. INGERSOLL A PRISONER ON PAROLE. CONCLUSION

THE news of the battle of Lexington, which arrived at New Haven April 21, 1775, stirred the community profoundly. The result was that a town meeting was called at the "Middle Brick" Church to determine what action, if any, should be taken. It appears that the group which for years had followed more or less consistently the leadership of Jared Ingersoll lacked only one vote of defeating Roger Sherman, the choice of the radicals, for moderator,[1] and in spite of this, finally succeeded in getting not only the appointment of a committee of strong conservative tendencies to care for the town interests in this crisis, but also a decision against taking up arms, at least for the present, against the king. But the radicals were not to be outdone, for they had found a leader in the impetuous Benedict Arnold, captain of the local militia company, known as the Second Company of the Governor's Guards. Arnold called out his company and proposed that they should march to the aid of the Massachusetts Minute Men. About fifty volunteered. However, in order to equip themselves for the journey it was necessary to have ammunition. When requested to furnish this from the town supply, the New Haven authorities at first refused; not until Arnold had drawn his men up

[1] E. E. Atwater, *History of the City of New Haven*, p. 42; see also footnote.

before the tavern where the town fathers were deliberating and threatened to break down the door of the powder-house, unless the keys were delivered up, did the over-awed conservatives give way.[1]

For months now after the Lexington alarm, there was comparative quiet in the town, although soldiers in goodly numbers were enlisted and sent on to Boston or into the Lake Champlain country.[2] Most of those in New Haven who were not in sympathy with the activities of this revolutionary program were discreetly keeping their peace and abiding quietly at home.[3] But the case of

---

[1] *History of the City of New Haven*, pp. 42, 649-650. The somewhat unbridled individualism of the Connecticut soldier is well known. Ebenezer Huntington wrote to Andrew Huntington of Norwich, Connecticut, on December 1, 1775, from Camp Roxbury, ''the Connecticut men have this day taken the liberty to leave camp without leave (I mean some of them). Major Trumbull and Captain Chester are sent after them to bring them back, they have not returned tho' 8 o'clock—A party went from Cambridge in the same manner among whom was a Sergeant, whom the General has determined to send to Connecticut in Irons with a label on his back telling of his Crime—to be dealt with as the authority of the Colony shall think proper—the men seem universally desirous of mutiny—fears the men had not a bounty.'' *The Correspondence of Samuel B. Webb* (edited by Mr. Worthington C. Ford), I, 123. Silas Deane, writing to his wife, on December 15, 1775, declared: ''The behaviour of our soldiers has made me sick, but little better could be expected from men trained up with notions of their right of saying how, and when and under whom, they will serve; and who have for certain dirty political purposes, been tampered with by their officers, among whom no less than a *general* has been *busy.''* *Ibid.*, I, 124 *et seq.*

[2] From beginning to end New Haven contributed about one thousand men; this included North Haven, East Haven, West Haven, Orange Hundred, Mt. Carmel, Woodbridge, Bethany, and Westville. But her losses were estimated to have been only sixty-one killed, twenty-three wounded and twenty-one prisoners. See estimates by W. S. Wells in *Revolutionary Characters of New Haven*. (Published by the Connecticut Society of the Sons of the American Revolution, 1911.)

[3] The treatment of loyalists at Farmington, Chatham, Torrington, New Hartford, Somers, Goshen, and other Connecticut towns in 1774, while not as drastic as the treatment meted out to them at some of the other colonies, had been of such a character and was so widely advertised that the effect

Abiathar Camp, Jr., shows that some, at least, felt deeply about the turn of affairs even if they did not act.

Abiathar, whose parents lived at New Haven, was a student at Yale College. He had, it seems, discussed freely and unwisely, among his fellows at the college, the pending issues. As a result, the members of his class appointed a committee to address to him a letter, "inquiring about his political principles, and asking him to clear up his character." His reply could hardly be called a dignified one: "New Haven, June 13, 1775: To the Hon. and Resp. Gentlemen of the Committee now residing at Yale College: May it please your honors, ham—ham—ham. Finis cum sistula popularum gig. A man without a head has no need of a wig." After this counterblast, a committee of the whole college met and prepared a statement against Camp. It was charged that he had stated before the beginning of hostilities that not only would he not stand by the doings of the Continental Congress but "that all those who did so or justified the destruction of tea at Boston were a pack of d—— Rebels." He was further accused of saying that if he were at home and "the Liberty Pole Men should rise against the Administration, he would fight on the ministerial side till he had killed a number of the Rebels." He was thereupon advertised as an enemy to his country and his name as such was posted upon "the Hall Door" of the college.[1]

To be able to determine more accurately who were for and against the cause of the colonies, the town meeting in September, 1775, unanimously voted in favor of the formation of an "Association" by the general assembly which should supplement the non-importation, non-ex-

must have been profound upon those at New Haven. See *Hartford Courant*, September 19, 26, and October 17, 1774.

[1] *Connecticut Journal*, August 30, 1775.

portation, and non-consumption association already adopted at the request of the Continental Congress. By this plan, there were to be sent to the different Connecticut towns papers to be signed by all the inhabitants which would allow the friends of American freedom to be distinguished from its enemies.[1] The action of the town meeting would seem to indicate that while this body had surrendered to the popular influences there were nevertheless a good many living in the community who had not placed themselves on record as yet, as to their political principles. But, for the time, it seems that nothing further was done to draw the lines between the loyal and disloyal.

What thoroughly aroused the town to a sense of peril in its situation was the wanton bombarding and subsequent burning of the little unfortified seaport of Falmouth on the Maine coast by an English fleet in October. As a result steps were taken to guard against danger both from without and from within. Among other things, steps were taken at a town meeting, held November 6, to erect a beacon of warning on Indian Hill in East Haven, and to provide the means for receiving the earliest possible warning of the appearance of any hostile fleet in the sound; arrangements were made with Captain Isaac Sears of New York to establish "a mode of intelligence in case of any danger by way of New York"; it was ordered that a fort should be erected at Black Rock; an artillery company was organized, the citizens at large were summoned to military drill, Yale College library was turned into an armory and a committee of public safety with large and indefinite powers was appointed. Before adjourning the town meeting also

[1] *Connecticut Journal*, September 20, 1775. For the organization of the defense associations see A. M. Schlesinger, *The Colonial Merchant and the American Revolution*, p. 542, et passim.

appointed a special committee, the members of which were empowered "to call before them all those who might be disposed to give aid to the enemy and who harbored unfriendly sentiments."[1]

This committee, it appears, in the course of its duty called upon Richard Woodhull and the other local Sandemanians, who, after having given a tentative answer, as a reply to the question of their allegiance, forwarded a letter to the committee in which among other things they declared, "We hold ourselves bound in conscience to yield obedience to the commands of his Majesty, King George III, so far as to take up arms against New Haven or the United Colonies." According to the report of the committee, the Sandemanians went on further to state in the letter that "in avoiding a plain answer to so plain a question at a time when the town and country were disavowing their allegiance to the king and were going into open rebellion against God and the king was evidence to them that they were influenced in their first answer by fear of man and not of God."[2]

Nothing, apparently, was done to molest Woodhull and his friends in spite of their highly unsatisfactory reply. There probably was a feeling that these men in reality were not dangerous but were desirous of living peacefully with their fellows; the committee must also have realized that many at heart felt as the Sandemanians did. Once local persecution was started where would it end? New Haven, however, was soon to come into the limelight as a harrower of Tories.

[1] The above measures were provided for at a town meeting held November 6, 1775. New Haven Town Records, V, 54-55.

[2] For an account of the Sandemanians see Chapter I of this study; E. E. Atwater, *History of the City of New Haven*, p. 139. According to the *Connecticut Journal*, the Sandemanians later on agreed to submit to "the laws of the government," but in 1777 they retracted, stating that they felt themselves bound to their king. *Connecticut Journal*, October 29, 1777.

It seems that Isaac Sears, referred to above, had taken up his abode in New Haven some months previous and had been most active in stirring up a martial spirit among the people. Sears was a native of Norwalk, Connecticut, but had gone to New York City to live and there had gained some reputation as a trader. At the time of the Stamp Act he had become zealous in the defense of the colonial claims and seems to have been especially active in organizing the Sons of Liberty, first in eastern Connecticut and later in New York. James Rivington, who in 1775 was the loyalist editor of the *New York Gazette,* it appears, had in September, 1765, lampooned Sears in a burlesque poem, entitled, ''Loyal York,'' to celebrate the refusal of New York to send delegates to the Stamp Act Congress. The first verse of the doggerel runs as follows:

''And, so my good master, I find 'tis no joke,
For York has stepped forward and thrown off the yoke,
Of Congress, Committees and even King Sears
Who shows you good nature by showing his ears.''[1]

Sears never forgot the insult and seized the first opportunity to repay it. This opportunity came in 1775.

On November 20 he left New Haven, on horseback, with a party of bold spirits who were increased by recruits from other Connecticut towns until they numbered about one hundred. The riders first made their way to Westchester, New York, where they made prisoner three of the most prominent men of the town, who were reputed to be ardent Tories, the Rev. Samuel Seabury, Judge

[1] *Memoirs of Jonathan Mix* (ed. by W. P. Black), pp. 30-31. Mix was married to Anna, Sears's sister. For further facts regarding the activities of Sears see Becker's *History of Political Parties in the Province of New York, 1760-1776,* and Andrews's *The Boston Merchants and the Non-Importation Movement.* In 1890 Samuel P. May wrote and published *Notes on Isaac Sears (King Sears),* which contains many facts regarding his life.

Jonathan Fowler, and "Lord" Underhill.[1] The main body then proceeded to New York City to execute a still more daring plan. On November 23 they suddenly rode into the city with fixed bayonets and drew up in close order before the printing office of Rivington, whereupon a small detachment entered the building and after demolishing the printing press loaded the type into bags prepared for the purpose, offering to pay the astonished proprietor for the same, by "An order on Lord Dunmore," who, at Norfolk, Virginia, had recently made way with the outfit of a patriotic printer there. Sears and his men having accomplished this, rode slowly out of the city to the tune of Yankee Doodle, cheered by a "vast concourse of people assembled at the Coffee House Bridge."[2] The party, in returning to New Haven, not only brought along Rivington's type but the Tories that had been apprehended on the way.[3]

[1] The Rev. Samuel Seabury later became the first bishop of the Episcopal Church in the United States, being consecrated in 1784 as bishop of the Episcopal Church of Connecticut; at the time he was rector of the West-chester Anglican Church, Jonathan Fowler was a judge of the superior court of the province of New York; after the war he went to live in Digby, Nova Scotia. Nathaniel Underhill was mayor of Westchester. J. T. Scharf, *History of Westchester County*, New York, II, 303-308. Scharf passionately arraigns the lawlessness of the Connecticut adventurers.

[2] *Memoirs of Jonathan Mix*, p. 14; *New London Gazette*, December 1, 1775; Forrest Morgan, *Connecticut as a Colony and as a State*, II, 71-72.

The feeling against Rivington among the people of the seaport of New York was reflected in an appeal, December, 1774, to Silas Deane, of the Connecticut committee of correspondence, on the part of the "Friends of Liberty" of that city to boycott both the *Gazette* and those who advertised in it. *Correspondence of Samuel Blachley Webb* (ed. by W. C. Ford), I, 45-46. Nevertheless, as ardent a champion of the popular side as Alexander Hamilton was so "filled with indignation at this violent suppression of opinion" that "if he could have got a few men to go with him would have ridden after the marauders and recaptured the property." H. C. Lodge, *Alexander Hamilton*, p. 11.

[3] Fowler and Underhill took an oath of allegiance to the American cause and were allowed to return home soon after their arrival in New Haven.

The importance of the incident, for the purpose of this study, is to show that erstwhile ultra-conservative New Haven, now under the inspiration of such leaders as Arnold and Sears, had become to all appearances most aggressively active in support of the revolt.

As for Jared Ingersoll, during the first two years of the war, he was well satisfied, by reason of the antagonism that he had aroused in Connecticut, to remain away from New Haven, continuing therefore to abide within the limits of the Quaker City. As soon as the revolutionary government assumed control in Philadelphia, upon the outbreak of hostilities, it was necessary, of course, for him to suspend the business of the vice-admiralty court for the middle colonies; but it should be understood that technically the court did not go out of existence until 1783, although there was no incumbent of the judgeship after the death of Ingersoll in 1781.[1] In spite of the sittings of the Continental Congress at Philadelphia, that place was by no means an uncomfortable one for those of loyalist leanings; men of conservative tendencies, such as John Dickinson, were placed in positions of responsibility; the Quakers "publicly dis-

Seabury, having refused the oath, was kept in confinement for over a month before he was finally released.

[1] Warrants in the Audit Office show that Ingersoll received his salary up to and including the official year ending October 17, 1779 (his commission, issued in 1768, was dated October 17). In 1772 Thomas Life of Basinghall Street, Cripplegate, London, was empowered to act as his attorney and to collect his salary; later his son Jared, who was studying at the Middle Temple, was given the responsibility, and upon his return to America apparently the exiled David Ingersoll cared for his cousin's interests until the appointment of Richard Jackson and James Brown, in 1778, to act as his legal representatives. After tne death of Judge Ingersoll his son appointed Dennis de Berdt to act as "the Administrator of the Effects" of his father. Audit Office, 15: 60, 355; 64, 51, 239, 673, 674; "Wills on file in the Surrogates' Office City of New York." New York Historical Society *Collections* (1900), p. 45.

avowed all *unwarrantable Combinations*";[1] and when the committees of the several counties of Pennsylvania, early in 1775, met to consider the question of arming the province, it was found that this measure was opposed by so many people of weight and influence that it was dropped.[2] How tolerant men were there of loyalist opinions is shown by the fact that Galloway did not hesitate to declare in the Provincial Congress that Rivington, the ardent Tory editor of the *New York Gazette,* was an honor to his country.[3] It is therefore not surprising that Ingersoll wrote in October, "I enjoy, thank Heaven, an undisturbed repose & have good reason to believe the same may Continue."[4] But it should be observed that he was exceedingly circumspect and quiet now that the crisis had arrived. He confessed that after his experience with his "pretty little stamp office," he had become careful about writing letters;[5] however, it is to be observed that he went so far on one occasion in writing to his nephew Jonathan, who was living, as has been noticed, in New Haven, as to counsel him that "in Case the Connecticut forces should be called forth against the Kings Troops, that you will not degrade yourself by going in a Caracter below that of a Colonel."[6] While he was not clear whether New Haven would be a "proper asylum next summer for a Tory," he did not fail to inquire both regarding the

[1] Jared Ingersoll to Jonathan Ingersoll, February 11, 1775, New Haven Col. Hist. Soc. *Papers,* IX ("Jared Ingersoll Papers"), 451.

[2] *Ibid.,* IX, 451.

[3] Jared Ingersoll to Jonathan Ingersoll, Jr., March 10, 1775, *ibid.,* IX, 454. In commenting upon this Ingersoll said, "I suppose no man in N. England dares say so much."

[4] Jared Ingersoll to Jonathan Ingersoll, Jr., October 7, 1775, *ibid.,* IX, 458.

[5] Jared Ingersoll to Jonathan Ingersoll, Jr., December 7, 1775, Ingersoll Papers.

[6] Jared Ingersoll to Jonathan Ingersoll, Jr., March 10, 1775, New Haven Col. Hist. Soc. *Papers,* IX ("Jared Ingersoll Papers"), 454.

terms of the Connecticut loyalty test act[1] and the fate of the Westchester Tories who had been brought to New Haven by Sears and his followers. As to the alarm beacon, set up by the town on a near-by hill, he facetiously asked of his nephew ''how far by the light of it you can discover a real patriot from a false?''[2]

As it became apparent that the country was destined to face the rigors of a long and bloody struggle, Mrs. Ingersoll, it seems, could no longer bear separation from the home ties of New Haven. It was, therefore, decided in the spring of 1776 that she should proceed to Connecticut; the house therefore that she and the judge had occupied in Philadelphia was given up and the furnishings, probably for precautionary reasons, were carted to Burlington, New Jersey, about twenty miles away from Philadelphia. The judge's desire to accompany Mrs. Ingersoll to New Haven in the family ''chariot'' found expression in a letter written some few weeks previous to her setting out, which also set forth his determination to do nothing that would hazard his various interests. ''May I come & live at N. Haven or may I not?'' he asked. ''It is not very likely to me that I shall ever again officiate in the office I hold, but I think I shall by all means Choose to draw the Salary until I shall be able to part with it upon some Composition with Government.—by the late law of Connecticut a person, I think, forfeits his Estate by taking refuge on Board a Man of War.[3] I think it must be rather hard for a Man who has an Estate in that Colony,

---

[1] It does not appear that any test act was passed in Connecticut prior to October 16, 1776. *Conn. State Records*, I, 4. However, December 15, 1775, an act to punish disloyalty was passed. *Conn. Col. Rec.*, XV, 192-195.

[2] Jared Ingersoll to Jonathan Ingersoll, Jr., November 26, 1775, Ingersoll Papers.

[3] ''An Act for restraining and punishing Persons who are inimical to the Liberties of this and the Rest of the United Colonies, and for directing Proceedings therein,'' passed December 15, 1775. *Conn. Col. Rec.*, XV, 194.

not to be allowed to live on it nor yet to leave it.'"[1] In spite of assurances given to him by Roger Sherman, Colonel Eliphalet Dyer, and others, that he might return to New Haven without difficulty, Ingersoll prudently chose to remain in Philadelphia. That he felt the growing isolation of his situation is evidenced by a line in one of his letters. He was now, he declared, "like a Saint of old, as a Pilgrim and Stranger in the Earth having no Abiding City.'"[2] Not until the fall of 1777 did Ingersoll return to New Haven,—when he arrived he was a prisoner on parole.

While in the name of liberty the New Haven "liberty" group took much satisfaction in rounding up prominent Tories, such as Rev. Samuel Seabury, the exultation of many of them was not unalloyed. They had gone into the struggle for freedom—freedom from all that seemed oppressive or onerous. To the chagrin of many of them the courts continued to grind away and the most "vociferous patriots" on various pretexts were rudely dragged before the bar of justice. Prosecutions for debt seem to have been especially frequent, even in a colony famed for its spirit of litigation. For, in spite of the war, numerous creditors were seeking payment of old debts, such, for example, as John Hotchkiss, who claimed to have among the people of New Haven several thousand pounds owing him and some of these obligations, he complained, had been neglected for ten or fifteen years, "an unremitting indulgence," as he called it. Very naturally, a cry was raised the moment that legal pressure was applied. Indeed, these exciting times did not offer an opportune moment for the settlement of accounts, when men were

[1] Jared Ingersoll to Jonathan Ingersoll, Jr., April 4, 1776, New Haven Col. Hist. Soc. *Papers*, IX ("Jared Ingersoll Papers"), 464.

[2] Jared Ingersoll to Jonathan Ingersoll, Jr., August 1, 1775, *ibid.*, IX, 456.

especially liable to neglect personal affairs. But in vain, appeals—prepared by both "Rusticus" and "Legion"— were sent forth by means of the press "that law suits, which threaten to overwhelm the province be discontinued."[1]

If the courts were active in harassing financially embarrassed Sons of Liberty, those who refused to support the popular cause were not, on the other hand, entirely neglected. During the years 1775 and 1776 especially, the "Association" was evidently enforced rather effectively and offenders against it were disciplined. For example, in March, 1776, William Glen and Freeman Huse were convicted of buying tea and selling it at an extortionate price and also of refusing the paper currency of the colony. The offenders accordingly were "advertised" so that no patriot should have any further dealings or inter-

---

[1] *Connecticut Journal*, February 21, 1776. How the creditor class, which was also the more conservative class, felt about the matter is recorded in a most interesting and richly ironical communication addressed to the printers of the *Connecticut Journal*. The author desires to appear in the guise of an irritated debtor. As it undoubtedly gives a valuable insight into the attitude of mind of no small proportion of the New Haven freemen, it would be well to present it in some fullness: "Why are sheriffs and constables," he asked, "allowed to seize and put in jail people for debt? What is all your liberty good for if a man is in jail? Why is a man to be forced to pay his debts if he does not so desire? You may talk of what you please but everybody knows if our courts were righted so that they could not dare to set and do business, we should not value the lawyers and sheriffs at three skips of a louse. . . . Why if you will believe it, Messrs. Printers, I am as good a Son of Liberty as ever breathed and have run around to the taverns and drunk as much flip in the common cause as e'er a soul of them, and yet I have had such an assortment of writs and executions out after me, that I dare hardly put my nose out of the door for fear your confounded Sheriffs coming for want thereof to take the body." The writer went on to declare that he would leave it to any man "who owes more money than he intends to pay, if times were not better when they could cock their hats in their creditors' faces and tell them to sue if they dare than to sit as he is now with the doors locked for fear a constable will enter. A fig, I say, for such liberty as this! More than half the people would be glad to do away with the Courts." *Connecticut Journal*, February 28, 1776.

course with them;[1] whether the guilty purchasers of this high-priced tea were likewise suitably punished is not recorded. It is to be noted that Glen, soon after being "advertised," begged the pardon of the public for his offense.

While the town proceeded against such petty traders as Glen and Huse, it seemed more reluctant to take any steps against men of prominence who were reported to be disloyal. As a result, one Lamberton Smith and others of New Haven, in 1776, were impelled to complain to the general assembly against the disloyal practices of Ralph Isaacs and Captain Abiathar Camp, two of the leading New Haven loyalists. It was declared against Isaacs that he had sent "some fine black fish" to Governor Montford Browne[2] and "tea and other luxuries" to Governor William Franklin,[3] who as Tory prisoners had been brought to Connecticut and were at that time confined at Middletown.[4] Camp, according to Smith and his friends, had used his vessels in a suspicious manner and had gen-

[1] *Connecticut Journal*, April 10, 1776. For a discussion of the enforcement of the Association in Connecticut see A. M. Schlesinger, *The Colonial Merchants and the American Revolution*, pp. 486-488.

[2] Governor Browne and others were brought from New Providence. He was governor of the Bahamas and later a brigadier general in the British army. In 1777 he was exchanged.

[3] Governor Franklin of New Jersey. He will be given further mention in the course of this chapter.

[4] R. R. Hinman, *A Historical Collection . . . of the Part Sustained by Connecticut during the war of the Revolution*, pp. 241, 297, 303; Jonathan Trumbull, "Defamation of Revolutionary Patriots," in the *Year Book* (for 1895) *of the Connecticut Society of the Sons of the American Revolution*, p. 183.

It is to be noted that "Ingersoll [presumably Jonathan, the nephew of Judge Ingersoll] and Botsford [later a Tory refugee] . . . acted for the respondents Camp and Isaacs in petitioning or memorializing the lower house against depriving them of their liberties by banishing them according to the request of the petitioners." The general assembly, however, acted favorably upon the petition of Lamberton Smith and Camp was sent to Eastbury. Conn. Archives, Revolutionary War, V, 429, 432, 443; VIII, 211.

erally shown disloyalty. As a result the two were declared by the assembly enemies of the state and imprisoned within the limits of Glastonbury.

In studying the revolutionary movement in a local way, it must not be forgotten that news of the military operations was continually coming to encourage or depress the public mind. With intense interest the tidings were received of the successful fighting about Boston, of the failure of the Canadian expedition and of the shifting of the struggle to the middle colonies, especially about New York. Although New Haven continued to contribute her quota of men and money, there was, nevertheless, a feeling abroad that the town was not as whole-souled as she might be in supporting the war against Great Britain. This was reflected in 1776 in a letter written by Joseph Webb of Wethersfield to Silas Deane. ''Our people,'' declared Webb, ''are afraid you adjourned to N. Haven. They do not think that N. Haven [h]as been Hearty eno[ugh] to deserve it.''[1]

Whether or not there was any basis for the charge of lukewarmness against New Haven in 1776, there nevertheless seems to be little doubt that during the spring of 1777 the patriotic fervor of the town sank to a low level. It is probably no exaggeration to say that every community in Connecticut, during the late months of 1776 and the earliest months of 1777, had searchings of heart after learning of the defeats at Long Island and White Plains, and the surrender of Forts Washington and Lee

In October Camp published a confession in the local paper, in which he asked forgiveness for disobeying an act of the committees of inspection by sending his ship to sea. He promised his utmost assistance to carry into execution all such measures as the Continental Congress might arrive at. *Connecticut Journal*, October 4, 1775.

[1] Webb was of course referring to the Continental Congress of which, until recently, Deane had been a member. *Correspondence of Samuel Blachley Webb*, I, 146.

on the Hudson, as well as of the exciting pursuit of Washington southward to the Delaware. The occupation of New York, so short a distance to the west, by the British and the news that New Jersey was returning to the king's allegiance, must have sounded very ominous. For it seemed logical that Connecticut would be the next colony to be overrun by the royal grenadiers. The conviction that the cause of independence, in spite of declarations and resolves, was doomed, took possession of the more timid. Even the general assembly could not escape the charge of weakening in its enthusiasm for American freedom. It is true that among other things the assembly called upon every male between the ages of sixteen and sixty, not otherwise exempted, to procure arms and enroll in a company "for an alarm list,"[1] yet when it came to exacting the oath of allegiance already provided for there was a strange hesitation. This oath had been prepared by the authority of the assembly during the fall of 1776; the act stated that all freemen should be enjoined to take a prescribed oath of fidelity and that after January 1, 1777, no person should execute any office or have the right to vote until he had taken the oath.[2] The assembly, however, at an adjourned meeting, held in November, in the midst of the general gloom of disaster, decided to suspend the operation of the law until April; and then in December, when the cause seemed still more hopeless, the act was repealed in its entirety.[3] The formal reason assigned for the repeal was that "the separatists could not in conscience subscribe to all the laws of the state (which would include those ecclesiastical) as was enjoined

[1] *Conn. State Records*, I, 92. The meeting was held at Middletown, December 18, 1776.

[2] *Ibid.*, I, 5.

[3] *Ibid.*, I, 63, 100.

by the oath.'"¹ Apparently, for the first time in their lives, many of the members of the general assembly had become profoundly impressed with the unfortunate situation of the separatists.²

However, there was a minority group in the assembly made up of ardent ''liberty men,'' which was anxious to put everyone on record so that the friends of independence might be made known to all. These members prepared a new bill to meet the religious objections but it was vigorously and successfully opposed. According to an anonymous writer, signing himself ''Plain Dealer,'' the majority took the ground that now was no time for such an act. ''Our affairs are in a fluctuating, unsettled state—We know not what the event of War will be—We had better wait until the Articles of Confederation are agreed upon. When the war is over we can make one at our leisure that will give general satisfaction.'' ''Plain Dealer'' declared that translated into plain English the argument of the majority meant: ''It is quite probable that we shall be conquered. General Howe is already in possession of New Jersey, and I expect he will be here next, and then those of us who have taken the test oath adjuring the authority of the King and swearing to support the independence of this State will lose our estates and it's five to one our heads also.'"³ Such men in the assembly as endorsed these views, according to this New Haven critic, could never be expected to push the war

¹ *Connecticut Journal*, March 19, 1777. The ''separatists'' were those Congregationalists who, repudiating the Saybrook platform, refused to conform to the church regulations established by the Connecticut government. For over thirty years they had suffered persecution, sometimes of an extreme type. E. P. Parker, ''The Congregationalist Separates of the Eighteenth Century in Connecticut.'' New Haven Col. Hist. Soc. *Papers*, VIII, 151-161.

² *Connecticut Journal* of March 26, 1777, has a valiant defense of the action of the legislature.

³ *Ibid.*, March 19, 1777.

vigorously, nor could they be depended upon to make decisions for the people of the state. "Seclude them from your councils," he appealed, "avoid them as you would a cockatrice den—they will desert your cause at the first approach of danger." What was the actual situation in New Haven and elsewhere in Connecticut? he asked. In reply, he affirmed that Tories who were freemen had as good a right to vote as other freemen. The consequence was that in some towns the Tory influence was such as to allow them to send to the general assembly, "Either men of their own Kidney, or at best half saved Whigs who in Council and everywhere else are as bad as Tories." He then concluded significantly, "And in our town they actually do send Tory representatives."[1]

Both "A Freeman" and "Junius" used the local New Haven paper to express similar views. "I have long wanted," said the latter ironically, "to have stated to the public the very great advantage of that extreme timidity which has for some time actuated every movement of this state."[2] On the other hand, contributors, under the pseudonyms "M. M.," "Aristides," and "Medicus" vied with one another in castigating the one who had written the communication signed by "A Freeman." He was accused of wanting to get his New Haven friends into the legislature. "Medicus" even compared him to a mad dog.[3]

The situation certainly appeared so full of peril for the commonwealth that many only looked for an opportunity to make peace with the enemy and thereby secure themselves from the impending ruin. Not only is it clear

[1] *Connecticut Journal.* The New Haven representatives were Samuel Bishop and Colonel Jonathan Fitch. The latter, in 1774, had been attacked for showing loyalist sympathies, and was defended in the *Connecticut Journal* (see issue of August 25, 1774) by one signing himself "Z."

[2] *Ibid.*, March 26, 1777.

[3] *Ibid.*, April 4, 1777.

354   JARED INGERSOLL

that large numbers of Connecticut people at this time
"absconded" and fled to New York, but three of the
most prominent men in the state, General Erastus Wolcott of East Windsor, William Hillhouse of New London,
a member of the council of safety, and Thomas Seymour,
a leading financier of the general assembly, were publicly
accused of securing "protections" of General Howe in
command of New York. General Wolcott was defended
both by General Parsons and by the writer "Aristides."
But in reply the editor of the *Connecticut Journal* said:
"The character of Mr. Wolcott I have ever esteemed.
Whether he has been unjustly aspersed or not I am ignorant. It is, however, certain that no person who opposes
the existence of an oath of fidelity to his state can be head
and heart a sincere friend of its interests."[1]

[1] *Connecticut Gazette*, March 21, 1777; *Connecticut Journal*, April 7,
1777.

It may be pointed out in this connection that General Parsons, the defender of General Wolcott, was himself in after years accused of inclining
to the enemy in the year 1781 (see Justin Winsor, *Narrative and Critical
History of America*, VI, 460). This charge is based upon General Sir
Henry Clinton's "A Record of Private Intelligence" (edited by E. F.
DeLancey and printed in the *Magazine of American History*, vols. X, XI,
and XII), which contains a series of secret communications from the loyalist, William Heron of Redding, Connecticut. The evidence against General Parsons is very damaging in spite of the able defense in his behalf by
both G. B. Loring, in 1888 ("Vindication of General Samuel Holden Parsons," *Magazine of American History*, XX, 286-304), and J. G. Woodward,
in 1895 (an examination of the charge of Treason against General Samuel
Holden Parsons, *Year Book* (for 1895) *of the Connecticut Sons of the
American Revolution*). Woodward falls into difficulties in attempting to
prove that it was not generally known among the people of Redding that
Heron was loyalist in sympathy; he also takes it for granted that Heron,
who was a representative in the general assembly, had taken the oath of
fidelity of 1776, repudiating the government of the empire. Neither of the
writers apparently sees anything extraordinarily significant in the fact that
Parsons, having retired from the service meanwhile, should in 1782 write
to Washington for the purpose of influencing him to make use of Heron in
the secret service. According to Clinton it was Heron who was the intermediary between Parsons and the British headquarters at New York. In

Whether or not these gentlemen really secured "protections" has never been determined. They continued in their offices and appeared to have the confidence of people rather generally in the state. That this latter fact might not argue necessarily in favor of their unswerving devotion to the idea of American independence is shown by the case of such men as William Heron of Redding, Connecticut, who, although in the assembly, "was an enemy to the Declaration of American Independency," and George Wyllys, who was secretary of the colony and later secretary of state. "It is a significant fact," writes Dr. Franklin B. Dexter, concerning Wyllys, "that, though his tenure of office was not interrupted at the Revolution, he was in active sympathy with the loyalist element."[1]

While this conservative reaction was taking place in Connecticut, Jared Ingersoll was living in seclusion in Philadelphia. In fact, after the outbreak of the war almost nothing is known of his activities until the summer

---

spite of what Parsons wrote in 1782 to Washington, it is not clear that Heron really furnished the Continentals with secret information. There is manifest weakness in the light of available evidence in the attempt to paint the character of Heron entirely black and that of his associate, Parsons, blamelessly white. Indeed, it would not be at all surprising had Parsons, like many another man during this period of confusion and of conflicting issues, desired to secure his future. As C. B. Todd brings out in his *History of Redding*, Heron bore the highest reputation among his fellow townsmen until his death in 1819. For further facts regarding the life of Parsons, the reader should consult C. S. Hall, *Life and Letters of Samuel Holden Parsons* (1905), which is an ardent and able brief for this soldier; in this connection the discriminating review of Hall's book by Professor Andrew C. McLaughlin (*Amer. Hist. Rev.*, XI, 914-916) should not be neglected.

[1] Regarding the case of Heron, see page 354, note 1, and also *New York Col. Doc.*, VIII, 804. As to the case of George Wyllys, see F. B. Dexter, *Yale Biographies and Annals*, 1701-1745, p. 400; and Jonathan Trumbull's reply to the charge against Wyllys in "The Defamation of Revolutionary Patriots," in the *Year Book* (for 1895) *of the Connecticut Society of the Sons of the American Revolution*, pp. 183-184.

of 1777. Early in 1776 he wrote of riding into the country and of stopping for an hour at the home of his loyalist friend, ex-Governor James Hamilton.[1] John Adams,
attending the Continental Congress, found him the following year living at a family hotel, which was presided
over by a buxom Mrs. Cheesman. It is of no little interest to note that the fiery Samuel Adams was also stopping there and that the two seemed to be living together
on the best of terms. Indeed, the year 1777 was no time
for baiting the Tory element. John Adams whimsically
describes his cousin's situation:

"Mr. Adams has removed to Mrs. Cheesman's in
Fourth Street, near the corner of Market Street, where
he has a curious group of company consisting of characters, as opposite as North and South. Ingersoll, the
stamp man and Judge of Admiralty; Sherman, an old
Puritan, as honest as an angel and as firm in the cause
of American Independence as Mount Atlas; and Col.
Thornton, as droll and funny as Tristan Shandy. Between the fun of Thornton, the gravity of Sherman, the
formal toryism of Ingersoll, Adams will have a curious
life of it. The landlady too, who has buried four hus-
bands, one tailor, two shoemakers and Gilbert Tenant,
and still is ready for a fifth and still deserves him too,
will add to the entertainment."[2]

In the summer of 1777 Ingersoll emerged from his obscurity. For, the early part of July the British fleet,
loaded with soldiers, sailed from New York, and the Continental Congress anticipating that a blow might be delivered against Philadelphia resolved, on July 31, that
it was expedient to arrest all late proprietary and crown

[1] Jared Ingersoll to Jonathan Ingersoll, February 20, 1776, New Haven
Col. Hist. Soc. *Papers*, IX ("Jared Ingersoll Papers"), 461.

[2] March 16, 1777. *Familiar Letters of John Adams and his Wife, Abigail
Adams, During the Revolution*, p. 251.

office holders, and all other disaffected persons in and near that city. In fulfillment of this policy, on August 4 a warrant was issued by the supreme executive council of Pennsylvania for the arrest of "certain persons."[1] According to this warrant, Judge Ingersoll was to be arrested and was thereupon to be sent "on his parole to Winchester in Virginia there to confine himself within six miles of that town or at his option to be sent to Hartford in Connecticut under like restrictions." However, this warrant was countermanded on August 8, when the supreme council sent to Ingersoll a request by its secretary that "from the present situation of affairs as well on your own account as from other considerations, it will be most proper for you to remain in this city for a few weeks and they [the council] recommend it to you to do so."[2] For about a month longer, therefore, the judge continued to reside in Philadelphia. However, early in September, when Howe's plan to capture the city was clearly evident, the decision was reached to rid it of the Tory element; in accordance with the determination the more aggressive loyalists were confined under guard in the Free Mason's Lodge,[3] and later were transported to Staunton, Virginia; Ingersoll, on the contrary, and probably by reason of his intimate relations with such men of influence in revolutionary circles as Joseph Reed of Philadelphia, was allowed his freedom until September 4, when he was instructed to depart immediately for Connecticut in conformity with his parole.[4] Arriving in this

1 *Penn. Archives*, V, 484; acts of the Executive Council under date August 4, 1777, *Penn. Col. Rec.*, XI, 284.

2 *Penn. Archives*, V, 503.

3 There has survived an interesting pamphlet, entitled, "*An Address to the Inhabitants of Pennsylvania by those . . . confined to the Mason's Lodge.* (1777.)

4 *Penn. Col. Rec.*, XI, 291. Copy of parole signed by J. Ingersoll.
"Philadelphia, August 5th, 1777.
"I, Jared Ingersoll, late of New Haven in the State of Connecticut Esq.—

state he was granted the privilege by the authorities of settling down once again at New Haven, where he and Mrs. Ingersoll reëstablished themselves in their old home near the green.

Meanwhile young Jared, who was residing at the Inner Temple in London when the Revolution began, found his sympathies enlisted on the side of the colonies. "I am now suffering," he wrote to his cousin Jonathan, in August, 1775, "the most humilating News of a Defeat of the Provincials by the King's Troops."[1] Nevertheless, he was not prepared to sacrifice the family interests and apparently continued his residence in London, where his uncle David was a Tory refugee, until late in the spring of 1777. The latter part of February of that year he is found petitioning Lord North and the rest of the Commissioners of the Treasury, in behalf of his father, for two years' arrears of salary that became due October 17, 1776.[2] Sometime after this event it seems that he passed over to the Continent in order to secure a passage to America. In April, 1778, he wrote from

but now of the City of Philadelphia Do declare upon my honour that I will not do any Thing injurious to the United States of *America*, by Writing, Speaking, or otherwise, nor give any Intelligence to the commander in chief of the *British* Forces, nor any person under him, or to any other Person whatever, respecting public affairs, but will in every respect conduct myself according to the Rules which are accustomed to be observed by Prisoners of War on their parole, and that I will immediately repair to Connecticut and there deliver myself to His Excellency the Governor to be disposed of as the Governor & Council of said State shall direct." The following was printed, but crossed out. "Without special permission from the President in Council, or the Board of War of the United States, signified by their Secretary." Trumbull Papers.

[1] Jared Ingersoll to Jonathan Ingersoll, August 2, 1775, Dartmouth Papers, Intercepted Letters, B. F. Stevens, *Catalogue Index of Manuscripts in Europe relative to America* (Library of Congress), vol. XXXIII.

[2] "The Petition of Jared Ingersoll of the Middle Temple." This was received by the board, February 27, 1777, and read July 22, 1777. Treasury, 1: 533, fos. 184-185.

Calais to Silas Deane asking his "advice respecting a continued residence" at that place,[1] and at last succeeded in reaching America and joining his parents at New Haven in September of that year.[2]

In returning to New Haven, Judge Ingersoll by no means found himself in a hostile atmosphere—in spite of the fact that he was a declared political enemy. The general reaction that took place in Connecticut during the winter of 1776-1777 quite naturally operated with peculiar force at New Haven by reason of her traditions. The lukewarmness of the authorities of the town was repeatedly held up to criticism. In February, 1777, an "impeachment," signed by about thirty inhabitants, was presented to the selectmen, charging William McCracken, John Miles, Jr., Ralph Earle, and Nicholas Calahan with having positively declared "that they were friends of George III and would not take up arms against him and his troops." Calahan even declared, according to these protestators, that he would take arms for the crown. The town authorities were accused of ignoring not only this but the actions also of Joshua Chandler, Ingersoll's old friend, who was one of the most prominent freemen of the town, and who, as was previously stated, had represented the town in the general assembly in 1774 and in 1775, but had become a pronounced loyalist. Chandler, it seems, was summoned in March to appear before the authorities as a delinquent. He was charged not only with refusing to appear when summoned but also with threatening to go among those who had smallpox, and then in case the constable attempted to force him from

[1] Jared Ingersoll, Jr., to Silas Deane, at Passy, April 12, 1778, L. M. Hays, *Calendar of the Franklin Papers*, IV, 255.

[2] Under date of September 9, 1778, Ezra Stiles records in his Diary: "Mr. Ingersoll Jun. arrived here 5th inst. from Paris. He left France the 28th Sept. Ult." *Literary Diary*, II, 312. If Dr. Stiles is correct, Jared could not have been in Calais in April.

his home in North Haven, to go without changing his clothes with the idea of spreading the infection, which at that time was a serious menace to Connecticut.[1] Chandler, it would appear, was left unmolested at his home until his departure with the British troops the following year.

Another incident that took place the latter part of March, 1777, throws additional light upon the conservative attitude of the New Haven authorities. Three soldiers belonging to an artillery battalion stationed within the town, according to the account, "committed a riot" at the expense of Archibald and Elijah Austin, who were reputed to be unfriendly to the cause of American freedom. These soldiers were promptly ordered to be punished and, in order to escape imprisonment, they disappeared. This led to a public protest from their sympathizers on the ground that "the most trivial complaints against the Whigs are taken up by the authorities and vigorously carried into execution and no notice taken of enemies when complaints of the most flagrant breaches of the law . . . are exhibited."[2] In April, the *Connecticut Journal* was constrained to publish an indictment against a New Haven justice of the peace, whose name is not disclosed, for absolutely refusing, and that with impunity, to grant to one of Washington's cou-

[1] *Connecticut Journal*, April 23, 1777. Cf. Professor Dexter, "Notes on Some of the New Haven Loyalists," in New Haven Hist. Soc. *Papers*, IX, 39-40.

The Tories living at New Haven apparently were inoculated against this disease but "none of the Whigs who observed the orders of the General Assembly about innoculation." *Connecticut Journal*, April 23, 1777. It appears that at Lebanon Tories actually attempted, in February, to spread the smallpox by visiting infected houses, so that the Committee of Safety had to take steps. See R. R. Hinman, *Historical Collection of the Part Sustained by Connecticut during the Revolution*, p. 417.

[2] *Connecticut Journal*, April 2, 1777.

It is very significant to notice that those who prepared this protest were obliged to pay for it at advertising rates in order to get it printed.

riers,—carrying dispatches to Governor Cook and General Spencer at Providence,—a warrant to impress a horse in order to proceed on his journey.[1]

For almost a year after the arrival of Ingersoll, in the fall of 1777, there is little to record respecting the affairs of the community which is other than prosaic and unromantic in the extreme. The writhing of the people in their efforts to rid themselves of the pressure of taxation is the one thing that is reflected in almost every page of the annals of the town during the year 1778;[2] the revenue features, alone, among the proposed Articles of Confederation could awaken discussion in town meeting.[3] The members of the general assembly were loudly accused of supporting methods of taxation for personal advantage, the press was full of bitter complaint and the New Haven freemen, after choosing deputies, gave them "particular instructions" regarding the manner in which they should vote on the financial issues in order to remedy a situation where "poor men with large families paid greater taxes than some of the most affluent families" and as a result would "soon be obliged to sell their estates and become tenants of their rich neighbors; thus one main part of that slavery against which the present war was professedly undertaken will be established among us."[4] It was even maintained that this inequitable financial drain was ruining more than one-third of the families of the state.[5]

[1] *Connecticut Journal*, April 8, 1777. Curiously enough the name of the justice is not mentioned. The indictment was anonymously written; however, there appeared a postscript declaring that "the Printers are at liberty to mention the author's name whenever the Justice pleases to call upon them; likewise the names of the persons ready to testify to the above charge."

[2] For example, see *ibid.*, March 12, 1777.

[3] New Haven Town Records, V, 77-78.

[4] *Connecticut Journal*, May 6, 1778.

[5] *Ibid.*, April 8, 1778.

Yet with all the discontent, New Haven, by the spring of 1778, had recovered a good deal of its zeal for the cause of American independence which had been at so low an ebb, especially during the winter and spring of 1777. The news of Burgoyne's surrender at Saratoga, late in the fall of that year, naturally inspirited the doubting, lagging ones. In March, 1778, there was organized "by a large number of respectable inhabitants" a society "for the promotion of friendship and unanimity, in order to strengthen the hands of the civil authority in the execution of the laws; and to detect and frustrate the designs of enemies in their midst";[1] in April, when the news came of the recognition of the independence of America by France, the town gave itself over to rejoicing, the bells were rung, the "respectable inhabitants" met for a big dinner, and people generally gathered together to drink "thirteen toasts";[2] while in May, upon his arrival home, Major General Arnold was met on the road by continental and militia officers and the cadet company, as well as by a number of the "respectable inhabitants," to testify their esteem, and upon entering the town he was greeted by a salute from thirteen cannon.[3]

On the other hand, it is worthy of notice that Jared Ingersoll, in October, was, it seems, allowed to entertain at his home ex-Governor William Franklin[4] and other

[1] *Connecticut Journal.*

[2] *Ibid.*

[3] *Ibid.*, May 8, 1778.

[4] William Franklin, natural son of Benjamin Franklin, was appointed governor of New Jersey in 1763 and continued in that office until 1776, when he was sent to Connecticut as a prisoner. He was confined at Wallingford, East Windsor, and Litchfield. At the latter place he was confined in the jail under guard. Through the efforts of Clinton he was exchanged in 1778. *Conn. State Rec.*, I, 217, 511; *Literary Diary of Ezra Stiles*, II, 29; Lorenzo Sabine, *American Loyalists*, I, 440-442.

prisoners who were on their way to be exchanged.[1] On this occasion Ingersoll made out a writ of attorney empowering his old friend, Richard Jackson, and James Brown, a banker, who also was living in London, to act as his agents and to collect his salary as judge of vice-admiralty. Franklin and one Joseph Webb signed the writ as witnesses and upon the former's arrival in New York he took care to see that it was properly recorded.[2]

As was previously noticed, the younger Jared had reached his home in New Haven in September and was stopping with his parents, when in December, Joseph Reed, president of the supreme executive council of Pennsylvania, wrote to Judge Ingersoll, his "ancient and valued friend," in reply to a communication from the latter. In this letter Reed declared that his election to office had left a vacancy in Philadelphia to be filled by some gentleman who would consult the interests of his clients and upon whom he could depend for that assistance which a young man of parts could give to one in his station. He also went on to make the interesting remark that "Our lawyers here, of any considerable abilities, are all, as I may say, in one interest, and not the popular one.'"[3] Reed, therefore, bade the young man hasten to Philadelphia, promising that he would receive "every assistance and advantage . . . which his merit and my sincere esteem for him will justly claim." Needless to say, young Ingersoll, who was now twenty-nine years of age and well qualified to undertake the work in hand,

[1] New Haven Town Records, V, 97.

[2] This is to be found among the abstracts of "Wills on file in the surrogate's office City of New York." New York Historical Society *Collections* (1900), p. 45. The power of attorney was given in New Haven, October 28, 1778.

[3] Joseph Reed to Jared Ingersoll, December 15, 1778. W. B. Reed, *Life and Correspondence of Joseph Reed,* II, 39-40.

accepted the flattering offer and it was not long before he had achieved great eminence at the Philadelphia bar.[1]

The war had been going on now for three years, and New Haven had been left in undisturbed peace. The fear of invasion subsided as time went on. During the dark hours of 1777 little real interest had been taken in the plans that previously had been laid for repelling the British, and it is probable that little resistance would have been made. Apparently, even the fort at Black Rock, with its cannon, was left for a time in a deserted, neglected condition. However, the latter part of 1777 the town meeting plucked up sufficient energy to vote that ten men be hired, six for the purpose of taking care of the fort, four to look after the cannon and other military equipment "in the town Platt," until the assembly should furnish guards for these tasks;[2] in the spring of 1778 additional measures were taken to provide for the security of the town.[3] In spite of this, New Haven was in no position to sustain the attack which came at last in the month of July, 1779.

On the morning of the fifth of that month, a British fleet, consisting of some forty-eight vessels, including transports and tenders, appeared off the coast and came to anchor close to the shore line of West Haven. This armada was under the command of Sir George Collier

[1] In a letter to an unknown party, Jared, Jr., wrote from Philadelphia, on February 23, 1779, "I have clients, two clerks and am engaged in the most important causes now pending." Ingersoll Papers. In 1780 he was sent to the Continental Congress; in 1787 he was a delegate to the Constitutional Convention, and in 1812 he was the Federalist candidate for Vice-President of the United States. At the time of his death in 1822 he was acting as chief judge of the district court for the City and County of Philadelphia. It may also be added that he was the attorney for the great merchant prince, Stephen Girard. McMaster, *Life and Times of Stephen Girard*, I, 289, 349.

[2] New Haven Town Records, V, 76.

[3] *Ibid.*, V, 83.

and carried three thousand troops under Major General Tryon. It would seem that the purpose of the visit was to attempt to win the town back to the king's allegiance, for reports had been repeatedly carried to the British commanders respecting the pronounced loyalist leanings of many of the people. Clinton, in his instructions to Tryon, had declared "the country is populous and there are many friends there."[1] In conformity with this plan an address to the people of New Haven was drawn up and printed. "We offer you," ran the declaration, "a refuge against the distress which you universally acknowledge broods with increasing and intolerable weight over your country. . . . Leaving you to consult with each other upon this invitation, we do now declare that whoever shall be found and remain in peace at his usual place of residence shall be shielded from any insult either to his person or his property."[2]

Needless to say, the town was thrown into great confusion at the sight of the British ships. Men were confronted with the problem of making a decision as to which side to support; many in the dilemma remained in a state of total indecision. About five o'clock in the morning boats laden with troops from the ships put off to West Haven and it was not long until some 1500 soldiers, under the command of Brigadier General Garth, began their march around the cove in the direction of the town by way of the Milford road. "All then knew our Fate," wrote President Stiles of Yale College, a witness of the scene. "Perhaps one Third of the Adult male Inhab. flew to Arms & went out to meet them! A quar-

[1] G. H. Ford, "The Defense of New Haven," in *Revolutionary Characters of New Haven* (1911), p. 33; Chauncey Goodrich, "Invasion of New Haven by the British Troops, July 5, 1779." New Haven Hist. Soc. *Papers*, II, 31-92.

[2] A copy of this is printed in Hinman's *Historical Collections of Connecticut*, p. 771.

ter moved out of T° doing nothing, the rest remained un-
moved partly Tories partly timid Whigs. Sundry of the
Tories armed & went forth. About 90 or an hundred Men
finally stayed in T°.'''[1]

At West Bridge the British were checked by a small
body of determined militia-men under Captain James
Hillhouse. Uncertain of the strength of the latter force,
the invaders, guided by William Chandler, son of Joshua
Chandler, now made a wide detour to the west until they
came to the Derby road, which they then followed toward
New Haven. Meanwhile, most of the ·women and children had betaken themselves to the two high promontories
beyond the town known as East Rock and West Rock.
Some of the women, however, bravely insisted on remaining at home in order to help in the work of casting bullets. Over seventy Yale College students, under their
leader, George Welles, a member of the senior class,
joined in the fray. The defenders were, it is interesting
to note, assisted by Aaron Burr of New York, who happened to be in New Haven at the time and who was
placed in charge of a portion of the troops. The spirit
of the occasion has been well preserved in a pen picture
which Ezra Stiles has left of old ex-President Naphtali
Daggett of Yale College, with his gray hair flying,
mounted on his faithful black mare, with a fowling piece
across the pommel of the saddle, riding out to meet the
enemy, followed by Welles and the student volunteers.[2]
What made the task of resistance utterly hopeless was
that while General Garth was approaching the town from
the west, General Tryon landed another large division

[1] *The Literary Diary of Ezra Stiles,* II, 352-353.

[2] Professor Daggett unfortunately was captured by the enemy and subjected to many brutalities from which he was long in recovering. It is
related that William Chandler, one of his former students, who, as was
stated above, was guiding the British, saved him from being put to death.

of troops at East End near Morris Cove and marched upon the town from that direction. In fact, the only real resistance to Tryon came from the fort at Black Rock, held by nineteen men and three cannon, and even this was soon evacuated, when it came under fire of the enemy's gunboats.

About noon Garth's troops, after some skirmishing, brushed aside the raw levies and entered the town, firing by volley as they marched down the streets. Then followed plundering and a certain amount of wanton violence and bloodshed. In spite of the address that had been issued, promising that those who should be found at their usual place of residence should be shielded from insult either in person or property, many peaceably inclined people lukewarm toward the cause of independence were made to suffer indignities. The fact that the soldiers found in the town a large store of Santa Cruz rum did not improve the situation, for it is related that the royal troops on that hot July day "sweated, swore, fought and got dreadfully drunk." While this was going on, the Connecticut troops took an advantageous position on the outskirts of the town from which point they continued to annoy the enemy throughout the remainder of the day. The attempt to restore New Haven to the loyalist fold had clearly failed. How near the town came to being delivered over to the torch can now be appreciated, for at half past one in the afternoon General Garth reported to Tryon, who was encamped to the north of the town across the neck of water, that as soon as the bridge connecting the two forces had been secured he would begin burning the town.[1] He was, however, led

[1] This communication is printed in C. H. Townshend, *A Pictorial History of "Raynham," New Haven*, p. 10. Lieutenant Colonel Stephen Kemple, in his Journals, under date of July 7, wrote: "Landed at New Haven, opposed by the Militia of the Town and Country. A few Store houses

to desist in this plan, probably through the influence of local loyalists and, it is alleged, especially through the intercession of Edmund Fanning, a Yale graduate who was on Tryon's staff.[1] Garth is said to have been taken to the top of the state house and, after surveying the scene, was heard to remark that it was too beautiful a town to burn. The quiet behavior of the local militia on the following day, it would seem, also helped to save the town. "The next morning," General Tryon reported, "as there was not a shot fired to molest the retreat, General Garth changed his design and destroyed only the public stores."[2] The British troops were not only guided into New Haven by William Chandler, who showed the way for Garth, and by Thomas Chandler, who aided Tryon, but were, according to accounts, entertained by Joshua Chandler, by Madam Hillhouse, an ardent loyalist, although the foster mother of Captain Hillhouse, and by one Ogden, the proprietor of a coffee house that bore his name. The Chandlers, the Camps, the Botsfords, and also a few others went much farther in their devotion to the empire and determined to tie their fortunes irrevocably to that of the king and to desert their homes.[3]

burnt, but by some fatality the Troops were not able to reembark at the time proposed; the Boats were aground and I fear Drunkenness was the cause of several Men being left behind wounded. . . . The Town by unaccountable accident not burnt, tho the troops were fired at from the houses till they got off.'' New York Hist. Soc. *Coll.* (1883), I, 179-180.

1 F. B. Dexter, *Yale Biographies and Annals,* 1778-1792, p. 89; New Haven Hist. Soc. *Papers,* IX, 44.

2 J. W. Barber, *Connecticut Historical Collections,* p. 172.

3 Two of the brothers of Amos Botsford acted as guides for General Tryon on the expedition. Botsford after leaving New Haven settled in New York and then in 1782 went to England. Cf. Alexander Fraser, *Second Report of the Bureau of Archives for Ontario,* p. 310. The fate of the Chandlers was most tragic. After leaving New Haven they settled temporarily at Long Island and when the British evacuated New York in

The enemy, who had entered the town on Monday, quietly departed the next day about nine o'clock in the morning, taking with them not only the group of Tory families just mentioned, but some thirty or forty other residents of the town, mostly as prisoners, among them John Whiting, Jared Ingersoll's brother-in-law, who was judge of probate and clerk of the county court. It appears that Whiting was asked, previous to the entering of the town by the royal troops, whether he would flee. He is said to have replied that not only had he not borne arms but that he was loyal to the king, and pointing to an engraving of King George which hung on the wall of his home, said, "This will protect me." But it seems that his loyalty was suspected by reason of the fact that he was holding office and was a leader in the Congregational church, and he was taken away from home so quickly,

1783 they removed to Nova Scotia. The hardships encountered were too much for Mrs. Chandler, who died soon after reaching the latter section. The next few years were spent by Chandler in a vain attempt to get compensation for his losses; in this connection he went to England. Early in 1787 he decided to lay his case before Commissioners sitting at St. John's and attempted to cross the Bay of Fundy with a daughter and son. The small sailboat was struck by a violent storm and was cast upon the rocks some miles distant from St. John's. In the attempt to land the son was drowned; although the others reached the shore, they were benumbed with the cold; in this condition Joshua Chandler fell to his death while attempting to climb a rocky point; his daughter and a companion wandered about in the woods until they succumbed. F. B. Dexter, *Yale Biographies and Annals*, 1745-1763, p. 109; Alexander Fraser, *The First Report of the Bureau of Archives for Ontario*, p. 286; Sabine also should be consulted. An account of the estate of Joshua Chandler has been written by A. M. Davis.

Apparently others were obliged to leave New Haven after the invasion. For instance, Zedicia Cook testified before the Loyalist Commission sitting in Canada, after the war, that he had been so tormented in New Haven that he was obliged to leave there in 1779, deserting his home and personal property, among which was "a stage wagon and two fine horses." Alexander Fraser, *Second Report of the Bureau of Archives for Ontario*, pp. 825-826.

according to reports, that the astonished man did not have time to put on his wig.[1]

An amusing account has come down from that period of the reoccupation of New Haven by the fugitives after the departure of the British. It seems that crowds of curious-minded country people flocked into the town, in order to view the havoc wrought by the enemy. Suddenly a report was circulated that the British army was surrounding the place. In an instant the multitude stampeded, fleeing into the country at breakneck speed; it is chronicled that "their progress could be traced for miles by the immense clouds of dust which arose in all directions."[2]

As was previously pointed out, among the things which the British soldiers either consumed or carried away was most of the town's abundant supply of rum. It would appear that this put the sturdy New Haven fathers in a position of most extraordinary inconvenience, so much so that in town meeting it was voted, shortly after the invasion, to "treat with proper contempt all persons who either would refuse to sell their rum or would sell it for more than $32.00 per gallon by retail."[3]

After quiet had been restored and the civil authority was again in control, the town meeting appointed a series

[1] E. E. Atwater, *History of the City of New Haven*, p. 59. The American loss during the invasion was estimated at twenty-seven killed and eleven wounded. R. R. Hinman, *A Historical Collection of the Part Sustained by Connecticut during the War of the Revolution*, p. 609.

[2] J. W. Barber, *Connecticut Historical Collections*, p. 174. "It is said, that some of the country people were base enough to take advantage of the general confusion, and carried off goods to a large amount." *Ibid.*

[3] New Haven Town Records, V, 95. The estimated total loss to the community by reason of this invasion was £15,660.8.9. There has survived a list of those who suffered losses with the amounts. Jared Ingersoll suffered a loss of £2, while Amos Morriss, who probably was an importer of rum, suffered a loss of £1293.17. Conn. Archives, Revolutionary War, XV, 234.

of committees to readjust affairs; one was entrusted with the responsibility of procuring an exchange of those who were taken as prisoners from the town during the invasion; another was delegated to call upon certain people who stayed in town when the others had fled; while still another was to question those who had neglected to oppose the enemy in the defense of the town. At this same meeting, moreover, it was thought necessary to appoint a fourth committee to wait upon Judge Ingersoll in order to ascertain the reason ''why he entertained the prisoners who were lately in this town.''[1] This, without doubt, had reference to the loyalist prisoners, among whom was ex-Governor Franklin, who, as has been noticed, were in New Haven the preceding fall en route to be exchanged. It probably was felt that there was some connection between Franklin's meeting with Ingersoll and this rather extraordinary attempt to win back New Haven to the royal allegiance, especially since Franklin, after going to New York, had become president of the Board of Associated Loyalists, which set on foot the expedition against New Haven. It would appear that Ingersoll was able to make a satisfactory explanation to the committee.

The British invasion not only failed of its objective but undoubtedly resulted in a reaction in the direction of greater opposition to a reconciliation with the mother country. The town had for years been the center of conflict, as has been seen, between the conservative and the radical elements, with the balance under normal conditions inclining strongly in favor of the former, and it is a fact worthy of notice that at this crisis apparently only about one-third of the men of the town were disposed to resist the approach of the British by force of arms. To such patriots as President Ezra Stiles of Yale College this was a source of surprise and disappointment,

[1] New Haven Town Records, V, 97.

for it goes without saying that the approach of an enemy
such as a body of Indians would have seen every able-
bodied man on the outskirts of town, musket in hand.
Yet, on the other hand, it would appear that there were
not many of these townsmen sufficiently devout in their
loyalty to the empire to leave their homes and go aboard
the royal fleet. To most of the conservatives of New
Haven, who were as a rule men of some wealth, especially
in landed property, such a step was not to be contemplated; even Jared Ingersoll found the disadvantages too
great. While these mild loyalists were not at all disposed
to risk their lives in fighting in the cause of American
independence, they were, on the other hand, not disposed,
in following their sentiments and convictions, to sacrifice
their property and stations in life in overtly supporting
the king. The men who made up this group—and the
number must have been large in every colony—had not
started the war; personally they had no deep-laid grievances; they had in fact been living happily under colonial conditions, and, in spite of the taxation controversy,
had not favored rebellion, and contemplated with great
uneasiness the idea of seeing the extreme anti-British
radicals in charge of the destinies of the commonwealth.
Even after the signing of the treaty of peace and the
successful termination of the war, a feeling of distrust
of the liberty group continued to be manifested. This
came to the surface in 1784, in New Haven, when that
city, having secured incorporation, held its first city election. Ezra Stiles, an eyewitness, writes regarding this:

''The City Politics are founded in an endeavor silently
to bring the Tories into a Equality & Supremacy among
the Whigs. The Episcopalians are all Tories but two,
and all qualified on this occasion, tho' dispise Congress
gov't before—they may perhaps be 40 Voters. There may
be 20 or 30 of Mr Whitty's Meet added to these. Perhaps

one third of the Citizens may be hearty Tories, one third Whigs. one third Indifferent. Mixing all up together, the election has come out, Mayor and two Aldermen, Whigs; 2 Ald. Tories. Of the Common Council 5 Whigs, 5 Flexibles but in heart Whigs, 8 Tories.''[1] Although

[1] Besides the Episcopalians, Stiles, it will be noticed, counts some twenty or thirty ''tory'' members of the Old Light Congregation, which met in the Brick Meeting House. *The Literary Diary of Ezra Stiles*, III, 109-112. Rev. Jonathan Edwards, writing to Sherman shortly after the election, begged him not to refuse the office of mayor. ''If you should refuse it, Mr. Howell would certainly be chosen. I cannot bear that the first Mayor of this infant city should be a tory.'' L. H. Boutell, *The Life of Roger Sherman*, p. 43. Thomas Howell, referred to in Edwards's letter, received one hundred and ten votes, while Thomas Darling, ''who was probably the choice of the extreme Tories,'' received twenty-two. C. H. Levermore, ''The Town and City Government of New Haven,'' p. 10. (*Johns Hopkins University Studies*, Fourth Series, No. X.)

The loyalist, William Heron, of Redding, Connecticut, for years a member of the lower house of the assembly and on the board of accounts as late as September 4, 1780, stated at British headquarters, where he came under a flag of truce, ''Undoubtedly the majority of the Continent have long been for a reunion with Great Britain. From his intimate knowledge of *Connecticut*, he is firmly persuaded that *not a tenth* of the Inhabitants are for contending for Independency, if well assured by the Government, that the Charter shall stand good. The greater part of *the loyalists* are for preserving the Charter, and many became loyalists, because they conceived the Independent Party, exposed it to dissolution, by their intemperate measures. Others now listen to *them* as men of wisdom and patriotism, and execrate the danger to which an indiscreet heat has exposed the Charter.'' *N. Y. Col. Doc.*, VIII, 807.

The following New Haven men forfeited their estates for ''joining the enemy'': ''Chas. Thomas, Thomas Thomas, John Crittenden, John Leak, Benjamin Anderson, Mere Todd, Nicholas Callahan, Enoch Malthrop, Nathe Cook, Stephen Mix, Wm Cook, Joseph Tyneham, Joshua Chandler, Abiathar Camp, Amos Botsford, Leml Esther, Bradley, Jedediah Cook, Wm Chandler, Gad Miller, Benedict Arnold, Saml Pierpont Jr, Tos Peck, Jr., Philo Lansford, and Wm Glen.'' ''List of Confiscated Estates in New Haven County.'' Conn. Archives, Revolutionary War, XXXIV, 456. The list for the entire county is, of course, very much larger than this.

Rev. Samuel Peters drew up a list of New Haven loyalists, which is as follows: ''Ralph Isaacs, John Shipman, Jared Ingersoll (L.), Joshua Chandler (L.), Mr. Woodhull, Joseph Peechem, Daniel Humphrey (L.), Mr. Gold, Rev. Mr. Chamberlain, Rev. Bela Hubbard, Botsford (L.), Capt.

Roger Sherman was chosen mayor at this election by a vote of one hundred and twenty-five, there were one hundred and twenty-four votes cast against him.

The conservatives, swept along in the train of revolution, at last had come to a point where there appeared to be no turning back to the old order of things. They therefore had come to accept the new situation as inevitable while never ceasing to oppose what seemed to them an irresponsible popular element and its leaders, who had helped to plunge the country into war. In this general shifting of ground, it appears that even their old leader, Jared Ingersoll, gradually came to accept the idea that the separation of America from Great Britain would be for the best, and what is more, actually gave his aid secretly, in 1780, in bringing this to pass. In that year, in spite of the fact that he was enjoying his vice-admiralty commission and through his agents in England was soliciting his pay of £600 sterling, in spite of the fact that he was an acknowledged Tory prisoner on parole, he actually prepared a treatise, according to his son, upon the perplexing question of the proper solution of America's financial problem which the Continental Congress was hopelessly struggling to solve. This he forwarded to Philadelphia with the expectation that it would be given publicity in the papers,—anonymously, of course,— as was his confirmed practice in getting his ideas before the public. The treatise, however, according to the younger Ingersoll, was too extensive to publish; it was, however, privately circulated among some of the influential men then in Philadelphia, such as President Joseph

Camp, Capt. Dan¹ Lyman, Rev. Arebᵈ Strong, Rev. Mr. Woodbridge, Dr. Daniel Bonham, Isaac Jones, Elias Dibbles, Capt. Beecher, Mr. Pierpont.'' ''List of Connecticut Loyalists (As Found Among Rev. Samuel Peters's Papers).'' Conn. Archives, Revolutionary War (second series), V, 3 a and 4 b.

Reed, and the suggestions contained in it seem to have made a favorable impression upon them.[1] Although, unfortunately, it is not possible to speak with any certainty regarding the contents of the manuscript in question, for the purpose of this study the most important thing is the knowledge of the fact that one of the most highly paid and important officials in the British colonial service in America should have become so vitally interested in the welfare of the revolutionary government as to offer a plan whereby it might survive in its struggle against the authority of the government which he was supposed to be serving. Ingersoll's position in 1780 was, to say the least, an anomalous one.

It is indeed food for thought that by the beginning of 1780, Benedict Arnold, the former leader of the extreme pro-liberty radicals at New Haven, was secretly serving against the cause of American independence, while Jared Ingersoll, the former leader of the extreme pro-loyalist group within the same community, was as truly secretly serving against the cause of loyalism and the continued unity of the British empire. In the case of Arnold, personal ambition and pique and an untamed individualism seem to have been the mainspring of his action; in the case of Ingersoll, it was undoubtedly the result of solicitude for the welfare of all that was most dear to him, the upwelling of a deep-seated Americanism which now warred against his old imperial conceptions, as well as against his personal interests. At the parting of the ways

[1] These facts appear in a letter written by Jared Ingersoll, Jr., to Jonathan Ingersoll, March 14, 1780. Ingersoll Papers. ''You will perceive by our newspapers, if they reach you, that all the world here are busy in speculations and plans, in devising ways and means for the Grand purpose of retrieving the credit of our Continental currency. . . . I have shown my Father's Manuscript to the President and Coll. Petit who is, I believe as good a financier as any we have, they approve of it very much, but it is too long for a newspaper.''

he sought the impossible—to go in both directions. A lonely and repudiated champion of the old order of things which was passing away before his eyes never to return, he yet sought to adjust himself to the new conditions. "But all this made him unhappy," in the words of his friend, Ezra Stiles;[1] his soul had become a battle ground and he wearied of life. He did not see the outcome of the struggle which terminated in October, 1781, at Yorktown, for on August 25 of that year he passed away. Paradoxical as it may seem, it was perhaps not entirely unfitting that revolutionary New Haven paused for a moment in the conflict then raging to pay her respects to one who had stood for so many years in her midst as a foremost American representative of the British imperial administrative system and that there gathered to the funeral sermon "the Gentlemen of the town and a very large Assembly with much decency and respect."

[1] *Literary Diary of Ezra Stiles*, II, 552.

On October 8, 1779, Ingersoll's wife, Hannah, died; on January 6, 1780, he married Hannah, the widow of Enos Alling, who had been a prosperous merchant. In the *Connecticut Journal* for March 8, 1780, there appeared the following interesting notice:

"All persons indebted to the estate of Enos Alling Esq., late of New Haven, deceased, or have demands on the same, are desired to apply for settlement unto the subscriber, administrator in right of his wife."

The question arises, How could Ingersoll perform this office of administrator, not having taken the oath of fidelity provided for in October, 1777, and enjoined upon those who could act in the capacity of administrators? Professor Simeon E. Baldwin of Yale University Law School takes the view that probably Ingersoll claimed that the statute as to the oath of fidelity did not apply to a case where the widow was entitled to administration by another statute and her husband simply qualified in her right. As the probate court, which could rule upon this, was presided over by Judge Whiting, Ingersoll's brother-in-law, who was a mild loyalist, it is not likely that the question of Ingersoll's ability to act in this case was called in question.

BIBLIOGRAPHICAL NOTE

GUIDES AND OTHER BIBLIOGRAPHICAL AIDS

Among the most important bibliographical aids that have been employed in the preparation of this work are C. M. Andrews's *Guide to the Materials for American History to 1783 in the Public Record Office of Great Britain*, C. M. Andrews and F. G. Davenport's *Guide to the Manuscript Materials for the History of the United States to 1783 in the British Museum, in minor London Archives, and in the Libraries of Oxford and Cambridge*, Charles Evans's *American Bibliography*, A. P. C. Griffin's ''Bibliography of American Historical Societies'' (Amer. Hist. Assoc. *Report*, 1905, vol. II), A. R. Hasse's ''Materials for a Bibliography of the Public Archives of the Thirteen Original Colonies'' (*ibid.*, for 1906, vol. III), N. P. Mead's ''Public Archives of Connecticut. County, Probate and Local Records'' (*ibid.*), together with the ''Guide to Items relating to American History in the Reports of the English Historical Manuscript Commission and their Appendices'' (*ibid.*, 1898), the ''List of Printed Guides to and Descriptions of Archives and other Repositories of Historical Manuscript'' (*ibid.*, 1896, vol. I), and a ''Report on the Public Archives of Connecticut (*ibid.*, 1900, vol. II).

BRITISH MANUSCRIPTS

Among the materials in the Public Record Office many of the Colonial Office Papers, Treasury Board Papers, Admiralty Papers, and Audit Office Papers covering the late colonial period have been found exceedingly valuable. Of the Colonial Office Papers, the most important for my purpose are those in Class 5; among the Treasury Papers, a number of the ''In-Letters'' are of especial importance, while among the

Admiralty Papers certain of the "Out-Letters" and admiralty warrants, and among the Audit Office Papers certain of the warrants and declared accounts are of the highest value. In the British Museum, among the Additional Manuscripts are two collections—the Newcastle Papers and the Hardwicke Papers—which have shed much light upon certain of the activities of Ingersoll.

AMERICAN MANUSCRIPTS

The most important body of manuscript relating to the life of Jared Ingersoll is the collection of Ingersoll Papers in the possession of the New Haven Colony Historical Society. These papers are divided into two groups, one, a chronologically arranged body of documents, mostly letters to or from Jared Ingersoll; the other, a large number of miscellaneous papers, mostly of a legal nature, gathered into bundles. A few Ingersoll letters are in the possession of Mr. George Pratt Ingersoll of Ridgefield, Connecticut, and in the Emmett Collection of manuscripts in the New York Public Library, while the Yale University Library possesses two of Jared Ingersoll's account books.

I also found that the Fitch Papers and the William Samuel Johnson Papers in the Connecticut Historical Society archives, and the Trumbull Papers in the Massachusetts Historical Society archives contain highly important unpublished materials. In the Connecticut State Library are the Connecticut Archives, a veritable mine of useful information, although I have found especially illuminating those volumes classified under the titles, "Foreign Correspondence," "Crimes and Misdemeanors," "Revolutionary War," and "Towns and Lands." In the office of the Secretary of State the records of the Superior Court of the Colony of Connecticut (vols. XIII to XVIII, inclusive) have yielded much valuable data. Several collections that are preserved at New Haven have also been very serviceable: in the office of the Clerk of the Superior Court the New Haven County Court Records, the first seven volumes of which cover the colonial period; in the office of the Judge of the Probate Court, the District of New Haven Probate Court Records, dating from 1719; in the office of the Town Clerk, the New Haven Town Records, dating from 1638; and scattered through these volumes the records also of the Freemen's meetings as well as the records of the Proprietors' meetings; there are, in addition, two separate volumes of Proprietors' Records.

BRITISH OFFICIAL DOCUMENTS, PRINTED

Among the most useful of the printed sources for my purpose are the *Acts of the Privy Council of England, Colonial Series* (1908-1912), the *Statutes at Large* (London, 1762-1800), *The Journals of the Lords* (vols. XXX-XXXIV), *The Journals of the House of Commons* (vols. XXIX-XXXV), Cobbett-Hansard's *The Parliamentary History of England from the Earliest Period to the Year 1803, The Annual Register* for the years 1760 to 1780, and the *Historical Manuscripts Commission Reports.* Among the latter the calendar of the Marquis of Shelburne Manuscripts (Appendix to the Fifth Report), the calendar of the Lord Lecomfield Manuscripts (Appendix to the Sixth Report), and the calendar of the Earl of Dartmouth Manuscripts (Fourth part of Appendix to the Eleventh Report and the Tenth part of the Appendix to the Fourteenth Report) shed a good deal of light upon certain of the questions herein considered.

AMERICAN OFFICIAL DOCUMENTS, PRINTED

Among printed documents bearing upon Connecticut colonial history, none are more important than the *Public Records of the Colony of Connecticut,* compiled by J. H. Trumbull and C. J. Hoadly (Hartford, 1850-1890). For my purpose the first two volumes of the *Public Records of the State of Connecticut* are also useful, as are the *Acts and Laws of His Majesty's English Colony of Connecticut, 1750,* with the revision of 1769, and the *Acts and Laws of the State of Connecticut, in America, 1784*

Outside of the Connecticut documents, mentioned above, none of the printed colonial official documents have been of greater general service to me than the *Documents Relative to the Colonial History of State of New York, Procured in Holland, England, and France,* edited by E. B. O'Callaghan (Albany, 1856-1861). To these should be added *Documents and Records relating to the Province of New Hampshire,* edited by N. Bouton and others (Concord, 1867-1907); *Archives of the State of New Jersey,* edited by W. A. Whitehead and others (Newark, 1880-1906); *Minutes of the Provincial Council of Pennsylvania,* followed by the *Minutes of the Supreme Executive Council* (Philadelphia, 1852-1853); *Pennsylvania Archives,* compiled by Samuel Hazard and others (Philadelphia and Harrisburg, 1852-1899); *Colonial Records of North Carolina,* edited by W. L. Saunders (Raleigh, 1886-1890), which, as in the case of the *New York Colonial Documents,* contain much useful material bearing upon general colonial conditions and are especially valuable for this study because they include certain representations of the Board of Trade.

CORRESPONDENCE, MEMOIRS, PAPERS, PRINTED

In 1766 Jared Ingersoll published for private distribution a collection of twelve letters written between the spring of 1764 and the spring of 1766, under title of *Mr. Ingersoll's Letters Relating to the Stamp Act;* the explanatory footnotes that accompany these letters are illuminating. These letters were included in the *Jared Ingersoll Papers,* edited by Dr. Franklin B. Dexter, published in 1918 in volume IX of the *Papers* of the New Haven Colony Historical Society, and since reprinted as a separate volume. These *Papers* represent a selection from the correspondence and miscellaneous papers of Jared Ingersoll and show the result of painstaking and discriminating editing. Some one hundred and sixty-four documents are printed in this collection.

Several collections of printed correspondence have been published, for the most part by the Connecticut Historical Society, which are of the highest value in studying the late colonial period of Connecticut history. Among these are *Letters from English Kings and Queens to the Governors of the Colony of Connecticut together with the Answers thereto from 1635 to 1749*, collected by R. R. Hinman (Hartford, 1836), "Correspondence of the Connecticut Governors with the British Government, 1755-1758" (Conn. Hist. Soc. *Collections*, vol. I, Hartford, 1860), "Roger Wolcott's Memoir" (Conn. Hist. Soc. *Collections*, vol. III, Hartford), *Talcott Papers: Correspondence and Documents (chiefly official) during Joseph Talcott's governorship of the colony of Connecticut, 1724-1741*, edited by M. K. Talcott (Conn. Hist. Soc. *Collections*, vol. V, Hartford, 1892-1896), *Law Papers, correspondence and documents during Jonathan Law's Governorship of the Colony of Connecticut, 1741-1750* (Conn. Hist. Soc. *Collections*, vols. XI, XIII, XV, Hartford, 1907-1914), *Wolcott Papers. Correspondence and Documents during Roger Wolcott's Governorship of the Colony of Connecticut, 1750-1754*, edited by A. C. Bates (Conn. Hist. Soc. *Collections*, vol. XVI, Hartford, 1916), which includes a large number of documents of great importance for the purpose of the present study, as do the *Fitch Papers, Correspondence and Documents during Thomas Fitch's Governorship of the Colony of Connecticut, 1754-1766*, I, edited by A. C. Bates (Conn. Hist. Soc. *Collections*, vol. XVII, Hartford, 1918), which is to be followed by a second volume, the manuscript of which Mr. Bates kindly allowed me to examine.

Several of Jared Ingersoll's contemporaries, besides those previously mentioned, have left correspondence, memoirs, or diaries which have been published and which in varying degree are useful in this connection. The recently printed *Extracts from the Itineraries and other Miscellanies of Ezra Stiles, D.D., LL.D., 1755-1795, with a Selection from his Correspondence*, edited by Dr. F. B. Dexter (New Haven, 1916), although almost a wilderness of unrelated observations recorded by the learned divine, is really invaluable; less important has been the more pretentious and logically developed *Literary Diary of Ezra Stiles*, also edited by Dr. Dexter (New York, 1901), as well as the *Diary of Joshua Hempstead of New London, Connecticut* (New London, 1901), another literary wilderness, and the "Letters of William Samuel Johnson to the Governors of Connecticut" (Mass. Hist.

Soc. *Collections,* fifth series, vol. IX). The *Writings of Benjamin Franklin,* edited by A. H. Smyth (10 vols., New York, 1905-1907), *The Grenville Papers,* edited by W. J. Smith (4 vols., London, 1853), the "Letters of Charles Garth" (*Maryland Hist. Magazine,* vol. V), the *Correspondence of William Pitt,* edited by G. S. Kimball (3 vols., New York, 1906), *The Montresor Journals,* edited by G. D. Scull (New York Hist. Soc. *Collections,* second series, vol. XIV, New York, 1881), the *Memoirs and Letters of Captain W. Glanville Evelyn,* also edited by G. D. Scull (Oxford, 1879), the *Journal Kept by Hugh Finlay* (Brooklyn, 1867), the *Familiar Letters of John Adams,* edited by C. F. Adams (Boston, 1876), and the *Collection of . . . Papers Relative to the Dispute between Great Britain and America . . . ,* made by John Almon (London, 1777), should be especially mentioned.

CONTEMPORARY TRACTS AND BOOKS

The *Tracts and other Papers,* collected by Peter Force (Washington, 1836-1846), as well as the John Almon *Collection of the most interesting Tracts* (London, 1766-1767) contains useful material. In connection with the Stamp Act crisis, among the vast number of pamphlets issued at that time, I am most indebted to Thomas Whately's (?) *Considerations on the Trade and Finances of this Kingdom and on the Measures of Administration with Respect to those great National Objects since the Conclusion of the Peace* (London, 1766), Samuel Cooper's *The Crisis* (London, 1766), Timothy Cunningham's *The History of our Customs, Acts, Subsidies, National Debts and Taxes* (London, 1761), J. Cunningham's *An Essay on Trade and Commerce Containing Observations on Taxes as they are supposed to affect the price of Labour in our Manufactories: Together with some Interesting Reflections on the Importance of our Trade to America* (London, 1770), Henry McCulloh's *Miscellaneous Representations relative to Our Concerns in America,* Thomas Fitch's *Some Reasons that Influenced the Governor to Take and the Councillors to Administer the oath required by Parliament, commonly called the Stamp Act* (Hartford, 1766), the famous Connecticut *Reasons Why the British Colonies should not be charged with Internal Taxes* (New Haven, 1764), and Benjamin Church's (?) *Liberty and Property Vindicated and the St—pm—n burnt* (New London, 1765).

Regarding the political and social conditions in Connecticut of this period, much valuable information can be gleaned from Timothy Dwight's *A Statistical Account of the Towns and Parishes in the State of Connecticut* (New Haven, 1811) and his *Travels in New England and New York* (New Haven, 1821), Benjamin Gale's *The Present State of the Colony of Connecticut* (New London, 1755), and *Doctor Gale's letter to J. W. Esq.* (Hartford, 1769), Eliphalet Dyer's *Remarks on Dr. Gale's letter to J. W. Esq.* (Hartford, 1769), and Thomas Clap's *Answer of the Friend in the West from a Gentleman in the East* (New Haven, 1755); the principal sources of information relative to these conditions are of course the private correspondence and the newspapers of that period.

In studying the Susquehanna controversy, I have found especialy useful *The State of the lands said to be Once within the Bounds of the Charter of the Colony of Connecticut, west of the Province of New York, Considered. By the Public's humble Servant* (New York, 1770), Dr. William Smith's (?) *An Examination of the Connecticut Claim to the Lands in Pennsylvania, with an Appendix Containing Extracts and Copies taken from Original Papers*, by Jared Ingersoll (Philadelphia, 1774), the *Report of the Commissioners Appointed by the General Assembly of Connecticut to Treat with the Proprietors of Pennsylvania respecting the Boundaries of this Colony* (Norwich, 1774), Barnabas Bidwell's *The Susquehanna Title Stated and Examined* (Catskill, N. Y., 1796), and the *Charge of Judge Paterson to the Jury in the Case of Van Horne's lessee vs. Dorrance* (Philadelphia, 1796).

NEWSPAPERS

The *Connecticut Gazette*, established in New Haven in 1755 and published until 1786 by J. Parker & Co. and Benjamin Mecom, successively, is a source of first importance; this paper was followed by the *Connecticut Journal* and *New Haven News Boy*, published by Thomas and Samuel Green, which is also invaluable; hardly less so are the *New London Gazette*, which became, in 1763, the *Connecticut Gazette and Universal Intelligencer*, and the *Connecticut Courant*, established at Hartford in 1764 by Thomas Green. Outside of Connecticut, the Philadelphia newspapers have been the most helpful; the files of the *Pennsylvania Journal or Weekly Advertiser*, published by William and Thomas Bradford, contain the significant ''Russel'' letters and Ingersoll's replies, while the *Pennsylvania Gazette*, controlled during this period by Hall and Sellers, and the *Pennsylvania Chronicle and Universal Advertiser*, shed additional light on Ingersoll's activities while in Philadelphia. Serviceable but of less importance have been the *Boston Evening Post*, the *Boston Gazette and Country Journal*, the *Boston Post Boy and Advertiser*, and the *Massachusetts Gazette* and *Boston News Letter*, the *New Hampshire Gazette and Historical Chronicle*, the *Newport Mercury or Weekly Advertiser*, the *New York Gazette or Weekly Post-Boy*, the *New York Mercury*, which was changed to the *New York Gazette and Weekly Mercury* in 1768, *Rivington's New York Gazatteer*, which appeared in 1777 as *Rivington's New York Loyal Gazette* and later as the *Royal Gazette*, the *Providence Gazette and Country Journal*, and the *Portsmouth Mercury and Weekly Advertiser*.

INDEX